DATA MINING

DATA MINING

Concepts, Models, Methods, and Algorithms

Mehmed Kantardzic

J. B. Speed Scientific School
University of Louisville

IEEE Computer Society, *Sponser*

IEEE Press

A JOHN WILEY & SONS, INC., PUBLICATION

For general information on our other products and services please contact our Customer Care Department within the U.S. at 877-762-2974, outside the U.S. at 317-572-3993 or fax 317-572-4002.

Wiley also publishes its books in a variety of electronic formats. Some content that appears in print, however, may not be available in electronic format.

Library of Congress Cataloging-in-Publication Data is available

ISBN 0–471–22852–4

Printed in the United States of America.

10 9 8 7 6 5 4

To Belma and Nermin

Contents

Preface

Traditionally, analysts have performed the task of extracting useful information from recorded data. But, the increasing volume of data in modern business and science calls for computer-based approaches. As data sets have grown in size and complexity, there has been an inevitable shift away from direct hands-on data analysis toward indirect, automatic data analysis using more complex and sophisticated tools. The modern technologies of computers, networks, and sensors have made data collection and organization an almost effortless task. However, the captured data needs to be converted into information and knowledge from recorded data to become useful. Data mining is the entire process of applying computer-based methodology, including new techniques for knowledge discovery, from data.

The modern world is a data-driven one. We are surrounded by data, numerical and otherwise, which must be analyzed and processed to convert it into information that informs, instructs, answers, or otherwise aids understanding and decision-making. This is the age of the Internet, intranets, data warehouses and data marts, and the fundamental paradigms of classical data analysis are ripe for change. Very large collections of data – sometimes hundreds of millions of individual records – are being stored in centralized data warehouses, allowing analysts to use more comprehensive, powerful data mining methods. While the quantity of data is huge, and growing, the number of sources is unlimited, and the range of areas covered is vast: industrial, commercial, financial, and scientific.

In recent years there has been an explosive growth of methods for discovering new knowledge from raw data. In response to this, a new discipline of data mining has been specially developed to extract valuable information from such huge data sets. Given the proliferation of low-cost computers (for software implementation), low-cost sensors, communications, database technology (to collect and store data), and computer-literate application experts who can pose "interesting" and "useful" application problems, this is not surprising.

Data mining technology has recently become a hot topic for decision-makers because it provides valuable, hidden business and scientific "intelligence" from a large amount of historical data. Fundamentally however, data mining is not a new technology. Extracting information and knowledge from recorded data is a well-established concept in scientific and medical studies. What is new is the convergence of several disciplines and corresponding technologies that have created a unique opportunity for data mining in a scientific and corporate world.

Originally, this book was intended to fulfill a wish for a single, introductory source to direct students to. However, it soon became apparent that people from a wide variety of backgrounds and positions, confronted by the need to make sense of large amounts of raw data, would also appreciate a compilation of some of the most important methods, tools, and algorithms in data mining. Thus, this book was written for a range of readers; from students wishing to learn about basic processes and techniques in data mining, to analysts and programmers who will be engaged directly in interdisciplinary teams for selected data mining applications. This book reviews state-of-the-art techniques for analyzing enormous quantities of raw data in high-dimensional data spaces to extract new information useful to the decision-making process. Most of the definitions, classifications, and explanations of the techniques covered in this book are not new, and they are presented in references at the end of the book. One of my main goals was to concentrate on systematic and balanced approach to all phases of a data mining process, and present them with enough illustrative examples. I expect that carefully prepared examples should give the reader additional arguments and guidelines in the selection and structure of techniques and tools for their own data mining applications. Better understanding of implementation details for most of the introduced techniques challenge the reader to build their own tools or to improve the applied methods and techniques.

To teach data mining, one has to emphasize the concepts and properties of the applied methods, rather than the mechanical details of applying different data mining tools. Despite all of their attractive bells and whistles, computer-based tools alone will never replace the practitioner who makes important decisions on how the process will be designed, and how and what tools will be employed. A deeper understanding of methods and models, how they behave, and why, is a prerequisite for efficient and successful application of data mining technology. Any researcher or practitioner in this field needs to be aware of these issues in order to successfully apply a particular methodology, understand a method's limitations, or develop new techniques. This is an attempt to present and discuss such issues and principles, and then describe representative and popular methods originating from statistics, machine learning, computer graphics, databases, information retrieval, neural networks, fuzzy logic, and evolutionary computation. It discusses approaches that have proven critical in revealing important patterns, trends, and models in large data sets.

Although it is easy to focus on technologies, as you read through the book keep in mind that technology alone does not provide the entire solution. One of my goals in writing this book was to minimize the hype associated with data mining, rather than making false promises of what can reasonably be expected. I have tried to take a more objective approach. I describe the processes and algorithms that are necessary to produce reliable, useful results in data mining applications.

I do not advocate the use of any particular product or technique over another; the designer of data mining process has to have enough background to select the appropriate methodologies and software tools. I expect that once a reader has completed this text, he or she will be able to initiate and perform basic activities in all phases of a data mining process successfully and effectively.

Louisville, KY   Mehmed Kantardzic
August, 2002

1 Data-Mining Concepts

CHAPTER OBJECTIVES

- Understand the need for analyses of large, complex, information-rich data sets.
- Identify the goals and primary tasks of the data-mining process.
- Describe the roots of data-mining technology.
- Recognize the iterative character of a data-mining process and specify its basic steps.
- Explain the influence of data quality on a data-mining process.
- Establish the relation between data warehousing and data mining.

1.1 INTRODUCTION

Modern science and engineering are based on using *first-principle models* to describe physical, biological, and social systems. Such an approach starts with a basic scientific model, such as Newton's laws of motion or Maxwell's equations in electromagnetism, and then builds upon them various applications in mechanical engineering or electrical engineering. In this approach, experimental data are used to verify the underlying first-principle models and to estimate some of the parameters that are difficult or sometimes impossible to measure directly. However, in many domains the underlying first principles are unknown, or the systems under study are too complex to be mathematically formalized. With the growing use of computers, there is a great amount of data being generated by such systems. In the absence of first-principle models, such readily available data can be used to derive models by estimating useful relationships between a system's variables (i.e., unknown input–output dependencies). *Thus there is currently a paradigm shift from classical modeling and analyses based on first principles to developing models and the corresponding analyses directly from data.*

We have grown accustomed gradually to the fact that there are tremendous volumes of data filling our computers, networks, and lives. Government agencies, scientific institutions, and businesses have all dedicated enormous resources to collecting and storing data. In reality, only a small amount of these data will ever be used because, in many cases, the volumes are simply too large to manage, or the data structures themselves are too complicated to be analyzed effectively. How could this happen? The primary reason is that the original effort to create a data set is often focused on issues such as storage efficiency; it does not include a plan for how the data will eventually be used and analyzed.

The need to understand large, complex, information-rich data sets is common to virtually all fields of business, science, and engineering. In the business world, corporate and customer data are becoming recognized as a strategic asset. The ability to extract useful knowledge hidden in these data and to act on that knowledge is becoming increasingly important in today's competitive world. The entire process of applying a computer-based methodology, including new techniques, for discovering knowledge from data is called data mining.

Data mining is an iterative process within which progress is defined by discovery, through either automatic or manual methods. Data mining is most useful in an exploratory analysis scenario in which there are no predetermined notions about what will constitute an "interesting" outcome. Data mining is the search for new, valuable, and nontrivial information in large volumes of data. It is a cooperative effort of humans and computers. Best results are achieved by balancing the knowledge of human experts in describing problems and goals with the search capabilities of computers.

In practice, the two primary goals of data mining tend to be *prediction* and *description*. *Prediction* involves using some variables or fields in the data set to predict unknown or future values of other variables of interest. *Description*, on the other hand, focuses on finding patterns describing the data that can be interpreted by humans. Therefore, it is possible to put data-mining activities into one of two categories:

1) Predictive data mining, which *produces the model* of the system described by the given data set, or
2) Descriptive data mining, which *produces new, nontrivial information* based on the available data set.

On the predictive end of the spectrum, the goal of data mining is to produce a model, expressed as an executable code, which can be used to perform classification, prediction, estimation, or other similar tasks. On the other, descriptive, end of the spectrum, the goal is to gain an understanding of the analyzed system by uncovering patterns and relationships in large data sets. The relative importance of prediction and description for particular data-mining applications can vary considerably. The goals of prediction and description are achieved by using data-mining techniques, explained later in this book, for the following *primary data-mining tasks:*

1. *Classification* – discovery of a predictive learning function that classifies a data item into one of several predefined classes.
2. *Regression* – discovery of a predictive learning function, which maps a data item to a real-value prediction variable.
3. *Clustering* – a common descriptive task in which one seeks to identify a finite set of categories or clusters to describe the data.
4. *Summarization* – an additional descriptive task that involves methods for finding a compact description for a set (or subset) of data.
5. *Dependency Modeling* – finding a local model that describes significant dependencies between variables or between the values of a feature in a data set or in a part of a data set.
6. *Change and Deviation Detection* – discovering the most significant changes in the data set.

The more formal approach, with graphical interpretation of data-mining tasks for complex and large data sets and illustrative examples, is given in Chapter 4. Current introductory classifications and definitions are given here only to give the reader a feeling of the wide spectrum of problems and tasks that may be solved using data-mining technology.

The success of a data-mining engagement depends largely on the amount of energy, knowledge, and creativity that the designer puts into it. In essence, data mining is like solving a puzzle. The individual pieces of the puzzle are not complex structures in and of themselves. Taken as a collective whole, however, they can constitute very elaborate systems. As you try to unravel these systems, you will probably get frustrated, start forcing parts together, and generally become annoyed at the entire process; but once you know how to work with the pieces, you realize that it was not really that hard in the first place. The same analogy can be applied to data mining. In the beginning, the designers of the data-mining process probably do not know much about the data sources; if they did, they would most likely not be interested in performing data mining. Individually, the data seem simple, complete, and explainable. But collectively, they take on a whole new appearance that is intimidating and difficult to comprehend, like the puzzle. Therefore, being an analyst and designer in a data-mining process requires, besides thorough professional knowledge, creative thinking and a willingness to see problems in a different light.

Data mining is one of the fastest growing fields in the computer industry. Once a small interest area within computer science and statistics, it has quickly expanded into a field of its own. One of the greatest strengths of data mining is reflected in its wide range of methodologies and techniques that can be applied to a host of problem sets. Since data mining is a natural activity to be performed on large data sets, one of the largest target markets is the entire data warehousing, data-mart, and decision-support community, encompassing professionals from such industries as retail, manufacturing, telecommunications, healthcare, insurance, and transportation. In the business community, data mining can be used to discover new purchasing trends, plan investment strategies, and detect unauthorized expenditures in the accounting system. It can improve marketing campaigns and the outcomes can be used to provide customers with more focused support and attention. Data-mining techniques can be applied to problems of business process reengineering, in which the goal is to understand interactions and relationships among business practices and organizations.

Many law enforcement and special investigative units, whose mission is to identify fraudulent activities and discover crime trends, have also used data mining successfully. For example, these methodologies can aid analysts in the identification of critical behavior patterns in the communication interactions of narcotics organizations, the monetary transactions of money laundering and insider trading operations, the movements of serial killers, and the targeting of smugglers at border crossings. Data-mining techniques have also been employed by people in the intelligence community who maintain many large data sources as a part of the activities relating to matters of national security. Appendix B of the book gives a brief overview of typical commercial applications of data-mining technology today.

1.2 DATA-MINING ROOTS

Looking at how different authors describe data mining, it is clear that we are far from a universal agreement on the definition of data mining or even what constitutes data mining. Is data mining a form of statistics enriched with learning theory or is it a revolutionary new concept? In our view, most data-mining problems and corresponding solutions have roots in classical data analysis. Data mining has its origins in various disciplines, of which the two most important are *statistics* and *machine learning*. Statistics has its roots in mathematics, and therefore, there has been an emphasis on mathematical rigor, a desire to establish that something is sensible on theoretical grounds before testing it in practice. In contrast, the machine-learning community has its origins very much in computer practice. This has led to a practical orientation, a willingness to test something out to see how well it performs, without waiting for a formal proof of effectiveness.

If the place given to mathematics and formalizations is one of the major differences between statistical and machine-learning approaches to data mining, another is in the relative emphasis they give to models and algorithms. Modern statistics is almost entirely driven by the notion of a model. This is a postulated structure, or an approximation to a structure, which could have led to the data. In place of the statistical emphasis on models, machine learning tends to emphasize algorithms. This is hardly surprising; the very word "learning" contains the notion of a process, an implicit algorithm.

Basic modeling principles in data mining also have roots in *control theory*, which is primarily applied to engineering systems and industrial processes. The problem of determining a mathematical model for an unknown system (also referred to as the target system) by observing its input–output data pairs is generally referred to as system identification. The purposes of system identification are multiple and, from a standpoint of data mining, the most important are to predict a system's behavior and to explain the interaction and relationships between the variables of a system.

System identification generally involves two top-down steps:

1. *Structure identification* – In this step, we need to apply a priori knowledge about the target system to determine a class of models within which the search for the most suitable model is to be conducted. Usually this class of models is denoted by a parametrized function $y = f(u,t)$, where y is the model's output, u is an input vector, and t is a parameter vector. The determination of the function f is problem-dependent, and the function is based on the designer's experience, intuition, and the laws of nature governing the target system.

2. *Parameter identification* – In the second step, when the structure of the model is known, all we need to do is apply optimization techniques to determine parameter vector t such that the resulting model $y^* = f(u,t^*)$ can describe the system appropriately.

In general, system identification is not a one-pass process: both structure and parameter identification need to be done repeatedly until a satisfactory model is found. This iterative process is represented graphically in Figure 1.1. Typical steps in every iteration are as follows:

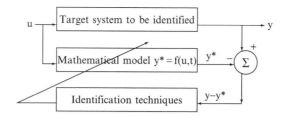

FIGURE 1.1   Block diagram for parameter identification

1. Specify and parametrize a class of formalized (mathematical) models, $y^* = f(u,t)$, representing the system to be identified.
2. Perform parameter identification to choose the parameters that best fit the available data set (the difference $y - y^*$ is minimal).
3. Conduct validation tests to see if the model identified responds correctly to an unseen data set (often referred as test, validating, or checking data set).
4. Terminate the process once the results of the validation test are satisfactory.

If we do not have any *a priori* knowledge about the target system, then structure identification becomes difficult, and we have to select the structure by trial and error. While we know a great deal about the structures of most engineering systems and industrial processes, in a vast majority of target systems where we apply data-mining techniques, these structures are totally unknown, or they are so complex that it is impossible to obtain an adequate mathematical model. Therefore, new techniques were developed for parameter identification and they are today a part of the spectra of data-mining techniques.

Finally, we can distinguish between how the terms "model" and "pattern" are interpreted in data mining. A model is a "large scale" structure, perhaps summarizing relationships over many (sometimes all) cases, whereas a pattern is a local structure, satisfied by few cases or in a small region of a data space. It is also worth noting here that the word "pattern", as it is used in pattern recognition, has a rather different meaning for data mining. In pattern recognition it refers to the vector of measurements characterizing a particular object, which is a point in a multidimensional data space. In data mining, a pattern is simply a local model. In this book we refer to n-dimensional vectors of data as *samples*.

1.3   DATA-MINING PROCESS

Without trying to cover all possible approaches and all different views about data mining as a discipline, let us start with one possible, sufficiently broad definition of data mining:

DEF: Data Mining is a process of discovering various models, summaries, and derived values from a given collection of data.

The word "process" is very important here. Even in some professional environments there is a belief that data mining simply consists of picking and applying a computer-based tool to match the presented problem and automatically obtaining a solution. This is a misconception based on an artificial idealization of the world. There are several reasons why this is incorrect. One reason is that data mining is not simply a collection of isolated tools, each completely different from the other, and waiting to be matched to the problem. A second reason lies in the notion of matching a problem to a technique. Only very rarely is a research question stated sufficiently precisely that a single and simple application of the method will suffice. In fact, what happens in practice is that data mining becomes an iterative process. One studies the data, examines it using some analytic technique, decides to look at it another way, perhaps modifying it, and then goes back to the beginning and applies another data-analysis tool, reaching either better or different results. This can go round and round many times; each technique is used to probe slightly different aspects of data—to ask a slightly different question of the data. What is essentially being described here is a voyage of discovery that makes modern data mining exciting. Still, data mining is not a random application of statistical, machine learning, and other methods and tools. It is not a random walk through the space of analytic techniques but a carefully planned and considered process of deciding what will be most useful, promising, and revealing.

It is important to realize that the problem of discovering or estimating dependencies from data or discovering totally new data is only one part of the general experimental procedure used by scientists, engineers, and others who apply standard steps to draw conclusions from the data. The general experimental procedure adapted to data-mining problems involves the following steps:

1. State the problem and formulate the hypothesis

Most data-based modeling studies are performed in a particular application domain. Hence, domain-specific knowledge and experience are usually necessary in order to come up with a meaningful problem statement. Unfortunately, many application studies tend to focus on the data-mining technique at the expense of a clear problem statement. In this step, a modeler usually specifies a set of variables for the unknown dependency and, if possible, a general form of this dependency as an initial hypothesis. There may be several hypotheses formulated for a single problem at this stage. The first step requires the combined expertise of an application domain and a data-mining model. In practice, it usually means a close interaction between the data-mining expert and the application expert. In successful data-mining applications, this cooperation does not stop in the initial phase; it continues during the entire data-mining process.

2. Collect the data

This step is concerned with how the data are generated and collected. In general, there are two distinct possibilities. The first is when the data-generation process is under the control of an expert (modeler): this approach is known as a *designed experiment*. The second possibility is when the expert cannot influence the data-generation process: this is known as the *observational approach*. An observational setting, namely, random data generation, is assumed in most data-mining applications. Typically, the sampling distribution is completely unknown after data are collected, or it is partially and implicitly given in the data-collection procedure. It is very important, however, to understand how data collection affects its theoretical distribution, since such a priori knowledge can be very useful for modeling and, later, for the final interpretation of results. Also, it is important to make sure that the data used for estimating a model and the data used later for testing and applying a model come from the same, unknown, sampling distribution. If this is not the case, the estimated model cannot be successfully used in a final application of the results.

3. Preprocessing the data

In the observational setting, data are usually "collected" from the existing databases, data warehouses, and data marts. Data preprocessing usually includes at least two common tasks:

1. *Outlier detection (and removal)* – Outliers are unusual data values that are not consistent with most observations. Commonly, outliers result from measurement errors, coding and recording errors, and, sometimes, are natural, abnormal values. Such nonrepresentative samples can seriously affect the model produced later. There are two strategies for dealing with outliers:

   a) Detect and eventually remove outliers as a part of the preprocessing phase, or
   b) Develop robust modeling methods that are insensitive to outliers.

2. *Scaling, encoding, and selecting features* – Data preprocessing includes several steps such as variable scaling and different types of encoding. For example, one feature with the range [0, 1] and the other with the range [−100, 1000] will not have the same weights in the applied technique; they will also influence the final data-mining results differently. Therefore, it is recommended to scale them and bring both features to the same weight for further analysis. Also, application-specific encoding methods usually achieve dimensionality reduction by providing a smaller number of informative features for subsequent data modeling.

These two classes of preprocessing tasks are only illustrative examples of a large spectrum of preprocessing activities in a data-mining process.

Data-preprocessing steps should not be considered completely independent from other data-mining phases. In every iteration of the data-mining process, all activities, together, could define new and improved data sets for subsequent iterations. Generally, a good preprocessing method provides an optimal representation for a data-mining technique by incorporating a priori knowledge in the form of application-specific scaling and encoding. More about these techniques and the preprocessing phase in general will be given in Chapters 2 and 3, where we have functionally divided preprocessing and its corresponding techniques into two subphases: data preparation and data-dimensionality reduction.

4. Estimate the model

The selection and implementation of the appropriate data-mining technique is the main task in this phase. This process is not straightforward; usually, in practice, the implementation is based on several models, and selecting the best one is an additional task. The basic principles of learning and discovery from data are given in Chapter 4 of this book. Later, Chapters 5 through 13 explain and analyze specific techniques that are applied to perform a successful learning process from data and to develop an appropriate model.

5. Interpret the model and draw conclusions

In most cases, data-mining models should help in decision making. Hence, such models need to be interpretable in order to be useful because humans are not likely to base their decisions on complex "black-box" models. Note that the goals of accuracy of the model and accuracy of its interpretation are somewhat contradictory. Usually, simple models are more interpretable, but they are also less accurate. Modern data-mining methods are expected to yield highly accurate results using high-dimensional models. The problem of interpreting these models, also very important, is considered a separate task, with specific techniques to validate the results. A user does not want hundreds of pages of numeric results. He does not understand them; he cannot summarize, interpret, and use them for successful decision-making.

Even though the focus of this book is on steps 3 and 4 in the data-mining process, we have to understand that they are just two steps in a more complex process. All phases, separately, and the entire data-mining process, as a whole, are highly iterative, as has been shown in Figure 1.2. A good understanding of the whole process is important for any successful application. No matter how powerful the data-mining method used in step 4 is, the resulting model will not be valid if the data are not collected and preprocessed correctly, or if the problem formulation is not meaningful.

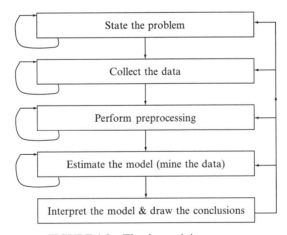

FIGURE 1.2   The data-mining process

1.4 LARGE DATA SETS

As we enter into the age of digital information, the problem of data overload looms ominously ahead. Our ability to analyze and understand massive *data sets*, as we call large data, is far behind our ability to gather and store the data. Large databases of digital information are ubiquitous. Data from the neighborhood store's checkout register, your bank's credit card authorization device, records in your doctor's office, patterns in your telephone calls, and many more applications generate streams of digital records archived in huge business databases. Scientists are at the higher end of today's data-collection machinery, using data from different sources—from remote-sensing platforms to microscope probing of cell details. Scientific instruments can easily generate terabytes of data in a short period of time and store them in the computer. The information age, with the expansion of the Internet, has caused an exponential growth in information sources and also in information-storage units. An illustrative example is given in Figure 1.3, where we can see a dramatic increase of Internet hosts in just the last three years, where these numbers are directly proportional to the amount of data stored on the Internet.

There is a rapidly widening gap between data-collection and data-organization capabilities and the ability to analyze the data. Current hardware and database technology allows efficient, inexpensive, and reliable data storage and access. However, whether the context is business, medicine, science, or government, the data sets themselves, in their raw form, are of little direct value. What is of value is the knowledge that can be inferred from the data and put to use. For example, the marketing database of a consumer goods company may yield knowledge of the correlation between sales of certain items and certain demographic groupings. This knowledge can be used to introduce new, targeted marketing campaigns with a predictable financial return, as opposed to unfocused campaigns.

The root of the problem is that the data size and dimensionality are too large for manual analysis and interpretation, or even for some semiautomatic computer-based analyses. A scientist or a business manager can work effectively with a few hundred or thousand records. Effectively mining millions of data points, each described with tens or hundreds of characteristics, is another matter. Imagine the analysis of terabytes of sky-image data with thousands of photographic high-resolution images (23,040 × 23,040 pixels per image), or human genome databases with billions of components. In theory, "big data" can lead to much stronger conclusions,

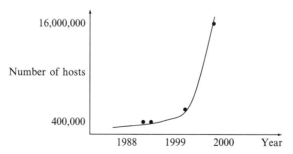

FIGURE 1.3 Growth of Internet hosts

but in practice many difficulties arise. The business community is well aware of today's information overload, and one analysis shows that

1. 61% of managers believe that information overload is present in their own workplace,
2. 80% believe the situation will get worse,
3. over 50% of the managers ignore data in current decision-making processes because of the information overload,
4. 84% of managers store this information for the future; it is not used for current analysis,
5. 60% believe that the cost of gathering information outweighs its value.

What are the solutions? Work harder. Yes, but how long can you keep up, because the limits are very close. Employ an assistant. Maybe, if you can afford it. Ignore the data. But then you are not competitive in the market. The only real solution will be to replace classical data analysis and interpretation methodologies (both manual and computer-based) with a new data-mining technology.

In theory, most data-mining methods should be happy with large data sets. Large data sets have the potential to yield more valuable information. If data mining is a search through a space of possibilities, then large data sets suggest many more possibilities to enumerate and evaluate. The potential for increased enumeration and search is counterbalanced by practical limitations. Besides the computational complexity of the data-mining algorithms that work with large data sets, a more exhaustive search may also increase the risk of finding some low-probability solutions that evaluate well for the given data set, but may not meet future expectations.

In today's multimedia-based environment that has a huge Internet infrastructure, different types of data are generated and digitally stored. To prepare adequate data-mining methods, we have to analyze the basic types and characteristics of datasets. The first step in this analysis is systematization of data with respect to their computer representation and use. Data that is usually the source for a data-mining process can be classified into structured data, semi-structured data, and unstructured data.

Most business databases contain structured data consisting of well-defined fields with numeric or alphanumeric values, while scientific databases may contain all three classes. Examples of semi-structured data are electronic images of business documents, medical reports, executive summaries, and repair manuals. The majority of web documents also fall in this category. An example of unstructured data is a video recorded by a surveillance camera in a department store. Such visual and, in general, multimedia recordings of events or processes of interest are currently gaining widespread popularity because of reduced hardware costs. This form of data generally requires extensive processing to extract and structure the information contained in it.

Structured data is often referred to as traditional data, while the semi-structured and unstructured data are lumped together as nontraditional data (also called multimedia data). Most of the current data-mining methods and commercial tools are applied to traditional data. However, the development of data-mining tools for nontraditional data, as well as interfaces for its transformation into structured formats, is progressing at a rapid rate.

The standard model of structured data for data mining is a collection of cases. Potential measurements called features are specified, and these features are uniformly measured over many cases. Usually the representation of structured data for data-mining problems is in a tabular form, or in the form of a single relation (term used in relational databases), where columns are features of objects stored in a table and rows are values of these features for specific entities. A simplified graphical representation of a data set and its characteristics is given in Figure 1.4. In the data-mining literature, we usually use the terms samples or cases for rows. Many different types of features (attributes or variables)— i.e., fields—in structured data records are common in data mining. Not all of the data-mining methods are equally good at dealing with different types of features.

There are several ways of characterizing features. One way of looking at a feature—or in a formalization process, the more often-used term; variable—is to see whether it is an *independent variable* or a *dependent variable*; i.e, whether or not it is a variable whose values depend upon values of other variables represented in a data set. This is a model-based approach to classifying variables. All dependent variables are accepted as outputs from the system for which we are establishing a model, and independent variables are inputs to the system, as represented in Figure 1.5.

There are some additional variables that influence system behavior, but the corresponding values are not available in a data set during a modeling process. The reasons are different: from high complexity and the cost of measurements for these features to a modeler's not understanding the importance of some factors and their influences on the model. These are usually called unobserved variables, and they are the main cause of ambiguities and estimations in a model.

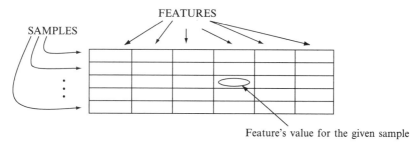

FIGURE 1.4   Tabular representation of a data set

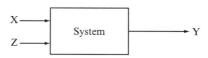

FIGURE 1.5   A real system, besides input (independent) variables X and (dependent) outputs Y, often has unobserved inputs Z

Today's computers and corresponding software tools support the processing of data sets with millions of samples and hundreds of features. Large data sets, including those with mixed data types, are a typical initial environment for application of data-mining techniques. When a large amount of data is stored in a computer, one cannot rush into data-mining techniques, because the important problem of data quality has first to be resolved. Also, it is obvious that a manual quality analysis is not possible at that stage. Therefore, it is necessary to prepare a data-quality analysis in the earliest phases of the data-mining process; usually it is a task to be undertaken in the data-preprocessing phase. The quality of data has a profound effect on the image of the system and determines the corresponding model that is implicitly described; it could also limit the ability of end users to make informed decisions. Using the available data-mining techniques, it will be difficult to undertake major qualitative changes in an organization if the data is of a poor quality; similarly, to make new sound discoveries from poor quality scientific data will be almost impossible. There are a number of indicators of data quality:

1. The data should be accurate. The analyst has to check that the name is spelled correctly, the code is in a given range, the value is complete, etc.
2. The data should be stored according to data type. The analyst must ensure that the numeric value is not presented in character form, that integers are not in the form of real numbers, etc.
3. The data should have integrity. Updates should not be lost because of conflicts among different users; robust backup and recovery procedures should be implemented if they are not already part of the Data Base Management System (DBMS).
4. The data should be consistent. The form and the content should be the same after integration of large data sets from different sources.
5. The data should not be redundant. In practice, redundant data should be minimized and reasoned duplication should be controlled. Duplicated records should be eliminated.
6. The data should be timely. The time component of data should be recognized explicitly from the data or implicitly from the manner of its organization.
7. The data should be well understood. Naming standards are a necessary but not the only condition for data to be well understood. The user should know that the data corresponds to an established domain.
8. The data set should be complete. Missing data, which occurs in reality, should be minimized. Missing data could reduce the quality of a global model. On the other hand, some data-mining techniques are robust enough to support analyses of data sets with missing values.

How to work with and solve some of these problems of data quality is explained in greater detail in Chapters 2 and 3 where basic data-mining preprocessing methodologies are introduced. These processes are performed very often using data-warehousing technology, briefly explained in Section 1.5.

1.5   DATA WAREHOUSES

Although the existence of a data warehouse is not a prerequisite for data mining, in practice, the task of data mining, especially for some large companies, is made a lot easier by having access to a data warehouse. A primary goal of a data warehouse is to increase the "intelligence" of a decision process and the knowledge of the people involved in this process. For example, the ability of product marketing executives to look at multiple dimensions of a product's sales performance—by region, by type of sales, by customer demographics—may enable better promotional efforts, increased production, or new decisions in product inventory and distribution. It should be noted that average companies work with averages. The superstars differentiate themselves by paying attention to the details. They may need to slice and dice the data in different ways to obtain a deeper understanding of their organization and to make possible improvements. To undertake these processes, users have to know what data exists, where it is located, and how to access it.

A data warehouse means different things to different people. Some definitions are limited to data; others refer to people, processes, software, tools, and data. One of the global definitions is that

> the data warehouse is a collection of integrated, subject-oriented databases designed to support the decision-support functions (DSF), where each unit of data is relevant to some moment in time.

Based on this definition, a data warehouse can be viewed as an organization's repository of data, set up to support strategic decision-making. The function of the data warehouse is to store the historical data of an organization in an integrated manner that reflects the various facets of the organization and business. The data in a warehouse are never updated but used only to respond to queries from end users who are generally decision-makers. Typically, data warehouses are huge, storing billions of records. In many instances, an organization may have several local or departmental data warehouses often called data marts. A data mart is a data warehouse that has been designed to meet the needs of a specific group of users. It may be large or small, depending on the subject area.

At this early time in the evolution of data warehouses, it is not surprising to find many projects floundering because of the basic misunderstanding of what a data warehouse is. What *does* surprise is the size and scale of these projects. Many companies err by not defining exactly what a data warehouse is, the business problems it will solve, and the uses to which it will be put. Two aspects of a data warehouse are most important for a better understanding of its design process: the first is the specific types (classification) of data stored in a data warehouse, and the second is the set of transformations used to prepare the data in the final form such that it is useful for decision making. A data warehouse includes the following categories of data, where the classification is accommodated to the time-dependent data sources:

1. Old detail data
2. Current (new) detail data

3. Lightly summarized data
4. Highly summarized data
5. Metadata (the data directory or guide).

To prepare these five types of elementary or derived data in a data warehouse, the fundamental types of data transformation are standardized. There are four main types of transformations, and each has its own characteristics:

1. *Simple transformations* – These transformations are the building blocks of all other more complex transformations. This category includes manipulation of data that is focused on one field at a time, without taking into account its values in related fields. Examples include changing the data type of a field or replacing an encoded field value with a decoded value.

2. *Cleansing and scrubbing* – These transformations ensure consistent formatting and usage of a field, or of related groups of fields. This can include a proper formatting of address information, for example. This class of transformations also includes checks for valid values in a particular field, usually checking the range or choosing from an enumerated list.

3. *Integration* – This is a process of taking operational data from one or more sources and mapping it, field by field, onto a new data structure in the data warehouse. The common identifier problem is one of the most difficult integration issues in building a data warehouse. Essentially, this situation occurs when there are multiple system sources for the same entities and there is no clear way to identify those entities as the same. This is a challenging problem, and in many cases it cannot be solved in an automated fashion. It frequently requires sophisticated algorithms to pair up probable matches. Another complex data-integration scenario occurs when there are multiple sources for the same data element. In reality, it is common that some of these values are contradictory, and resolving a conflict is not a straightforward process. Just as difficult as having conflicting values is having no value for a data element in a warehouse. All these problems and corresponding automatic or semiautomatic solutions are always domain-dependent.

4. *Aggregation and summarization* – These are methods of condensing instances of data found in the operational environment into fewer instances in the warehouse environment. Although the terms aggregation and summarization are often used interchangeably in the literature, we believe that they do have slightly different meanings in the data-warehouse context. Summarization is a simple addition of values along one or more data dimensions; e.g., adding up daily sales to produce monthly sales. Aggregation refers to the addition of different business elements into a common total; it is highly domain-dependent. For example, aggregation is adding daily product sales and monthly consulting sales to get the combined, monthly total.

These transformations are the main reason why we prefer a warehouse as a source of data for a data-mining process. If the data warehouse is available, the preprocessing phase in data mining is significantly reduced, sometimes even eliminated. Do not forget that this preparation of data is the most time-consuming phase.

Although the implementation of a data warehouse is a complex task, described in many texts in great detail, in this text we are giving only the basic characteristics. A three-stage data-warehousing development process is summarized through the following basic steps:

1. *Modeling* – In simple terms, to take the time to understand business processes, the information requirements of these processes, and the decisions that are currently made within processes.
2. *Building* – To establish requirements for tools that suit the types of decision support necessary for the targeted business process; to create a data model that helps further define information requirements; to decompose problems into data specifications and the actual data store, which will, in its final form, represent either a data mart or a more comprehensive data warehouse.
3. *Deploying* – To implement, relatively early in the overall process, the nature of the data to be warehoused and the various business intelligence tools to be employed; to begin by training users. The deploy stage explicitly contains a time during which users explore both the repository (to understand data that are and should be available) and early versions of the actual data warehouse. This can lead to an evolution of the data warehouse, which involves adding more data, extending historical periods, or returning to the build stage to expand the scope of the data warehouse through a data model.

Data mining represents one of the major applications for data warehousing, since the sole function of a data warehouse is to provide information to end users for decision support. Unlike other query tools and application systems, the data-mining process provides an end-user with the capacity to extract hidden, nontrivial information. Such information, although more difficult to extract, can provide bigger business and scientific advantages and yield higher returns on "data warehousing and data mining" investments.

How is data mining different from other typical applications of a data warehouse, such as structured query languages (SQL) and on-line analytical processing tools (OLAP), which are also applied to data warehouses? SQL is a standard relational database language that is good for queries that impose some kind of constraints on data in the database in order to extract an answer. In contrast, data-mining methods are good for queries that are exploratory in nature, trying to extract hidden, not so obvious information. SQL is useful when we know exactly what we are looking for and we can describe it formally. We will use data-mining methods when we know only vaguely what we are looking for. Therefore, these two classes of data-warehousing applications are complementary.

OLAP tools and methods have become very popular in recent years as they let users analyze data in a warehouse by providing multiple views of the data, supported by advanced graphical representations. In these views, different dimensions of data correspond to different business characteristics. OLAP tools make it very easy to look at dimensional data from any angle or to slice-and-dice it. Although OLAP tools, like data-mining tools, provide answers that are derived from data, the similarity between them ends here. The derivation of answers from data in OLAP is analogous to calculations in a spreadsheet; because they use simple and given-in-advance calculations, OLAP tools do not learn from data, nor do they create new knowledge. They are usually special-purpose visualization tools that can help end-users draw their own conclusions and decisions, based on graphically condensed data. OLAP tools are very useful for the data-mining process; they can be a part of it but they are not a substitute.

1.6 ORGANIZATION OF THIS BOOK

After introducing the basic concepts of data mining in Chapter 1, the rest of the book follows the basic phases of a data-mining process. In Chapters 2 and 3 are explained common characteristics of raw, large, data sets, and the typical techniques of data preprocessing. The text emphasizes the importance and influence of these initial phases on the final success and quality of data-mining results. Chapter 2 provides basic techniques for transforming raw data, including data sets with missing values and with time-dependent attributes. Outlier analysis is a set of important techniques for preprocessing of messy data, and is also explained in this chapter. Chapter 3 deals with reduction of large data sets and introduces efficient methods for reduction of features, values, and cases. When the data set is preprocessed and prepared for mining, a wide spectrum of data-mining techniques is available, and the selection of a technique or techniques depends on the type of application and the data characteristics. In Chapter 4, before introducing particular data-mining methods, we present the general theoretical background and formalizations applicable for all mining techniques. The essentials of the theory can be summarized with the question: How can one learn from data? The emphasis in Chapter 4 is on statistical learning theory and the different types of learning methods and learning tasks that may be derived from the theory.

Chapters 5 to 12 give an overview of common classes of data-mining techniques. Selected statistical inference methods are presented in Chapter 5, including Bayesian classifier, predictive and logistic regression, ANOVA analysis, and log-linear models. Chapter 6 explains the complexity of clustering problems and introduces agglomerative, partitional, and incremental clustering techniques. Chapter 7 summarizes the basic characteristics of the C4.5 algorithm as a representative of logic-based techniques for classification problems. Different aspects of local modeling in large data sets are addressed in Chapter 8, and common techniques of association-rules mining, Web mining, and text mining are presented. Chapter 9 discusses the basic components of artificial neural networks and introduces two classes: multilayer perceptrons and competitive networks as illustrative representatives of a neural-network technology. Most of the techniques explained in Chapters 10 and 11, about genetic algorithms and fuzzy systems, are not directly applicable in mining large data sets. The author believes that these technologies, derived from soft computing, become more important, perhaps not as separate techniques for data mining but as methodologies combined with other techniques, in better representing and computing with data. Finally, Chapter 12 recognizes the importance of data-mining visualization techniques, especially those for representation of large-dimensional samples.

It is our hope that we have succeeded in producing an informative and readable text supplemented with relevant examples and illustrations. All chapters in the book have a set of review problems and reading lists. The author is preparing a solutions manual for instructors, who might use the book for undergraduate or graduate classes. For an in-depth understanding of the various topics covered in this book, we recommend to the reader a fairly comprehensive list of references, given at the end of each chapter. Although many of these references are from various journals, magazines, conference and workshop proceedings, it is obvious that during the last few years there are many more books available, covering different aspects of data mining and knowledge discovery. Finally, the book has two appendices with useful background information for practical applications of data-mining technology. In Appendix A we provide an overview of commercial and publicly available data-mining tools, and in Appendix B an extensive list of important Web sites and data-mining vendors has been included.

The reader should have some knowledge of the basic concepts and terminology associated with data structures and databases. In addition, some background in elementary statistics and machine learning may also be useful, but it is not necessarily required, as the concepts and techniques discussed within the book can be utilized without knowledge of the underlying theory.

1.7 REVIEW QUESTIONS AND PROBLEMS

1. Explain why it is not possible to analyze some large data sets using classical modeling techniques.

2. Do you recognize in your business or academic environment some problems in which the solution can be obtained through classification, regression, or deviation? Explain with examples.

3. Explain the differences between statistical and machine-learning approaches to the analysis of large data sets.

4. Why are preprocessing and dimensionality reduction important phases in successful data-mining applications?

5. Give examples of data where the time component may be recognized explicitly, and other data where the time component is given implicitly in a data organization.

6. Why is it important that the data miner understand data well?

7. Give examples of structured, semi-structured, and unstructured data from everyday situations.

8. Can a set with 50,000 samples be called a large data set? Explain your answer.

9. Enumerate the tasks that a data warehouse may solve as a part of the data-mining process.

10. Many authors include OLAP tools as a standard data-mining tool. Give the arguments for and against this classification.

1.8 REFERENCES FOR FURTHER STUDY

1. Berson, A., S. Smith, K. Thearling, *Building Data Mining Applications for CRM*, McGraw-Hill, New York, 2000.

   The book is written primarily for the business community, explaining the competitive advantage of data-mining technology. It bridges the gap between understanding this vital technology and implementing it to meet a corporation's specific needs. Basic phases in a data-mining process are explained through real-world examples.

2. Han, J. and M. Kamber, *Data Mining: Concepts and Techniques*, Morgan Kaufmann, San Francisco, 2000.

   This book gives a sound understanding of data-mining principles. The primary orientation of the book is for database practitioners and professionals, with emphasis on OLAP and data warehousing. In-depth analysis of association rules and clustering algorithms is an additional strength of the book. All algorithms are presented in easily understood pseudocode and they are suitable for use in real-world, large-scale data-mining projects, including advanced applications such as Web mining and text mining.

3. Hand, D., H. Mannila, P. Smith, *Principles of Data Mining*, MIT Press, Cambridge: MA, 2001.

   The book consists of three sections. The first, foundations, provides a tutorial overview of the principles underlying data-mining algorithms and their applications. The second section, data-mining algorithms, shows how algorithms are constructed to solve specific problems in a principled manner. The third section shows how all of the preceding analyses fit together when applied to real-world data-mining problems.

4. Westphal, C. and T. Blaxton, *Data Mining Solutions: Methods and Tools for Solving Real-World Problems*, John Wiley, New York, 1998.

   This introductory book gives a refreshing "out-of-the-box" approach to data mining that will help the reader to maximize time and problem-solving resources, and prepare for the next wave of data-mining visualization techniques. An extensive coverage of data-mining software tools is valuable to readers who are planning to set up their own data-mining environment.

2 Preparing the Data

CHAPTER OBJECTIVES

- Analyze basic representations and characteristics of raw and large data sets.
- Apply different normalization techniques on numerical attributes.
- Recognize different techniques for data preparation, including attribute transformation.
- Compare different methods for elimination of missing values.
- Construct a method for uniform representation of time-dependent data.
- Compare different techniques for outlier detection.
- Implement some data preprocessing techniques.

2.1 REPRESENTATION OF RAW DATA

Data samples introduced as rows in Figure 1.4 are basic components in a data-mining process. Every sample is described with several features and there are different types of values for every feature. We will start with the two most common types: *numeric* and *categorical*. Numeric values include real-value variables or integer variables such as age, speed, or length. A feature with numeric values has two important properties: its values have an order relation ($2 < 5$ and $5 < 7$) and a distance relation ($d(2.3, 4.2) = 1.9$).

In contrast, categorical (often called symbolic) variables have neither of these two relations. The two values of a categorical variable can be either equal or not equal: they only support an equality relation (Blue = Blue, or Red $\neq$ Black). Examples of variables of this type are eye color, sex, or country of citizenship. A categorical variable with two values can be converted, in principle, to a numeric binary variable with two values: 0 or 1. A categorical variable with N values can be converted into N binary numeric variables, namely, one binary variable for each categorical value. These coded categorical variables are known as "dummy variables" in statistics. For example, if the variable eye-color has four values: black, blue, green, and brown, they can be coded with four binary digits.

Feature value	Code
Black	1000
Blue	0100
Green	0010
Brown	0001

Another way of classifying variable, based on its values, is to look at it as a continuous variable or a discrete variable.

Continuous variables are also known as *quantitative* or *metric variables*. They are measured using either an interval scale or a ratio scale. Both scales allow the underlying variable to be defined or measured theoretically with infinite precision. The difference between these two scales lies in how the zero point is defined in the scale. The zero point in *the interval scale* is placed arbitrarily and thus it does not indicate the complete absence of whatever is being measured. The best example of the interval scale is the temperature scale, where zero degrees Fahrenheit does not mean a total absence of temperature. Because of the arbitrary placement of the zero point, the ratio relation does not hold true for variables measured using interval scales. For example, 80 degrees Fahrenheit does not imply twice as much heat as 40 degrees Fahrenheit. In contrast, *a ratio scale* has an absolute zero point and, consequently, the ratio relation holds true for variables measured using this scale. Quantities such as height, length, and salary use this type of scale. Continuous variables are represented in large data sets with values that are numbers—real or integers.

Discrete variables are also called qualitative variables. Such variables are measured, or its values defined, using one of two kinds of nonmetric scales—*nominal* or *ordinal*. A nominal scale is an order-less scale, which uses different symbols, characters, and numbers to represent the different states (values) of the variable being measured. An example of a nominal variable, a utility, customer-type identifier with possible values is residential, commercial, and industrial. These values can be coded alphabetically as A, B, and C, or numerically as 1, 2, or 3, but they do not have metric characteristics as the other numeric data have. Another example of a nominal attribute is the zip-code field available in many data sets. In both examples, the numbers used to designate different attribute values have no particular order and no necessary relation to one another.

An *ordinal scale* consists of ordered, discrete gradations, e.g., rankings. An ordinal variable is a categorical variable for which an order relation is defined but not a distance relation. Some examples of an ordinal attribute are the rank of a student in a class and the gold, silver, and bronze medal positions in a sports competition. The ordered scale need not be necessarily linear; e.g., the difference between the students ranked 4th and 5th need not be identical to the difference between the students ranked 15th and 16th. All that can be established from an ordered scale for ordinal attributes is greater-than, equal-to, or less-than relations. Typically, ordinal variables encode a numeric variable onto a small set of overlapping intervals corresponding to the values of an ordinal variable. These ordinal variables are closely related to the linguistic or fuzzy variables commonly used in spoken English; e.g., AGE (with values young, middle-aged, and old) and INCOME (with values low, middle-class, upper-middle-class, and rich). More about the formalization and use of fuzzy values in a data-mining process has been given in Chapter 11.

A special class of discrete variables is periodic variables. A *periodic variable* is a feature for which the distance relation exists but there is no order relation. Examples are days of the week, days of the month, or year. Monday and Tuesday, as the values of a feature, are closer than Monday and Thursday, but Monday can come before or after Friday.

Finally, one additional dimension of classification of data is based on its behavior with respect to time. Some data do not change with time and we consider them *static data*. On the other hand, there are attribute values that change with time and this type of data we call *dynamic* or *temporal data*. The majority of the data-mining methods are more suitable for static data, and special consideration and some preprocessing are often required to mine dynamic data.

Most data-mining problems arise because there are large amounts of samples with different types of features. Besides, these samples are very often high dimensional, which means they have extremely large number of measurable features. This additional dimension of large data sets causes the problem known in data-mining terminology as "the curse of dimensionality". The "curse of dimensionality" is produced because of the geometry of high-dimensional spaces, and these kinds of data spaces are typical for data-mining problems. The properties of high-dimensional spaces often appear counterintuitive because our experience with the physical world is in a low-dimensional space, such as a space with two or three dimensions. Conceptually, objects in high-dimensional spaces have a larger surface area for a given volume than objects in low-dimensional spaces. For example, a high-dimensional hypercube, if it could be visualized, would look like a porcupine, as in Figure 2.1. As the dimensionality grows larger, the edges grow longer relative to the size of the central part of the hypercube. Four important properties of high-dimensional data are often the guidelines in the interpretation of input data and data-mining results.

1. The size of a data set yielding the same density of data points in an n-dimensional space increases exponentially with dimensions. For example, if a one-dimensional sample containing n data points has a satisfactory level of density, then to achieve the same density of points in k dimensions, we need n^k data points. If integers 1 to 100 are values of one-dimensional samples, where the domain of the dimension is [0, 100], then to obtain the same density of samples in a 5-dimensional space we will need $100^5 = 10^{10}$ different samples. This is true even for the largest real-world data sets; because of their large dimensionality, the density of samples is still relatively low and, very often, unsatisfactory for data-mining purposes.

2. A larger radius is needed to enclose a fraction of the data points in a high-dimensional space. For a given fraction of samples, it is possible to determine the edge length e of the hypercube using the formula

FIGURE 2.1 High-dimensional data looks conceptually like a porcupine

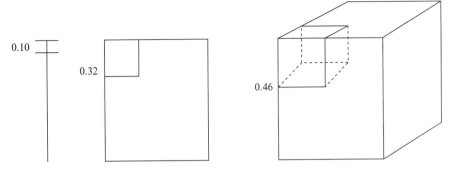

FIGURE 2.2   Regions enclose 10% of the samples for 1-, 2-, and 3-dimensional spaces

$$e(\mathrm{p}) = \mathrm{p}^{1/d}$$

where p is the prespecified fraction of samples and d is the number of dimensions. For example, if one wishes to enclose 10% of the samples (p = 0.1), the corresponding edge for a two-dimensional space will be $e_2(0.1) = 0.32$, for a three-dimensional space $e_3(0.1) = 0.46$, and for a 10-dimensional space $e_{10}(0.1) = 0.80$. Graphical interpretation of these edges is given in Figure 2.2.

This shows that a very large neighborhood is required to capture even a small portion of the data in a high-dimensional space.

3. Almost every point is closer to an edge than to another sample point in a high-dimensional space. For a sample size n, the expected distance D between data points in a d-dimensional space is

$$D(d, n) = 1/2(1/n)^{1/d}$$

For example, for a two-dimensional space with 10000 points the expected distance is D(2,10000) = 0.0005 and for a 10-dimensional space with the same number of sample points D(10,10000) = 0.4. Keep in mind that the maximum distance from any point to the edge occurs at the center of the distribution, and it is 0.5 for normalized values of all dimensions.

4. Almost every point is an outlier. As the dimension of the input space increases, the distance between the prediction point and the center of the classified points increases. For example, when d = 10, the expected value of the prediction point is 3.1 standard deviations away from the center of the data belonging to one class. When d = 20, the distance is 4.4 standard deviations. From this standpoint, the prediction of every new point looks like an outlier of the initially classified data. This is illustrated conceptually in Figure 2.1, where predicted points are mostly in the edges of the porcupine, far from the central part.

These rules of the "curse of dimensionality" most often have serious consequences when dealing with a finite number of samples in a high-dimensional space. From properties (1) and (2) we see the difficulty in making local estimates for high-dimensional samples; we need more and more samples to establish the required data density for performing planned mining activities. Properties (3) and (4) indicate the difficulty of predicting a response at a given point, since any new point will on average be closer to an edge than to the training examples in the central part.

2.2 CHARACTERISTICS OF RAW DATA

All raw data sets initially prepared for data mining are often large; many are related to human beings and have the potential for being messy. A priori, one should expect to find missing values, distortions, misrecording, inadequate sampling, and so on in these initial data sets. Raw data that do not appear to show any of these problems should immediately arouse suspicion. The only real reason for the high quality of data could be that the presented data have been cleaned up and preprocessed before the analyst sees them, as in data of a correctly designed and prepared data warehouse.

Let us see what the sources and implications of messy data are. First, data may be *missing* for a huge variety of reasons. Sometimes there are mistakes in measurements or recordings, but in many cases, the value is unavailable. To cope with this in a data-mining process, one must not only be able to model with the data that are presented, but even with their values missing. We will see later that some data-mining techniques are more or less sensitive to missing values. If the method is robust enough, then the missing values are not a problem. Otherwise, it is necessary to solve the problem of missing values before the application of a selected data-mining technique. The second cause of messy data is *misrecorded data*, and that is typical in large volumes of data. We have to have mechanisms to discover some of these "unusual" values; in some cases, even to work with them to eliminate their influence on the final results. Further, data may *not* be *from the population* they are supposed to be from. Outliers are typical examples here, and they require careful analysis before the analyst can decide whether they should be dropped from the data-mining process as anomalous or included as unusual examples from the population under study.

It is very important to examine the data thoroughly before undertaking any further steps in formal analysis. Traditionally, data-mining analysts had to familiarize themselves with their data before beginning to model them or use them with some data-mining algorithms. However, with the large size of modern data sets this is less feasible or even entirely impossible in many cases. Here we must rely on computer programs to check the data for us.

Distorted data, incorrect choice of steps in methodology, misapplication of data-mining tools, too idealized a model, a model which goes beyond the various sources of uncertainty and ambiguity in the data—all these represent possibilities for taking the wrong direction in a data-mining process. Therefore, data mining is not just a matter of simply applying a directory of tools to a given problem, but rather a process of critical assessments, exploration, testing, and evaluation. The data should be well-defined, consistent, and nonvolatile in nature. The quantity of data should be large enough to support data analysis, querying, reporting, and comparisons of historical data over a long period of time.

Many experts in data mining will agree that one of the most critical steps in a data-mining process is the preparation and transformation of the initial data set.

This task often receives little attention in the research literature, mostly because it is considered too application-specific. But, in most data-mining applications, some parts of a data-preparation process or, sometimes, even the entire process can be described independently of an application and a data-mining method. For some companies with extremely large and often distributed data sets, some of the data-preparation tasks can be performed during the design of the data warehouse, but many specialized transformations may be initialized only when a data-mining analysis is requested.

Raw data are not always (in our opinion very seldom!) the best data set prepared for data mining. Many transformations may be needed to produce features more useful for selected data-mining methods such as prediction or classification. Counting in different ways, using different sampling sizes, taking important ratios, varying data-window sizes for time-dependent data, and including changes in moving averages—all may contribute to better data-mining results. Do not expect that the machine will find the best set of transformations without human assistance and do not expect that transformations used in one-data mining application are the best for another.

The preparation of data is sometimes dismissed as a minor topic in the data-mining literature and as a phase in a data-mining process. In the real world of data-mining applications, the situation is reversed. More effort is expended preparing data than applying data-mining methods. There are two central tasks for the preparation of data:

1. To organize data into a standard form that is ready for processing by data-mining and other computer-based tools (a standard form is a relational table).
2. To prepare data sets that lead to the best data-mining performances.

2.3 TRANSFORMATION OF RAW DATA

We will review a few general types of transformations of data that are not problem-dependent and that may improve data-mining results. Selection of techniques and use in particular applications depend on types of data, amounts of data, and general characteristics of the data-mining task.

1. Normalizations

Some data-mining methods, typically those that are based on distance computation between points in an n-dimensional space, may need normalized data for best results. The measured values can be scaled to a specific range, e.g., [−1, 1], or [0, 1]. If the values are not normalized, the distance measures will overweight those features that have, on an average, larger values. There are many ways of normalizing data. Here are three simple and effective normalization techniques:

a) Decimal scaling   Decimal scaling moves the decimal point but still preserves most of the original digit value. The typical scale maintains the values in a range of

−1 to 1. The following equation describes decimal scaling, where v(i) is the value of the feature v for case i and v′(i) is a scaled value

$$v'(i) = v(i)/10^k$$

for the smallest k such that max$(|v'(i)|) < 1$.

First, the maximum $|v'(i)|$ is found in the data set and then, the decimal point is moved until the new, scaled, maximum absolute value is less than 1. The divisor is then applied to all other v(i). For example, if the largest value in the set is 455 and the smallest value is –834, then the maximum absolute value of the feature becomes .834, and the divisor for all v(i) is 1000 (k = 3).

*b) **Min–max normalization***   Suppose that the data for a feature v are in a range between 150 and 250. Then, the previous method of normalization will give all normalized data between .15 and .25; but it will accumulate the values on a small subinterval of the entire range. To obtain better distribution of values on a whole, normalized interval, e.g., [0, 1], we can use the min–max formula

$$v'(i) = (v(i) - min(v(i)))/(max(v(i)) - min(v(i)))$$

where the minimum and the maximum values for the feature v are computed on a set automatically, or they are estimated by an expert in a given domain. Similar transformation may be used for the normalized interval [−1, 1]. The automatic-computation of min and max values requires one additional search through the entire data set, but, computationally, the procedure is very simple. On the other hand, expert estimations of min and max values may cause unintentional accumulation of normalized values.

*c) **Standard deviation normalization***   Normalization by standard deviation often works well with distance measures, but transforms the data into a form unrecognizable from the original data. For a feature v, the mean value *mean*(v) and the standard deviation *sd*(v) are computed for the entire data set. Then, for a case *i*, the feature value is transformed using the equation

$$v'(i) = (v(i) - mean(v))/sd(v)$$

For example, if the initial set of values of the attribute is v = {1, 2, 3}, then *mean*(v) = 2, *sd*(v) = 1, and the new set of normalized values is v* = { − 1, 0, 1}.

Why not treat normalization as an implicit part of a data-mining method? The simple answer is that normalizations are useful for several diverse methods of data mining. Also very important is that the normalization is not a one-time or a one-phase event. If a method requires normalized data, available data will be transformed and prepared for the selected data-mining technique, but an identical normalization must be applied in all other phases of data-mining, and with all new and future data. Therefore, the normalization parameters must be saved along with a solution.

2. Data smoothing

A numeric feature, y, may range over many distinct values, sometimes as many as the number of training cases. For many data-mining techniques, minor differences between these values are not significant and may degrade the performance of the method and the final results. They may be considered as random variations of the same underlying value. Hence, it can be advantageous sometimes to smooth the values of the variable.

Many simple smoothers can be specified that average similar measured values. For example, if the values are real numbers with several decimal places, rounding the values to the given precision could be a simple smoothing algorithm for a large number of samples, where each sample has its own real value. If the set of values for the given feature F is {0.93, 1.01, 1.001, 3.02, 2.99, 5.03, 5.01, 4.98}, then it is obvious that smoothed values will be $F_{smoothed}$ = {1.0, 1.0, 1.0, 3.0, 3.0, 5.0, 5.0, 5.0}. This simple transformation is performed without losing any quality in a data set, and, at the same time, it reduces the number of different real values for the feature to only three.

Some of these smoothing algorithms are more complex, and they are explained in Section 3.2. Reducing the number of distinct values for a feature means reducing the dimensionality of the data space at the same time. Reduced values are particularly useful for logic-based methods of data mining, as will be explained in Chapter 6. Smoothers in this case can be used to discretize continuous features into a set of features with binary true–false values.

3. Differences and ratios

Even small changes to features can produce significant improvement in data-mining performances. The effects of relatively minor transformations of input or output features are particularly important in the specification of the data-mining goals. Two types of simple transformations, *differences* and *ratios*, could make improvements in goal specification, especially if they are applied to the output features.

These transformations sometimes produce better results than the simple, initial goal of predicting a number. In one application, e.g., the objective is to move the controls for a manufacturing process to an optimal setting. But instead of optimizing the absolute magnitude specification for the output $s(t + 1)$, it will be more effective to set the goal of a relative move from current value to a final optimal $s(t + 1) - s(t)$. The range of values for the relative moves is generally much smaller than the range of values for the absolute control setting. Therefore, for many data-mining methods, a smaller number of alternatives will improve the efficiency of the algorithm and will very often give better results.

Ratios are the second simple transformation of features. Using $s(t + 1)/s(t)$ as the output of a data-mining process instead of absolute value $s(t + 1)$ means that the level of increase or decrease in the values of a feature may also improve the performances of the entire mining process.

Differences and ratio transformations are not only useful for output features, but also for inputs. They can be used as changes in time for one feature or as a composition of different input features. For example, in many medical data sets, there are two features of a patient, height and weight, that are taken as input parameters for different diagnostic analyses. Many applications show that better diagnostic results are obtained when an initial transformation is performed using a new feature called the body–mass index (BMI), which is the weighted ratio between weight and height. This composite feature is better than the initial parameters to describe some of the characteristics of the patient, such as whether or not the patient is overweight.

Logical transformations can also be used to compose new features. For example, sometimes it is useful to generate a new feature which will determine the logical value of the relation A > B between existing features A and B. But there are no universally best data-transformation methods. The lesson to be learned is that a major role remains for human insight while defining the problem. Attention should be paid to composing features, because relatively simple transformations can sometimes be far more effective for the final performance than switching to some other techniques of data mining.

2.4 MISSING DATA

For many real-world applications of data mining, even when there are huge amounts of data, the subset of cases with complete data may be relatively small. Available samples and also future cases may have values missing. Some of the data-mining methods accept missing values and satisfactorily process data to reach a final conclusion. Other methods require that all values be available. An obvious question is whether these missing values can be filled in during data preparation, prior to the application of the data-mining methods. The simplest solution for this problem is the reduction of the data set and the elimination of all samples with missing values. That is possible when large data sets are available, and missing values occur only in a small percentage of samples. If we do not drop the samples with missing values, then we have to find values for them. What are the practical solutions?

First, a data miner, together with the domain expert, can manually examine samples that have no values and enter a reasonable, probable, or expected value, based on a domain experience. The method is straightforward for small numbers of missing values and relatively small data sets. But, if there is no obvious or plausible value for each case, the miner is introducing noise into the data set by manually generating a value.

The second approach gives an even simpler solution for elimination of missing values. It is based on a formal, often automatic replacement of missing values with some constants, such as:

1. Replace all missing values with a single global constant (a selection of a global constant is highly application-dependent).
2. Replace a missing value with its feature mean.
3. Replace a missing value with its feature mean for the given class (this approach is possible only for classification problems where samples are classified in advance).

These simple solutions are tempting. Their main flaw is that the substituted value is not the correct value. By replacing the missing value with a constant or changing the values for a few different features, the data are biased. The re-placed value (values) will homogenize the cases with missing values into a uniform subset directed toward the class with most missing values (an artificial class!). If missing values are replaced with a single global constant for all features, an unknown value may be implicitly made into a positive factor that is not objectively justified.

One possible interpretation of missing values is that they are "don't care" values. In other words, we suppose that these values do not have any influence on the final data-mining results. In that case, a sample with the missing value may be extended to the set of artificial samples, where, for each new sample, the missing value is replaced with one of the possible feature values of a given domain. Although this interpret-ation may look more natural, the problem with this approach is the combinatorial explosion of artificial samples. For example, if one three-dimensional sample X is given as $X = \{1, ?, 3\}$, where the second feature's value is missing, the process will generate five artificial samples for the feature domain [0, 1, 2, 3, 4]

$$X_1 = \{1, 0, 3\}, X_2 = \{1, 1, 3\}, X_3 = \{1, 2, 3\}, X_4 = \{1, 3, 3\}, \text{ and } X_5 = \{1, 4, 3\}$$

Finally, the data miner can generate a predictive model to predict each of the missing values. For example, if three features A, B, and C are given for each sample, then, based on samples that have all three values as a training set, the data miner can generate a model of correlation between features. Different techniques such as regression, Bayesian formalism, clustering, or decision-tree induction may be used depending on data types (all these techniques are explained later in this book in Chapters 5, 6, and 7). Once you have a trained model, you can present a new sample that has a value missing and generate a "predictive" value. For example, if values for features A and B are given, the model generates the value for the feature C. If a missing value is highly correlated with the other known features, this process will generate the best value for that feature. Of course, if you can always predict a missing value with certainty, this means that the feature is redun-dant in a data set and not necessary in further data-mining analyses. In real-world applications, you should expect an imperfect correlation between the feature with the missing value and other features. Therefore, all automatic methods fill in values that may not be correct. Such automatic methods, however, are among the most popular in the data-mining community. In comparison to the other methods, they use the most information from the present data to predict missing values.

In general, it is speculative and often misleading to replace missing values using a simple, artificial schema of data preparation. It is best to generate multiple solu-tions of data mining with and without features that have missing values and then analyze and interpret them.

2.5 TIME-DEPENDENT DATA

Practical data-mining applications will range from those having strong time-dependent relationships to those with loose or no time relationships. Real-world problems with time dependencies require special preparation and transformation of data, which are, in many cases, critical for successful data mining. We will start with the simplest case—a single feature measured over time. This feature has a series of values over fixed time units. For example, a temperature reading could be measured every hour, or the sales of a product could be recorded every day. This is the classical univariate time-series problem, where it is expected that the value of the variable X at a given time be related to previous values. Because the time series is measured at fixed units of time, the series of values can be expressed as

$$X = \{t(1), t(2), t(3), \ldots, t(n)\}$$

where t(n) is the most recent value.

For many time-series problems, the goal is to forecast $t(n + 1)$ from previous values of the feature, where these values are directly related to the predicted value. One of the most important steps in preprocessing of row, time-dependent data is the specification of a window or a time lag. This is the number of previous values that influence the prediction. Every window represents one sample of data for further analysis. For example, if the time series consists of the eleven measurements

$$X = \{t(0), t(1), t(2), t(3), t(4), t(5), t(6), t(7), t(8), t(9), t(10)\}$$

and if the window for analysis of the time-series is five, then it is possible to reorganize the input data into a tabular form with six samples, which is more convenient (standardized) for the application of data-mining techniques. Transformed data are given in Table 2.1.

The best time lag must be determined by the usual evaluation techniques for a varying complexity measure using independent test data. Instead of preparing the data once and turning them over to the data-mining programs for prediction, additional iterations of data preparation have to be performed. While the typical goal is to predict the next value in time, in some applications, the goal can be modified to predict values in the future, several time units in advance. More formally, given the time-dependent values $t(n - i), \ldots, t(n)$, it is necessary to predict the value $t(n + j)$. In the previous example, taking $j = 3$, the new samples are given in Table 2.2.

TABLE 2.1   Transformation of Time Series to standard tabular form (window = 5)

Sample	W I N D O W					Next Value
	M1	M2	M3	M4	M5	
1	t(0)	t(1)	t(2)	t(3)	t(4)	t(5)
2	t(1)	t(2)	t(3)	t(4)	t(5)	t(6)
3	t(2)	t(3)	t(4)	t(5)	t(6)	t(7)
4	t(3)	t(4)	t(5)	t(6)	t(7)	t(8)
5	t(4)	t(5)	t(6)	t(7)	t(8)	t(9)
6	t(5)	t(6)	t(7)	t(8)	t(9)	t(10)

TABLE 2.2   Time-series samples in standard tabular form (window = 5) with postponed predictions (j = 3)

Sample	W	I	N	D	O	W	Next Value
	M1	M2	M3	M4	M5		
1	t(0)	t(1)	t(2)	t(3)	t(4)		t(7)
2	t(1)	t(2)	t(3)	t(4)	t(5)		t(8)
3	t(2)	t(3)	t(4)	t(5)	t(6)		t(9)
4	t(3)	t(4)	t(5)	t(6)	t(7)		t(10)

In general, the further out in the future, the more difficult and less reliable is the forecast. The goal for a time series can easily be changed from predicting the next value in the time series to classification into one of predefined categories. From a data-preparation perspective there are no significant changes. For example, instead of predicted output value $t(i+1)$, the new classified output will be binary: T for $t(i+1) \geq$ threshold value and F for $t(i+1) <$ threshold value.

The time units can be relatively small, enlarging the number of artificial features in a tabular representation of time series for the same time period. The resulting problem of high dimensionality is the price paid for precision in the standard representation of the time-series data.

In practice, many older values of a feature may be historical relics that are no more relevant and should not be used for analysis. Therefore, for many business and social applications, new trends can make old data less reliable and less useful. This leads to a greater emphasis on recent data, possibly discarding the oldest portions of the time series. Now we are talking not only of a fixed window for the presentation of a time series, but also on a fixed size for the data set. Only the n most recent cases are used for analysis, and, even then, they may not be given equal weight. These decisions must be given careful attention and are somewhat dependent on knowledge of the application and past experience. For example, using 20-year-old data about cancer patients will not give the correct picture about the chances of survival today.

Besides standard tabular representation of time series, sometimes it is necessary to additionally preprocess raw data and summarize their characteristics before application of data-mining techniques. Many times it is better to predict the difference $t(n+1) - t(n)$ instead of the absolute value $t(n+1)$ as the output. Also, using a ratio, $t(n+1)/t(n)$, which indicates the percentage of changes, can sometimes give better prediction results. These transformations of the predicted values of the output are particularly useful for logic-based data-mining methods such as decision trees or rules. When differences or ratios are used to specify the goal, features measuring differences or ratios for input features may also be advantageous.

Time-dependent cases are specified in terms of a goal and a time lag or a window of size m. One way of summarizing features in the data set is to average them, producing "*moving averages*" (MA). A single average summarizes the most recent m feature values for each case, and for each increment in time moment i, its value is

$$MA(i, m) = 1/m \cdot \sum_{j=i-m+1}^{i} t(j)$$

Knowledge of the application can aid in specifying reasonable sizes for m. Error estimation should validate these choices. Moving averages weight all time points equally in the average. Typical examples are moving averages in the stock market such as 200-days moving average for DOW or NASDAQ. The objective is to smooth neighboring time points by a moving average to reduce the random variation and noise components

$$MA(i, m) = t(i) = \text{ mean}(i) + \text{error}$$

Another type of average is an *exponential moving average* (EMA) that gives more weight to the most recent time periods. It is described recursively as

$$EMA(i, m) = p*t(i) + (1 - p)*EMA(i - 1, m - 1)$$
$$EMA(i, 1) = t(i)$$

where p is a value between 0 and 1. For example, if $p = 0.5$, the most recent value t(i) is equally weighted with the computation for all previous values in the window, where the computation begins with averaging the first two values in the series. The computation starts with the following two equations:

$$EMA(i, 2) = 0.5t(i) + 0.5t(i - 1)$$
$$EMA(i, 3) = 0.5t(i) + 0.5[0.5t(i - 1) + 0.5t(i - 2)]$$

As usual, application knowledge or empirical validation determines the value of p. The exponential moving average has performed very well for many business-related applications, usually producing results superior to the moving average.

A moving average summarizes the recent past, but spotting a change in the trend of the data may additionally improve forecasting performances. Characteristics of a trend can be measured by composing features that compare recent measurements to those of the more distant past. Three simple comparative features are

1. $t(i) - MA(i, m)$, the difference between the current value and a moving average;
2. $MA(i, m) - MA(i - k, m)$, the difference between two moving averages, usually of the same window size, and
3. $t(i)/MA(i, m)$, the ratio between the current value and a moving average, which may be preferable for some applications.

In general, the main components of the summarizing features for a time series are

1. current values,
2. smoothed values using moving averages, and
3. derived trends, differences, and ratios.

The immediate extension of a univariate time series is to a multivariate one. Instead of having a single measured value at time i, t(i), multiple measurements t[a(i), b(j)] are taken at the same time. There are no extra steps in data preparation for the multivariate time series. Each series can be transformed into features, and the values of the features at each distinct time i are merged into a sample. The resultant transformations yield a standard tabular form of data such as the table given in Figure 2.3.

While some data-mining problems are characterized by a single time series, hybrid applications are more frequent in real-world problems, having both time series and features that are not dependent on time. In these cases, standard procedures for time-dependent transformation and summarization of attributes are performed. High dimensions of data generated during these transformations can be reduced through the next phase of a data-mining process: data reduction.

Some data sets do not include a time component explicitly, but the entire analysis is performed in the time domain (typically based on several dates that are attributes of described entities). One very important class of data belonging to this type is *survival data*. Survival data are data concerning how long it takes for a particular event to happen. In many medical applications the event is the death of a patient, and, therefore, we analyze the patient's survival time. In industrial applications, the event is often the failure of a component in a machine. Thus, the output in these sorts of problems is the survival time. The inputs are the patient's records in medical applications and characteristics of the machine component in industrial applications. There are two main characteristics of survival data that make them different from the data in other data-mining problems. The first characteristic is called *censoring*. In many studies, the event has not happened by the end of the study period. So, for some patients in a medical trial we might know that the patient was still alive after five years, but do not know when the patient died. This sort of observation would be called a censored observation. If the output is censored we do not know the value of the output, but we do have some information about it. The second characteristic of survival data is that the input values are *time-dependent*. Since collecting data entails waiting until the event happens, it is possible for the inputs to change its value during the waiting period. If a patient stops smoking or starts with a new drug during the study, it is important to know what data to include into the study and how to represent these changes in time. Data-mining analysis for these types of problems concentrates on the survivor

Time	a	b
1	5	117
2	8	113
3	4	116
4	9	118
5	10	119
6	12	120

Sample	a(n-2)	a(n-1)	a(n)	b(n-2)	b(n-1)	b(n)
1	5	8	4	117	113	116
2	8	4	9	113	116	118
3	4	9	8	116	118	119
4	9	10	12	118	119	120

a) Initial time-dependent data

b) Samples prepared for data mining with time window = 3

FIGURE 2.3 Tabulation of time-dependent features a and b

function or the hazard function. The survivor function is the probability of the survival time being greater than the time t. The hazard function indicates how likely a failure (of the industrial component) is at time t, given that a failure has not occurred before time t.

2.6 OUTLIER ANALYSIS

Very often, in large data sets, there exist samples that do not comply with the general behavior of the data model. Such samples, which are significantly different or inconsistent with the remaining set of data, are called outliers. Outliers can be caused by measurement error or they may be the result of inherent data variability. If, e.g., the display of a person's age in the database is −1 the value is obviously not correct, and the error could have been caused by a default setting of the field "unrecorded age" in the computer program. On the other hand, if, in the database, the number of children for one person is 25 this datum is unusual and has to be checked. The value could be a typographical error, or it could be correct and represent real variability for the given attribute.

Many data-mining algorithms try to minimize the influence of outliers on the final model, or to eliminate them in the preprocessing phases. The data-mining analyst has to be very careful in the automatic elimination of outliers because, if the data are correct, that could result in the loss of important hidden information. Some data-mining applications are focused on outlier detection, and it is the essential result of a data analysis. For example, while detecting fraudulent credit card transactions in a bank, the outliers are typical examples that may indicate fraudulent activity, and the entire data-mining process is concentrated on their detection. But, in most of the other data-mining applications, especially if they are supported with large data sets, outliers are not very useful, and they are more the result of errors in data collection than a characteristic of a data set.

Outlier detection and potential removal from a data set can be described as a process of the selection of k out of n samples that are considerably dissimilar, exceptional, or inconsistent with respect to the remaining data. The problem of defining outliers is nontrivial, especially in multidimensional samples. Data visualization methods that are useful in outlier detection for one to three dimensions are weaker in multidimensional data because of a lack of adequate visualization methodologies for these spaces. An example of a visualization of two-dimensional samples and visual detection of outliers is given in Figure 2.4.

The simplest approach to outlier detection for one-dimensional samples is based on statistics. Assuming that the distribution of values is given, it is necessary to find basic statistical parameters such as mean value and variance. Based on these values and the expected (or predicted) number of outliers, it is possible to establish the threshold value as a function of variance. All samples out of the threshold value are candidates for outliers. The main problem with this simple methodology is an a priori assumption about data distribution. In most real-world examples the data distribution may not be known.

For example, if the given data set represents the feature Age with twenty different values:

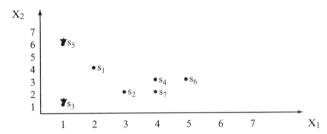

FIGURE 2.4   Visualization of two-dimensional data set for outlier detection

$$Age = \{3, 56, 23, 39, 156, 52, 41, 22, 9, 28, 139, 31, 55, 20,$$
$$-67, 37, 11, 55, 45, 37\}$$

then, the corresponding statistical parameters are

Mean = 39.9
Standard deviation = 45.65

If we select the threshold value for normal distribution of data as

$$Threshold = Mean \pm 2 \times Standard\ deviation$$

then, all data that are out of range $[-54.1, 131.2]$ will be potential outliers. Additional knowledge of the characteristics of the feature (Age is always greater then zero) may further reduce the range to $[0, 131.2]$. In our example there are three values that are outliers based on the given criteria: 156, 139, and -67. With a high probability we can conclude that all three of them are typo-errors (data entered with additional digits or an additional "$-$" sign).

Distance-based outlier detection is a second method that eliminates some of the limitations imposed by the statistical approach. The most important difference is that this method is applicable to multidimensional samples while statistical descriptors analyze only a single dimension, or several dimensions, but separately. The basic computational complexity of this method is the evaluation of distance measures between all samples in an n-dimensional data set. Then, a sample s_i in a data set S is an outlier if at least a fraction p of the samples in S lies at a distance greater than d. In other words, distance-based outliers are those samples which do not have enough neighbors, where neighbors are defined through the multidimensional distance between samples. Obviously, the criterion for outlier detection is based on two parameters, p and d, which may be given in advance using knowledge about the data, or which may be changed during the iterations (trial-and-error approach) to select the most representative outliers.

To illustrate the approach we can analyze a set of two-dimensional samples S, where the requirements for outliers are the values of thresholds $p \geq 4$ and $d \geq 3$

$$S = \{s_1, s_2, s_3, s_4, s_5, s_6, s_7\} = \{(2, 4), (3, 2), (1, 1), (4, 3), (1, 6), (5, 3), (4, 2)\}$$

The table of Euclidian distances, $d = [(x1 - x2)^2 + (y1 - y2)^2]^{1/2}$, for the set S is given in Table 2.3 and, based on this table, we can calculate a value for the parameter p with the given threshold distance (d = 3) for each sample. The results are represented in Table 2.4.

Using the results of the applied procedure and given threshold values, it is possible to select samples s_3 and s_5 as outliers (because their values for p is above the threshold value: p = 4). The same results could be obtained by visual inspection of a data set, represented in Figure 2.4. Of course, the given data set is very small and a two-dimensional graphical representation is possible and useful. For n-dimensional, real-world data analyses the visualization process is much more difficult, and analytical approaches in outlier detection are often more practical and reliable.

Deviation-based techniques are the third class of outlier-detection methods. These techniques simulate the way in which humans can distinguish unusual samples from a set of other similar samples. These methods define the basic characteristics of the sample set, and all samples that deviate from these characteristics are outliers. The sequential-exception technique is one possible approach that is based on a dissimilarity function. For a given set of n samples, a possible dissimilarity function is the total variance of the sample set. Now, the task is to define the smallest subset of samples whose removal results in the greatest reduction of the dissimilarity function for the residual set. The general task of finding outliers using this method can be very complex (combinational explosion of different

TABLE 2.3   **Table of distances for data set S**

	s_1	s_2	s_3	s_4	s_5	s_6	s_7
s_1		2.236	3.162	2.236	2.236	3.162	2.828
s_2			2.236	1.414	4.472	2.236	1.000
s_3				3.605	5.000	4.472	3.162
s_4					4.242	1.000	1.000
s_5						5.000	5.000
s_6							1.414

TABLE 2.4   **Number of points p with the distance greater then d for each given point in S**

Sample	p
s_1	2
s_2	1
s_3	5
s_4	2
s_5	5
s_6	3

selections of the set of potential outliners – the so called exception set), and it can be theoretically defined as an NP-hard problem (i.e., intractable). If we settle for a less-than-optimal answer, the algorithm's complexity can be reduced to the linear level, using a sequential approach. Using the greedy method, the algorithm reduces the size sequentially, sample by sample (or subset by subset), by selecting at each step the one that causes the greatest decrease in the total variance.

2.7 REVIEW QUESTIONS AND PROBLEMS

1. Generate the tree structure of data types explained in Section 2.1.

2. If one attribute in the data set is student-grade with values A, B, C, D, and F, what type is these attribute values? Give a recommendation for preprocessing of the given attribute.

3. Explain why "the curse of dimensionality" principles are especially important in understanding large data sets.

4. Every attribute in a 6-dimensional sample is described with one out of three numeric values {0, 0.5, 1}. If there exist samples for all possible combinations of attribute values, what will be the number of samples in a data set and what will be the expected distance between points in a 6-dimensional space?

5. Derive the formula for min–max normalization of data on [−1, 1] interval.

6. Given one-dimensional data set $X = \{-5.0, 23.0, 17.6, 7.23, 1.11\}$, normalize the data set using
   a) Decimal scaling on interval [−1, 1].
   b) Min–max normalization on interval [0, 1].
   c) Min–max normalization on interval [−1, 1].
   d) Standard deviation normalization.
   e) Compare the results of previous normalizations and discuss the advantages and disadvantages of different techniques.

7. Perform data smoothing using a simple rounding technique for a data set:

$$Y = \{1.17, 2.59, 3.38, 4.23, 2.67, 1.73, 2.53, 3.28, 3.44\}$$

and present the new data set when the rounding is performed to the precision of:
   a) 0.1
   b) 1.

8. Given a set of four-dimensional samples with missing values:

$$X1 = \{0, 1, 1, 2\}$$
$$X2 = \{2, 1, -, 1\}$$

$$X3 = \{1, -, -, 0\}$$
$$X4 = \{-, 2, 1, -\}$$

if the domains for all attributes are [0, 1, 2], what will be the number of "artificial" samples if missing values are interpreted as "don't care values" and they are replaced with all possible values for a given domain.

9. A twenty-four-hour, time-dependent data set X is collected as a training data set to predict values three hours in advance. If the data set X is

$$X = \{7, 8, 9, 10, 9, 8, 7, 9, 11, 13, 15, 17, 16, 15,$$
$$14, 13, 12, 11, 10, 9, 7, 5, 3, 1\}$$

a) what will be a standard tabular representation of data set X if
   i) the window width is 6, and a prediction variable is based on the difference between the current value and the value after three hours. What is the number of samples?
   ii) the window width is 12, and the prediction variable is based on ratio. What is the number of samples?
b) Plot discrete X values together with computed 6- and 12-hours moving averages (MA).
c) Plot time-dependent variable X and its 4-hours exponential moving average (EMA).

10. The number of children for different patients in a database is given with a vector

$$C = \{3, 1, 0, 2, 7, 3, 6, 4, -2, 0, 0, 10, 15, 6\}.$$

a) Find the outliers in the set C using standard statistical parameters mean and variance.
b) If the threshold value is changed from ±3 standard deviations to ±2 standard deviations, what additional outliers are found?

11. For a given data set X of three-dimensional samples,

$$X = [\{1, 2, 0\}, \{3, 1, 4\}, \{2, 1, 5\}, \{0, 1, 6\}, \{2, 4, 3\}, \{4, 4, 2\},$$
$$\{5, 2, 1\}, \{7, 7, 7\}, \{0, 0, 0\}, \{3, 3, 3\}].$$

a) find the outliers using the distance-based technique if
   i) the threshold distance is 4, and threshold fraction p for non-neighbor samples is 3.
   ii) the threshold distance is 6, and threshold fraction p for non-neighbor samples is 2.
b) Describe the procedure and interpret the results of outlier detection based on mean values and variances for each dimension separately.

12. Discuss the applications in which you would prefer to use exponential moving averages (EMA) instead of moving averages (MA).

13. If your data set contains missing values, discuss the basic analyses and corresponding decisions you will take in the preprocessing phase of the data-mining process.

14. Develop a software tool for the detection of outliers if the data for preprocessing are given in the form of a flat file with n-dimensional samples.

2.8   REFERENCES FOR FURTHER STUDY

1. Bischoff, J. and T. Alexander, *Data Warehouse: Practical Advice from the Experts*, Prentice Hall, Upper Saddle River, 1997.

   The objective of a data warehouse is to provide any data, anywhere, anytime in a timely manner at a reasonable cost. Different techniques used to preprocess the data in warehouses reduce the effort in initial phases of data mining.

2. Hand, D., Mannila H., Smith P., *Principles of Data Mining*, MIT Press, Cambridge: MA, 2001.

   The book consists of three sections. The first, foundations, provides a tutorial overview of the principles underlying data-mining algorithms and their applications. The second section, data-mining algorithms, shows how algorithms are constructed to solve specific problems in a principled manner. The third section shows how all of the preceding analysis fits together when applied to real-world data-mining problems.

3. Kennedy, R. L. et al., *Solving Data Mining Problems through Pattern Recognition*, Prentice Hall, Upper Saddle River: NJ, 1998.

   The book takes a practical approach to overall data mining–project development. The rigorous, multistep methodology includes defining the data set; collection, preparation and preprocessing of data; choosing the appropriate technique and tuning the parameters; training, testing, and troubleshooting.

4. Weiss, S. M. and N. Indurkhya, *Predictive Data Mining: a Practical Guide*, Morgan Kaufman Publishers, San Francisco, 1998.

   This book focuses on the data-preprocessing phase in successful data-mining applications. Preparation and organization of data and development of an overall strategy for data mining are not only time-consuming processes, but also fundamental requirements in real-world data mining. The simple presentation of topics with a large number of examples is an additional strength of the book.

3 Data Reduction

CHAPTER OBJECTIVES

- Identify the differences in dimensionality reduction based on features, cases, and reduction of value techniques.

- Explain the advantages of data reduction in the preprocessing phase of a data-mining process.

- Understand the basic principles of feature-selection and feature-composition tasks using corresponding statistical methods.

- Apply and compare entropy-based technique and principal component analysis for feature ranking.

- Understand the basic principles and implement ChiMerge and Bin-based techniques for reduction of discrete values.

- Distinguish approaches in cases where reduction is based on incremental and average samples.

For small or moderate data sets, the preprocessing steps mentioned in the previous chapter in preparation for data mining are usually enough. For really large data sets, there is an increased likelihood that an intermediate, additional step—data reduction—should be performed prior to applying the data-mining techniques. While large data sets have the potential for better mining results, there is no guarantee that they will yield better knowledge than small data sets. Given multidimensional data, a central question is whether it can be determined, prior to searching for all data-mining solutions in all dimensions, that the method has exhausted its potential for mining and discovery in a reduced data set. More commonly, a general solution is deduced from a subset of available features or cases, and it will remain the same even when the search space is enlarged.

The main theme for simplifying the data in this step is dimension reduction, and the main question is whether some of these prepared and preprocessed data can be discarded without sacrificing the quality of results. There is one additional question about techniques for data reduction: Can the prepared data be reviewed and a subset found in a reasonable amount of time and space? If the complexity of algorithms for data reduction increases exponentially, then there is little to gain in reducing dimensions in big data. In this chapter, we will present basic and relatively efficient techniques for dimension reduction applicable to different data-mining problems.

3.1 DIMENSIONS OF LARGE DATA SETS

The choice of data representation, and selection, reduction, or transformation of features is probably the most important issue that determines the quality of a data-mining solution. Besides influencing the nature of a data-mining algorithm, it can determine whether the problem is solvable at all, or how powerful the resulting model of data mining is. A large number of features can make available samples of data relatively insufficient for mining. In practice, the number of features can be as many as several hundreds. If we have only a few hundred samples for analysis, dimensionality reduction is required in order for any reliable model to be mined or to be of any practical use. On the other hand, data overload, because of high dimensionality, can make some data-mining algorithms nonapplicable, and the only solution is again a reduction of data dimensions. The three main dimensions of preprocessed data sets, usually represented in the form of flat files, are *columns* (features), *rows* (cases or samples), and *values* of the features.

Therefore, the three basic operations in a data-reduction process are delete a column, delete a row, and reduce the number of values in a column (smooth a feature). These operations attempt to preserve the character of the original data by deleting data that are nonessential. There are other operations that reduce dimensions, but the new data are unrecognizable when compared to the original data set, and these operations are mentioned here just briefly because they are highly application-dependent. One approach is the replacement of a set of initial features with a new composite feature. For example, if samples in a data set have two features, person-height and person-weight, it is possible for some applications in the medical domain to replace these two features with only one, body-mass-index, which is proportional to the quotient of the initial two features. Final reduction of data does not reduce the quality of results; in some applications, the results of data mining are even improved.

Performing standard data-reduction operations (deleting rows, columns, or values) as a preparation for data mining, we need to know what we gain and/or lose with these activities. The overall comparison involves the following parameters for analysis:

1. *Computing time* – Simpler data, a result of the data-reduction process, can hopefully lead to a reduction in the time taken for data mining. In most cases, we cannot afford to spend too much time on the data-preprocessing phases, including a reduction of data dimensions, although the more time we spend in preparation the better the outcome.

2. *Predictive/descriptive accuracy* – This is the dominant measure for most data-mining models since it measures how well the data is summarized and generalized into the model. We generally expect that by using only relevant features, a data-mining algorithm can not only learn faster but also with higher accuracy. Irrelevant data may mislead a learning process and a final model, while redundant data may complicate the task of learning and cause unexpected data-mining results.

3. *Representation of the data-mining model* – The simplicity of representation, obtained usually with data reduction, often implies that a model can be better understood. The simplicity of the induced model and other results depends on its representation. Therefore, if the simplicity of representation improves, a relatively small decrease in accuracy may be tolerable. The need for a balanced view between accuracy and simplicity is necessary, and dimensionality reduction is one of the mechanisms for obtaining this balance.

It would be ideal if we could achieve reduced time, improved accuracy, and simplified representation at the same time, using dimensionality reduction. More often, however, we gain in some and lose in others, and balance between them according to the application at hand. It is well known that no single data-reduction method can be best suited for all applications. A decision about method selection is based on available knowledge about an application (relevant data, noise data, meta-data, correlated features), and required time constraints for the final solution.

Algorithms that perform all basic operations for data reduction are not simple, especially when they are applied to large data sets. Therefore, it is useful to enumerate the desired properties of these algorithms before giving their detailed descriptions. Recommended characteristics of data-reduction algorithms that may be guidelines for designers of these techniques are as follows:

1. *Measurable quality* – the quality of approximated results using a reduced data set can be determined precisely.
2. *Recognizable quality* – the quality of approximated results can be easily determined at run time of the data-reduction algorithm, before application of any data-mining procedure.
3. *Monotonicity* – the algorithms are usually iterative, and the quality of results is a nondecreasing function of time and input data quality.
4. *Consistency* – the quality of results is correlated with computation time and input data quality.
5. *Diminishing returns* – the improvement in the solution is large in the early stages (iterations) of the computation, and it diminishes over time.
6. *Interruptability* – the algorithm can be stopped at any time and provide some answers.
7. *Preemptability* – the algorithm can be suspended and resumed with minimal overhead.

3.2 FEATURES REDUCTION

When we are talking about data quality and improved performances of reduced data sets, we can see that this issue is not only about noisy or contaminated data (problems mainly solved in the preprocessing phase), but also about irrelevant, correlated, and redundant data. Recall that data with corresponding features are not usually collected solely for data-mining purposes. Therefore, dealing with relevant features alone can be far more effective and efficient. Basically, we want to choose features that are relevant to our data-mining application in order to achieve maximum performance with the minimum measurement and processing effort. A feature-reduction process should result in

1. less data so that the data-mining algorithm can learn faster;
2. higher accuracy of a data-mining process so that the model can generalize better from data;
3. simple results of a data-mining process so that they are easier to understand and use; and

4. fewer features so that in the next round of data collection, a saving can be made by removing redundant or irrelevant features.

Let us start our detailed analysis of possible column-reduction techniques, where features are eliminated from the data set based on a given criterion. Two standard tasks are associated with producing a reduced set of features, and they are classified as

1. *Feature selection* – Based on the knowledge of the application domain and the goals of the mining effort, the human analyst may select a subset of the features found in the initial data set. The process of feature selection can be manual or supported by some automated procedures.

2. *Feature composition* – There are transformations of data that can have a surprisingly strong impact on the results of data-mining methods. In this sense, the composition of features is a greater determining factor in the quality of data-mining results than the specific mining technique. In most instances, feature composition is dependent on knowledge of the application, and an interdisciplinary approach to feature composition tasks produces significant improvements in the preparation of data.

Different feature-selection methods will give different reduced data sets, and we can globally classify all this methods into two: feature-ranking algorithms and minimum subset algorithms.

In the feature-ranking algorithm, one can expect a ranked list of features that are ordered according to a specific evaluation measure. A measure can be based on accuracy of available data, consistency, information content, distances between samples, and finally, statistical dependencies between features. These algorithms do not tell you what the minimum set of features for further analysis is; they indicate only the relevance of a feature compared to others. Minimum-subset algorithms, on the other hand, return a minimum feature subset and no differences are made among features in the subset—all have the same ranking. The features in the subset are relevant for the mining process; the others are irrelevant. In both types of algorithms, it is important to establish a feature-evaluation scheme: the way in which the features are evaluated and then ranked, or added to the selected subset.

Feature selection in general can be viewed as a search problem, with each state in the search space specifying a subset of the possible features. If, for example, a data set has three features $\{A_1, A_2, A_3\}$, and in the process of selecting features, the presence of a feature is coded with 1 and its absence with 0, then there should be a total of 2^3 reduced-feature subsets coded with $\{0, 0, 0\}$, $\{1, 0, 0\}$, $\{0, 1, 0\}$, $\{0, 0, 1\}$, $\{1, 1, 0\}$, $\{1, 0, 1\}$, $\{0, 1, 1\}$, and $\{1, 1, 1\}$. The problem of feature selection is relatively trivial if the search space is small, since we can analyze all subsets in any order and a search will get completed in a short time. However, the search space is usually not small. It is 2^N where the number of dimensions N in typical data-mining applications is large (N > 20). This makes the starting point and the search strategy very important. An exhaustive search of all subsets of features very often is replaced with some heuristic search procedures. Using knowledge of the problem, these procedures find near-optimal subsets of features that further improve the quality of the data-mining process.

The objective of feature selection is to find a subset of features with data-mining performances comparable to the full set of features. Given a set of features m, the number of subsets to be evaluated as candidates for column reduction is finite, but still very large for iterative analysis through all cases. For practical reasons, an optimal search is not feasible, and simplifications are made to produce reasonable, acceptable, and timely results. If the reduction task is to create a subset, one possibility—the so called bottom-up approach—starts with an empty set, and fills it in by choosing the most relevant features from the initial set of features. This process is based on some heuristic criteria for a feature evaluation. The top-down approach, on the other hand, begins with a full set of original features and then removes one-by-one those that are shown as irrelevant based on the selected heuristic evaluation measure. Additional approximations to the optimal approach are

1. to examine only promising subsets of features – promising subsets are usually obtained heuristically. This provides enough room for exploration of competing alternatives
2. to substitute computationally simple distance measures for the error measures – this approximation will reduce the computation time yet give satisfactory results for comparison of subset alternatives
3. to select features based only on subsets of large amounts of data, but the subsequent steps of data mining will be applied on the whole set.

The application of feature selection and reduction of data dimensionality helps all phases of the data-mining process for successful knowledge discovery. It has to be started in the preprocessing phase, but, on many occasions, feature selection and reduction is a part of the data-mining algorithm, even it is applied in postprocessing for better evaluation and consolidation of obtained results.

Let us return to the promising subsets of features. One possible technique for feature selection is based on comparison of *means* and *variances*. To summarize the key characteristics of the distribution of values for a given feature, it is necessary to compute the mean value and the corresponding variance. The main weakness in this approach is that the distribution for the feature is not known. If it is assumed to be a normal curve, the statistics can work out very well, but this may in fact be a poor assumption. Without knowing the shape of the distribution curve, the means and variances are viewed as heuristics for feature selection, not exact, mathematical modeling tools.

In general, if one feature describes different classes of entities, samples of different classes can be examined. The means of feature values are normalized by its variances and then compared. If the means are far apart, interest in a feature increases; it has potential, in terms of its use in distinguishing between two classes. If the means are indistinguishable, interest wanes in that feature. It is a heuristic, nonoptimal approach to feature selection, but it is consistent with practical experience in many data-mining applications in the triage of features. Next equations formalize the test, where A and B are sets of feature values measured for two different classes, and n_1 and n_2 are the corresponding number of samples:

$$SE(A - B) = \sqrt{(var(A)/n_1 + var(B)/n_2)}$$

$$TEST: |mean(A) - mean(B)|/SE(A - B) > \text{threshold-value}$$

The mean of a feature is compared in both classes without taking into consideration relationship to other features. In this approach to feature selection, we assumed a *priori* that the given feature is independent of the others. A comparison of means is a natural fit to classification problems. For the purpose of feature selection, a regression problem can be considered as a pseudo-classification problem. For k classes, k pairwise comparisons can be made, comparing each class to its complement. A feature is retained if it is significant for any of the pairwise comparisons.

We can analyze this approach in feature selection through one example. A simple data set is given in Table 3.1 with two input features X and Y, and an additional feature C that classifies samples into two classes A and B. It is necessary to decide whether the features X and Y are candidates for reduction or not. Suppose that the threshold value of the applied test is 0.5.

First, we need to compute a mean value and a variance for both classes and both features X and Y. The analyzed subsets of the feature's values are

$$X_A = \{0.3, 0.6, 0.5\}, X_B = \{0.2, 0.7, 0.4\}, Y_A = \{0.7, 0.6, 0.5\}, \text{ and}$$
$$Y_B = \{0.9, 0.7, 0.9\}$$

and the results of applied tests are

$$SE(X_A - X_B) = \sqrt{(var(X_A)/n_1 + var(X_B)/n_2)} = \sqrt{(0.0233/3 + 0.6333/3)} = 0.4678$$
$$SE(Y_A - Y_B) = \sqrt{(var(Y_A)/n_1 + var(Y_B)/n_2)} = \sqrt{(0.01/3 + 0.0133/3)} = 0.0875$$
$$|mean(X_A) - mean(X_B)| /SE(X_A - X_B) = |0.4667 - 0.4333| /0.4678 = 0.0735 < 0.5$$
$$|mean(Y_A) - mean(Y_B)| /SE(Y_A - Y_B) = |0.6 - 0.8333| /0.0875 = 2.6667 > 0.5$$

This analysis shows that X is a candidate for reduction because its mean values are close and, therefore, the final test is below the threshold value. On the other hand, the test for feature Y is significantly above the threshold value; this feature is not a candidate for reduction because it has the potential to be a distinguishing feature between two classes.

TABLE 3.1   Dataset with three features

X	Y	C
0.3	0.7	A
0.2	0.9	B
0.6	0.6	A
0.5	0.5	A
0.7	0.7	B
0.4	0.9	B

The previous simple method tests features separately. Several features may be useful when considered separately, but they may be redundant in their predictive ability. If the features are examined collectively, instead of independently, additional information can be obtained about their characteristics. Assuming normal distributions of values, it is possible to describe an efficient technique for selecting subsets of features. Two descriptors characterize a multivariate normal distribution:

1. M – a vector of the m feature means, and
2. C – an m × m covariance matrix of the means, where $C_{i,i}$ are simply the variance of feature i, and $C_{i,j}$ terms are correlations between each pair of features

$$C_{i,j} = 1/n \sum_{k=1}^{n} ((v(k,i) - m(i))*(v(k,j) - m(j)))$$

where
v(k,i) and v(k,j) are the values of features indexed with i and j,
m(i) and m(j) are feature means, and
n is the number of dimensions.

These two descriptors, M and C, provide a basis for detecting redundancies in a set of features. If two classes exist in a data set, then the heuristic measure, DM, for filtering features that separate the two classes is defined as

$$DM = (M_1 - M_2)\ (C_1 + C_2)^{-1} (M_1 - M_2)^T$$

where M_1 and C_1 are descriptors of samples for the first class, and M_2 and C_2 for the second class. Given the target of k best features, all subsets of k from m features must be evaluated to find the subset with the largest DM. With large data sets that have features, this can be a huge search space and alternative heuristic methods should be considered. One of these methods selects and ranks features based on an entropy measure. Detailed explanations are given in Section 3.3.

An alternative view of this process is to reduce feature dimensions by merging features instead of by deleting them. This process results in a new set of fewer features with totally new values. One well-known approach is merging by *principal components*. The features are examined collectively, merged, and transformed into a new set of features that, it is hoped, will retain the original information content in a reduced form. The basic transformation is linear. Given m features, they can be transformed into a single new feature F′ by the simple application of weights:

$$F' = \sum_{j=1}^{m} w(j) \cdot f(j)$$

Most likely, a single set of weights, w(j), will not be adequate transformation, and up to m transformations are generated. Each vector of m weights is called a principal component and it generates a new feature. The first vector of m weights is expected to be the strongest, and the remaining vectors are ranked according to their expected usefulness in reconstructing the original data. Eliminating the bottom-ranked transformation will reduce dimensions. The complexity of computation increases significantly with the number of features. The main weakness of the method is that it makes an advance assumption to a linear model that maximizes the variance of features. Formalization of principal component analysis and the basic steps of the corresponding algorithm for selecting features are given in Section 3.4.

With the size of data getting bigger and bigger, all feature-selection (and reduction) methods also face a problem of oversized data because of a computer's limited resources. But, do we really need so much data for selecting features as an initial process in data mining? Or can we settle for less data? We know that some portion of a huge data set can represent it reasonably well. The point is which portion and how large should it be. Instead of looking for the right portion, we can randomly select a part, P, of a data set, use that portion to find the subset of features that satisfy the evaluation criteria, and test this subset on a different part of the data. The results of this test will show whether the task has been successfully accomplished. If an inconsistency is found, we shall have to repeat the process with a slightly enlarged portion of the initial data set. What should be the initial size of the data subset P? Intuitively, we know that its size should not be too small or too large. A simple way to get out of this dilemma is to choose a percentage of data, say 10%. The right percentage can be determined experimentally.

What are the results of a feature-reduction process, and why do we need this process for every specific application? The purposes vary, depending upon the problem on hand, but, generally, we want

1. to *improve performances* of the model-generation process and the resulting model itself; (typical criteria are speed of learning, predictive accuracy, and simplicity of the model)
2. to *reduce dimensionality* of the model without reduction of its quality, through
   a) elimination of irrelevant features
   b) detection and elimination of redundant data and features
   c) identification of highly correlated features
   d) extraction of independent features that determine the model
3. to help the user *visualize* alternative results, which have fewer dimensions, to improve decision-making

3.3   ENTROPY MEASURE FOR RANKING FEATURES

A method for unsupervised feature selection or ranking based on entropy measure is a relatively simple technique; but with a large number of features its complexity increases significantly. The basic assumption is that all samples are given as vectors of a feature's values without any classification of output samples. The approach is based on the observation that removing an irrelevant feature, a redundant feature, or both from a set may not change the basic characteristics of the data set. The idea is to remove as many features as possible but yet maintain the level of distinction between the samples in the data set as if no features had been removed. The algorithm is based on a similarity measure S that is in inverse proportion to the distance D between two n-dimensional samples. The distance measure D is small for close samples (close to zero) and large for distinct pairs (close to one). When the features are numeric, the similarity measure S of two samples can be defined as

$$S_{ij} = e^{-\alpha D_{ij}}$$

where D_{ij} is the distance between samples x_i and x_j and α is a parameter mathematically expressed as

$$\alpha = -(\ln\ 0.5)/D$$

D is the average distance among samples in the data set. Hence, α is determined by the data. But, in a successfully implemented practical application, it was used a constant value of $\alpha = 0.5$. Normalized Euclidean distance measure is used to calculate the distance D_{ij} between two samples x_i and x_j:

$$D_{ij} = \left[\sum_{k=1}^{n} ((x_{ik} - x_{jk})/(max_k - min_k))^2 \right]^{1/2}$$

where n is the number of dimensions and max_k and min_k are maximum and minimum values used for normalization of the k-th dimension.

All features are not numeric. The similarity for nominal variables is measured directly using Hamming distance:

$$S_{ij} = \left(\sum_{k=1}^{n} |x_{ik} = x_{jk}| \right)/n$$

where $|x_{ik} = x_{jk}|$ is 1 if $x_{ik} = x_{jk}$, and 0 otherwise. The total number of variables is equal to n. For mixed data, we can discretize numeric values and transform numeric features into nominal features before we apply this similarity measure. Figure 3.1 is an example of a simple data set with three categorical features; corresponding similarities are given in Table 3.1.

Sample	F_1	F_2	F_3
R_1	A	X	1
R_2	B	Y	2
R_3	C	Y	2
R_4	B	X	1
R_5	C	Z	3

	R_1	R_2	R_3	R_4	R_5
R_1		0/3	0/3	2/3	0/3
R_2			2/3	1/3	0/3
R_3				0/3	1/3
R_4					0/3

a) Data set with three categorical features

b) A table of similarity measures S_{ij} between samples

FIGURE 3.1   A tabular representation of similarity measures S

The distribution of all similarities (distances) for a given data set is a characteristic of the organization and order of data in an n-dimensional space. This organization may be more or less ordered. Changes in the level of order in a data set are the main criteria for inclusion or exclusion of a feature from the features set; these changes may be measured by entropy.

From information theory, we know that entropy is a global measure, and that it is less for ordered configurations and higher for disordered configurations. The proposed technique compares the entropy measure for a given data set before and after removal of a feature. If the two measures are close, then the reduced set of features will satisfactorily approximate the original set. For a data set of N samples, the entropy measure is

$$E = -\sum_{i=1}^{N-1} \sum_{j=I+1}^{N} (S_{ij} \times \log S_{ij} + (1 - S_{ij}) \times \log (1 - S_{ij}))$$

where S_{ij} is the similarity between samples x_i and x_j. This measure is computed in each of the iterations as a basis for deciding the ranking of features. We rank features by gradually removing the least important feature in maintaining the order in the configurations of data. The steps of the algorithm are based on sequential backward ranking, and they have been successfully tested on several real-world applications

1. Start with the initial full set of features F.
2. For each feature f ∈ F, remove one feature f from F and obtain a subset F_f. Find the difference between entropy for F and entropy for all F_f. In our example in Figure 3.2, we have to compare the differences $(E_F - E_{F-F1})$, $(E_F - E_{F-F2})$, and $(E_F - E_{F-F3})$.
3. Let f_k be a feature such that the difference between entropy for F and entropy for F_{fk} is minimum.
4. Update the set of features $F = F - \{f_k\}$, where – is a difference operation on sets. In our example, if the difference $(E_F - E_{F-F1})$ is minimum, then the reduced set of features is $\{F_2, F_3\}$. F_1 becomes the bottom of the ranked list.
5. Repeat steps 2–4 until there is only one feature in F.

A ranking process may be stopped in any iteration, and may be transformed into a process of selecting features, using the additional criterion mentioned in step 4. This criterion is that the difference between entropy for F and entropy for F_f should be less then the approved threshold value to reduce feature f_k from set F. A computational complexity is the basic disadvantage of this algorithm, and its parallel implementation could overcome the problems of working with large data sets and large number of features sequentially.

3.4 PRINCIPAL COMPONENT ANALYSIS

The most popular statistical method for dimensionality reduction of a large data set is the Karhunen-Loeve (K-L) method, also called *Principal Component Analysis*.

Principal component analysis is a method of transforming the initial data set represented by vector samples into a new set of vector samples with derived dimensions. The goal of this transformation is to concentrate the information about the differences between samples into a small number of dimensions. More formally, the basic idea can be described as follows: A set of n-dimensional vector samples $X = \{x_1, x_2, x_3, \ldots, x_m\}$ should be transformed into another set $Y = \{y_1, y_2, \ldots, y_m\}$ of the same dimensionality, but y-s have the property that most of their information content is stored in the first few dimensions. This will allow us to reduce the data set to a smaller number of dimensions with low information loss.

The transformation is based on the assumption that high information corresponds to high variance. So, if we want to reduce a set of input dimensions X to a single dimension Y, we should transform X into Y as a matrix computation

$$Y = A \cdot X$$

choosing A such that Y has the largest variance possible for a given data set. The single dimension Y obtained in this transformation is called *the first principal component*. The first principal component is an axis in the direction of maximum variance. It minimizes the distance of the sum of squares between data points and their projections on the component axis, as it is shown in Figure 3.2 where a two-dimensional space is transformed into a one-dimensional space in which the data set has the highest variance.

In practice, it is not possible to determine matrix A directly, and therefore we compute the covariance matrix S as a first step in features transformation. Matrix S is defined as

$$S_{n \times n} = 1/(n-1)\left[\sum_{j=1}^{n}(x_j - x')^T(x_j - x')\right]$$

where $x' = (1/n)\sum_{j=1}^{n} x_j$.

The eigenvalues of the covariance matrix S for the given data should be calculated in the next step. Finally, the m eigenvectors corresponding to the m largest

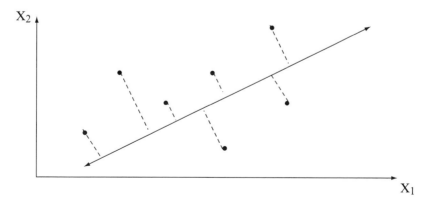

FIGURE 3.2 The first principal component is an axis in the direction of maximum variance

eigenvalues of S define a linear transformation from the n-dimensional space to an m-dimensional space in which the features are uncorrelated. To specify the principal components we need the following additional explanations about the notation in matrix S:

1. The eigenvalues of $S_{n \times n}$ are $\lambda_1, \lambda_2, \ldots, \lambda_n$, where

$$\lambda_1 \geq \lambda_2 \geq \ldots \geq \lambda_n \geq 0.$$

2. The eigenvectors $e_1, e_2, \ldots, e_n$ correspond to eigenvalues $\lambda_1, \lambda_2, \ldots, \lambda_n$, and they are called the principal axes.

Principal axes are new, transformed axes of n-dimensional space, where the new variables are uncorrelated, and variance for the i-th component is equal to the i-th eigenvalue. Because λ_i's are sorted, most of the information about the data set is concentrated in a few first principal components. The fundamental question is how many of the principal components are needed to get a good representation of the data? In other words, what is the effective dimensionality of the data set? The easiest way to answer the question is to analyze the proportion of variance. Dividing the sum of the first m eigenvalues by the sum of all the variances (all eigenvalues), we will get the measure for the quality of representation based on the first m principal components. The result is expressed as a percentage, and if, e.g., the projection accounts for over 90% of the total variance, it is considered to be good. More formally, we can express this ratio in the following way. The criterion for features selection is based on the ratio of the sum of the m largest eigenvalues of S to the trace of S. That is a fraction of the variance retained in the m-dimensional space. If the eigenvalues are labeled so that $\lambda_1 \geq \lambda_2 \geq \ldots \geq \lambda_n$, then the ratio can be written as

$$R = \left(\sum_{i=1}^{m} \lambda_i \right) / \left(\sum_{i=1}^{n} \lambda_i \right)$$

When the ratio R is sufficiently large (greater than the threshold value), all analyses of the subset of m features represent a good initial estimate of the n-dimensionality space. This method is computationally inexpensive, but it requires characterizing data with the covariance matrix S.

We will use one example from the literature to show the advantages of principal component analysis. The initial data set is the well-known set of Iris data, available on the Internet for data-mining experimentation. This data set has four features, so every sample is a 4-dimensional vector. The correlation matrix, calculated from the Iris data after normalization of all values, is given in Table 3.2.

Based on the correlation matrix, it is a straightforward calculation of eigenvalues (in practice, usually, one of the standard statistical packages is used), and these final results for the Iris data are given in Table 3.3.

By setting a threshold value for $R^* = 0.95$, we choose the first two features as the subset of features for further data-mining analysis, because

TABLE 3.2   The correlation matrix for Iris data

	Feature 1	Feature 2	Feature 3	Feature 4
Feature 1	1.0000	−0.1094	0.8718	0.8180
Feature 2	−0.1094	1.0000	−0.4205	−0.3565
Feature 3	0.8718	−0.4205	1.0000	0.9628
Feature 4	0.8180	−0.3565	0.9628	1.0000

TABLE 3.3   The eigenvalues for Iris data

Feature	Eigenvalue
Feature 1	2.91082
Feature 2	0.92122
Feature 3	0.14735
Feature 4	0.02061

$$R = (2.91082 + 0.92122)/(2.91082 + 0.92122 + 0.14735 + 0.02061)$$
$$= 0.958 > 0.95$$

For the Iris data, the first two principal components should be adequate description of the characteristics of the data set. The third and fourth components have small eigenvalues and therefore, they contain very little variation; their influence on the information content of the data set is thus minimal. Additional analysis shows that, based on the reduced set of features in the Iris data, the model has the same quality using different data-mining techniques (sometimes the results were even better than with the original features).

3.5   VALUES REDUCTION

A reduction in the number of discrete values for a given feature is based on the second set of techniques in the data-reduction phase; these are the *feature-discretization techniques*. The task of feature-discretization techniques is to discretize the values of continuous features into a small number of intervals, where each interval is mapped to a discrete symbol. The benefits of these techniques are simplified data description and easy-to-understand data and final data-mining results. Also, more data-mining techniques are applicable with discrete feature values. An "old fashioned" discretization is made manually, based on our a priori knowledge about the feature. For example, using common sense or consensus, a person's age, given at the beginning of a data-mining process as a continuous value (between 0 and 150 years) may be classified into categorical segments: child, adolescent, adult, middle age, and elderly. Cut off points are subjectively defined (Figure 3.3). Two main questions exist about this reduction process:

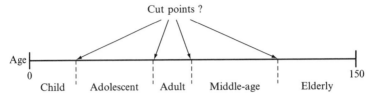

FIGURE 3.3   Discretization of the *age* feature

1. What are the cut-off points?
2. How does one select representatives of intervals?

Without any knowledge about a feature, a discretization is much more difficult and, in many cases, arbitrary. A reduction in feature values usually is not harmful for real-world data-mining applications, and it leads to a major decrease in computational complexity. Therefore, we will introduce, in the next two sections, several automated discretization techniques.

Within a column of a data set (set of feature values), the number of distinct values can be counted. If this number can be reduced, many data-mining methods, especially the logic-based methods explained in Chapter 7, will increase the quality of a data analysis. Reducing the number of values by smoothing feature values does not require a complex algorithm because each feature is smoothed independently of other features and the process is performed only once, without iterations.

Suppose that a feature has a range of numeric values, and that these values can be ordered from the smallest to the largest using standard greater-than and less-than operators. This leads naturally to the concept of *placing the values in bins—*partitioning into groups with close values. Typically, these bins have a close number of elements. All values in a bin will be merged into a single concept represented by a single value—usually either the mean or median of the bin's values. The mean or the mode is effective for a moderate or large number of bins. When the number of bins is small, the closest boundaries of each bin can be candidates for representatives in a given bin.

For example, if a set of values for a given feature f is {3, 2, 1, 5, 4, 3, 1, 7, 5, 3}, then, after sorting, these values will be organized into an ordered set:

$$\{1, 1, 2, 3, 3, 3, 4, 5, 5, 7\}$$

Now, it is possible to split the total set of values into three bins with a close number of elements:

$$\{1, 1, 2, \quad 3, 3, 3, \quad 4, 5, 5, 7\}$$
$$\text{BIN}_1 \qquad \text{BIN}_2 \qquad \text{BIN}_3$$

In the next step, different representatives can be selected for each bin. If the smoothing is performed based on bin modes, the new set of values for each bin will be

$$\{1, 1, 1, \quad 3, 3, 3, \quad 5, 5, 5, 5\}$$
$$\text{BIN}_1 \qquad \text{BIN}_2 \qquad \text{BIN}_3$$

If the smoothing is performed based on mean values, then the new distribution for reduced set of values will be

$$\{1.33, 1.33, 1.33, \quad 3, 3, 3, \quad 5.25, 5.25, 5.25, 5.25\}$$
$$\text{BIN}_1 \qquad\qquad \text{BIN}_2 \qquad\qquad \text{BIN}_3$$

and finally, if all the values in a bin are replaced by the closest of the boundary values, the new set will be

$$\{1, 1, 2, \quad 3, 3, 3, \quad 4, 4, 4, 7\}$$
$$\text{BIN}_1 \qquad \text{BIN}_2 \qquad \text{BIN}_3$$

One of the main problems of this method is to find the best cutoffs for bins. In theory, a decision about cutoffs cannot be made independently of other features. Still, heuristic decisions for every feature independently give good results in many data-mining applications. The value-reduction problem can be stated as an optimization problem in the selection of k bins: given the number of bins k, distribute the values in the bins to minimize the average distance of a value from its bin mean or median. The distance is usually measured as the squared distance for a bin mean and as the absolute distance for a bin median. This algorithm can be computationally very complex, and a modified heuristic procedure is used to produce a near-optimum solution. The procedure consists of the following steps:

1. Sort all values for a given feature.
2. Assign approximately equal numbers of sorted adjacent values (v_i) to each bin, where the number of bins is given in advance.
3. Move a border element v_i from one bin to the next (or previous) when that reduces the global distance error (ER) (the sum of all distances from each v_i to the mean or mode of its assigned bin).

A simple example of the dynamic bin procedure for feature discretization is given next. The set of values for a feature f is $\{5, 1, 8, 2, 2, 9, 2, 1, 8, 6\}$. Split them into three bins (k = 3), where the bins will be represented by their modes. The computations in the first iteration of the algorithm are

a) Sorted set of values for feature f is $\{1, 1, 2, 2, 2, 5, 6, 8, 8, 9\}$

b) Initial bins (k = 3) are $\begin{array}{ccc} \{1, 1, 2, & 2, 2, 5, & 6, 8, 8, 9\} \\ \text{BIN}_1 & \text{BIN}_2 & \text{BIN}_3 \end{array}$

c) (i) Modes for the three selected bins are $\{1, 2, 8\}$. After initial distribution, the total error, using absolute distance for modes, is

$$\text{ER} = 0 + 0 + 1 + 0 + 0 + 3 + 2 + 0 + 0 + 1 = 7.$$

.
.
.

(iv) After moving two elements from BIN_2 into BIN_1 and one element from BIN_3 to BIN_2 in the next three iterations and obtaining smaller and smaller ER, the new and final distribution of elements will be

$$\text{Final bins} \Rightarrow \quad \begin{array}{ccc} f = \{1, 1, 2, 2, 2, & 5, 6, & 8, 8, 9\} \\ BIN_1 & BIN_2 & BIN_3 \end{array}$$

The corresponding modes are $\{2, 5, 8\}$, and the total minimized error ER is 4. Any additional move of elements between bins will cause an increase in the ER value. The final distribution, with medians as representatives, will be the solution for a given value-reduction problem.

Another very simple method of smoothing feature values is *number approximation by rounding*. Rounding is a natural operation for humans; it is also natural for a computer, and it involves very few operations. First, numbers with decimals are converted to integers prior to rounding. After rounding, the number is divided by the same constant. Formally, these steps are described with the following computations applied to the feature value X:

1. Integer division $Y = int \, (X/10^k)$
2. Rounding   *If* $(mod \, (X, 10^k) \geq (10^k/2))$ *then* $Y = Y + 1$
3. Integer multiplication $X = Y*10^k$

where k is the number of rightmost decimal places to round. For example, the number 1453 is rounded to 1450 if $k = 1$, rounded to 1500 if $k = 2$, and rounded to 1000 if $k = 3$.

Given a number of values for a feature as an input parameter of the procedure, this simple rounding algorithm can be applied in iterations to reduce these values in large data sets. First, a feature's values are sorted so that the number of distinct values after rounding can be counted. Starting at $k = 1$, rounding is performed for all values, and the number of distinct values counted. Parameter k is increased in the next iteration until the number of values in the sorted list is reduced to less than the allowable maximum, typically in real-world applications between 50 and 100.

3.6 FEATURE DISCRETIZATION: CHIMERGE TECHNIQUE

ChiMerge is one automated discretization algorithm that analyzes the quality of multiple intervals for a given feature by using χ^2 statistics. The algorithm determines similarities between distributions of data in two adjacent intervals based on output classification of samples. If the conclusion of the χ^2 test is that the output class is independent of the feature's intervals, then the intervals should be merged; otherwise, it indicates that the difference between intervals is statistically significant, and no merger will be performed.

ChiMerge algorithm consists of three basic steps for discretization:

1. Sort the data for the given feature in ascending order.
2. Define initial intervals so that every value of the feature is in a separate interval.
3. Repeat until no χ^2 of any two adjacent intervals is less then threshold value.

After each merger, χ^2 tests for the remaining intervals are calculated, and two adjacent features with the smallest χ^2 values are found. If the calculated χ^2 is less than the threshold, merge these intervals. If no merge is possible, and the number of intervals is greater than the user-defined maximum, increase the threshold value.

The χ^2 test or contingency-table test is used in the methodology for determining the independence of two adjacent intervals. When the data are summarized in a contingency table (its form is represented in Table 3.4), the χ^2 test is given by the formula:

$$\chi^2 = \sum_{i=1}^{2} \sum_{j=1}^{k} (A_{ij} - E_{ij})^2 / E_{ij}$$

where
  k = the number of classes,
  A_{ij} = the number of instances in the i-th interval, j-th class,
  E_{ij} = the expected frequency of A_{ij}, which is computed as $(R_i \cdot C_j)/N$,
  R_i = the number of instances in the i-th interval = ΣA_{ij}, j = 1, ..., k,
  C_j = the number of instances in the j-th class = ΣA_{ij}, i = 1, 2,
  N = the total number of instances = ΣR_i, i = 1, 2.

If either R_i or C_j in the contingency table is 0, E_{ij} is set to a small value, e.g., $E_{ij} = 0.1$. The reason for this modification is to avoid very small values in the denominator of the test. The degree of freedom of the χ^2 test for the given data set is for one less than the number of classes. When more then one feature has to be discretized, a threshold for the maximum number of intervals and a confidence interval for the χ^2 test should be defined separately for each feature. If the number of intervals exceeds the maximum, the algorithm ChiMerge may continue with a new, reduced value for confidence.

For a classification problem with two classes (k = 2), where the merging of two intervals is analyzed, the contingency table for 2×2 data has the form given in Table 3.4. A_{11} represents the number of samples in the first interval belonging to the first class, A_{12} is the number of samples in the first interval belonging to the second class, A_{21} is the number of samples in the second interval belonging to the first class, and finally A_{22} is the number of samples in the second interval belonging to the second class.

We will analyze the ChiMerge algorithm using one relatively simple example, where the database consists of 12 two-dimensional samples with only one continuous feature (F) and an output classification feature (K). The two values 1 and 2 for the feature K represent the two classes to which the samples belong. The initial data set, already sorted with respect to the continuous numeric feature F, is given in Table 3.5.

We can start the algorithm of a discretization by selecting the smallest χ^2 value for intervals on our sorted scale for F. We define a middle value in the given data

TABLE 3.4   A contingency table for 2×2 categorical data

	Class 1	Class 2	Σ
Interval-1	A_{11}	A_{12}	R_1
Interval-2	A_{21}	A_{22}	R_2
Σ	C_1	C_2	N

TABLE 3.5   Data on the sorted continuous feature F with corresponding classes K

Sample:	F	K
1	1	1
2	3	2
3	7	1
4	8	1
5	9	1
6	11	2
7	23	2
8	37	1
9	39	2
10	45	1
11	46	1
12	59	1

as a splitting interval point. For our example, interval points for feature F are 0, 2, 5, 7.5, 8.5, 10, etc. Based on this distribution of intervals, we analyze all adjacent intervals trying to find a minimum for the χ^2 test. In our example, χ^2 was the minimum for intervals [7.5, 8.5] and [8.5, 10]. Both intervals contain only one sample, and they belong to class K = 1. The initial contingency table is given in Table 3.6.

Based on the values given in the table, we can calculate the expected values

$$E_{11} = 2/2 = 1$$

$$E_{12} = 0/2 \approx 0.1$$

TABLE 3.6   Contingency table for intervals [7.5, 8.5] and [8.5, 10]

	K = 1	K = 2	Σ
Interval [7.5, 8.5]	$A_{11} = 1$	$A_{12} = 0$	$R_1 = 1$
Interval [8.5, 9.5]	$A_{21} = 1$	$A_{22} = 0$	$R_2 = 1$
Σ	$C_1 = 2$	$C_2 = 0$	N = 2

$$E_{21} = 2/2 = 1 \quad \text{and}$$

$$E_{22} = 0/2 \approx 0.1$$

and the corresponding χ^2 test

$$\chi^2 = (1-1)^2/1 + (0-0.1)^2/0.1 + (1-1)^2/1 + (0-0.1)^2/0.1 = 0.2$$

For the degree of freedom $d = 1$, and $\chi^2 = 0.2 < 2.706$ (the threshold value from the tables for Chi-Squared distribution for $\alpha = 0.1$), we can conclude that there are no significant differences in relative class frequencies and that the selected intervals can be merged. The merging process will be applied in one iteration only for two adjacent intervals with a minimum χ^2 and, at the same time, with $\chi^2 <$ threshold value. The iterative process will continue with the next two adjacent intervals that have the minimum χ^2. We will just show one additional step, somewhere in the middle of the merging process, where the intervals [0, 7.5] and [7.5, 10] are analyzed. The contingency table is given in Table 3.7, and expected values are

$$E_{11} = 12/5 = 2.4$$
$$E_{12} = 3/5 = 0.6$$
$$E_{21} = 8/5 = 1.6$$
$$E_{22} = 2/5 = 0.4$$

while the χ^2 test is

$$\chi^2 = (2-2.4)^2/2.4 + (1-0.6)^2/0.6 + (2-1.6)^2/1.6 + (0-0.4)^2/0.4 = 0.834$$

Selected intervals should be merged into one because, for the degree of freedom $d = 1$, $\chi^2 = 0.834 < 2.706$ (for $\alpha = 0.1$). In our example, with the given threshold value for χ^2, the algorithm will define a final discretization with three intervals: [0, 10], [10, 42], and [42, 60], where 60 is supposed to be the maximum value for the feature F. We can assign to these intervals coded values 1, 2, and 3 or descriptive linguistic values low, medium, and high.

Additional merging is not possible because the χ^2 test will show significant differences between intervals. For example, if we attempt to merge the intervals

TABLE 3.7   Contingency table for intervals [0, 7.5] and [7.5, 10]

	$K = 1$	$K = 2$	Σ
Interval [0, 7.5]	$A_{11} = 2$	$A_{12} = 1$	$R_1 = 3$
Interval [7.5, 10]	$A_{21} = 2$	$A_{22} = 0$	$R_2 = 2$
Σ	$C_1 = 4$	$C_2 = 1$	$N = 5$

TABLE 3.8   Contingency table for intervals [0, 10] and [10, 42]

	K = 1	K = 2	Σ
Interval [0, 10.0]	$A_{11} = 4$	$A_{12} = 1$	$R_1 = 5$
Interval [10.0, 42.0]	$A_{21} = 1$	$A_{22} = 3$	$R_2 = 4$
Σ	$C_1 = 5$	$C_2 = 4$	$N = 9$

[0, 10] and [10, 42]—contingency table is given in Table 3.8—and the test results are $E_{11} = 2.78$, $E_{12} = 2.22$, $E_{21} = 2.22$, $E_{22} = 1.78$, and $\chi^2 = 2.72 > 2.706$, the conclusion is that significant differences between two intervals exist, and merging is not recommended.

3.7   CASES REDUCTION

Data mining can be characterized as a secondary data analysis in the sense that data miners are not involved directly with the data-collection process. That fact may sometimes explain the poor quality of raw data. Seeking the unexpected or the unforeseen, the data-mining process is not concerned with optimal ways to collect data and to select the initial set of samples; they are already given, usually in large numbers, with a high or low quality, and with or without prior knowledge of the problem at hand.

The largest and the most critical dimension in the initial data set is the number of cases or samples or, in other words, the number of rows in the tabular representation of data. Case reduction is the most complex task in data reduction. Already, in the preprocessing phase, we have elements of case reduction through the elimination of outliers and, sometimes, samples with missing values. But the main reduction process is still ahead. If the number of samples in the prepared data set can be managed by the selected data-mining techniques, then there is no technical or theoretical reason for case reduction. In real-world data-mining applications, however, with millions of samples available, that is not the case.

Let us specify two ways in which the sampling process arises in data analysis. First, sometimes the data set itself is merely a sample from a larger, unknown population, and sampling is a part of the data-collection process. Data mining is not interested in this type of sampling. Second , and more characteristic of data mining, the initial data set represents an extremely large population and the analysis of the data is based only on a subset of samples. After the subset of data is obtained, it is used to provide some information about entire data set. It is often called estimator and its quality depends on the elements in the selected subset. A sampling process always causes a sampling error. Sampling error is inherent and unavoidable for every approach and every strategy. This error, in general, will decrease when the size of subset increases, and it will theoretically become nonexistent in the case of a complete data set. Compared to data mining with the entire data set, practical sampling possesses one or more of the following advantages: reduced cost, greater speed, greater scope, and sometimes even higher accuracy. As yet there is no known method of sampling that ensures with certainty that the estimates of the subset will be equal to the characteristics of the entire data set. Relying on sampling nearly always involve the risk of reaching incorrect conclusions. Sampling theory and the correct selection of a sampling technique can assist in reducing that risk, but not eliminating it.

There are various strategies for drawing a representative subset of samples from a data set. The size of a suitable subset is determined by taking into account the cost of computation, memory requirements, accuracy of the estimator, and other characteristics of the algorithm and data. Generally, a subset size can be determined so that the estimates for the entire data set do not differ by more than a stated margin error in more than δ of the samples. By setting up a probability inequality $P(|e - e_0| \geq \varepsilon) \leq \delta$, we solve it for the subset of sample size n, and for a given value ε (confidence limit) and δ (where $1 - \delta$ is the confidence level). The parameter e stands for an estimate from the subset and it is generally a function of the subset size n, while e_0 stands for the true value obtained from entire data set. However, e_0 is usually unknown too. In this case, a practical way to determine the required size of the data subset can be done as follows: In the first step we select a small preliminary subset of samples of size m. Observations made based on this subset of data will be used to estimate e_0. After replacing e_0 in the inequality, it is solved for n. If $n \geq m$, then additional **n − m** samples are selected in the final subset for analysis. If $n \leq m$, then no more samples are selected and the preliminary subset of data is used as the final.

One possible classification of sampling methods in data mining is based on the scope of application of these methods, and the main classes are

1) general-purpose sampling methods
2) sampling methods for specific domains.

In this text we will introduce only some of the techniques that belong to the first class because they do not require specific knowledge about the application domain and may be used for a variety of data-mining applications.

Systematic sampling is the simplest sampling technique. For example, if we want to select 50% of a data set, we could take every other sample in a database. This approach is adequate for many applications and it is a part of many data-mining tools. However, it can also lead to unpredicted problems when there are some regularities in the database. Therefore, the data miner has to be very careful in applying this sampling technique.

Random sampling is a method by which every sample from an initial data set has the same chance of being selected in the subset. The method has two variants: *random sampling without replacement* and *random sampling with replacement*. Random sampling without replacement is a popular technique in which n distinct samples are selected from N initial samples in the data set without repetition (a sample may not occur twice). The advantages of the approach are simplicity of the algorithm and nonexistence of any bias in a selection. In random sampling with replacement, the samples are selected from a data set such that all samples are given an equal chance of being selected, no matter how often they already have been drawn, i.e. any of the samples may be selected more than once. Random sampling is not a one-time activity in a data-mining process. It is an iterative process, resulting in several randomly selected subsets of samples. The two basic forms of a random sampling process are

1. Incremental sampling – Mining incrementally larger random subsets of samples in real-world applications helps spot trends in error and complexity. Experience has shown that the performance of the solution may level off rapidly after some percentage of the available samples has been examined. A principal approach to case reduction is to perform a data-mining process on increasingly larger random subsets, to observe the trends in performances, and to stop when no progress is made. The subsets should take big increments in data sets, so that the expectation of improving performance with more data is reasonable. A typical pattern of incremental subsets might be 10%, 20%, 33%, 50%, 67%, and 100%. These percentages are reasonable, but can be adjusted based on knowledge of the application and the number of samples in the data set. The smallest subset should be substantial: typically, no fewer than 1000 samples.

2. Average sampling – When the solutions found from many random subsets of samples are *averaged* or *voted*, the combined solution can do as well or even better than the single solution found on the full collection of data. The price of this approach is the repetitive process of data mining on smaller sets of samples and, additionally, a heuristic definition of criteria to compare the several solutions of different subsets of data. Typically, the process of voting between solutions is applied for classification problems (if three solutions are class1 and one solution is class2, then the final voted solution is class1) and averaging for regression problems (if one solution is 6, the second is 6.5, and the third 6.7, then the final averaged solution is 6.4). When the new sample is to be presented and analyzed by this methodology, an answer should be given by each solution, and a final result will be obtained by comparing and integrating these solutions with the proposed heuristics.

Two additional techniques, *stratified sampling* and *inverse sampling*, may be convenient for some data-mining applications. Stratified sampling is a technique in which the entire data set is split into nonoverlapping subsets or strata, and sampling is performed for each different strata independently of another. The combination of all the small subsets from different strata forms the final, total subset of data samples for analysis. This technique is used when the strata are relatively homogeneous and the variance of the overall estimate is smaller than that arising from a simple random sample. Inverse sampling is used when a feature in a data set occurs with rare frequency, and even a large subset of samples may not give enough information to estimate a feature value. In that case, sampling is dynamic; it starts with the small subset and it continues until some conditions about the required number of feature values are satisfied.

For some specialized types of problems, alternative techniques can be helpful in reducing the number of cases. For example, for time-dependent data the number of samples is determined by the frequency of sampling. The sampling period is specified based on knowledge of the application. If the sampling period is too short, most samples are repetitive and few changes occur from case to case.

For some applications, increasing the sampling period causes no harm and can even be beneficial in obtaining a good data-mining solution. Therefore, for time-series data the windows for sampling and measuring features should be optimized, and that requires additional preparation and experimentation with available data.

3.8 REVIEW QUESTIONS AND PROBLEMS

1. Explain what we gain and what we lose with dimensionality reduction in large data sets in the preprocessing phase of data mining.

2. Use one typical application of data mining in a retail industry to explain monotonicity and interruptability of data-reduction algorithms.

3. Given the data set X with three input features and one output feature representing the classification of samples

X:

I_1	I_2	I_3	O
2.5	1.6	5.9	0
7.2	4.3	2.1	1
3.4	5.8	1.6	1
5.6	3.6	6.8	0
4.8	7.2	3.1	1
8.1	4.9	8.3	0
6.3	4.8	2.4	1

rank the features using a comparison of means and variances.

4. Given four-dimensional samples where the first two dimensions are numeric and last two are categorical

X_1	X_2	X_3	X_4
2.7	3.4	1	A
3.1	6.2	2	A
4.5	2.8	1	B
5.3	5.8	2	B
6.6	3.1	1	A
5.0	4.1	2	B

apply a method for unsupervised feature selection based on entropy measure to reduce one dimension from the given data set.

5. (a) Perform Bin-based values reduction with the best cutoffs for the following:
   i) The feature I_3 in problem #3 using mean values as representatives for two bins.
   ii) The feature X_2 in problem #4 using the closest boundaries for two bin representatives

5. (b) Discuss the possibility of applying approximation by rounding to reduce the values of numeric attributes in problems #3 and #4.

6. Apply the ChiMerge technique to reduce the number of values for numeric attributes in problem #3
   a) Reduce the number of numeric values for feature I_1 and find the final, reduced number of intervals.
   b) Reduce the number of numeric values for feature I_2 and find the final, reduced number of intervals.
   c) Reduce the number of numeric values for feature I_3 and find the final, reduced number of intervals.
   d) Discuss the results and benefits of dimensionality reduction obtained in a), b), and c).

7. Explain the differences between averaged and voted combined solutions when random samples are used to reduce dimensionality of a large data set.

8. How can the-incremental samples approach and the average-samples approach be combined to reduce cases in large data sets.

9. Develop a software tool for feature ranking based on means and variances. Input data set is represented in the form of flat file with several features.

10. Develop a software tool for ranking features using entropy measure. The input data set is represented in the form of a flat file with several features.

11. Implement the ChiMerge algorithm for automated discretization of selected features in a flat input file.

3.9   REFERENCES FOR FURTHER STUDY

1. Liu, H. and H. Motoda, eds., *Instance Selection and Construction for Data Mining*, Kluwer Academic Publishers, Boston: MA, 2001.

   Many different approaches have been used to address the data-explosion issue, such as algorithm scale-up and data reduction. Instance, sample, or tuple selection pertains to methods that select or search for a representative portion of data that can fulfill a data-mining task as if the whole data were used. This book brings researchers and practitioners together to report new developments and applications in instance-selection techniques, to share hard-learned experiences in order to avoid similar pitfalls, and to shed light on future development.

2. Liu, H. and H. Motoda, *Feature Selection for Knowledge Discovery and Data Mining*, (Second Printing), Kluwer Academic Publishers, Boston: MA, 2000.

   The book offers an overview of feature-selection methods and provides a general framework in order to examine these methods and categorize them. The book uses simple examples to show the essence of methods and suggests guidelines for using different methods under various circumstances.

3. Liu, H. and H. Motoda, eds., *Feature Extraction, Construction and Selection: A Data Mining Perspective*, Kluwer Academic Publishers, Boston: MA, 1998.

   The book compiles contributions from many leading and active researchers in the field of feature processing. It paints a picture of the state-of-the-art techniques that can boost the capabilities of many existing data-mining tools. This book attempts to create synergy among seemingly different methods and pave the way for developing meta-systems and novel approaches.

4. Weiss, S. M. and N. Indurkhya , *Predictive Data Mining: a Practical Guide*, Morgan Kaufman, San Francisco, 1998.

This book focuses on the data-preprocessing phase in successful data-mining applications. Preparation and organization of data and development of an overall strategy for data mining are not only time-consuming processes but fundamental requirements in real-world data mining. A simple presentation of topics with a large number of examples is an additional strength of the book.

4 Learning from Data

CHAPTER OBJECTIVES

- Analyze the general model of inductive learning in observational environments.
- Explain how the learning machine selects an approximating function from the set of functions it supports.
- Introduce the concepts of risk functional for regression and classification problems.
- Identify the basic concepts in statistical learning theory (SLT) and discuss the differences between inductive principles, empirical risk minimization (ERM), and structural risk minimization (SRM).
- Discuss the practical aspects of the Vapnik-Chervonenkis (VC) dimension concept as an optimal structure for inductive-learning tasks.
- Compare different inductive learning tasks using graphical interpretation of approximating functions in a 2D space.
- Introduce methods for validation of inductive-learning results.

Many recent approaches to developing models from data have been inspired by the learning capabilities of biological systems and, in particular, those of humans. In fact, biological systems learn to cope with the unknown, statistical nature of the environment in a data-driven fashion. Babies are not aware of the laws of mechanics when they learn how to walk, and most adults drive a car without knowledge of the underlying laws of physics. Humans as well as animals also have superior pattern-recognition capabilities for such tasks as identifying faces, voices, or smells. People are not born with such capabilities, but learn them through data-driven interaction with the environment.

It is possible to relate the problem of learning from data samples to the general notion of inference in classical philosophy. Every predictive-learning process consists of two main phases:

1. Learning or estimating unknown dependencies in the system from a given set of samples, and
2. Using estimated dependencies to predict new outputs for future input values of the system.

These two steps correspond to the two classical types of inference known as *induction* (progressing from particular cases—training data—to a general mapping or model) and *deduction* (progressing from a general model and given input values to particular cases of output values). These two phases are shown graphically in Figure 4.1.

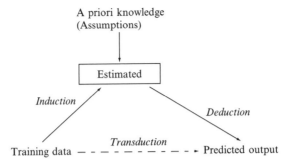

FIGURE 4.1   Types of inference: *induction, deduction,* and *transduction*

A unique estimated model implies that a learned function can be applied everywhere, i.e., for all possible input values. Such global-function estimation can be overkill, because many practical problems require one to deduce estimated outputs only for a few given input values. In that case, a better approach may be to estimate the outputs of the unknown function for several points of interest directly from the training data without building a global model. Such an approach is called *transductive* inference in which a local estimation is more important than a global one. An important application of the *transductive* approach is a process of mining association rules, which has been described in detail in Chapter 8. It is very important to mention that the standard formalization of machine learning does not apply to this type of inference.

The process of inductive learning and estimating the model may be described, formalized, and implemented using different learning methods. A learning method is an algorithm (usually implemented in software) that estimates an unknown mapping (dependency) between a system's inputs and outputs from the available data set, namely, from known samples. Once such a dependency has been accurately estimated, it can be used to predict the future outputs of the system from the known input values. Learning from data has been traditionally explored in such diverse fields as statistics, engineering, and computer science. Formalization of the learning process and a precise, mathematically correct description of different inductive-learning methods were the primary tasks of disciplines such as statistical learning theory and artificial intelligence. In this chapter, we will introduce the basics of these theoretical fundamentals for inductive learning.

4.1 LEARNING MACHINE

Machine learning, as a combination of artificial intelligence and statistics, has proven to be a fruitful area of research, spawning a number of different problems and algorithms for their solution. These algorithms vary in their goals, in the available training data sets, and in the learning strategies and representation of data. All of these algorithms, however, learn by searching through an n-dimensional space of a given data set to find an acceptable generalization. One of the most fundamental machine-learning tasks is *inductive machine learning* where a generalization is obtained from a set of samples, and it is formalized using different techniques and models.

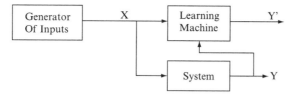

FIGURE 4.2   A learning machine uses observations of the system to form an approximation of its output

We can define inductive learning as the process of estimating an unknown input–output dependency or structure of a system, using limited number of observations or measurements of inputs and outputs of the system. In the theory of inductive learning, all data in a learning process are organized, and each instance of input–output pairs we use a simple term known as a sample. The general learning scenario involves three components, represented in Figure 4.2

1. A generator of random input vectors X,
2. A system which returns an output Y for a given input vector X, and
3. A learning machine, which estimates an unknown (input X, output Y') mapping of the system from the observed (input X, output Y) samples.

This formulation is very general and describes many practical, inductive-learning problems such as interpolation, regression, classification, clustering, and density estimation. The generator produces a random vector X, which is drawn independently from any distribution. In statistical terminology, this situation is called an observational setting. It differs from the designed-experiment setting, which involves creating a deterministic sampling scheme, optimal for a specific analysis according to experimental design theory. The learning machine has no control over which input values were supplied to the system, and therefore, we are talking about an observational approach in inductive machine learning systems.

The second component of the inductive-learning model is the system that produces an output value Y for every input vector X according to the conditional probability $p(Y/X)$, which is unknown. Note that this description includes the specific case of a deterministic system where $Y = f(X)$. Real-world systems rarely have truly random outputs; however, they often have unmeasured inputs. Statistically, the effects of these unobserved inputs on the output of the system can be characterized as random and represented with a probability distribution.

An inductive-learning machine tries to form generalizations from particular, true facts, which we call the training data set. These generalizations are formalized as a set of functions that approximate a system's behavior. This is an inherently difficult problem, and its solution requires a priori knowledge in addition to data. All inductive-learning methods use a priori knowledge in the form of the selected class of approximating functions of a learning machine. In the most general case, the learning machine is capable of implementing a set of functions $f(X, w)$, $w \in W$, where X is an input, w is a parameter of the function, and W is a set of abstract parameters used only to index the set of functions. In this formulation, the set of functions implemented by the learning machine can be any set of functions. Ideally, the choice of a set of approximating functions reflects a priori knowledge, about the system and its unknown dependencies. However, in practice, because of the complex and often informal nature of a priori knowledge, specifying such approximating functions may be, in many cases, difficult or impossible.

To explain the selection of approximating functions, we can use a graphical interpretation of the inductive-learning process. The task of inductive inference is this: given a collection of samples $(x_i, f(x_i))$, return a function $h(x)$ that approximates $f(x)$. The function $h(x)$ is often called a hypothesis. Figure 4.3 shows a simple example of this task, where the points in 2D are given in Figure 4.3a, and it is necessary to find "the best" function through these points. The true $f(x)$ is unknown, so there are many choices for $h(x)$. Without more knowledge, we have no way to prefer one of three suggested solutions (Figure 4.3 b, c, or d). Because there is almost always a large number of possible, consistent hypotheses, all learning algorithms search through the solution space based on given criteria. For example, the criterion may be a linear approximating function that has a minimum distance from all given data points. This a priori knowledge will restrict the search space to the functions in the form given in Figure 4.3b.

There is also an important distinction between the two types of approximating functions we usually use in an inductive-learning process. Their parameters could be *linear* or *nonlinear*. Note that the notion of linearity is with respect to parameters rather than input variables. For example, polynomial regression in a form

$$Y = w_1 x^n + w_2 x^{n-1} + \ldots + w_0$$

is a linear method, because the parameters w_i in the function are linear (even if the function by itself is nonlinear). We will see later that some learning methods such as multilayer, artificial neural networks provide an example of nonlinear parametrization, since the output of an approximating function depends nonlinearly on parameters. A typical factor in these functions is e^{-ax}, where a is a parameter and x is the input value. Selecting the approximating functions $f(X, w)$ and estimating the values of parameters w are typical steps for every inductive-learning method.

Before further formalization of a learning process, it is necessary to make a clear distinction between two concepts that are highly connected with a learning process. Let us discuss the differences between *statistical dependency and causality*. The statistical dependency between input X and output Y is expressed with the approximating functions of the learning method. The main point is that causality cannot be inferred from data analysis alone and concluded with some inductive, learned model using input–output approximating functions, $Y = f(X, w)$; instead, it must

  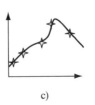 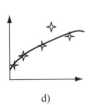

a)   b)   c)   d)

FIGURE 4.3 Three hypotheses for a given data set

be assumed or demonstrated by arguments outside the results of inductive-learning analysis. For example, it is well known that people in Florida are on average older than in the rest of the United States. This observation may be supported by inductive-learning dependencies, but it does not imply, however, that the climate in Florida causes people to live longer. The cause is totally different; people just move there when they retire and that is possibly the cause, and maybe not the only one, of people being older in Florida than elsewhere. Similar misinterpretation could be based on the data analysis of life expectancy for a married versus a single man. Statistics show that the married man lives longer than the single man. But do not hurry with sensational causality and conclusions: that marriage is good for one's health and increases life expectancy. It can be argued that males with physical problems and/or socially deviant patterns of behavior are less likely to get married, and this could be one of possible explanations why married men live longer. Unobservable factors such as a person's health and social behavior are more likely the cause of changed life expectancy, and not the observed variable, marriage status. These illustrations should lead us to understand that inductive-learning processes build the model of dependencies but they should not automatically be interpreted as causality relations. Only experts in the domain where the data are collected may suggest additional, deeper semantics of discovered dependencies.

Let us return again to the learning machine and its task of system modeling. The problem encountered by the learning machine is to select a function from the set of functions this machine supports, which best approximates the system's responses. The learning machine is limited to observing a finite number of samples n in order to make this selection. The finite number of samples, which we call a training data set, is denoted by (X_i, y_i), where $i = 1, \ldots, n$. The quality of an approximation produced by the learning machine is measured by the *loss function $L(y, f(X, w))$* where

   y is the output produced by the system,
   X is a set of inputs,
   $f(X, w)$ is the output produced by the learning machine for a selected approximating function, and
   w is the set of parameters in the approximating functions.

L measures the difference between the outputs produced by the system y_i and that produced by the learning machine $f(X_i, w)$ for every input point X_i. By convention, the loss function is nonnegative, so that large positive values correspond to poor approximation and small positive values close to zero show a good approximation. The expected value of the loss is called the *risk functional $R(w)$*

$$R(w) = \int \int L(y, f(X, w)) \, p(X, y) \, dX \, dy$$

where $L(y, f(X, w))$ is a loss function and $p(X, y)$ is a probability distribution of samples. The $R(w)$ value, for a selected approximating functions, is dependent only on a set of parameters w. Inductive learning can be now defined as the process of estimating the function $f(X, w_{opt})$, which minimizes the risk functional $R(w)$ over the set of functions supported by the learning machine, using only the training data set, and not knowing the probability distribution p(X, y). With finite data, we cannot expect to find $f(X, w_{opt})$ exactly, so we denote $f(X, w_{opt}*)$ as the estimate of parameters $w_{opt}*$ of the optimal solution w_{opt} obtained with finite training data using some learning procedure.

For common learning problems such as classification or regression, the nature of the loss function and the interpretation of risk functional are different. In a two-class classification problem, where the output of the system takes on only two symbolic values, y = {0, 1}, corresponding to the two classes, a commonly used loss function measures the classification error.

$$L(y, f(X, w)) = \begin{cases} 0 & \text{if } y = f(X, w) \\ 1 & \text{if } y \neq f(X, w) \end{cases}$$

Using this loss function, the risk functional quantifies the *probability of misclassification*. Inductive learning becomes a problem of finding the classifier function f(X, w), which minimizes the probability of misclassification using only the training data set.

Regression is a process of estimating a real-value function based on a finite data set of noisy samples. A common loss function for regression is the squared error measure

$$L(y, f(X, w)) = (y - f(X, w))^2$$

The corresponding risk functional measures the *accuracy* of the learning machine's predictions of the system output. Maximum accuracy will be obtained by minimizing the risk functional because, in that case, the approximating function will describe the best set of given samples. Classification and regression are only two of many typical learning tasks. For the other data-mining tasks, different loss functions may be selected and they are supported with different interpretations of a risk functional.

What is a learning procedure? Or how should a learning machine use training data? The answer is given by the concept known as *inductive principle*. An inductive principle is a general prescription for obtaining an estimate $f(X, w_{opt}*)$ in the class of approximating functions from the available finite training data. An inductive principle tells us *what* to do with the data, whereas the learning method specifies *how* to obtain an estimate. Hence a learning method or learning algorithm is a constructive implementation of an inductive principle. For a given inductive principle, there are many learning methods corresponding to a different set of functions of a learning machine. The important issue here is to choose the candidate models (approximating functions of a learning machine) of the right complexity to describe the training data.

The mathematical formulation and formalization of the learning problem explained in this section may give the unintended impression that learning algorithms do not require human intervention, but this is clearly not the case. Even though available literature is concerned with the formal description of learning methods, there is an equally important, informal part of any practical learning system. This part involves such practical and human-oriented issues as selection of the input and output variables, data encoding and representation, and incorporating a priori domain knowledge into the design of a learning system. In many cases, the user also has some influence over the generator in terms of the sampling rate or distribution. The user very often selects the most suitable set of functions for the learning machine based on his/her knowledge of the system. This part is often more critical for an overall success than the design of the learning machine itself. Therefore, all formalizations in a learning theory are useful only if we keep in mind that inductive learning is a process in which there is some overlap between activities that can be formalized and others that are not a part of formalization.

4.2 STATISTICAL LEARNING THEORY

Statistical learning theory (SLT) is relatively new, but it is perhaps one of the best currently available formalized theories for finite-sample inductive learning. It is also known as the Vapnik-Chervonenkis (VC) theory. It rigorously defines all the relevant concepts for inductive learning and provides mathematical proofs for most inductive-learning results. In contrast, other approaches such as neural networks, Bayesian inference, and decision rules are more engineering-oriented, with an emphasis on practical implementation without needing strong theoretical proofs and formalizations.

Statistical learning theory effectively describes statistical estimation with small samples. It explicitly takes into account the sample size and provides quantitative description of the trade-off between the complexity of the model and the available information. The theory includes, as a special case, classical statistical methods developed for large samples. Understanding SLT is necessary for designing sound, constructive methods of inductive learning. Many nonlinear learning procedures recently developed in neural networks, artificial intelligence, data mining, and statistics can be understood and interpreted in terms of general SLT principles. Even though SLT is quite general, it was originally developed for pattern recognition or classification problems. Therefore, the widely known, practical applications of the theory are mainly for classification tasks. There is growing empirical evidence, however, of successful application of the theory to other types of learning problems.

The goal of inductive learning is to estimate unknown dependencies in a class of approximating functions using available data. The optimal estimate corresponds to the minimum expected risk functional that includes general distribution of data. This distribution is unknown, and the only available information about distribution is the finite training sample. Therefore, the only possibility is to substitute an unknown *true risk functional* with its approximation given as *empirical risk*, which is computable based on the available data set. This approach is called *empirical risk minimization* (ERM) and it represents the basic inductive principle. Using the ERM inductive principle, one seeks to find a solution $f(X, w^*)$ that minimizes the empirical risk expressed through the training error as a substitute for the unknown true risk, which is a measure of the true error on the entire population. Depending on the chosen loss function and the chosen class of approximating functions, the ERM inductive principle can be implemented by a variety of methods defined in statistics, neural networks, automatic learning, etc. The ERM inductive principle is typically used in a learning setting where the model is given or approximated first and then its parameters are estimated from the data. This approach works well only when the number of training samples is large relative to the prespecified model complexity, expressed through the number of free parameters.

A general property necessary for any inductive principle including ERM is asymptotic *consistency*, which is a requirement that the estimated model converge to the true model or the best-possible estimation, as the number of training samples grows large. An important objective of the statistical learning theory is to formulate the conditions under which the ERM principle is consistent. The notion of consistency is illustrated in Figure 4.4. When the number of samples increases, empirical risk also increases while true, expected risk decreases. Both risks approach the common minimum value of the risk functional: *min R(w)* over the set of approximating functions, and for an extra large number of samples. If we take the classification problem as an example of inductive learning, the empirical risk corresponds to the probability of misclassification for the training data, and the expected risk is the probability of misclassification averaged over a large amount of data not included into a training set, and with unknown distribution.

Even though it can be intuitively expected that for n → ∞ the empirical risk converges to the true risk, this by itself does not imply the consistency property, which states that minimizing one risk for a given data set will also minimize the other risk. To ensure that the consistency of the ERM method is always valid and does not depend on the properties of the approximating functions, it is necessary that consistency requirement should hold for all approximating functions. This requirement is known as nontrivial consistency. From a practical point of view, conditions for consistency are at the same time prerequisites for a good generalization obtained with the realized model. Therefore, it is desirable to formulate conditions for convergence of risk functions in terms of the general properties of a set of the approximating functions.

Let us define the concept of a *growth function* G(n) as a function that is either linear or bounded by a logarithmic function of the number of samples n. Typical behavior of the growth function G(n) is given in Figure 4.5. Every approximating function that is in the form of the growth function G(n) will have a consistency property and potential for a good generalization under inductive learning, because empirical and true risk functions converge. The most important characteristic of the growth function G(n) is the concept of *VC-dimension*. At a point n = h where

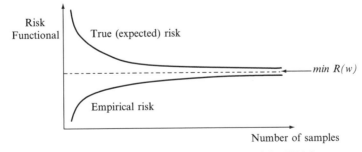

FIGURE 4.4 Asymptotic consistency of the ERM

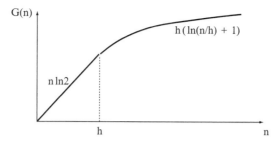

FIGURE 4.5   Behavior of the growth function G(n)

the growth starts to slow down, it is a characteristic of a set of functions. If h is finite, then the G(n) function does not grow linearly for enough large training data sets, and it is bounded by a logarithmic function. If G(n) is only linear, then h → ∞, and no valid generalization through selected approximating functions is possible. The finiteness of h provides necessary and sufficient conditions for the quick convergence of risk functions, consistency of ERM, and potentially good generalization in the inductive-learning process. These requirements place analytic constraints on the ability of the learned model to generalize, expressed through the empirical risk. All theoretical results in the statistical learning theory use the VC-dimension defined on the set of loss functions. But, it has also been proved that the VC-dimension for theoretical loss functions is equal to the VC-dimension for approximating functions in typical, inductive-learning tasks such as classification or regression.

The ERM inductive principle is intended for relatively large data sets, namely, when the ratio n/h is large and the empirical risk converges close to the true risk. However, if n/h is small, namely, when the ratio n/h is less than 20, then a modification of the ERM principle is necessary. The inductive principle called *structural risk minimization* (SRM) provides a formal mechanism for choosing a model with optimal complexity in finite and small data sets. According to SRM, solving a learning problem with a finite data set requires a priori specification of a structure on a set of approximating functions. For example, a set of functions S_1 is a subset of S_2, S_2 is subset of S_3, etc. The set of approximating functions S_1 has the lowest complexity, but the complexity increases with each new superset S_2, S_3, ..., S_k. A simplified graphical representation of the structure is given in Figure 4.6.

For a given data set, the optimal model estimation is performed through two steps:

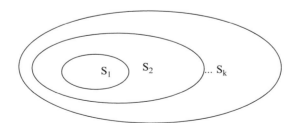

FIGURE 4.6   Structure of a set of approximating functions

1) selecting an element of a structure having optimal complexity, and
2) estimating the model based on the set of approximating functions defined in a selected element of the structure.

Through these two steps the SRM provides a quantitative characterization of the trade-off between the complexity of approximating functions and the quality of fitting the training data. As the complexity increases (increase of the index k for S_k), the minimum empirical risk decreases, and the quality of fitting the data improves. But estimated true risk, measured through the additional testing data set, has a convex form, and in one moment it moves in a direction opposite that of the empirical risk, as shown in Figure 4.7. The SRM chooses an optimal element of the structure that yields the minimal guaranteed bound on the true risk.

In practice, to implement the SRM approach, it is necessary to be able to

1) calculate or estimate the VC-dimension for any element S_k of the structure, and then
2) minimize the empirical risk for each element of the structure.

For most practical inductive-learning methods that use nonlinear approximating functions, finding the VC-dimension analytically is difficult, as is the nonlinear optimization of empirical risk. Therefore, rigorous application of the SRM principle can not only be difficult but, in many cases, impossible with nonlinear approximations. This does not, however, imply that the statistical learning theory is impractical. There are various heuristic procedures that are often used to implement SRM implicitly. Examples of such heuristics include early stopping rules and weight initialization, which are often used in artificial neural networks. These heuristics will be explained together with different learning methods in the following chapters. The choice of an SRM-optimization strategy suitable for a given learning problem depends on the type of approximating functions supported by the learning machine. There are three commonly used optimization approaches:

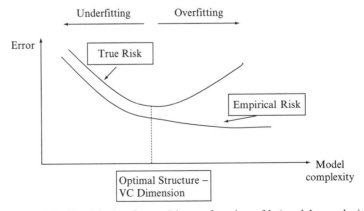

FIGURE 4.7   Empirical and true risk as a function of h (model complexity)

1. *Stochastic approximation (or gradient descent)* – Given an initial estimate of the values of parameter w for the approximating functions, the optimal parameter values are found by repeatedly updating them. In each step, while computing the gradient of the risk function, the updated values of the parameters cause a small movement in the direction of the steepest descent along the risk (error) function.

2. *Iterative methods* – Parameter values w are estimated iteratively so that at each iteration the value of the empirical risk is decreased. In contrast to stochastic approximation, iterative methods do not use gradient estimates; instead they rely on a particular form of approximating functions with a special iterative parameter.

3. *Greedy optimization* – The greedy method is used when the set of approximating functions is a linear combination of some basic functions. Initially, only the first term of the approximating functions is used and the corresponding parameters optimized. Optimization corresponds to minimizing the differences between the training data set and the estimated model. This term is then held fixed, and the next term is optimized. The optimization process is repeated until values are found for all parameters w and for all terms in the approximating functions.

These typical optimization approaches and also other more specific techniques have one or more of the following problems:

1. *Sensitivity to initial conditions* – The final solution is very sensitive to the initial values of the approximation function parameters.

2. *Sensitivity to stopping rules* – Nonlinear approximating functions often have regions that are very flat, where some optimization algorithms can become "stuck" for a long time (for a large number of iterations). With poorly designed stopping rules these regions can be interpreted falsely as local minima by the optimization algorithm.

3. *Sensitivity to multiple local minima* – Nonlinear functions may have many local minima, and optimization methods can find, at best, one of them without trying to reach global minimum. Various heuristics can be used to explore the solution space and move from a local solution toward a globally optimal solution.

Working with finite data sets, SLT reaches several conclusions that are important guidelines in a practical implementation of data-mining techniques. Let us briefly explain two of these useful principles. First, when solving a problem of inductive learning based on finite information, one should keep in mind the following general commonsense principle: Do not attempt to solve a specified problem by indirectly solving a harder general problem as an intermediate step. We are interested in solving a specific task, and we should solve it directly. Following statistical learning theory results, we stress that for estimation with finite samples, it is always better to solve a specific learning problem rather than attempt a general one. Conceptually, this means that posing the problem directly will then require fewer samples for a specified level of accuracy in the solution. This point, while obvious, has not been clearly stated in most of the classical textbooks on data analysis.

Second, there is a general belief that for inductive-learning methods with finite data sets, the best performance is provided by a model of optimal complexity, where the optimization is based on the general philosophical principle known as Occam's razor. According to this principle, limiting the model complexity is more important than using true assumptions with all details. We should seek simpler models over complex ones and optimize the trade-off between model complexity and the accuracy of the model's description and fit to the training data set. Models that are too complex and fit the training data very well or too simple and fit the data poorly are both not good models because they often do not predict future data very well. Model complexity is usually controlled in accordance with Occam's razor principle by a priori knowledge.

Summarizing SLT, in order to form a unique model of a system from finite data, any inductive-learning process requires the following:

1. A wide, flexible set of *approximating functions* f(X, w), w ∈ W, that can be linear or nonlinear in parameters w.
2. *A priori knowledge* (or assumptions) used to impose constraints on a potential solution. Usually such a priori knowledge orders the functions, explicitly or implicitly, according to some measure of their flexibility to fit the data. Ideally, the choice of a set of approximating functions reflects a priori knowledge about a system and its unknown dependencies.
3. *An inductive principle*, or method of inference, specifying what has to be done. It is a general prescription for combining a priori knowledge with available training data in order to produce an estimate of an unknown dependency.
4. *A learning method*, namely, a constructive, computational implementation of an inductive principle for a given class of approximating functions. There is a general belief that for learning methods with finite samples, the best performance is provided by a model of optimum complexity, which is selected based on the general principle known as Occam's razor. According to this principle, we should seek simpler models over complex ones and optimize the model that is the trade-off between model complexity and the accuracy of fit to the training data.

4.3   TYPES OF LEARNING METHODS

There are two common types of the inductive-learning methods known as

1. *supervised learning (or learning with a teacher)*, and
2. *unsupervised learning (or learning without a teacher)*.

Supervised learning is used to estimate an unknown dependency from known input–output samples. Classification and regression are common tasks supported by this type of inductive learning. Supervised learning assumes the existence of a teacher—fitness function or some other external method of estimating the proposed model. The term "supervised" denotes that the output values for training samples are known (i.e., provided by a "teacher").

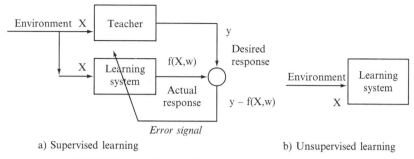

a) Supervised learning   b) Unsupervised learning

FIGURE 4.8   Two main types of inductive learning

Figure 4.8a shows a block diagram that illustrates this form of learning. In conceptual terms, we may think of the teacher as having knowledge of the environment, with that knowledge being represented by a set of input–output examples. The environment with its characteristics and model is, however, unknown to the learning system. The parameters of the learning system are adjusted under the combined influence of the training samples and the error signal. The error signal is defined as the difference between the desired response and the actual response of the learning system. Knowledge of the environment available to the teacher is transferred to the learning system through the training samples, which adjust the parameters of the learning system. It is a closed-loop feedback system, but the unknown environment is not in the loop. As a performance measure for the system, we may think in terms of the mean-square error or the sum of squared errors over the training samples. This function may be visualized as a multidimensional error surface, with the free parameters of the learning system as coordinates. Any learning operation under supervision is represented as a movement of a point on the error surface. For the system to improve the performance over time and therefore learn from the teacher, the operating point on an error surface has to move down successively toward a minimum of the surface. The minimum point may be a local minimum or a global minimum. The basic characteristics of optimization methods such as stochastic approximation, iterative approach, and greedy optimization have been given in the previous section. An adequate set of input–output samples will move the operating point toward the minimum, and a supervised learning system will be able to perform such tasks as pattern classification and function approximation. Different techniques support this kind of learning, and some of them such as logistic regression, multilayered perceptron, and decision rules and trees will be explained with more details in Chapters 5, 7, and 9.

Under the unsupervised learning scheme, only samples with input values are given to a learning system, and there is no notion of the output during the learning process. Unsupervised learning eliminates the teacher and requires that the learner forms and evaluates the model on its own. The goal of unsupervised learning is to discover "natural" structure in the input data. In biological systems, perception is a task learned via unsupervised techniques.

The simplified schema of unsupervised or self-organized learning, without an external teacher to oversee the learning process, is indicated in Figure 4.8b. The emphasis in this learning process is on a task-independent measure of the quality of representation that is learned by the system. The free parameters w of the learning system are optimized with respect to that measure. Once the system has become tuned to the regularities of the input data, it develops the ability to form internal representations for encoding features of the input examples. This representation can be *global*; applicable to the entire input data set. These results are obtained with methodologies such as cluster analysis or some artificial neural networks, explained in Chapters 6 and 9. On the other hand, learned representation for some learning tasks can be only *local*, applicable to the specific subsets of data from the environment; association rules are a typical example of an appropriate method- ology. It has been explainedwith more details in Chapter 8.

4.4   COMMON LEARNING TASKS

The generic inductive-learning problem can be subdivided into several common learning tasks. The fundamentals of inductive learning, along the with classification of common learning tasks, have already been given in the introductory chapter of this book. Here, we would like to analyze these tasks in detail, keeping in mind that for each of these tasks, the nature of the loss function and the output differ. However, the goal of minimizing the risk based on training data is common to all tasks. We believe that visualization of these tasks will give the reader the best feeling about the complexity of the learning problem and the techniques required for its solution.

To obtain a graphical interpretation of the learning tasks, we start with the formalization and representation of data samples that are the "infrastructure" of the learning process. Every sample used in data mining represents one entity de- scribed with several attribute–value pairs. That is one row in a tabular representa- tion of a training data set, and it can be visualized as a point in an n-dimensional space, where n is the number of attributes (dimensions) for a given sample. This graphical interpretation of samples is illustrated in Figure 4.9, where a student with the name John represents a point in a four-dimensional space that has four add- itional attributes.

STUDENT-NAME	SEX	YEAR OF BIRTH	MAYOR	CREDITS
John	M	1982	CS	64

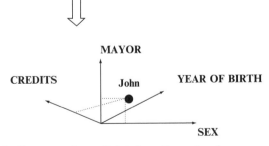

FIGURE 4.9   Data samples = Points in n-dimensional space

When we have a basic idea of the representation of each sample, the training data set can be interpreted as a set of points in the n-dimensional space. Visualization of data and a learning process is difficult for large number of dimensions. Therefore, we will explain and illustrate the common learning tasks in a 2D space, supposing that the basic principles are the same for a higher number of dimensions. Of course, this approach is an important simplification that we have to take care of, especially keeping in mind all the characteristics of large, multidimensional data sets, explained earlier under the topic "the curse of dimensionality".

Let us start with the first and most common task in inductive learning: classification. This is a learning function that classifies a data item into one of several predefined classes. The initial training data set is given in Figure 4.10a. Samples belong to different classes and therefore we use different graphical symbols to visualize each class. The final result of classification in a 2D space is the curve shown in Figure 4.10b, which best separates samples into two classes. Using this function, every new sample, even without a known output (the class to which it belongs), may be classified correctly. Similarly, when the problem is specified with more than two classes, it results in more complex functions. For an n-dimensional space of samples the complexity of the solution increases exponentially, and the classification function is represented in the form of hypersurfaces in the given space.

The second learning task is *regression*. The result of the learning process in this case is a learning function, which maps a data item to a real-value prediction variable. The initial training data set is given in Figure 4.11a. The regression function in Figure 4.11b was generated based on some predefined criteria built inside a data-mining technique. Based on this function, it is possible to estimate the value of a prediction variable for each new sample. If the regression process is performed in the time domain, specific subtypes of data and inductive-learning techniques can be defined.

Clustering is the most common unsupervised learning task. It is a descriptive task in which one seeks to identify a finite set of categories or clusters to describe the data. Figure 4.12a shows the initial data, and they are grouped into clusters, as shown in Figure 4.12b, using one of the standard distance measures for samples as

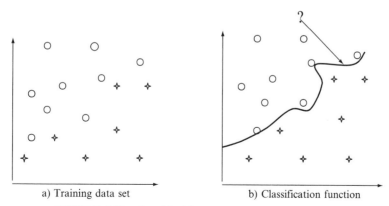

a) Training data set   b) Classification function

FIGURE 4.10 Graphical interpretation of classification

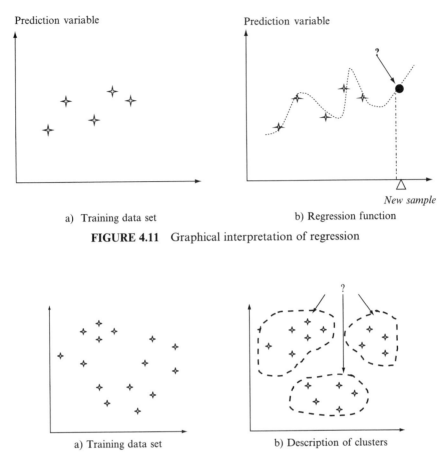

a) Training data set   b) Regression function

FIGURE 4.11   Graphical interpretation of regression

a) Training data set   b) Description of clusters

FIGURE 4.12   Graphical interpretation of clustering

points in an n-dimensional space. All clusters are described with some general characteristics, and the final solutions differ for different clustering techniques. Based on results of the clustering process, each new sample may be assigned to one of the previously found clusters, using its similarity with the cluster characteristics of the sample as a criterion.

Summarization is also a typical descriptive task, where the inductive-learning process is without a teacher. It involves methods for finding a *compact description* for a set (or subset) of data. If a description is formalized, as given in Figure 4.13b, that information may simplify and therefore improve the decision-making process in a given domain.

Dependency-modeling is a learning task that discovers local models based on a training data set. The task consists of finding a model that describes significant dependency between features or between values in a data set covering not the entire data set, but only some specific subsets. An illustrative example is given in Figure 4.14b, where the ellipsoidal relation is found for one subset and a linear relation for the other subset of the training data. These types of modeling are especially useful in large data sets that describe very complex systems. Discovering general models

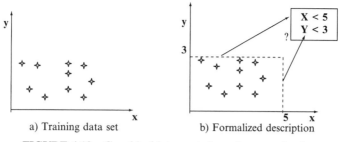

FIGURE 4.13   Graphical interpretation of summarization

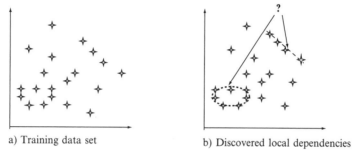

FIGURE 4.14   Graphical interpretation of dependency-modeling task

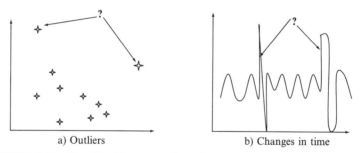

FIGURE 4.15   Graphical interpretation of change and detection of deviation

based on the entire data set is, in many cases, almost impossible, because of the computational complexity of the problem at hand.

Change and deviation detection is a learning task, and we have been introduced already to some of its techniques in Chapter 2. These are the algorithms that detect outliers. In general, this task focuses on discovering the most significant changes in a large data set. Graphical illustrations of the task are given in Figure 4.15. In Figure 4.15a the task is to discover outliers in a given, data set with discrete values of features. The task in Figure 4.15b is detection of time-dependent deviations for the variable in a continuous form.

The list of inductive-learning tasks is not exhausted with these six classes that are common specifications for data-mining problems. With wider and more intensive applications of the data-mining technology, new specific tasks are being developed, together with the corresponding techniques for inductive learning.

Whatever the learning task and whatever the available data-mining techniques, we have to accept that the foundation for successful data-mining processes is data-preprocessing and data-reduction methods. They transform raw and usually messy data into valuable data sets for mining, using methodologies explained in Chapters 2 and 3. As a review, we will enumerate some of these techniques just to show how many alternatives the data-mining designer has in the beginning phases of the process: scaling and normalization, encoding, outliers detection and removal, feature selection and composition, data cleansing and scrubbing, data smoothing, missing-data elimination, and cases reduction by sampling.

When the data are preprocessed and when we know what kind of learning task is defined for our application, a list of data-mining methodologies and corresponding computer-based tools are available. Depending on the characteristics of the problem at hand and the available data set, we have to make a decision about the application of one or more of the data-mining and knowledge-discovery techniques, which can be classified as follows:

1. *Statistical Methods* where the typical techniques are Bayesian inference, logistic regression, ANOVA analysis, and log-linear models.

2. *Cluster Analysis*, the common techniques of which are divisible algorithms, agglomerative algorithms, partitional clustering, and incremental clustering.

3. *Decision Trees and Decision Rules* are the set of methods of inductive learning developed mainly in artificial intelligence. Typical techniques include the CLS method, the ID3 algorithm, the C4.5 algorithm and the corresponding pruning algorithms.

4. *Association Rules* represent a set of relatively new methodologies that include algorithms such as market basket analysis, apriori algorithm, and WWW path-traversal patterns.

5. *Artificial Neural Networks*, where the emphasis is on multilayer perceptrons with backpropagation learning and Kohonen networks.

6. *Genetic Algorithms* are very useful as a methodology for solving hard-optimization problems.

7. *Fuzzy Inference Systems* are based on the theory of fuzzy sets and fuzzy logic. Fuzzy modeling and fuzzy decision making are steps very often included in the data-mining process.

8. *N-dimensional Visualization Methods* are usually skipped in the literature as a standard data-mining methodology, although useful information may be discovered using these techniques and tools. Typical data-mining visualization techniques are geometric, icon-based, pixel-oriented, and hierarchical techniques.

This list of data-mining and knowledge-discovery techniques is not exhaustive, and the order does not suggest any priority in the application of these methods. Iterativity and interactivity are basic characteristics of these data-mining techniques. Also, with more experience in data-mining applications, the reader will understand the importance of not relying on a single methodology. Parallel application of several techniques that cover the same inductive-learning task is a standard approach in this phase of data mining. In that case, for every iteration in a data-mining process, the results of the different techniques must additionally be evaluated and compared.

4.5   MODEL ESTIMATION

In the final phase of the data-mining process, when the model is obtained using one or more inductive-learning techniques, one important question still exists. How does one verify and validate the model? At the outset, let us differentiate between *validation* and *verification*.

Model *validation* is substantiating that the model, within its domain of applicability, behaves with satisfactory accuracy consistent with the objectives defined by the users. In other words, in model validation, we substantiate that the data has transformed into the model and that it has sufficient accuracy in representing the observed system. Model validation deals with building the *right* model, the model that corresponds to the system. Model *verification* is substantiating that the model is transformed from the data as intended into new representations with sufficient accuracy. Model verification deals with building the model *right*, the model that corresponds correctly to the data.

Model validity is a necessary but insufficient condition for the credibility and acceptability of data-mining results. If, for example, the initial objectives are incorrectly identified or the data set is improperly specified, the data-mining results expressed through the model will not be useful; however, we may still find the model valid. We can claim that we conducted an "excellent" data-mining process, but the decision-makers will not accept our results and we cannot do anything about it. Therefore, we have always to keep in mind, as it has been said, that a problem correctly formulated is a problem half-solved. Albert Einstein once indicated that the correct formulation and preparation of a problem was even more crucial than its solution. The ultimate goal of a data-mining process should not be just to produce a model for a problem at hand, but to provide one that is sufficiently credible and accepted and implemented by the decision-makers.

The data-mining results are validated and verified by the testing process. Model testing is demonstrating that inaccuracies exist or revealing the existence of errors in the model. We subject the model to test data or test cases to see if it functions properly. "Test failed" implies the failure of the model, not the test. Some tests are devised to evaluate the behavioral accuracy of the model (i.e., validity), and some tests are intended to judge the accuracy of data transformation into the model (i.e., verification).

The objective of a model obtained through the data-mining process is to classify/ predict new instances correctly. The commonly used measure of a model's quality is predictive accuracy. Since new instances are supposed not to be seen by the model in its learning phase, we need to estimate it's predictive accuracy using the true error rate. The true error rate is statistically defined as the error rate of the model on an asymptotically large number of new cases, where this number converge to the actual population distribution. In practice, the true error rate of a data-mining model must be estimated from all the available samples, which are usually split into training and testing sets. The model is first designed using training samples, and then it is evaluated based on its performance on the test samples. In order for this error estimate to be reliable in predicting future model performance, not only should the training and the testing sets be sufficiently large, they must also be independent. This requirement of independent training and test samples is still often overlooked in practice.

How should the available samples be split to form training and test sets? If the training set is small, then the resulting model will not be very robust and will have low generalization ability. On the other hand, if the test set is small, then the confidence in the estimated error rate will be low. Various methods are used to estimate the error rate. They differ in how they utilize the available samples as training and test sets. If the number of available samples is extremely large (say, 1 million), then all these methods are likely to lead to the same estimate of the error rate. If the number of samples is smaller, then the designer of the data-mining experiments has to be very careful in splitting data. There are no good guidelines available on how to divide the samples into subsets. No matter how the data are split, it should be clear that different random splits, even with the specified size of training and testing sets, would result in different error estimates.

Let us discuss different techniques, usually called *resampling methods*, for splitting data sets into training and test samples. The main advantage of using the resampling approach over the analytical approach for estimating and selecting models is that the former does not depend on assumptions about the statistical distribution of the data or specific properties of approximating functions. The main disadvantages of resampling techniques are their high computational effort and the variation in estimates depending on the resampling strategy.

The basic approach in model estimation is first to prepare or to discover a model using a portion of the data set and then to use the remaining samples to estimate the prediction risk for this model. The first portion of the data is called a learning set, and the second portion is a validation set, also called a testing set. This *naïve strategy* is based on the assumption that the learning set and the validation set are chosen as representatives of the same, unknown distribution of data. This is usually true for large data sets, but the strategy has an obvious disadvantage for smaller data sets. With a smaller number of samples, the specific method of splitting the data starts to have an impact on the accuracy of the model. The various methods of resampling are used for smaller data sets, and they differ according to the strategies used to divide the initial data set. We will give a brief description of the resampling methods that are common in today's data-mining practice, and a designer of a data-mining system will have to make a selection based on the characteristics of the data and the problem.

1. Resubstitution Method – This is the simplest method. All the available data are used for training as well as for testing. In other words, the training and testing sets are the same. Estimation of the error rate for this "data distribution" is optimistically biased (estimated error is often smaller than could be expected in real applications of the model), and therefore the method is very seldom used in real-world data-mining applications. This is especially the case when the ratio of sample size to dimensionality is small.

2. Holdout Method – Half the data, or sometimes two-thirds of the data, is used for training and the remaining data is used for testing. Training and testing sets are independent and the error estimation is pessimistic. Different partitioning will give different estimates. A repetition of the process, with different training and testing sets randomly selected, and integration of the error results into one standard parameter, will improve the estimate of the model.

3. Leave-one-out Method – A model is designed using (n−1) samples for training and evaluated on the one remaining sample. This is repeated n times with different training sets of size (n−1). This approach has large computational requirements because n different models have to be designed and compared.

4. Rotation Method (n-fold cross validation) – This approach is a compromise between holdout and leave-one-out methods. It divides the available samples into P disjoint subsets, where $1 \leq P \leq n$. (P−1) subsets are used for training and the remaining subset for testing. This is the most popular method in practice, especially for problems where the number of samples is relatively small.

5. Bootstrap method – This method resamples the available data with replacements to generate a number of "fake" data sets of the same size as the given data set. The number of these new sets is typically several hundreds. These new training sets can be used to define so called bootstrap estimates of the error rate. Experimental results have shown that the bootstrap estimates can outperform the cross-validation estimates. This method is especially useful in small data set situations.

A model realized through the data-mining process using different inductive-learning techniques might be estimated using the standard error rate parameter as a measure of its performance. This value expresses an approximation of the true error rate, a parameter defined in statistical learning theory. The error rate is computed using a testing data set obtained through one of applied resampling techniques. In addition to the accuracy measured by the error rate, data-mining models can be compared with respect to their speed, robustness, scalability, and interpretability, and all these parameters may have an influence on the final verification and validation of the model. In the short overview that follows, we will illustrate the characteristics of the error-rate parameter for classification tasks; similar approaches and analyses are possible for other common data-mining tasks.

The computation of error rate is based on counting of errors in a testing process. These errors are, for a classification problem, simply defined as misclassification (wrongly classified samples). If all errors are of equal importance, an error rate R is the number of errors E divided by the number of samples S in the testing set:

$$R = E/S$$

The accuracy A of a model is a part of the testing data set that is classified correctly, and it is computed as one minus the error rate:

$$A = 1 - R = (S - E)/S$$

For standard classification problems, there can be as many as $m^2 - m$ types of errors, where m is the number of classes. If there are only two classes (positive and negative samples, symbolically represented with T and F or with 1 and 0), we can have only two types of errors:

1. It is expected to be T, but it is classified as F: these are false negative errors, and

2. It is expected to be F, but it is classified as T: these are false positive errors.

If there are more than two classes, the types of errors can be summarized in a confusion matrix, as shown in Figure 4.16. For the number of classes m = 3, there are six types of errors ($m^2 - m = 3^2 - 3 = 6$), and they are represented in bold type in Table 4.1. Every class contains thirty samples in this example, and the total is ninety testing samples.

The error rate for this example is

$$R = E/S = 10/90 = 0.11$$

and the corresponding accuracy is

$$A = 1 - R = 1 - 0.11 = 0.89 \text{ (or as a percentage: } A = 89\%).$$

So far we have considered that every error is equally bad. In many data-mining applications, the assumption that all errors have the same weight is unacceptable. So, the differences between various errors should be recorded, and the final measure of the error rate will take into account these differences. When different types of errors are associated with different weights, we need to multiply every error type with the given weight factor c_{ij}. If the error elements in the confusion matrix are e_{ij}, then the total cost function C (which replaces the number of errors in the accuracy computation) can be calculated as

TABLE 4.1   Confusion matrix for three classes

Classification model	True class 0	1	2	Total
0	28	**1**	**4**	33
1	**2**	28	**2**	32
2	**0**	**1**	24	25
Total	*30*	*30*	*30*	*90*

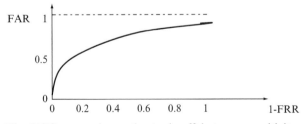

FIGURE 4.16   The ROC curve shows the trade-off between sensitivity and 1-specificity values

$$C = \sum_{i=1}^{m} \sum_{j=1}^{m} c_{ij}\ e_{ij}$$

In many data-mining applications, it is not adequate to characterize the performance of a model by a single number that measures the overall error rate. More complex and global measures are necessary to describe the quality of the model. Consider a classification problem where all samples have to be labeled with one of two possible classes. A typical example is a diagnostic process in medicine, where it is necessary to classify the patient as being with or without disease. For these types of problems, two different yet related error rates are of interest. The False Acceptance Rate (FAR) is the ratio of the number of test cases that are incorrectly "accepted" by a given model to the total number of training cases. For example, in medical diagnostics, these are the cases in which the patient is wrongly predicted as having a disease. On the other hand, the False Reject Rate (FRR) is the ratio of the number of test cases that are incorrectly "rejected" by a given model to the total number of cases. In the previous medical example, these are the cases of test patients who are wrongly classified as healthy, without any diagnosed disease.

For the most of the available data-mining methodologies, a classification model can be tuned by setting an appropriate threshold value to operate at a desired value of FAR. If we try to decrease the FAR parameter of the model, however, it would increase the FRR and vice versa. To analyze both characteristics at the same time, a new parameter was developed, the Receiver Operating Characteristic (ROC) Curve. It is a plot of FAR versus FRR for different threshold values in the model. This curve permits one to assess the performance of the model at various operating points (thresholds in a decision process using the available model) and the performance of the model as a whole (using as a parameter the area below the ROC curve). The ROC curve is especially useful for a comparison of the performances of two models obtained by using different data-mining methodologies. The typical shape of an ROC curve is given in Figure 4.16 where the axes are *sensitivity* (FAR) and *1-specificity* (1 − FRR).

4.6   REVIEW QUESTIONS AND PROBLEMS

1. Explain the differences between the basic types of inferences: induction, deduction, and transduction.

2. Why do we use the observational approach in most data-mining tasks?

3. Discuss situations in which we would use the interpolated functions given in Figures 4.3b, 4.3c, and 4.3d as "the best" data-mining model.

4. Which of the functions have linear parameters and which nonlinear? Explain why.

   a) $y = ax^5 + b$
   b) $y = a/x$
   c) $y = ae^x$
   d) $y = e^{ax}$

5. Explain the difference between interpolation of loss function for classification problems and for regression problems.

6. Is it possible that empirical risk becomes higher than expected risk? Explain.

7. Why is it so difficult to estimate the VC-dimension for real-world data-mining applications?

8. What will be the practical benefit of determining the VC-dimension in real-world data-mining applications?

9. Classify the common learning tasks explained in Section 4.4 as supervised or unsupervised learning tasks. Explain your classification.

10. Analyze the differences between validation and verification of inductive-based models.

11. In which situations would you recommend the Leave-one-out method for validation of data-mining results?

12. Develop a program for generating "fake" data sets using the bootstrap method.

13. Develop a program for plotting an ROC curve based on a table of FAR–FRR results.

14. Develop an algorithm for computing the area below the ROC curve (that is a very important parameter in the evaluation of inductive-learning results for classification problems).

4.7   REFERENCES FOR FURTHER STUDY

1. Berthold, M. and D. J. Hand, eds., *Intelligent Data Analysis – An Introduction*, Springer, Berlin: Germany, 1999.

    The book is a detailed, introductory presentation of the key classes of intelligent data-analysis methods including all common data-mining techniques. The first half of the book is devoted to the discussion of classical statistical issues, ranging from basic concepts of probability and inference to advanced multivariate analyses and Bayesian methods. The second part of the book covers theoretical explanations of data-mining techniques that have their roots in disciplines other than statistics. Numerous illustrations and examples enhance the reader's knowledge about theory and practical evaluations of data-mining techniques.

2. Cherkassky, V. and F. Mulier, *Learning from Data: Concepts, Theory and Methods*, John Wiley, New York, 1998.

    The book provides a unified treatment of the principles and methods for learning dependencies from data. It establishes a general conceptual framework in which various learning methods from statistics, machine learning, and other disciplines can be applied—showing that a few fundamental principles underlie most new methods being proposed today. An additional strength of this primarily theoretical book is the large number of case studies and examples that simplify and make understandable concepts in statistical learning theory.

3. Engel, A. and C. Van den Broeck, *Statistical Mechanics of Learning*, Cambridge University Press, Cambridge: UK, 2001.

The subject of this book is the contribution of machine learning over the last decade by researchers applying the techniques of statistical mechanics. The authors provide a coherent account of various important concepts and techniques that are currently only found scattered in papers. They include many examples and exercises, making this a book that can be used with courses, or for self-teaching, or as a handy reference.

4. Haykin, S., *Neural Networks: A Comprehensive Foundation*, Prentice Hall, Upper Saddle River: NJ, 1999.

The book provides a comprehensive foundation for the study of artificial neural networks, recognizing the multidisciplinary nature of the subject. The introductory part explains the basic principles of statistical learning theory and the concept of VC-dimension. The main part of the book classifies and explains artificial neural networks as learning machines with and without a teacher. The material presented in the book is supported with a large number of examples, problems, and computer-oriented experiments.

5 Statistical Methods

CHAPTER OBJECTIVES

- Explain methods of statistical inference commonly used in data-mining applications.
- Identify different statistical parameters for assessing differences in data sets.
- Describe the components and the basic principles of Naïve Bayesian Classifier and the logistic regression method.
- Introduce log–linear models using correspondence analysis of contingency tables.
- Discuss the concepts of ANOVA analysis and linear discriminant analysis of multidimensional samples.

Statistics is the science of collecting and organizing data and drawing conclusions from data sets. The organization and description of the general characteristics of data sets is the subject area of *descriptive statistics*. How to draw conclusions from data is the subject of *statistical inference*. In this chapter, the emphasis is on the basic principles of statistical inference; other related topics will be described briefly, only enough to understand the basic concepts.

Statistical data analysis is the most well-established set of methodologies for data mining. Historically, the first computer-based applications of data analysis were developed with the support of statisticians. Ranging from one-dimensional data analysis to multivariate data analysis, statistics offered a variety of methods for data mining, including different types of regression and discriminant analysis. In this short overview of statistical methods that support the data-mining process, we will not cover all approaches and methodologies; a selection has been made of the techniques used most often in real-world data-mining applications.

5.1 STATISTICAL INFERENCE

The totality of the observations with which we are concerned in statistical analysis, whether their number is finite or infinite, constitutes what we call a *population*. The term refers to anything of statistical interest, whether it is a group of people, objects, or events. The number of observations in the population is defined as the size of the population. In general, populations may be finite or infinite, but some finite populations are so large that, in theory, we assume them to be infinite.

In the field of statistical inference, we are interested in arriving at conclusions concerning a population when it is impossible or impractical to observe the entire set of observations that make up the population. For example, in attempting to determine the average length of the life of a certain brand of light bulbs, it would be practically impossible to test all such bulbs. Therefore, we must depend on a subset of observations from the population for most statistical-analysis applications. In statistics, a subset of a population is called a *sample* and it describes a finite data set of n-dimensional vectors. Throughout this book, we will call this subset of population just simply *data set*, to eliminate confusion between the two definitions of sample: one, explained earlier, denoting the description of a single entity in the population, and the other, given here, referring to the subset of a population. From a given data set, we build a statistical model of the population that will help us to make inferences concerning that same population. If our inferences from the data set are to be valid, we must obtain samples that are representative of the population. Very often, we are tempted to choose a data set by selecting the most convenient members of the population. But such an approach may lead to erroneous inferences concerning the population. Any sampling procedure that produces inferences that consistently overestimate or underestimate some characteristics of the population is said to be biased. To eliminate any possibility of bias in the sampling procedure, it is desirable to choose a random data set in the sense that the observations are made independently and at random. The main purpose of selecting random samples is to elicit information about unknown population parameters.

The relation between data sets and the system they describe may be used for inductive reasoning: from observed data to knowledge of a (partially) unknown system. Statistical inference is the main form of reasoning relevant to data analysis. The theory of statistical inference consists of those methods by which one makes inferences or generalizations about a population. These methods may be categorized into two major areas: *estimation*, and *tests of hypotheses*.

In *estimation*, one wants to come up with a plausible value or a range of plausible values for the unknown parameters of the system. The goal is to gain information from a data set T in order to estimate one or more parameters w belonging to the model of the real-world system f(X, w). A data set T is described by the ordered n-tuples of values for variables: $X = \{X_1, X_2, \ldots, X_n\}$ (attributes of entities in population):

$$T = \{(x_{11}, \ldots, x_{1n}), (x_{21}, \ldots, x_{2n}), \ldots, (x_{m1}, \ldots, x_{mn})\}$$

It can be organized in a tabular form as a set of samples with its corresponding feature values. Once the parameters of the model are estimated, we can use them to make predictions about the random variable Y from the initial set of attributes $Y \in X$, based on other variables or sets of variables $X^* = X - Y$. If Y is numeric, we speak about *regression* and if it takes its values from a discrete, unordered data set, we speak about *classification*.

Once we have obtained estimates for the model parameters w from some dataset T, we may use the resulting model (analytically given as a function f(X*, w)) to make predictions about Y when we know the corresponding value of the vector X*. The difference between the prediction f(X*, w) and the real value Y is called the prediction error. It should preferably take values close to zero. A natural quality measure of a model f(X*, w), as a predictor of Y, is the expected mean squared error for the entire data set T:

$$E_T[(Y - f(X^*, w))^2].$$

In *statistical testing*, on the other hand, one has to decide whether a hypothesis concerning the value of the population characteristic should be accepted or rejected in the light of an analysis of the data set. A statistical hypothesis is an assertion or conjecture concerning one or more populations. The truth or falsity of a statistical hypothesis can never be known with absolute certainty, unless we examine the entire population. This, of course, would be impractical in most situations, sometimes even impossible. Instead, we test a hypothesis on a randomly selected data set. Evidence from the data set that is inconsistent with the stated hypothesis leads to a rejection of the hypothesis, whereas evidence supporting the hypothesis leads to its acceptance, or more precisely, it implies that the data do not contain sufficient evidence to refute it. The structure of hypothesis testing is formulated with the use of the term *null hypothesis*. This refers to any hypothesis that we wish to test and is denoted by H_0. H_0 is only rejected if the given data set, on the basis of the applied statistical tests, contains strong evidence that the hypothesis is not true. The rejection of H_0 leads to the acceptance of an alternative hypothesis about the population.

In this chapter, some statistical estimation and hypothesis-testing methods are described in great detail. These methods have been selected primarily based on the applicability of the technique in a data-mining process on a large data set.

5.2 ASSESSING DIFFERENCES IN DATA SETS

For many data-mining tasks, it would be useful to learn the more general characteristics about the given data set, regarding both central tendency and data dispersion. These simple parameters of data sets are obvious descriptors for assessing differences between different data sets. Typical measures of central tendency include *mean*, *median*, and *mode*, while measures of data dispersion include *variance* and *standard deviation*.

The most common and effective numeric measure of the center of the data set is the *mean* value (also called the arithmetic mean). For the set of n numeric values $x_1, x_2, \ldots, x_n$, for the given feature X, the mean is

$$mean = 1/n \sum_{i=1}^{n} x_i$$

and it is a built-in function (like all other descriptive statistical measures) in most modern, statistical software tools. For each numeric feature in the n-dimensional set of samples, it is possible to calculate the mean value as a central tendency characteristic for this feature. Sometimes, each value x_i in a set may be associated with a weight w_i, which reflects the frequency of occurrence, significance, or importance attached to the value. In this case, the weighted arithmetic mean or the weighted average value is

$$mean = \sum_{i=1}^{n} w_i\, x_i \Big/ \sum_{i=1}^{n} w_i$$

Although the mean is the most useful quantity that we use to describe a set of data, it is not the only one. For skewed data sets, a better measure of the center of data is the *median*. It is the middle value of the ordered set of feature values if the set consists of an odd number of elements and it is the average of the middle two values if the number of elements in the set is even. If $x_1, x_2, \ldots, x_n$ represents a data set of size n, arranged in increasing order of magnitude, then the median is defined by

$$median = \begin{cases} x_{(n+1)/2} & \text{if n is odd} \\ (x_{n/2} + x_{(n/2)+1})/2 & \text{if n is even} \end{cases}$$

Another measure of the central tendency of a data set is the *mode*. The mode for the set of data is the value that occurs most frequently in the set. While mean and median are characteristics of primarily numeric data sets, the mode may be applied also to categorical data, but it has to be interpreted carefully because the data are not ordered. It is possible for the greatest frequency to correspond to several different values in a data set. That results in more than one mode for a given data set. Therefore, we classify data sets as unimodal (with only one mode) and multimodal (with two or more modes). Multimodal data sets may be precisely defined as bimodal, trimodal, etc. For unimodal frequency curves that are moderately asymmetrical, we have the following useful empirical relation for numeric data sets:

$$mean - mode = 3 \times (mean - median)$$

that may be used for an analysis of data set distribution and the estimation of one central-tendency measure based on the other two.

As an example, let us analyze these three measures on the simple data set T that has the following numeric values:

$$T = \{3, 5, 2, 9, 0, 7, 3, 6\}$$

After a sorting process the same data set is given as

$$T = \{0, 2, 3, 3, 5, 6, 7, 9\}$$

The corresponding descriptive statistical measures for central tendency are

$$mean_T = (0 + 2 + 3 + 3 + 5 + 6 + 7 + 9)/8 = 4.375$$
$$median_T = (3 + 5)/2 = 4$$
$$mode_T = 3$$

The degree to which numeric data tend to spread is called dispersion of the data, and the most common measures of dispersion are the *standard deviation* σ and the *variance* σ^2. The variance of n numeric values $x_1, x_2, \ldots, x_n$ is

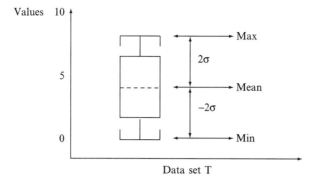

Figure 5.1 A boxplot representation of the data set T based on mean value, variance, and min and max values.

$$\sigma^2 = (1/(n-1)) \sum_{i=1}^{n} (x_i - mean)^2$$

The standard deviation σ is the square root of the variance σ^2. The basic properties of the standard deviation σ as a measure of spread are

1. σ measures spread about the *mean* and should be used only when the *mean* is chosen as a measure of the center.
2. $\sigma = 0$ only when there is no spread in the data, i.e., when all measurements have the same value. Otherwise $\sigma > 0$.

For the data set given in our example, *variance* σ^2 and *standard deviation* σ are

$$\sigma^2 = 1/8 \cdot \sum_{i=1}^{7} (x_i - 4.375)^2$$
$$\sigma^2 = 8.5532$$
$$\sigma = 2.9246$$

In many statistical software tools, a popularly used visualization tool of descriptive statistical measures for central tendency and dispersion is a *boxplot* that is typically determined by the mean value, variance, and sometimes max and min values of the data set. In our example, the minimal and maximal values in the T set are $min_T = 0$, and $max_T = 9$. Graphical representation of statistical descriptors for the data set T has a form of a boxplot, given in Figure 5.1.

5.3 BAYESIAN INFERENCE

It is not hard to imagine situations in which the data are not the only available source of information about the population or about the system to be modeled. The Bayesian method provides a principled way to incorporate this external information into the data-analysis process. This process starts with an already given probability distribution for the analyzed data set. As this distribution is given before any data is considered, it is called a *prior distribution*. The new data set updates this prior distribution into a *posterior distribution*. The basic tool for this updating is the Bayes Theorem.

The Bayes Theorem represents a theoretical background for a statistical approach to inductive-inferencing classification problems. We will first explain the basic concepts defined in the Bayes Theorem and then use this theorem in the explanation of the Naïve Bayesian Classification Process, or the Simple Bayesian Classifier.

Let X be a data sample whose class label is unknown. Let H be some hypothesis: such that the data sample X belongs to a specific class C. We want to determine $P(H/X)$, the probability that the hypothesis H holds given the observed data sample X. $P(H/X)$ is the posterior probability representing our confidence in the hypothesis after X is given. In contrast, $P(H)$ is the prior probability of H for any sample, regardless of how the data in the sample looks. The posterior probability $P(H/X)$ is based on more information then the prior probability $P(H)$. The Bayesian Theorem provides a way of calculating the posterior probability $P(H/X)$ using probabilities $P(H)$, $P(X)$, and $P(X/H)$. The basic relation is

$$P(H/X) = [P(X/H) \cdot P(H)]/P(X)$$

Suppose now that there are a set of m samples $S = \{S_1, S_2, \ldots, S_m\}$ (the training data set) where every sample S_i is represented as an n-dimensional vector $\{x_1, x_2, \ldots, x_n\}$. Values x_i correspond to attributes $A_1, A_2, \ldots, A_n$, respectively. Also, there are k classes $C_1, C_2, \ldots, C_k$, and every sample belongs to one of these classes. Given an additional data sample X (its class is unknown), it is possible to predict the class for X using the highest conditional probability $P(C_i/X)$, where $i = 1, \ldots, k$. That is the basic idea of Naïve Bayesian Classifier. These probabilities are computed using Bayes Theorem:

$$P(C_i/X) = [P(X/C_i) \cdot P(C_i)]/P(X)$$

As $P(X)$ is constant for all classes, only the product $P(X/C_i) \cdot P(C_i)$ needs to be maximized. We compute the prior probabilities of the class as

$P(C_i) =$ number of training samples of class C_i/m (m is total number of training samples).

Because the computation of $P(X/C_i)$ is extremely complex, especially for large data sets, the naïve assumption of conditional independence between attributes is made. Using this assumption, we can express $P(X/C_i)$ as a product:

$$P(X/C_i) = \prod_{t=1}^{n} P(x_t/C_i)$$

where x_t are values for attributes in the sample X. The probabilities $P(x_t/C_i)$ can be estimated from the training data set.

TABLE 5.1 Training data set for a classification using Naïve Bayesian Classifier

Sample	Attribute1 A_1	Attribute2 A_2	Attribute3 A_3	Class C
1	1	2	1	1
2	0	0	1	1
3	2	1	2	2
4	1	2	1	2
5	0	1	2	1
6	2	2	2	2
7	1	0	1	1

A simple example will show that the Naïve Bayesian Classification is a computationally simple process even for large training data sets. Given a training data set of seven four-dimensional samples (Table 5.1), it is necessary to predict classification of the new sample $X = \{1, 2, 2, \text{class} = ?\}$. For each sample, A_1, A_2, and A_3 are input dimensions and C is the output classification.

In our example, we need to maximize the product $P(X/C_i) \cdot P(C_i)$ for $i = 1, 2$ because there are only two classes. First, we compute prior probabilities $P(C_i)$ of the class:

$$P(C = 1) = 4/7 = 0.5714$$
$$P(C = 2) = 3/7 = 0.4286$$

Second, we compute conditional probabilities $P(x_t/C_i)$ for every attribute value given in the new sample $X = \{1, 2, 2, C = ?\}$, (or more precisely, $X = \{A_1 = 1, A_2 = 2, A_3 = 2, C = ?\}$) using training data sets:

$$P(A_1 = 1/C = 1) = 2/4 = 0.50$$
$$P(A_1 = 1/C = 2) = 1/3 = 0.33$$

$$P(A_2 = 2/C = 1) = 1/4 = 0.25$$
$$P(A_2 = 2/C = 2) = 2/3 = 0.66$$

$$P(A_3 = 2/C = 1) = 1/4 = 0.25$$
$$P(A_3 = 2/C = 2) = 2/3 = 0.66$$

Under the assumption of conditional independence of attributes, the conditional probabilities $P(X/C_i)$ will be

$$P(X/C = 1) = P(A_1 = 1/C = 1) \cdot P(A_2 = 2/C = 1) \cdot P(A_3 = 2/C = 1)$$
$$= 0.50 \cdot 0.25 \cdot 0.25 = 0.03125$$

$$P(X/C = 2) = P(A_1 = 1/C = 2) \cdot P(A_2 = 2/C = 2) \cdot P(A_3 = 2/C = 2)$$
$$= 0.33 \cdot 0.66 \cdot 0.66 = 0.14375$$

Finally, multiplying these conditional probabilities with corresponding priori probabilities, we can obtain values proportional ($\approx$) to $P(C_i/X)$ and find their maximum:

$$P(C_1/X) \approx P(X/C = 1) \cdot P(C = 1) = 0.03125 \cdot 0.5714 = 0.0179$$
$$P(C_2/X) \approx P(X/C = 2) \cdot P(C = 2) = 0.14375 \cdot 0.4286 = 0.0616$$
$$\Downarrow$$
$$P(C_2/X) = Max \{P(C_1/X), P(C_2/X)\} = Max\{0.0179, 0.0616\} = 0.0616$$

Based on the previous two values that are the final results of the Naive Bayesian Classifier, we can predict that the new sample X belongs to the class $C = 2$. The product of probabilities for this class $P(X/C = 2) \cdot P(C = 2)$ is higher, and therefore $P(C = 2/X)$ is higher because it is directly proportional to the computed probability product.

In theory, the Bayesian classifier has the minimum error rate compared to all other classifiers developed in data mining. In practice, however, this is not always the case because of inaccuracies in the assumptions of attributes and class-conditional independence.

5.4   PREDICTIVE REGRESSION

The prediction of continuous values can be modeled by a statistical technique called *regression*. The objective of regression analysis is to determine the best model that can relate the output variable to various input variables. More formally, regression analysis is the process of determining how a variable Y is related to one or more other variables $X_1, X_2, \ldots, X_n$. Y is usually called the response output or dependent variable, and $X_i - Y$ are called inputs, regressors, explanatory variables, or independent variables. Common reasons for performing regression analysis include

1. the output is expensive to measure but the inputs are not, and so a cheap prediction of the output is sought;
2. the values of the inputs are known before the output is known, and a working prediction of the output is required;
3. controlling the input values, we can predict the behavior of corresponding outputs;
4. there might be a causal link between some of the inputs and the output, and we want to identify the links.

Generalized linear models are currently the most frequently applied statistical techniques. They are used to describe the relationship between the trend of one variable and the values taken by several other variables. Modeling this type of relationship is often called linear regression. Fitting models is not the only task in statistical modeling. We often want to select one of several possible models as being the most appropriate. An objective method for choosing between different models is called analysis of variance, and it is described in Section 5.5.

The relationship that fits a set of data is characterized by a prediction model called a *regression equation*. The most widely used form of the regression model is the general linear model formally written as

$$Y = \alpha + \beta_1 \cdot X_1 + \beta_2 \cdot X_2 + \beta_3 \cdot X_3 + \ldots + \beta_n \cdot X_n$$

Applying this equation to each of the given samples we obtain a new set of equations

$$y_j = \alpha + \beta_1 \cdot x_{1j} + \beta_2 \cdot x_{2j} + \beta_3 \cdot x_{3j} + \ldots + \beta_n \cdot x_{nj} + \varepsilon_j \quad j = 1, \ldots, m$$

where ε_j's are errors of regression for each of m given samples. The linear model is called linear because the expected value of y_j is a linear function: the weighted sum of input values.

Linear regression with one input variable is the simplest form of regression. It models a random variable Y (called a response variable) as a linear function of another random variable X (called a predictor variable). Given n samples or data points of the form $(x_1, y_1), (x_2, y_2), \ldots, (x_n, y_n)$, where $x_i \in X$ and $y_i \in Y$, linear regression can be expressed as

$$Y = \alpha + \beta \cdot X$$

where α and β are regression coefficients. With the assumption that the variance of Y is a constant, these coefficients can be solved by the method of least squares, which minimizes the error between the actual data points and the estimated line. The residual sum of squares is often called the sum of squares of the errors about the regression line and it is denoted by SSE:

$$SSE = \sum_{i=1}^{n} e_i^2 = \sum_{i=1}^{n} (y_i - y_i')^2 = \sum_{i=1}^{n} (y_i - \alpha - \beta x_i)^2$$

where y_i is the real output value given in the data set, and y_i' is a response value obtained from the model. Differentiating SSE with respect to α and β, we have

$$\partial(SEE)/\partial\alpha = -2 \sum_{i=1}^{n} (y_i - \alpha - \beta x_i)$$

$$\partial(SEE)/\partial\beta = -2 \sum_{i=1}^{n} ((y_i - \alpha - \beta x_i) \cdot x_i)$$

Setting the partial derivatives equal to zero (minimization of the total error) and rearranging the terms, we obtain the equations

$$n\alpha + \beta \sum_{i=1}^{n} x_i = \sum_{i=1}^{n} y_i$$

$$\alpha \sum_{i=1}^{n} x_i + \beta \sum_{i=1}^{n} x_i^2 = \sum_{i=1}^{n} x_i \, y_i$$

which may be solved simultaneously to yield computing formulas for α and β. Using standard relations for the mean values, regression coefficients for this simple case of optimization are

$$\beta = \left[\sum_{i=1}^{n} (x_i - \text{mean}_x) \cdot (y_i - \text{mean}_y) \right] / \left[\sum_{i=1}^{n} (x_i - \text{mean}_x)^2 \right]$$

$$\alpha = \text{mean}_y - \beta \cdot \text{mean}_x$$

where mean_x and mean_y are the mean values for random variables X and Y given in a training data set. It is important to remember that our values of α and β, based on a given data set, are only estimates of the true parameters for the entire population. The equation $y = \alpha + \beta x$ may be used to predict the mean response y_0 for the given input x_0, which is not necessarily from the initial set of samples.

For example, if the sample data set is given in the form of a table, (Table 5.2), and we are analyzing the linear regression between two variables (predictor variable A and response variable B), then the linear regression can be expressed as

$$B = \alpha + \beta \cdot A$$

where α and β coefficients can be calculated based on previous formulas (using $\text{mean}_A = 5$, and $\text{mean}_B = 6$), and they have the values

$$\alpha = 0.8$$

$$\beta = 1.04$$

The optimal regression line is

$$B = 0.8 + 1.04 \cdot A$$

The initial data set and the regression line are graphically represented in Figure 5.2 as a set of points and a corresponding line.

Multiple regression is an extension of linear regression with one input variable, and involves more than one predictor variable. The response variable Y is modeled as a

TABLE 5.2   A database for the application of regression methods

A	B
1	3
8	9
11	11
4	5
3	2

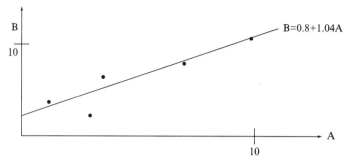

FIGURE 5.2   Linear regression for the data set given in Figure 4.3

linear function of several predictor variables. For example, if the predictor attributes are X_1, X_2, and X_3, then the multiple linear regression is expressed as

$$Y = \alpha + \beta_1 \cdot X_1 + \beta_2 \cdot X_2 + \beta_3 \cdot X_3$$

where α, β_1, β_2, β_3 are coefficients that are found by using the method of least squares. For a linear regression model with more than two input variables, it is useful to analyze the process of determining β parameters through a matrix calculation:

$$Y = \beta \cdot X$$

where $\beta = \{\beta_0, \beta_1, \ldots, \beta_n\}$, $\beta_0 = \alpha$, and X and Y are input and output matrices for a given training data set. The residual sum of the squares of errors SSE will also have the matrix representation

$$SSE = (Y - \beta \cdot X)' \cdot (Y - \beta \cdot X)$$

and after optimization

$$\partial(SSE)/\partial\beta = 0 \;\Rightarrow\; (X' \cdot X)\beta = X' \cdot Y$$

the final β vector satisfies the matrix equation

$$\beta = (X' \cdot X)^{-1}(X' \cdot Y)$$

where β is the vector of estimated coefficients in a linear regression. Matrices X and Y have the same dimensions as the training data set. Therefore, an optimal solution for β vector is relatively easy to find in problems with several hundred training samples. For real-world data-mining problems, the number of samples may increase to several millions. In these situations, because of the extreme dimensions of matrices and the exponentially increased complexity of the algorithm, it is necessary to find modifications and/or approximations in the algorithm, or to use totally different regression methods.

There is a large class of regression problems, initially nonlinear, that can be converted into the form of the general linear model. For example, a polynomial relationship such as

$$Y = \alpha + \beta_1 \cdot X_1 + \beta_2 \cdot X_2 + \beta_3 \cdot X_1 X_3 + \beta_4 \cdot X_2 X_3$$

can be converted to the linear form by setting new variables $X_4 = X_1 \cdot X_3$ and $X_5 = X_2 \cdot X_3$. Also, polynomial regression can be modeled by adding polynomial terms to the basic linear model. For example, a cubic polynomial curve has a form

$$Y = \alpha + \beta_1 \cdot X + \beta_2 \cdot X^2 + \beta_3 \cdot X^3$$

By applying transformation to the predictor variables ($X_1 = X$, $X_2 = X^2$, and $X_3 = X^3$), it is possible to linearize the model and transform it into a multiple-regression problem, which can be solved by the method of least squares. It should be noted that the term linear in the general linear model applies to the dependent variable being a linear function of the unknown parameters. Thus, a general linear model might also include some higher-order terms of independent variables, e.g., terms such as X_1^2, $e^{\beta X}$, $X_1 \cdot X_2$, $1/X$, or X_2^3. The basis is, however, to select the proper transformation of input variables or their combinations. Some useful transformations for linearization of the regression model are given in Table 5.3.

The major effort, on the part of a user, in applying multiple-regression techniques lies in identifying the *relevant* independent variables from the initial set and in selecting the regression model using only relevant variables. Two general approaches are common for this task:

1. *Sequential search approach* – which consists primarily of building a regression model with an initial set of variables and then selectively adding or deleting variables until some overall criterion is satisfied or optimized.

2. *Combinatorial approach* – which is, in essence, a brute-force approach, where the search is performed across all possible combinations of independent variables to determine the best regression model.

TABLE 5.3 Some useful transformations to linearize regression

Function	Proper transformation	Form of simple Linear regression
Exponential: $Y = \alpha e^{\beta x}$	$Y^* = \ln Y$	Regress Y^* against x
Power: $Y = \alpha x^\beta$	$Y^* = \log Y$; $x^* = \log x$	Regress Y^* against x^*
Reciprocal: $Y = \alpha + \beta(1/x)$	$x^* = 1/x$	Regress Y against x^*
Hyperbolic: $Y = x/(\alpha + \beta x)$	$Y^* = 1/Y$; $x^* = 1/x$	Regress Y^* against x^*

Irrespective of whether the sequential or combinatorial approach is used, the maximum benefit to model building occurs from a proper understanding of the application domain.

Additional postprocessing steps may estimate the quality of the linear-regression model. Correlation analysis attempts to measure the strength of a relationship between two variables (in our case this relationship is expressed through the linear regression equation). One parameter, which shows this strength of linear association between two variables by means of a single number, is called a *correlation coefficient r*. Its computation requires some intermediate results in a regression analysis.

$$r = \beta \cdot \sqrt{(S_{xx}/S_{yy})} = S_{xy}/\sqrt{(S_{xx} \cdot S_{yy})}$$

where

$$S_{xx} = \sum_{i=1}^{n} (x_i - mean_x)^2$$

$$S_{yy} = \sum_{i=1}^{n} (y_i - mean_y)^2$$

$$S_{xy} = \sum_{i=1}^{n} (x_i - mean_x)(y_i - mean_y)$$

The value of r is between -1 and 1. Negative values for r correspond to regression lines with negative slopes and a positive r shows a positive slope. We must be very careful in interpreting the r value. For example, values of r equal to 0.3 and 0.6 only mean that we have two positive correlations, the second somewhat stronger than the first. It is wrong to conclude that $r = 0.6$ indicates a linear relationship twice as strong as that indicated by the value $r = 0.3$.

For our simple example of linear regression given at the beginning of this section, the model obtained was $B = 0.8 + 1.04A$. We may estimate the quality of the model using the correlation coefficient r as a measure. Based on the available data in Figure 4.3, we obtained intermediate results

$$S_{AA} = 62$$

$$S_{BB} = 60$$

$$S_{AB} = 52$$

and the final correlation coefficient :

$$r = 52/\sqrt{62 \cdot 60} = 0.85$$

A correlation coefficient $r = 0.85$ indicates a good linear relationship between two variables. Additional interpretation is possible. Because $r^2 = 0.72$, we can say that approximately 72% of the variations in the values of B is accounted for by a linear relationship with A.

5.5 ANALYSIS OF VARIANCE

Often the problem of analyzing the quality of the estimated regression line and the influence of the independent variables on the final regression is handled through an *analysis-of-variance* approach. This is a procedure where the total variation in the dependent variable is subdivided into meaningful components that are then observed and treated in a systematic fashion. The analysis of variance is a powerful tool that is used in many data-mining applications.

The analysis of variance, or ANOVA, is a primarily a method of identifying which of the β's in a linear regression model are non-zero. Suppose that the β parameters have already been estimated by the least-square error algorithm. Then the residuals are differences between the observed output values and the fitted values:

$$R_i = y_i - f(x_i)$$

The size of the residuals, for all m samples in a data set, is related to the size of variance σ^2 and it can be estimated by:

$$S^2 = \left[\sum_{i=1}^{m} (y_i - f(x_i))^2 \right] / (m - (n - 1))$$

assuming that the model is not overparametrized. The numerator is called the residual sum while the denominator is called the residual degree of freedom.

The key fact about S^2 is that it allows us to compare different linear models. If the fitted model is adequate, then S^2 is a good estimate of σ^2. If the fitted model includes redundant terms (some β's are really zero), S^2 is still good and close to σ^2. Only if the fitted model does not include one or more of the inputs that it ought to, will S^2 tend to be significantly larger than the true value of σ^2. These criteria are basic decision steps in the ANOVA algorithm, in which we analyze the influence of input variables on a final model. First, we start with all inputs and compute S^2 for this model. Then, we omit inputs from the model one by one. If we omit a useful input the estimate S^2 will significantly increase, but if we omit a redundant input the estimate should not change much. Note that omitting one of the inputs from the model is equivalent to forcing the corresponding β to the zero. In principle, in each iteration we compare two S^2 values and analyze the differences between them. For this purpose, we introduce an F-ratio or F-statistic test in the form

$$F = S_{new}^2 / S_{old}^2$$

If the new model (after removing one or more inputs) is adequate, then F will be close to 1; a value of F significantly larger than one will signal that the model is not adequate. Using this iterative ANOVA approach, we can identify which inputs are related to the output and which are not. The ANOVA procedure is only valid if the models being compared are nested; in other words, one model is special case of the other.

TABLE 5.4 ANOVA analysis for a data set with three inputs x_1, x_2, and x_3

Case	Set of inputs	S_i^2	F
1	x_1, x_2, x_3	3.56	
2	x_1, x_2	3.98	$F_{21} = 1.12$
3	x_1, x_3	6.22	$F_{31} = 1.75$
4	x_2, x_3	8.34	$F_{41} = 2.34$
5	x_1	9.02	$F_{52} = 2.27$
6	x_2	9.89	$F_{62} = 2.48$

Suppose that the data set has three input variables x_1, x_2, and x_3 and one output Y. In preparation for the use of the linear regression method, it is necessary to estimate the simplest model, in the sense of the number of required inputs. Suppose that after applying the ANOVA methodology, the results given in Table 5.4. are obtained.

The results of ANOVA analysis show that the input attribute x_3 does not have an influence on the output estimation because the F-ratio value is close to 1:

$$F_{21} = S_2/S_1 = 3.98/3.56 = 1.12$$

In all other cases, the subsets of inputs increase the F-ratio significantly, and therefore, there is no possibility of reducing the number of input dimensions further without influencing the quality of the model. The final linear regression model for this example will be

$$Y = \alpha + \beta_1 \cdot x_1 + \beta_2 \cdot x_2$$

Multivariate analysis of variance is a generalization of the previously explained ANOVA analysis, and it concerns data-analysis problems in which the output is a vector rather than a single value. One way to analyze this sort of data would be to model each element of the output separately but this ignores the possible relationship between different outputs. In other words, the analysis would be based on the assumption that outputs are not related. Multivariate analysis of variance is a form of analysis that *does* allow correlation between outputs. Given the set of input and output variables, we might be able to analyze the available data set using a multivariate linear model:

$$Y_j = \alpha + \beta_1 \cdot x_{1j} + \beta_2 \cdot x_{2j} + \beta_3 \cdot x_{3j} + \ldots + \beta_n \cdot x_{nj} + \varepsilon_j \qquad j = 1, 2, \ldots, m$$

where n is the number of input dimensions, m is the number of samples, Y_j is a vector with dimensions $c \times 1$, and c is the number of outputs. This model can be fitted in using least square estimation the same way as a linear model. One way to do this fitting would be to fit a linear model to each of c dimensions of the output, one at a time. The corresponding residuals for each dimension will be $(y_j - y_j')$ where y_j is the exact value for a given dimension and y_j' is the estimated value.

The analogue of the residual sum of squares for the univariate linear model is the matrix of the residual sums of squares for the multivariate linear model. This matrix R is defined as

$$R = \sum_{j=1}^{m} (y_j - y_j')(y_j - y_j')^T$$

The matrix R has the residual sum of squares for each of the c dimensions stored on its leading diagonal. The off-diagonal elements are the residual sums of cross-products for pairs of dimensions. If we wish to compare two nested linear models to determine whether certain β's are equal to zero, then we can construct an extra sum of squares matrix and apply a method similar to ANOVA—multivariate ANOVA or MANOVA. While we had an F-statistic in the ANOVA methodology, MANOVA is based on matrix R with four commonly used test statistics: Roy's greatest root, the Lawley-Hotteling trace, the Pillai trace, and Wilks' lambda. Computational details of these tests are not explained in the book, but most textbooks on statistics will explain these; also, most standard statistical packages that support MANOVA analysis support all four statistical tests and explain which one to use under what circumstances.

Classical multivariate analysis also includes the method of principal component analysis, where the set of vector samples is transformed into a new set with a reduced number of dimensions. This method has been explained in Chapter 3 when we were talking about data reduction and data transformation as preprocessing phases for data mining.

5.6 LOGISTIC REGRESSION

Linear regression is used to model continuous-value functions. Generalized regression models represent the theoretical foundation on which the linear regression approach can be applied to model categorical response variables. A common type of a generalized linear model is *logistic regression*. Logistic regression models the probability of some event occurring as a linear function of a set of predictor variables.

Rather than predicting the value of the dependent variable, the logistic regression method tries to estimate the probability p that the dependent variable will have a given value. For example, in place of predicting whether a customer has a good or bad credit rating, the logistic regression approach tries to estimate the probability of a good credit rating. The actual state of the dependent variable is determined by looking at the estimated probability. If the estimated probability is greater than 0.50 then the prediction is closer to *YES* (a good credit rating), otherwise the output is closer to *NO* (a bad credit rating is more probable). Therefore, in logistic regression, the probability p is called the success probability.

We use logistic regression only when the output variable of the model is defined as a binary categorical. On the other hand, there is no special reason why any of the inputs should not also be quantitative, and, therefore, logistic regression supports a more general input data set. Suppose that output Y has two possible categorical values coded as 0 and 1. Based on the available data we can compute the probabilities for both values for the given input sample: $P(y_j = 0) = 1 - p_j$ and $P(y_j = 1) = p_j$. The model that we will fit these probabilities is accommodated linear regression:

$$\log(p_j/(1 - p_j)) = \alpha + \beta_1 \cdot X_{1j} + \beta_2 \cdot X_{2j} + \beta_3 \cdot X_{3j} + \ldots + \beta_n \cdot X_{nj}$$

This equation is known as the *linear logistic model*. The function $\log(p_j/(1 - p_j))$ is often written as logit(p). The main reason for using the logit form of output is to prevent the predicting probabilities p_j from going out of range, where the required range for p_j is [0,1]. Suppose that the estimated model, based on a training data set and using the linear regression procedure, is given with a linear equation

$$\text{logit}(p) = 1.5 - 0.6 \cdot x_1 + 0.4 \cdot x_2 - 0.3 \cdot x_3$$

and also suppose that the new sample for classification has input values $\{x_1, x_2, x_3\} = \{1, 0, 1\}$. Using the linear logistic model, it is possible to estimate the probability of the output value 1, $(p(Y = 1))$ for this sample. First, calculate the corresponding logit(p):

$$\text{logit}(p) = 1.5 - 0.6 \cdot 1 + 0.4 \cdot 0 - 0.3 \cdot 1 = 0.6$$

and then the probability of the output value 1 for the given inputs:

$$\log(p/(1 - p)) = 0.6$$

$$p = e^{-0.6}/(1 + e^{-0.6}) = 0.35$$

Based on the final value for probability p, we may conclude that output value $Y = 1$ is less probable than the other categorical value $Y = 0$. Even this simple example shows that logistic regression is a very simple but powerful classification tool in data-mining applications. With one set of data (training set) it is possible to establish the logistic regression model and with other set of data (testing set) we may analyze the quality of the model in predicting categorical values. The results of logistic regression may be compared with other data-mining methodologies for classification tasks such as decision rules, neural networks, and Bayesian classifier.

5.7 LOG–LINEAR MODELS

Log–linear modeling is a way of analyzing the relationship between categorical (or quantitative) variables. The log–linear model approximates discrete, multidimensional probability distributions. It is a type of generalized linear model where the output Yi is assumed to have a Poisson distribution, with expected value μ_j. The natural logarithm of μ_j is assumed to be the linear function of inputs

$$\log(\mu_j) = \alpha + \beta_1 \cdot X_{1j} + \beta_2 \cdot X_{2j} + \beta_3 \cdot X_{3j} + \ldots + \beta_n \cdot X_{nj}$$

Since all the variables of interest are categorical variables, we use a table to represent them, a frequency table that represents the global distribution of data. The aim in log–linear modeling is to identify associations between categorical variables. Association corresponds to the interaction terms in the model; so our problem becomes a problem of finding out which of all β's are 0 in the model. A similar problem can be stated in ANOVA analysis. If there is an interaction between the variables in a log–linear mode, it implies that the variables involved in the interaction are not independent but related, and the corresponding β is not equal to zero. There is no need for one of the categorical variables to be considered as an output in this analysis. If the output is specified, then instead of the log–linear models, we can use logistic regression for analysis. Therefore, we will next explain log–linear analysis when a data set is defined without output variables. All given variables are categorical, and we want to analyze the possible associations between them. That is the task for *correspondence analysis*.

Correspondence analysis represents the set of categorical data for analysis within incidence matrices, also called *contingency tables*. The result of an analysis of the contingency table answers the question: "Is there a relationship between analyzed attributes or not?" An example of 2×2 contingency table, with cumulative totals, is shown in Table 5.5. The table is a result of a survey to examine the relative attitude of males and females about abortion. The total set of samples is 1100 and every sample consists of two categorical attributes with corresponding values. For the attribute *sex*, the possible values are male and female, and for attribute *support* the values are yes and no. Cumulative results for all the samples are represented in four elements of the contingency table.

"Are there any differences in the extent of support for abortion between the male and the female populations?" This question may be translated into: "What is the level of dependency (if any) between the two given attributes: sex and support?" If an association exists, then there are significant differences in opinion between the male and the female populations; otherwise both populations have a similar opinion.

Having seen that log–linear modeling is concerned with association of categorical variables, we might attempt to find some quantity (measure) based on this model using data in the contingency table. But we don't do this. Instead, we define the algorithm for feature association based on a comparison of two contingency tables:

1. The first step in the analysis is to transform a given contingency table into a table with *expected* values. These values are calculated under assumption that the variables are independent.

TABLE 5.5   A 2×2 contingency table for 1100 samples surveying attitudes about abortion.

		Support		
		Yes	No	Total
Sex	Female	309	191	500
	Male	319	281	600
	Total	628	472	1100

2. In the second step, we compare these two matrices using the squared distance measure and the chi-square test as criteria of association for two categorical variables.

The computational process for these two steps is very simple for a 2 × 2 contingency table. The process is also applicable for increased dimensions of a contingency table (analysis of categorical variables with more than two values, such as 3 × 4 or 6 × 9).

Let us introduce the notation. Denote the contingency table as $X_{m \times n}$. The row totals for the table are

$$X_{j+} = \sum_{i=1}^{n} X_{ji}$$

and they are valid for every row ($j = 1, \ldots, m$). Similarly, we can define the column totals as

$$X_{+i} = \sum_{j=1}^{m} X_{ji}$$

The grand total is defined as a sum of row totals:

$$X_{++} = \sum_{j=1}^{m} X_{j+}$$

or as a sum of column totals:

$$X_{++} = \sum_{i=1}^{n} X_{+i}$$

Using these totals, we can calculate the contingency table of expected values under the assumption that there is no association between the row variable and the column variable. The expected values are

$$E_{ji} = (X_{j+} \cdot X_{+i})/X_{++} \qquad \text{for} \quad j = 1, \ldots, m, \ i = 1, \ldots, n$$

and they are computed for every position in the contingency table. The final result of this first step will be a totally new table that consists only of expected values, and the two tables will have the same dimensions.

For our example in Figure 4.7, all sums (columns, rows, and grand total) are represented already in the contingency table. Based on these values we can construct the contingency table of expected values. The expected value on the intersection of the first row and the first column will be

$$E_{11} = (X_{1+} \cdot X_{+1})/X_{++} = 500 \cdot 628/1100 = 285.5$$

TABLE 5.6 2×2 contingency table of expected values for the data given in Table 5.5

		Support		Total
		Yes	No	
Sex	Female	285.5	214.5	500
	Male	342.5	257.5	600
	Total	628	472	1100

Similarly, we can compute the other expected values and the final contingency table with expected values will be as given in Table 5.6.

The next step in the analysis of categorical-attributes dependency is application of the chi-squared test of association. The initial hypothesis H_0 is the assumption that the two attributes are unrelated, and it is tested by Pearson's chi-squared formula:

$$\chi^2 = \sum_{j=1}^{m} \sum_{i=1}^{n} ((X_{ji} - E_{ji})^2 / E_{ji})$$

The greater the value of χ^2, the greater the evidence against the hypothesis H_0. For our example, comparing the tables in Tables 5.5 and 5.6, the test gives the following result:

$$\chi^2 = 8.2816$$

with the degrees of freedom for an $m \times n$ dimensional table computed as

$$d.f.(\text{degrees of freedom}) = (m - 1) \cdot (n - 1) = (2 - 1)(2 - 1) = 1$$

In general, the hypothesis H_0 is rejected at the level of significance α if

$$\chi^2 \geq T(\alpha)$$

where $T(\alpha)$ is the threshold value from the χ^2 distribution table usually given in textbooks on statistics. For our example, selecting $\alpha = 0.05$ we obtain the threshold

$$T(0.05) = \chi^2(1 - \alpha, d.f.) = \chi^2(0.95, 1) = 3.84.$$

A simple comparison shows that

$$\chi^2 = 8.2816 \geq T(0.05) = 3.84$$

and therefore, we can conclude that hypothesis H_0 is rejected; the attributes analyzed in the survey have a high level of dependency. In other words, the attitude about abortion shows differences between the male and the female populations.

TABLE 5.7 Contingency tables for categorical attributes with three values

		Attribute1 Low	Med.	High	Totals
	Excell.	21	11	4	36
Attribute2	Good	3	2	2	7
	Poor	7	1	1	9
	Total	31	14	7	52

a) A 3 × 3 contingency table of observed values

		Attribute1 Low	Med.	High	Totals
	Excell.	21.5	9.7	4.8	36
Attribute2	Good	4.2	1.9	0.9	7
	Poor	5.4	2.4	1.2	9
	Total	31	14	7	52

b) A 3 × 3 Contingency table of expected values under H_0

The same procedure may be generalized and applied to contingency tables where the categorical attributes have more than two values. The next example shows how the previously explained procedure can be applied without modifications to the contingency table 3 × 3. The initial table given in Table 5.7a is compared with the table of estimated values that is given in Table 5.7b, and the corresponding test is calculated as $\chi^2 = 3.229$. Note that in this case parameter

$$d.f. = (n - 1)(m - 1) = (3 - 1) \cdot (3 - 1) = 4.$$

We have to be very careful about drawing additional conclusions and further analyzing the given data set. It is quite obvious that the sample size is not large. The number of observations in many cells of the table is small. This is a serious problem and additional statistical analysis is necessary to check if the sample is a good representation of the total population or not. We do not cover this analysis here because in most real-world data-mining problems the data set is enough large to eliminate the possibility of occurrence of these deficiencies.

That was one level of generalization for an analysis of contingency tables with categorical data. The other direction of generalization is inclusion into analysis of more than two categorical attributes. The methods for three- and high-dimensional contingency-table analysis are described in many books on advanced statistics; they explain the procedure of discovered dependencies between several attributes that are analyzed simultaneously.

5.8 LINEAR DISCRIMINANT ANALYSIS

Linear discriminant analysis (LDA) is concerned with classification problems where the dependent variable is categorical (nominal or ordinal) and the independent variables are metric. The objective of LDA is to construct a discriminant function that yields different scores when computed with data from different output classes. A linear discriminant function has the following form:

$$z = w_1x_1 + w_2x_2 + \ldots + w_kx_k$$

where x_1, x_2, ..., x_k are independent variables. The quantity z is called the discriminant score and w_1, w_2, ..., w_k are called weights. A geometric interpretation of the discriminant score is shown in Figure 5.3. As the figure shows, the discriminant score for a data sample represents its projection onto a line defined by the set of weight parameters.

The construction of a discriminant function z involves finding a set of weight values w_i that maximizes the ratio of the *between-class* to the *within-class* variance of the discriminant score for a preclassified set of samples. Once constructed, the discriminant function z is used to predict the class of a new nonclassified sample. Cutting scores serve as the criteria against which each individual discriminant score is judged. The choice of cutting scores depends upon a distribution of samples in classes. Letting z_a and z_b be the mean discriminant scores of preclassified samples from class A and B, respectively, the optimal choice for the cutting score z_{cut-ab} is given as

$$z_{cut-ab} = (z_a + z_b)/2$$

when the two classes of samples are of equal size and are distributed with uniform variance. A new sample will be classified to one or another class depending on its score $z > z_{cut-ab}$ or $z < z_{cut-ab}$. A weighted average of mean discriminant scores is used as an optimal cutting score when the set of samples for each of the classes are not of equal size:

$$z_{cut-ab} = (n_a \cdot z_a + n_b \cdot z_b)/(n_a + n_b)$$

The quantities n_a and n_b represent the number of samples in each class. Although a single discriminant function z with several discriminant cuts can separate samples into several classes, *multiple discriminant analysis* is used for more complex problems. The term multiple discriminant analysis is used in situations when separate discriminant

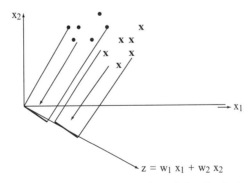

FIGURE 5.3   Geometric interpretation of the discriminant score

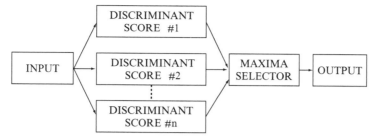

FIGURE 5.4   Classification process in multiple discriminant analysis

functions are constructed for each class. The classification rule in such situations takes the following form: "Decide in favor of the class whose discriminant score is the highest." This is illustrated in Figure 5.4.

5.9   REVIEW QUESTIONS AND PROBLEMS

1. What are the differences between statistical testing and estimation as basic areas in statistical inference theory?

2. A data set for analysis includes only one attribute X:

    $$X = \{7, 12, 5, 18, 5, 9, 13, 12, 19, 7, 12, 12, 13, 3, 4, 5, 13, 8, 7, 6\}.$$

   a) What is the mean of the data set X?
   b) What is the median?
   c) What is the mode, and what is the modality of the data set X?
   d) Find the standard deviation for X.
   e) Give a graphical summarization of the data set X using a boxplot representation.
   f) Find outliers in the data set X. Discuss the results.

3. For the training set given in Figure 4.2, predict the classification of the following samples using Simple Bayesian Classifier.

    a)   {2, 1, 1}

    b)   {0, 1, 1}

4. Given a data set with two dimensions X and Y:

X	Y
1	5
4	2.75
3	3
5	2.5

STATISTICAL METHODS

a) Use a linear-regression method to calculate the parameters α and β where $y = \alpha + \beta x$.

b) Estimate the quality of the model obtained in a) using the correlation coefficient r.

c) Use an appropriate nonlinear transformation (one of those represented in Figure 4.5) to improve regression results. What is the equation for a new, improved, and nonlinear model? Discuss a reduction of the correlation coefficient value.

5. A logit function, obtained through logistic regression, has the form:

$$\text{Logit}(p) = 1.2 - 1.3x1 + 0.6x2 + 0.4x3$$

Find the probability of output values 0 and 1 for the following samples:

a) $\{1, -1, -1\}$

b) $\{-1, 1, 0\}$

c) $\{0, 0, 0\}$

6. Analyze the dependency between categorical attributes X and Y if the data set is summarized in a 2×3 contingency table:

		Y	
		T	F
	A	128	7
X	B	66	30
	C	42	55

7. Implement the algorithm for a boxplot representation of each numeric attribute in an input flat file.

8. What are the basic principles in the construction of a discriminant function applied in a linear discriminant analysis?

9. Implement the algorithm to analyze a dependency between categorical variables using 2-dimensional contingency tables.

5.10   REFERENCES FOR FURTHER STUDY

1. Berthold, M. and D. J. Hand, eds., *Intelligent Data Analysis – An Introduction*, Springer, Berlin, 1999.

The book is a detailed introductory presentation of the key classes of intelligent data-analysis methods including all common data-mining techniques. The first half of the book is devoted to the discussion of classical statistical issues, ranging from basic concepts of probability and inference to advanced multivariate analyses and Bayesian methods. The second part of the book covers theoretical explanations of data-mining techniques with their roots in disciplines other than statistics. Numerous illustrations and examples will enhance a reader's knowledge about the theory and practical evaluations of data-mining techniques.

2. Brandt, S., *Data Analysis: Statistical and Computational Methods for Scientists and Engineers*, 3rd ed., Springer, New York, 1999.

   This text bridges the gap between statistical theory and practice. It emphasizes concise but rigorous mathematics while retaining the focus on applications. After introducing probability and random variables, the book turns to the generation of random numbers and important distributions. Subsequent chapters discuss statistical samples, the maximum- likelihood method, and the testing of statistical hypotheses. The text concludes with a detailed discussion of several important statistical methods such as least square minimization, analysis of variance, regressions, and analysis of time series.

3. Cherkassky, V. and F. Mulier, *Learning from Data: Concepts, Theory and Methods*, John Wiley, New York, 1998.

   The book provides a unified treatment of the principles and methods for learning dependencies from data. It establishes a general conceptual framework in which various learning methods from statistics, machine learning, and other disciplines can be applied— showing that a few fundamental principles underlie most new methods being proposed today. An additional strength of this primary theoretical book is a large number of case studies and examples that simplifies and makes understandable statistical learning theory concepts.

4. Hand, D., Mannila H., Smith P., *Principles of Data Mining*, MIT Press, Cambridge: MA, 2001.

   The book consists of three sections. The first, foundations, provides a tutorial overview of the principles underlying data-mining algorithms and their applications. The second section, data-mining algorithms, shows how algorithms are constructed to solve specific problems in a principled manner. The third section shows how all of the preceding analyses fit together when applied to real-world data-mining problems.

6 Cluster Analysis

CHAPTER OBJECTIVES

- Distinguish between different representations of clusters and different measures of similarities.
- Compare basic characteristics of agglomerative- and partitional-clustering algorithms.
- Implement agglomerative algorithms using single-link or complete-link measures of similarity.
- Derive the K-means method for partitional clustering and analysis of its complexity.
- Explain the implementation of incremental-clustering algorithms and its advantages and disadvantages.

Cluster analysis is a set of methodologies for automatic classification of samples into a number of groups using a measure of association, so that the samples in one group are similar and samples belonging to different groups are not similar. The input for a system of cluster analysis is a set of samples and a measure of similarity (or dissimilarity) between two samples. The output from cluster analysis is a number of groups (clusters) that form a partition, or a structure of partitions, of the data set. One additional result of cluster analysis is a generalized description of every cluster, and this is especially important for a deeper analysis of the data set's characteristics.

6.1 CLUSTERING CONCEPTS

Samples for clustering are represented as a vector of measurements, or more formally, as a point in a multidimensional space. Samples within a valid cluster are more similar to each other than they are to a sample belonging to a different cluster. Clustering methodology is particularly appropriate for the exploration of interrelationships among samples to make a preliminary assessment of the sample structure. Humans perform competitively with automatic-clustering procedures in one, two, or three dimensions, but most real problems involve clustering in higher dimensions. It is very difficult for humans to intuitively interpret data embedded in a high-dimensional space.

Table 6.1 shows a simple example of clustering information for nine customers, distributed across three clusters. Two features describe customers: the first feature is the number of items the customers bought, and the second feature shows the price they paid for each.

TABLE 6.1   Sample set of clusters consisting of similar objects

	# of items	Price
	2	1700
Cluster 1	3	2000
	4	2300
	10	1800
Cluster 2	12	2100
	11	2500
	2	100
Cluster 3	3	200
	3	350

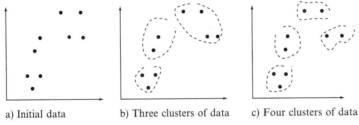

a) Initial data   b) Three clusters of data   c) Four clusters of data

FIGURE 6.1   Cluster analysis of points in a 2D-space

Customers in Cluster 1 purchase few high-priced items; customers in Cluster 2 purchase many high-priced items, and customers in Cluster 3 purchase few low-priced items. Even this simple example and interpretation of a cluster's characteristics shows that clustering analysis (in some references also called unsupervised classification) refers to situations in which the objective is to construct decision boundaries (classification surfaces) based on unlabeled training data set. The samples in these data sets have only input dimensions, and the learning process is classified as unsupervised.

Clustering is a very difficult problem because data can reveal clusters with different shapes and sizes in an n-dimensional data space. To compound the problem further, the number of clusters in the data often depends on the resolution (fine vs. coarse) with which we view the data. The next example illustrates these problems through the process of clustering points in the Euclidean 2D space. Figure 6.1a shows a set of points (samples in a two-dimensional space) scattered on a 2D-plane. Let us analyze the problem of dividing the points into a number of groups. The number of groups N is not given beforehand. Figure 6.1b shows the natural clusters G1, G2, and G3 bordered by broken curves. Since the number of clusters is not given, we have another partition of four clusters in Figure 6.1c that is as natural as the groups in Figure 6.1b. This kind of arbitrariness for the number of clusters is a major problem in clustering.

Note that the above clusters can be recognized by sight. For a set of points in a higher-dimensional Euclidean space, we cannot recognize clusters visually.

Accordingly, we need an objective criterion for clustering. To describe this criterion, we have to introduce a more formalized approach in describing the basic concepts and the clustering process.

An input to a cluster analysis can be described as an ordered pair (X, s), or (X, d), where X is a set of descriptions of samples, and s and d are measures for similarity or dissimilarity (distance) between samples, respectively. Output from the clustering system is a partition $\Lambda = \{G_1, G_2, \ldots, G_N\}$ where G_k, k = 1, ..., N is a crisp subset of X such that

$$G_1 \cup G_2 \cup \ldots \cup G_N = X, \text{ and}$$
$$G_i \cap G_j = \phi, \quad i \neq j$$

The members $G_1, G_2, \ldots, G_N$ of Λ are called clusters. Every cluster may be described with some characteristics. In discovery-based clustering, both the cluster (a separate set of points in X) and its descriptions or characterizations are generated as a result of a clustering procedure. There are several schemata for a formal description of discovered clusters:

1. Represent a cluster of points in an n-dimensional space (samples) by their centroid or by a set of distant (border) points in a cluster.
2. Represent a cluster graphically using nodes in a clustering tree.
3. Represent clusters by using logical expression on sample attributes.

Figure 6.2 illustrates these ideas. Using the centroid to represent a cluster is the most popular schema. It works well when the clusters are compact or isotropic. When the clusters are elongated or non-isotropic, however, this schema fails to represent them properly.

The availability of a vast collection of clustering algorithms in the literature and also in different software environments can easily confound a user attempting to select an approach suitable for the problem at hand. It is important to mention that there is no clustering technique that is universally applicable in uncovering the variety of structures present in multidimensional data sets. The user's understanding of the problem and the corresponding data types will be the best criteria to select the appropriate method. Most clustering algorithms are based on the following two popular approaches:

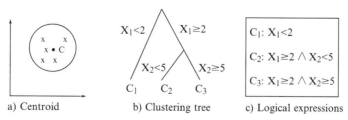

a) Centroid   b) Clustering tree   c) Logical expressions

FIGURE 6.2   Different schemata for cluster representation

1. Hierarchical clustering
2. Iterative square-error partitional clustering

Hierarchical techniques organize data in a nested sequence of groups, which can be displayed in the form of a dendrogram or a tree structure. Square-error partitional algorithms attempt to obtain that partition which minimizes the within-cluster scatter or maximizes the between-cluster scatter. These methods are nonhierarchical because all resulting clusters are groups of samples at the same level of partition. To guarantee that an optimum solution has been obtained, one has to examine all possible partitions of N samples of n-dimensions into K clusters (for a given K), but that retrieval process is not computationally feasible. Notice that the number of all possible partitions of a set of N objects into K clusters is given by:

$$1/K! \sum_{j=1}^{K} \binom{K}{j} j^N$$

So various heuristics are used to reduce the search space, but then there is no guarantee that the optimal solution will be found.

Hierarchical methods that produce a nested series of partitions are explained in Section 6.3, while partitional methods that produce only one level of data grouping are given with more details in section 6.4. The next section introduces different measures of similarity between samples; these measures are the core component of every clustering algorithm.

6.2 SIMILARITY MEASURES

To formalize the concept of a similarity measure, the following terms and notation are used throughout this chapter. A sample x (or feature vector, observation) is a single data vector used by the clustering algorithm in a space of samples X. In many other texts, the term pattern is used. We do not use this term because of a collision in meaning with patterns as in pattern-association analysis, where the term has a totally different meaning. Most data samples for clustering take the form of finite dimensional vectors, and it is unnecessary to distinguish between an object or a sample x_i, and the corresponding vector. Accordingly, we assume that each sample $x_i \in X$, $i = 1, \ldots, n$, is represented by a vector $x_i = \{x_{i1}, x_{i2}, \ldots, x_{im}\}$. The value m is the number of dimensions (features) of samples, while n is the total number of samples prepared for a clustering process that belongs to the sample domain X.

A sample can describe either a physical object (a chair) or an abstract object (a style of writing). Samples, represented conventionally as multidimensional vectors, have each dimension as a single feature. These features can be either quantitative or qualitative descriptions of the object. If the individual scalar component x_{ij} of a sample x_i is a feature or attribute value, then each component x_{ij}, $j = 1, \ldots, m$, is an element of a domain P_j, where P_j could belong to different types of data such as binary ($P_j = \{0, 1\}$), integer ($P_j \subseteq Z$), real number ($P_j \subseteq R$), or a categorical set of symbols. In the last case, for example, P_j may be a set of colors: $P_j = \{$white, black, red, blue, green$\}$. If weight and color are two features used to describe samples, then the sample (20, black) is the representation of a black object with 20 units of weight. The first feature is quantitative and the second one is qualitative. In general, both feature types can be further subdivided and details of this taxonomy are already given in Chapter 1.

Quantitative features can be subdivided as

1. *continuous values* (e.g., real numbers where $P_j \subseteq R$),
2. *discrete values* (e.g., binary numbers $P_j = \{0, 1\}$, or integers $P_j \subseteq Z$), and
3. *interval values* (e.g., $P_j = \{x_{ij} \leq 20, 20 < x_{ij} < 40, x_{ij} \geq 40\}$.

Qualitative features can be

1. *nominal or unordered* (e.g., color is "blue" or "red"), and
2. *ordinal* (e.g., military rank with values "general", "colonel", etc.).

Since similarity is fundamental to the definition of a cluster, a measure of the similarity between two patterns drawn from the same feature space is essential to most clustering algorithms. This measure must be chosen very carefully because the quality of a clustering process depends on this decision. It is most common to calculate, instead of the similarity measure, the dissimilarity between two samples using a distance measure defined on the feature space. A distance measure may be a metric or a quasi-metric on the sample space, and it is used to quantify the dissimilarity of samples.

The word "similarity" in clustering means that the value of $s(x, x')$ is large when x and x' are two similar samples; the value of $s(x, x')$ is small when x and x' are not similar. Moreover, a similarity measure s is symmetric:

$$s(x, x') = s(x', x), \quad \forall x, x' \in X$$

For most clustering techniques, we say that a similarity measure is normalized:

$$0 \leq s(x, x') \leq 1, \quad \forall x, x' \in X$$

Very often a measure of dissimilarity is used instead of a similarity measure. A dissimilarity measure is denoted by $d(x, x')$, $\forall x, x' \in X$. Dissimilarity is frequently called a distance. A distance $d(x, x')$ is small when x and x' are similar; if x and x' are not similar $d(x, x')$ is large. We assume without loss of generality that

$$d(x, x') \geq 0, \quad \forall x, x' \in X$$

Distance measure is also symmetric:

$$d(x, x') = d(x', x), \quad \forall x, x' \in X$$

and if it is accepted as a *metric distance measure*, then a triangular inequality is required:

$$d(x, x'') \leq d(x, x') + d(x', x''), \quad \forall x, x', x'' \in X$$

The most well known metric distance measure is the Euclidean distance in an m-dimensional feature space:

$$d_2(x_i, x_j) = \left(\sum_{k=1}^{m} (x_{ik} - x_{jk})^2 \right)^{1/2}$$

Another metric that is frequently used is called the L_1 metric or city block distance:

$$d_1(x_i, x_j) = \sum_{k=1}^{m} |x_{ik} - x_{jk}|$$

and finally, the Minkowski metric includes the Euclidean distance and the city block distance as special cases:

$$d_p(x_i, x_j) = \left(\sum_{k=1}^{m} (x_{ik} - x_{jk})^p \right)^{1/p}$$

It is obvious that when $p = 1$, then d coincides with L_1 distance, and when $p = 2$, d is identical with the Euclidean metric. For example, for 4-dimensional vectors $x_1 = \{1, 0, 1, 0\}$ and $x_2 = \{2, 1, -3, -1\}$ these distance measures are $d_1 = 1 + 1 + 4 + 1 = 7$, $d_2 = (1 + 1 + 16 + 1)^{1/2} = 4.36$, and $d_3 = (1 + 1 + 64 + 1)^{1/3} = 4.06$.

The Euclidian n-dimensional space model offers not only the Euclidean distance but also other measures of similarity. One of them is called the cosine-correlation:

$$s_{cos}(x_i, x_j) = \left[\sum_{k=1}^{m} (x_{ik} \cdot x_{jk}) \right] / \left[\sum_{k=1}^{m} x_{ik}^2 \cdot \sum_{k=1}^{m} x_{jk}^2 \right]^{1/2}$$

It is easy to see that

$$s_{cos}(x_i, x_j) = 1 \iff \forall i, j \text{ and } \lambda > 0 \text{ where } x_i = \lambda \cdot x_j$$
$$s_{cos}(x_i, x_j) = -1 \iff \forall i, j \text{ and } \lambda < 0 \text{ where } x_i = \lambda \cdot x_j$$

For the previously given vectors x_1 and x_2, the corresponding cosine measure of similarity is $s_{cos}(x_1, x_2) = (2 + 0 - 3 + 0)/(2^{1/2} \cdot 15^{1/2}) = -0.18$.

Computing distances or measures of similarity between samples that have some or all features that are noncontinuous is problematic, since the different types of features are not comparable and one standard measure is not applicable. In practice, different distance measures are used for different features of heterogeneous samples. Let us explain one possible distance measure for binary data. Assume that each sample is represented by the n-dimensional vector x_i, which has components with binary values ($v_{ij} \in \{0, 1\}$). A conventional method for obtaining a distance measure between two samples x_i and x_j represented with binary features is to use the 2×2 contingency table for samples x_i and x_j, as shown in Table 6.2.

TABLE 6.2   The 2 ×2 contingency table

		X_j	
		1	0
X_i	1	a	b
	0	c	d

The meaning of the table parameters a, b, c, and d given in Figure 6.2 is

1. *a* is the number of binary attributes of samples x_i and x_j such that $x_{ik} = x_{jk} = 1$.
2. *b* is the number of binary attributes of samples x_i and x_j such that $x_{ik} = 1$ and $x_{jk} = 0$.
3. *c* is the number of binary attributes of samples x_i and x_j such that $x_{ik} = 0$ and $x_{jk} = 1$.
4. *d* is the number of binary attributes of samples x_i and x_j such that $x_{ik} = x_{jk} = 0$.

For example, if x_i and x_j are 8-dimensional vectors with binary feature values

$$x_i = \{0, 0, 1, 1, 0, 1, 0, 1\}$$
$$x_j = \{0, 1, 1, 0, 0, 1, 0, 0\}$$

then the values of the parameters introduced are

$$a = 2, b = 2, c = 1, \text{ and } d = 3.$$

Several similarity measures for samples with binary features are proposed using the values in the 2×2 contingency table. Some of them are

1. Simple Matching Coefficient (SMC)

$$S_{smc}(x_i, x_j) = (a + d)/(a + b + c + d)$$

2. Jaccard Coefficient

$$S_{jc}(x_i, x_j) = a/(a + b + c)$$

3. Rao's Coefficient

$$S_{rc}(x_i, x_j) = a/(a + b + c + d)$$

For the previously given 8-dimensional samples x_i and x_j these measures of similarity will be $S_{smc}(x_i, x_j) = 5/8$, $S_{jc}(x_i, x_j) = 2/5$, and $S_{rc}(x_i, x_j) = 2/8$.

There are some advanced distance measures that take into account the effect of the surrounding or neighboring points in the n-dimensional spaces of samples. These surrounding points are called contexts. The similarity between two points x_i and x_j, with the given context, is measured using the *mutual neighbor distance* (MND), which is defined as

$$MND(x_i, x_j) = NN(x_i, x_j) + NN(x_j, x_i)$$

where $NN(x_i, x_j)$ is the neighbor number of x_j with respect to x_i. If x_i is the closest point to x_j, then $NN(x_i, x_j)$ is equal to 1, if it is the second closest point, $NN(x_i, x_j)$ is equal to 2 etc. Figures 6.3 and 6.4 give an example of the computation and basic characteristics of the MND measure.

Points in Figures 6.3 and 6.4, denoted by A, B, C, D, E, and F, are two-dimensional samples with features x_1 and x_2. In figure 6.3, the nearest neighbor of A is B using Euclidian distance, and B's nearest neighbor is A. So,

$$NN(A, B) = NN(B, A) = 1 \Rightarrow MND(A, B) = 2$$

If we compute the distance between points B and C, the results will be

$$NN(B, C) = 1, NN(C, B) = 2 \Rightarrow MND(B, C) = 3$$

Figure 6.4 was obtained from Figure 6.3 by adding three new points D, E, and F (samples in the data set). Now, because the context has changed, the distances between the same points A, B, and C have also changed:

$$NN(A, B) = 1, \quad NN(B, A) = 4 \Rightarrow MND(A, B) = 5$$
$$NN(B, C) = 1, \quad NN(C, B) = 2 \Rightarrow MND(B, C) = 3$$

The MND between A and B has increased by introducing additional points close to A, even though A and B have not moved. B and C points become more similar than A and B. The MND measure is not a metric because it does not satisfy the triangle inequality. Despite this, MND has been successfully applied in several real-world clustering tasks.

In general, based on a distance measure between samples, it is possible to define a distance measure between clusters (set of samples). These measures are an essential

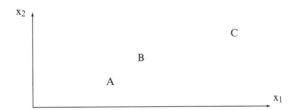

FIGURE 6.3   A and B are more similar than B and C using the MND measure

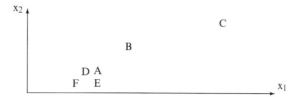

FIGURE 6.4   After changes in the context, B and C are more similar than A and B using the MND measure

part in estimating the quality of a clustering process, and therefore they are part of clustering algorithms. The widely used measures for distance between clusters C_i and C_j are

1) $D_{min}(C_i, C_j) = \min |p_i - p_j|$ where $p_i \in C_i$ and $p_j \in C_j$.
2) $D_{mean}(C_i, C_j) = |m_i - m_j|$ where m_i and m_j are centriods of C_i and C_j
3) $D_{avg}(C_i, C_j) = 1/(n_i n_j) \sum \sum |p_i - p_j|$ where $p_i \in C_i$ and $p_j \in C_j$, and n_i and n_j are the numbers of samples in clusters C_i and C_j
4) $D_{max}(C_i, C_j) = \max |p_i - p_j|$ where $p_i \in C_i$ and $p_j \in C_j$.

6.3   AGGLOMERATIVE HIERARCHICAL CLUSTERING

In hierarchical-cluster analysis, we do not specify the number of clusters as a part of the input. Namely, the input to a system is (X, s), where X is a set of samples, and s is a measure of similarity. An output from a system is a hierarchy of clusters. Most procedures for hierarchical clustering are not based on the concept of optimization, and the goal is to find some approximate, suboptimal solution, using iterations for improvement of partitions until convergence. Algorithms of hierarchical cluster analysis are divided into the two categories divisible algorithms and agglomerative algorithms. A *divisible algorithm* starts from the entire set of samples X and divides it into a partition of subsets, then divides each subset into smaller sets, and so on. Thus, a divisible algorithm generates a sequence of partitions that is ordered from a coarser one to a finer one. An *agglomerative algorithm* first regards each object as an initial cluster. The clusters are merged into a coarser partition, and the merging process proceeds until the trivial partition is obtained: all objects are in one large cluster. This process of clustering is a bottom-up process, where partitions from a finer one to a coarser one. In general, agglomerative algorithms are more frequently used in real-world applications than divisible methods, and therefore we will explain the agglomerative approach in greater detail.

Most agglomerative hierarchical clustering algorithms are variants of the *single-link* or *complete-link* algorithms. These two basic algorithms differ only in the way they characterize the similarity between a pair of clusters. In the single-link method, the distance between two clusters is the *minimum* of the distances between all pairs of samples drawn from the two clusters (one element from the first cluster, the other from the second). In the complete-link algorithm, the distance between two clusters is the *maximum* of all distances between all pairs drawn from the two clusters. A graphical illustration of these two distance measures is given in Figure 6.5.

In either case, two clusters are merged to form a larger cluster based on minimum-distance criteria. Although the single-link algorithm is computationally more simple, from a practical viewpoint it has been observed that the complete-link algorithm produces more useful hierarchies in most applications.

As explained earlier, the only difference between the single-link and complete-link approaches is in the distance computation. For both, the basic steps of the agglomerative clustering algorithm are the same. These steps are

1. Place each sample in its own cluster. Construct the list of inter-cluster distances for all distinct unordered pairs of samples, and sort this list in ascending order.
2. Step through the sorted list of distances, forming for each distinct threshold value d_k a graph of the samples where pairs of samples closer than d_k are connected into a new cluster by a graph edge. If all the samples are members of a connected graph, stop. Otherwise, repeat this step.
3. The output of the algorithm is a nested hierarchy of graphs, which can be cut at the desired dissimilarity level forming a partition (clusters) identified by simple connected components in the corresponding subgraph.

Let us consider five points $\{x_1, x_2, x_3, x_4, x_5\}$ with the following coordinates as a two-dimensional sample for clustering:

$$x_1 = (0, 2), x_2 = (0, 0), x_3 = (1.5, 0), x_4 = (5, 0), \text{ and } x_5 = (5, 2).$$

For this example, we selected two-dimensional points because it is easier to graphically represent these points and to trace all the steps in the clustering algorithm. The points are represented graphically in Figure 6.6.

The distances between these points using the Euclidian measure are

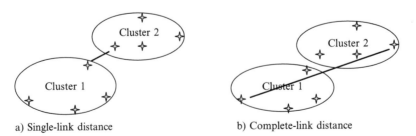

a) Single-link distance   b) Complete-link distance

FIGURE 6.5 Distances for a single-link and a complete-link clustering algorithm

$d(x_1, x_2) = 2$, $d(x_1, x_3) = 2.5$, $d(x_1, x_4) = 5.39$, $d(x_1, x_5) = 5$
$d(x_2, x_3) = 1.5$, $d(x_2, x_4) = 5$, $d(x_2, x_5) = 5.29$
$d(x_3, x_4) = 3.5$, $d(x_3, x_5) = 4.03$
$d(x_4, x_5) = 2$

The distances between points as clusters in the first iteration are the same for both single-link and complete-link clustering. Further computation for these two algorithms is different. Using agglomerative single-link clustering, the following steps are performed to create a cluster and to represent the cluster structure as a dendrogram.

First x_2 and x_3 samples are merged and a cluster $\{x_2, x_3\}$ is generated with a minimum distance equal to 1.5. Second, x_4 and x_5 are merged into a new cluster $\{x_4, x_5\}$ with a higher merging level of 2.0. At the same time, the minimum single-link distance between clusters $\{x_2, x_3\}$ and $\{x_1\}$ is also 2.0. So, these two clusters merge at the same level of similarity as x_4 and x_5. Finally, the two clusters $\{x_1, x_2, x_3\}$ and $\{x_4, x_5\}$ are merged at the highest level with a minimum single-link distance of 3.5. The resulting dendrogram is shown in Figure 6.7.

The cluster hierarchy created by using an agglomerative complete-link clustering algorithm is different compared to the single-link solution. First, x_2 and x_3 are merged and a cluster $\{x_2, x_3\}$ is generated with the minimum distance equal to 1.5. Also, in the second step, x_4 and x_5 are merged into a new cluster $\{x_4, x_5\}$ with a higher merging level of 2.0. Minimal complete-link distance is between clusters

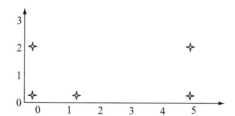

FIGURE 6.6   Five two-dimensional samples for clustering

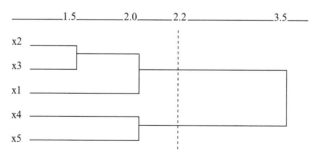

FIGURE 6.7   Dendrogram by single-link method for the data set in Figure 6.6

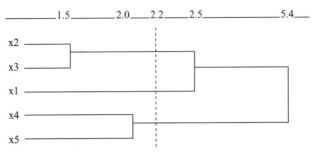

FIGURE 6.8 Dendrogram by complete-link method for the data set in Figure 6.6

$\{x_2, x_3\}$, and $\{x_1\}$ is now 2.5, so these two clusters merge after the previous two steps. Finally, the two clusters $\{x_1, x_2, x_3\}$ and $\{x_4, x_5\}$ are merged at the highest level with a minimal complete-link distance of 5.4. The resulting dendrogram is shown in Figure 6.8.

Selecting, e.g., a threshold measure of similarity s = 2.2, we can recognize from the dendograms in Figures 6.7 and 6.8 that the final clusters for single-link and complete-link algorithms are not the same. A single-link algorithm creates only two clusters: $\{x_1, x_2, x_3\}$ and $\{x_4, x_5\}$, while a complete-link algorithm creates three clusters: $\{x_1\}$, $\{x_2, x_3\}$, and $\{x_4, x_5\}$.

Unlike traditional agglomerative methods, *Chameleon* is a clustering algorithm that tries to improve the clustering quality by using a more elaborate criterion when merging two clusters. Two clusters will be merged if the interconnectivity and closeness of the merged clusters is very similar to the interconnectivity and closeness of the two individual clusters before merging.

To form the initial subclusters, Chameleon first creates a graph $G = (V, E)$, where each node $v \in V$ represents a data sample, and a weighted edge $e(v_i, v_j)$ exists between two nodes v_i and v_j if v_j is one of the k-nearest neighbors of v_i. The weight of each edge in G represents the closeness between two samples, i.e., an edge will weight more if the two data samples are closer to each other. *Chameleon* then uses a graph-partition algorithm to recursively partition G into many small, unconnected subgraphs by doing a min-cut on G at each level of recursion. Here, a min-cut on a graph G refers to a partitioning of G into two parts of close, equal size such that the total weight of the edges being cut is minimized. Each subgraph is then treated as an initial subcluster, and the algorithm is repeated until a certain criterion is reached.

In the second phase, the algorithm goes bottom up. *Chameleon* determines the similarity between each pair of elementary clusters C_i and C_j according to their relative interconnectivity $RI(C_i, C_j)$ and their relative closeness $RC(C_i, C_j)$. Given that the interconnectivity of a cluster is defined as the total weight of edges that are removed when a min-cut is performed, the relative interconnectivity $RI(C_i, C_j)$ is defined as the ratio between the interconnectivity of the merged cluster C_i and C_j to the average interconnectivity of C_i and C_j. Similarly, the relative closeness $RC(C_i, C_j)$ is defined as the ratio between the closeness of the merged cluster of C_i and C_j to the average internal closeness of C_i and C_j. Here the closeness of a cluster refers to the average weight of the edges that are removed when a min-cut is performed.

The similarity function is then computed as a product: $RC(C_i, C_j)*RI(C_i, C_j)^\alpha$ where α is a parameter between 0 and 1. A value of 1 for α will give equal weight to both measures while decreasing α will place more emphasis on $RI(C_i, C_j)$. Chameleon can automatically adapt to the internal characteristics of the clusters and it is effective in discovering arbitrarily-shaped clusters of varying density. However, algorithm is ineffective for high-dimensional data because its time complexity for n samples is $O(n^2)$.

6.4 PARTITIONAL CLUSTERING

Every partitional-clustering algorithm obtains a single partition of the data instead of the clustering structure, such as a dendrogram, produced by a hierarchical technique. Partitional methods have the advantage in applications involving large data sets for which the construction of a dendrogram is computationally very complex. The partitional techniques usually produce clusters by optimizing a criterion function defined either locally (on a subset of samples) or globally (defined over all of the samples). Thus we say that a clustering criterion can be either global or local. A global criterion, such as the Euclidean square-error measure, represents each cluster by a prototype or centroid and assigns the samples to clusters according to the most similar prototypes. A local criterion, such as the minimal mutual neighbor distance (MND), forms clusters by utilizing the local structure or context in the data. Therefore, identifying high-density regions in the data space is a basic criterion for forming clusters.

The most commonly used partitional-clustering strategy is based on the square-error criterion. The general objective is to obtain the partition that, for a fixed number of clusters, minimizes the total square-error. Suppose that the given set of N samples in an n-dimensional space has somehow been partitioned into K clusters $\{C_1, C_2, \ldots, C_k\}$. Each C_k has n_k samples and each sample is in exactly one cluster, so that $\sum n_k = N$, where $k = 1, \ldots, K$. The mean vector M_k of cluster C_k is defined as the *centroid* of the cluster or

$$M_k = (1/n_k) \sum_{i=1}^{n_k} x_{ik}$$

where x_{ik} is the ith sample belonging to cluster C_k. The square-error for cluster C_k is the sum of the squared Euclidean distances between each sample in C_k and its centroid. This error is also called the *within-cluster variation*:

$$e_k^2 = \sum_{i=1}^{n_k} (x_{ik} - M_k)^2$$

The square-error for the entire clustering space containing K clusters is the sum of the within-cluster variations:

$$E_k^2 = \sum_{k=1}^{K} e_k^2$$

The objective of a square-error clustering method is to find a partition containing K clusters that minimize E_k^2 for a given K.

The *K-means partitional-clustering algorithm* is the simplest and most commonly used algorithm employing a square-error criterion. It starts with a random, initial partition and keeps reassigning the samples to clusters, based on the similarity between samples and clusters, until a convergence criterion is met. Typically, this criterion is met when there is no reassignment of any sample from one cluster to another that will cause a decrease of the total squared error. K-means algorithm is popular because it is easy to implement, and its time and space complexity is relatively small. A major problem with this algorithm is that it is sensitive to the selection of the initial partition and may converge to a local minimum of the criterion function if the initial partition is not properly chosen.

The simple K-means partitional-clustering algorithm is computationally efficient and gives surprisingly good results if the clusters are compact, hyperspherical in shape, and well separated in the feature space. The basic steps of the K-means algorithm are

1. select an initial partition with K clusters containing randomly chosen samples, and compute the centroids of the clusters,
2. generate a new partition by assigning each sample to the closest cluster center,
3. compute new cluster centers as the centroids of the clusters,
4. repeat steps 2 and 3 until an optimum value of the criterion function is found (or until the cluster membership stabilizes).

Let us analyze the steps of the K-means algorithm on the simple data set given in Figure 6.6. Suppose that the required number of clusters is two, and initially, clusters are formed from random distribution of samples: $C_1 = \{x_1, x_2, x_4\}$ and $C_2 = \{x_3, x_5\}$. The centriods for these two clusters are

$$M_1 = \{(0 + 0 + 5)/3, (2 + 0 + 0)/3\} = \{1.66, 0.66\}$$
$$M_2 = \{(1.5 + 5)/2, (0 + 2)/2\} = \{3.25, 1.00\}$$

Within-cluster variations, after initial random distribution of samples, are

$$e_1^2 = [(0 - 1.66)^2 + (2 - 0.66)^2] + [(0 - 1.66)^2 + (0 - 0.66)^2]$$
$$+ [(5 - 1.66)^2 + (0 - 0.66)^2] = 19.36$$
$$e_2^2 = [(1.5 - 3.25)^2 + (0 - 1)^2] + [(5 - 3.25)^2 + (2 - 1)^2] = 8.12$$

And the total square error is

$$E^2 = e_1^2 + e_2^2 = 19.36 + 8.12 = 27.48$$

When we reassign all samples, depending on a minimum distance from centroids M_1 and M_2, the new redistribution of samples inside clusters will be

$$d(M_1, x_1) = (1.66^2 + 1.34^2)^{1/2} = 2.14 \quad \text{and } d(M_2, x_1) = 3.40 \;\Rightarrow\; x_1 \in C_1$$
$$d(M_1, x_2) = 1.79 \qquad\qquad\qquad\quad \text{and } d(M_2, x_2) = 3.40 \;\Rightarrow\; x_2 \in C_1$$
$$d(M_1, x_3) = 0.83 \qquad\qquad\qquad\quad \text{and } d(M_2, x_3) = 2.01 \;\Rightarrow\; x_3 \in C_1$$
$$d(M_1, x_4) = 3.41 \qquad\qquad\qquad\quad \text{and } d(M_2, x_4) = 2.01 \;\Rightarrow\; x_4 \in C_2$$
$$d(M_1, x_5) = 3.60 \qquad\qquad\qquad\quad \text{and } d(M_2, x_5) = 2.01 \;\Rightarrow\; x_5 \in C_2$$

New clusters $C_1 = \{x_1, x_2, x_3\}$ and $C_2 = \{x_4, x_5\}$ have new centroids

$$M_1 = \{0.5, 0.67\}$$
$$M_2 = \{5.0, 1.0\}$$

The corresponding within-cluster variations and the total square error are

$$e_1^2 = 4.17$$
$$e_2^2 = 2.00$$
$$E^2 = 6.17$$

We can see that after the first iteration, the total square error is significantly reduced (from the value 27.48 to 6.17). In this simple example, the first iteration was at the same time the final one because if we analyze the distances between the new centroids and the samples, the latter will all be assigned to the same clusters. There is no reassignment and therefore the algorithm halts.

In summary, only the K-means algorithm and its equivalent in an artificial neural networks domain—the Kohonen net—have been applied for clustering on large data sets. Other approaches have been tested, typically, on small data sets. The reasons behind the popularity of the K-means algorithm are as follows:

1. Its time complexity is O(nkl), where n is the number of samples, k is the number of clusters, and l is the number of iterations taken by the algorithm to converge. Typically, k and l are fixed in advance and so the algorithm has linear time complexity in the size of the data set.

2. Its space complexity is O(k + n), and if it is possible to store all the data in the primary memory, access time to all elements is very fast and the algorithm is very efficient.

3. It is an order-independent algorithm. For a given initial distribution of clusters, it generates the same partition of the data at the end of the partitioning process irrespective of the order in which the samples are presented to the algorithm.

A big frustration in using iterative partitional-clustering programs is the lack of guidelines available for choosing K-number of clusters apart from the ambiguity about the best direction for initial partition, updating the partition, adjusting the number of clusters, and the stopping criterion. The K-means algorithm is very sensitive to noise and outlier data points, because a small number of such data can substantially influence the mean value. Unlike the K-means, the *K-mediods* method, instead of taking the mean value of the samples, uses the most centrally located object (mediods) in a cluster to be the cluster representative. Because of this, the K-mediods method is less sensitive to noise and outliers.

6.5 INCREMENTAL CLUSTERING

There are more and more applications where it is necessary to cluster a large collection of data. The definition of "large" has varied with changes in technology. In the 1960s, "large" meant several thousand samples for clustering. Now, there are applications where millions of samples of high dimensionality have to be clustered. The algorithms discussed above work on large data sets, where it is possible to accommodate the entire data set in the main memory. However, there are applications where the entire data set cannot be stored in the main memory because of its size. There are currently three possible approaches to solve this problem:

1. The data set can be stored in a secondary memory and subsets of this data are clustered independently, followed by a merging step to yield a clustering of the entire set. We call this approach the divide-and-conquer approach.
2. An incremental-clustering algorithm can be employed. Here, data are stored in the secondary memory and data items are transferred to the main memory one at a time for clustering. Only the cluster representations are stored permanently in the main memory to alleviate space limitations.
3. A parallel implementation of a clustering algorithm may be used where the advantages of parallel computers increase the efficiency of the divide-and-conquer approach.

An incremental-clustering approach is most popular, and we will explain its basic principles. The following are the global steps of the incremental-clustering algorithm.

1. Assign the first data item to the first cluster.
2. Consider the next data item. Either assign this item to one of the existing clusters or assign it to a new cluster. This assignment is done based on some criterion, e.g., the distance between the new item and the existing cluster centroids. In that case, after every addition of a new item to an existing cluster, recompute a new value for the centroid.
3. Repeat step 2 till all the data samples are clustered.

The space requirements of the incremental algorithm are very small, necessary only for the centroids of the clusters. Typically, these algorithms are noniterative and therefore their time requirements are also small. But, even if we introduce iterations into the incremental-clustering algorithm, computational complexity and corresponding time requirements do not increase significantly. On the other hand, there is one obvious weakness of incremental algorithms that we have to be aware of. Most incremental algorithms do not satisfy one of the most important characteristics of a clustering process: order-independence. An algorithm is order-independent if it generates the same partition for any order in which the data set is presented. Incremental algorithms are very sensitive to the order of samples, and for different orders they generate totally different partitions.

Let us analyze the incremental-clustering algorithm with the sample set given in Figure 6.6. Suppose that the order of samples is x_1, x_2, x_3, x_4, x_5 and the threshold level of similarity between clusters is $\delta = 3$.

1. The first sample x_1 will become the first cluster $C_1 = \{x_1\}$. The coordinates of x_1 will be the coordinates of the centroid $M_1 = \{0, 2\}$.
2. Start analysis of the other samples.
   a) Second sample x_2 is compared with M_1, and the distance d is determined

   $$d(x_2, M_1) = (0^2 + 2^2)^{1/2} = 2.0 < 3$$

   Therefore, x_2 belongs to the cluster C_1. The new centroid will be

   $$M_1 = \{0, 1\}$$

   b) The third sample x_3 is compared with the centroid M_1 (still the only centroid!):

   $$d(x_3, M_1) = (1.5^2 + 1^2)^{1/2} = 1.8 < 3$$
   $$x_3 \in C_1 \quad \Rightarrow \quad C_1 = \{x_1, x_2, x_3\} \quad \Rightarrow \quad M_1 = \{0.5, 0.66\}$$

   c) The fourth sample x_4 is compared with the centroid M_1:

   $$d(x_4, M_1) = (4.5^2 + 0.66^2)^{1/2} = 4.55 > 3$$

   Because the distance of the sample from the given centroid M_1 is larger than the threshold value δ, this sample will create its own cluster $C_2 = \{x_4\}$ with the corresponding centroid $M_2 = \{5, 0\}$.
   d) The fifth sample x_5 is compared with both cluster centroids:

   $$d(x_5, M_1) = (4.5^2 + 1.44^2)^{1/2} \quad = 4.72 > 3$$
   $$d(x_5, M_2) = (0^2 + 2^2)^{1/2} \quad\quad = 2 < 3$$

   The sample is closer to the centroid M_2, and its distance is less than the threshold value δ. Therefore, sample x_5 is added to the second cluster C_2:

   $$C_2 = \{x_4, x_5\} \quad \Rightarrow \quad M_2 = \{5, 1\}$$

3. All samples are analyzed and a final clustering solution of two clusters is obtained:

   $$C_1 = \{x_1, x_2, x_3\} \text{ and } C_2 = \{x_4, x_5\}$$

The reader may check that the result of the incremental-clustering process will not be the same if the order of the samples is different. Usually, this algorithm is not iterative (although it could be!) and the clusters generated after all the samples have been analyzed in one iteration are the final clusters. If the iterative approach is used, the centroids of the clusters computed in the previous iteration are used as a basis for the partitioning of samples in the next iteration.

For most partitional-clustering algorithms, including the iterative approach, a summarized representation of the cluster is given through its cluster feature vector *CF*. This vector of parameters is given for every cluster as a triple, consisting of the number of points (samples) of the cluster, the centroid of the cluster, and the radius of the cluster. The cluster's radius is defined as the square root of the average mean-squared distance from the centroid to the points in the cluster (averaged within-cluster variation). When a new point is added or removed from a cluster, the new CF can be computed from the old CF. It is very important that we do not need the set of points in the cluster to compute a new CF. Working with cluster features is the fundamental approach in the new clustering alogorithm, the *Birch* clustering algorithm. We have to mention that this technique is very efficient for two reasons: 1) CFs occupy less space than any other representation of clusters, and 2) CFs are sufficient for calculating all the values involved in making clustering decisions. This approach is especially applicable if extremely large data sets have to be clustered, and time and space constraints are critical.

If samples are with categorical data, then we do not have a method to calculate centroids as representatives of the clusters. In that case, an additional algorithm called *K-nearest neighbor* may be used to estimate distances (or similarities) between samples and existing clusters. The basic steps of the algorithm are

1. to compute the distances between the new sample and all previous samples, already classified into clusters;
2. to sort the distances in increasing order and select K samples with the smallest distance values;
3. to apply the voting principle. A new sample will be added (classified) to the largest cluster out of K selected samples.

For example, given six 6-dimensional categorical samples

$$X_1 = \{A, B, A, B, C, B\}$$
$$X_2 = \{A, A, A, B, A, B\}$$
$$X_3 = \{B, B, A, B, A, B\}$$
$$X_4 = \{B, C, A, B, B, A\}$$
$$X_5 = \{B, A, B, A, C, A\}$$
$$X_6 = \{A, C, B, A, B, B\}$$

they are gathered into two clusters $C_1 = \{X_1, X_2, X_3\}$ and $C_2 = \{X_4, X_5, X_6\}$. How does one to classify the new sample $Y = \{A, C, A, B, C, A\}$?

To apply the K-nearest neighbor algorithm, it is necessary, as the first step, to find all distances between the new sample and the other samples already clustered.

Using the SMC measure, we can find similarities instead of distances between samples.

Similarities with elements in C_1	Similarities with elements in C_2
$SMC(Y, X_1) = 4/6 = 0.66$	$SMC(Y, X_4) = 4/6 = 0.66$
$SMC(Y, X_2) = 3/6 = 0.50$	$SMC(Y, X_5) = 2/6 = 0.33$
$SMC(Y, X_3) = 2/6 = 0.33$	$SMC(Y, X_6) = 2/6 = 0.33$

Using the 1-nearest neighbor rule ($K = 1$), the new sample cannot be classified because there are two samples (X_1 and X_4) with the same, highest similarity (smallest distances), and one of them is in the class C_1 and the other in the class C_2. On the other hand, using the 3-nearest neighbor rule ($K = 3$) and selecting the three largest similarities in the set, we can see that two samples (X_1 and X_2) belongs to the class C_1, and only one sample to the class C_2. Therefore, using a simple voting system we can classify the new sample Y into the C_1 class.

How is the output of a clustering algorithm evaluated? What characterizes a 'good' clustering result and a 'poor' one? All clustering algorithms will, when presented with data, produce clusters regardless of whether the data contain clusters or not. Therefore, the first step in evaluation is actually an assessment of the data domain rather than the clustering algorithm itself. Data that we do not expect will contain clusters should not be processed by any clustering algorithm. If the data does contain clusters, some clustering algorithms may obtain a 'better' solution than others. Cluster validity is the second step, when we expect to have our data clusters. A clustering structure is valid if it cannot reasonably have occurred by chance or as an artifact of a clustering algorithm. Applying some of the available cluster methodologies, we assess the outputs. This analysis uses a specific criterion of optimality that usually contains knowledge about the application domain and therefore is subjective. There are three types of validation studies for clustering algorithms. An *external* assessment of validity compares the discovered structure to an a priori structure. An *internal* examination of validity tries to determine if the discovered structure is intrinsically appropriate for the data. Both assessments are subjective and domain-dependent. A *relative* test, as a third approach, compares the two structures obtained either from different cluster methodologies or by using the same methodology but with different clustering parameters, such as the order of input samples. This test measures their relative merit but we still need to resolve the question how to select the structures for comparison.

Theory and practical applications both show that all approaches in the validation of clustering results have a subjective component. Hence, little in the way of "gold standards" exists in clustering evaluation. Recent studies in cluster analysis suggest that a user of a clustering algorithm should keep always the following issues in mind:

1. Every clustering algorithm will find clusters in a given data set whether they exist or not; the data should, therefore, be subjected to tests for clustering tendency before applying a clustering algorithm, followed by a validation of the clusters generated by the algorithm.
2. There is no best clustering algorithm; therefore a user is advised to try several algorithms on a given data set.

6.6   REVIEW QUESTIONS AND PROBLEMS

1. Why is the validation of a clustering process highly subjective?

2. What increases the complexity of clustering algorithms?

3. a) Using MND distance, distribute the input samples given as 2D points A(2, 2), B(4, 4), and C(7, 7) into two clusters.

   b) What will be the distribution of samples in the clusters if samples D(1, 1), E(2, 0), and F(0, 0) are added?

4. Given 5-dimensional numeric samples $A = (1, 0, 2, 5, 3)$ and $B = (2, 1, 0, 3, -1)$, find

   a) the Eucledian distance between points.

   b) the city-block distance.

   c) the Minkowski distance for $p = 3$.

   d) the cosine-correlation distance.

5. Given 6-dimensional categorical samples $C = (A, B, A, B, A, A)$ and $D = (B, B, A, B, B, A)$, find

   a) a Simple Matching Coefficient (SMC) of the similarity between samples.

   b) Jaccard's Coefficient.

   c) Rao's Coefficient.

6. Given a set of 5-dimensional categorical samples

$$A = (1, 0, 1, 1, 0)$$
$$B = (1, 1, 0, 1, 0)$$
$$C = (0, 0, 1, 1, 0)$$
$$D = (0, 1, 0, 1, 0)$$
$$E = (1, 0, 1, 0, 1)$$
$$F = (0, 1, 1, 0, 0)$$

   a) Apply agglomerative hierarchical clustering using
      i) Single-link similarity measure based on Rao's coefficient.
      ii) Complete-link similarity measure based on simple matching coefficient SMC.

   b) Plot the dendrograms for the solutions to part i) and ii) of a)

7. Given the samples $X1 = \{1, 0\}, X2 = \{0, 1\}, X3 = \{2, 1\}$, and $X4 = \{3, 3\}$, suppose that the samples are randomly clustered into two clusters $C1 = \{X1, X3\}$ and $C_2 = \{X2, X4\}$.

   a) Apply one iteration of the K-means partitional-clustering algorithm, and find a new distribution of samples in clusters. What are the new centroids? How can you prove that the new distribution of samples is better than the initial one?

   b) What is the change in the total square error?

c) Apply the second iteration of the K-means algorithm and discuss the changes in clusters.

8. For the samples in Example #7, apply iterative clustering with the threshold value for cluster radius $T = 2$. What is the number of clusters and samples distribution after the first iteration?

9. Suppose that the samples in Problem #6 are distributed into two clusters:

$$C1 = \{A, B, E\} \text{ and } C_2 = \{C, D, F\}.$$

Using K-nearest neighbor algorithm, find the classification for the following samples:

a) $Y = \{1, 1, 0, 1, 1\}$ using $K = 1$
b) $Y = \{1, 1, 0, 1, 1\}$ using $K = 3$
c) $Z = \{0, 1, 0, 0, 0\}$ using $K = 1$
d) $Z = \{0, 1, 0, 0, 0\}$ using $K = 5$.

10. Implement the hierarchical agglomerative algorithm for samples with categorical values using the SMC measure of similarity.

11. Implement the partitional K-means clustering algorithm. Input samples are given in the form of a flat file.

12. Implement the incremental-clustering algorithm with iterations. Input samples are given in the form of a flat file.

6.7 REFERENCES FOR FURTHER STUDY

1. Han, J. and M. Kamber, *Data Mining: Concepts and Techniques*, Morgan Kaufmann, San Francisco, 2000.
   This book gives a sound understanding of data-mining principles. The primary orientation of the book is for database practitioners and professionals with emphasis on OLAP and data warehousing. In-depth analysis of association rules and clustering algorithms is the additional strength of the book. All algorithms are presented in easily understood pseudocode and they are suitable for use in real-world, large-scale data-mining projects including advanced applications such as Web mining and text mining.
2. Hand, D., Mannila H., Smith P., *Principles of Data Mining*, MIT Press, Cambridge: MA, 2001.
   The book consists of three sections. The first, foundations, provides a tutorial overview of the principles underlying data-mining algorithms and their applications. The second section, data-mining algorithms, shows how algorithms are constructed to solve specific problems in a principled manner. The third section shows how all of the preceding analyses fit together when applied to real-world data-mining problems.
3. Jain, A. K., M. N. Murty, P. J. Flynn. **Data Clustering: A Review**, *ACM Computing Surveys*. 31, no. 3, (September 1999): 264–323.

Although there are several excellent books on clustering algorithms, this review paper will give the reader enough details about the state-of-the-art techniques in data clustering, with an emphasis on large data sets problems. The paper presents the taxonomy of clustering techniques and identifies cross-cutting themes, recent advances, and some important applications. For readers interested in practical implementation of some clustering methods, the paper offers useful advice and a large spectrum of references.

4. Miyamoto S., *Fuzzy Sets in Information Retrieval and Cluster Analysis*, Cluver Academic Publishers, Dodrecht: Germany, 1990.

This book offers an in-depth presentation and analysis of some clustering algorithms and reviews the possibilities of combining these techniques with fuzzy representation of data. Information retrieval, which, with the development of advanced Web-mining techniques, is becoming more important in the data-mining community, is also explained in the book.

7 Decision Trees and Decision Rules

CHAPTER OBJECTIVES

- Analyze the characteristics of a logic-based approach to classification problems.
- Describe the differences between decision-tree and decision-rule representations in a final classification model.
- Explain in-depth the C4.5 algorithm for generating decision trees and decision rules.
- Identify the required changes in the C4.5 algorithm when missing values exist in training or testing data set.
- Know when and how to use pruning techniques to reduce the complexity of decision trees and decision rules.
- Summarize the limitations of representing a classification model by decision trees and decision rules.

Decision trees and decision rules are data-mining methodologies applied in many real-world applications as a powerful solution to classification problems. Therefore, at the beginning, let us briefly summarize the basic principles of classification. In general, classification is a process of learning a function that maps a data item into one of several predefined classes. Every classification based on inductive-learning algorithms is given as input a set of samples that consist of vectors of attribute values (also called feature vectors) and a corresponding class. The goal of learning is to create a classification model, known as a *classifier*, which will predict, with the values of its available input attributes, the class for some entity (a given sample). In other words, classification is the process of assigning a discrete label value (class) to an unlabeled record, and a classifier is a model (a result of classification) that predicts one attribute—class of a sample—when the other attributes are given. In doing so, samples are divided into predefined groups. For example, a simple classification might group customer billing records into two specific classes: those who pay their bills within thirty days and those who takes longer than thirty days to pay. Different classification methodologies are applied today in almost every discipline where the task of classification, because of the large amount of data, requires automation of the process. Examples of classification methods used as a part of data-mining applications include classifying trends in financial market and identifying objects in large image databases.

A more formalized approach to classification problems is given through its graphical interpretation. A data set with N features may be thought of as a collection of discrete points (one per example) in an N-dimensional space. A classification rule is a hypercube in this space, and the hypercube contains one or more of these points. When there is more than one cube for a given class, all the cubes are

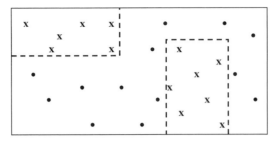

FIGURE 7.1   Classification of samples in a 2D space

OR-ed to provide a complete classification for the class, such as the example of two 2D classes in Figure 7.1. Within a cube the conditions for each part are AND-ed. The size of a cube indicates its generality, i.e., the larger the cube the more vertices it contains and potentially covers more sample-points.

In a classification model, the connection between classes and other properties of the samples can be defined by something as simple as a flowchart or as complex and unstructured as a procedure manual. Data-mining methodologies restrict discussion to formalized, "executable" models of classification, and there are two very different ways in which they can be constructed. On the one hand, the model might be obtained by interviewing the relevant expert or experts, and most knowledge-based systems have been built this way despite the well-known difficulties attendant on taking this approach. Alternatively, numerous recorded classifications might be examined and a model constructed inductively by generalizing from specific examples that are of primary interest for data-mining applications.

The statistical approach to classification explained in Chapter 5 gives one type of model for classification problems: summarizing the statistical characteristics of the set of samples. The other approach is based on logic. Instead of using math operations like addition and multiplication, the logical model is based on expressions that are evaluated as true or false by applying Boolean and comparative operators to the feature values. These methods of modeling give accurate classification results compared to other nonlogical methods, and they have superior explanatory characteristics. Decision trees and decision rules are typical data-mining techniques that belong to a class of methodologies that give the output in the form of logical models.

7.1   DECISION TREES

A particularly efficient method for producing classifiers from data is to generate a decision tree. The decision-tree representation is the most widely used logic method. There is a large number of decision-tree induction algorithms described primarily in the machine-learning and applied-statistics literature. They are supervised learning methods that construct decision trees from a set of input–output samples. A typical decision-tree learning system adopts a top-down strategy that searches for a solution in a part of the search space. It guarantees that a simple, but not necessarily the simplest, tree will be found. A decision tree consists of *nodes* that where attributes are tested. The outgoing *branches* of a node correspond to all the possible outcomes of the test at the node. A simple decision tree for classification of samples with two

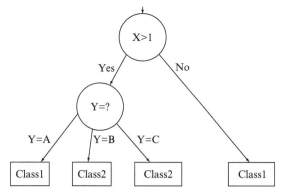

FIGURE 7.2   A simple decision tree with the tests on attributes X and Y

input attributes X and Y is given in Figure 7.2. All samples with feature values X>1 and Y=B belong to Class2, while the samples with values X<1 belong to Class1, whatever the value for feature Y. The samples, at a nonleaf node in the tree structure, are thus partitioned along the branches and each child node gets its corresponding subset of samples. Decision trees that use univariate splits have a simple representational form, making it relatively easy for the user to understand the inferred model; at the same time, they represent a restriction on the expressiveness of the model. In general, any restriction on a particular tree representation can significantly restrict the functional form and thus the approximation power of the model. A well-known tree-growing algorithm for generating decision trees based on univariate splits is Quinlan's *ID3* with an extended version called *C4.5*. Greedy search methods, which involve growing and pruning decision-tree structures, are typically employed in these algorithms to explore the exponential space of possible models.

The ID3 algorithm starts with all the training samples at the root node of the tree. An attribute is selected to partition these samples. For each value of the attribute a branch is created, and the corresponding subset of samples that have the attribute value specified by the branch is moved to the newly created child node. The algorithm is applied recursively to each child node until all samples at a node are of one class. Every path to the leaf in the decision tree represents a classification rule. Note that the critical decision in such a top-down decision tree–generation algorithm is the choice of attribute at a node. Attribute selection in ID3 and C4.5 algorithms are based on minimizing an information entropy measure applied to the examples at a node.

The approach based on information theory insists on minimizing the number of tests that will allow a sample to classify in a database. The attribute-selection part of ID3 is based on the assumption that the complexity of the decision tree is strongly related to the amount of information conveyed by the value of the given attribute. An information-based heuristic selects the attribute providing the highest information gain, i.e., the attribute that minimizes the information needed in the resulting subtree to classify the sample. An extension of ID3 is the C4.5 algorithm, which extends the domain of classification from categorical attributes to numeric ones. The measure favors attributes that result in partitioning the data into subsets that have low class entropy, i.e., when the majority of examples in it belong to a single class. The algorithm basically chooses the attribute that provides the maximum degree of discrimination between classes locally. More details about basic principles and implementation of these algorithms will be given in the following sections.

To apply some of the methods, which are based on the inductive-learning approach, several key requirements have to be satisfied:

1. *Attribute-value description* – The data to be analyzed must be in a flat-file form—all information about one object or example must be expressible in terms of a fixed collection of properties or attributes. Each attribute may have either discrete or numeric values, but the attributes used to describe samples must not vary from one case to another. This restriction rules out domains in which samples have an inherently variable structure.

2. *Predefined classes* – The categories to which samples are to be assigned must have been established beforehand. In the terminology of machine learning this is supervised learning.

3. *Discrete classes* – The classes must be sharply delineated: a case either does or does not belong to a particular class. It is expected that there will be far more samples than classes.

4. *Sufficient data* – Inductive generalization given in the form of decision tree proceeds by identifying patterns in data. The approach is valid if enough number of robust patterns can be distinguished from chance coincidences. As this differentiation usually depends on statistical tests, there must be sufficient number of samples to allow these tests to be effective. The amount of data required is affected by factors such as the number of properties and classes and the complexity of the classification model. As these factors increase, more data will be needed to construct a reliable model.

5. *"Logical" classification models* – These methods construct only such classifiers that can be expressed as decision trees or decision rules. These forms essentially restrict the description of a class to a logical expression whose primitives are statements about the values of particular attributes. Some applications require weighted attributes or their arithmetic combinations for a reliable description of classes. In these situations logical models become very complex and, in general, they are not effective.

7.2 *C4.5 ALGORITHM*: GENERATING A DECISION TREE

The most important part of the C4.5 algorithm is the process of generating an initial decision tree from the set of training samples. As a result, the algorithm generates a classifier in the form of a decision tree; a structure with two types of nodes: *a leaf*, indicating a class, or *a decision node* that specifies some test to be carried out on a single-attribute value, with one branch and subtree for each possible outcome of the test.

A decision tree can be used to classify a new sample by starting at the root of the tree and moving through it until a leaf is encountered. At each nonleaf decision node, the features' outcome for the test at the node is determined and attention shifts to the root of the selected subtree. For example, if the classification model of the problem is given with the decision tree in Figure 7.3a, and the sample for classification in Figure 7.3b, then the algorithm will create the path through the nodes **A**, **C**, and **F** (leaf node) until it makes the final classification decision: *CLASS2*.

The skeleton of the C4.5 algorithm is based on Hunt's *CLS* method for constructing a decision tree from a set T of training samples. Let the classes be denoted as $\{C_1, C_2, \ldots, C_k\}$. There are three possibilities for the content of the set T:

1. T contains one or more samples, all belonging to a single class C_j. The decision tree for T is a leaf identifying class C_j.
2. T contains no samples. The decision tree is again a leaf but the class to be associated with the leaf must be determined from information other than T, such as the overall majority class in T. The C4.5 algorithm uses as a criterion the most frequent class at the parent of the given node.
3. T contains samples that belong to a mixture of classes. In this situation, the idea is to refine T into subsets of samples that are heading towards a single-class collection of samples. Based on single attribute, an appropriate test that has one or more mutually exclusive outcomes $\{O_1, O_2, \ldots, O_n\}$ is chosen. T is partitioned into subsets $T_1, T_2, \ldots, T_n$ where T_i contains all the samples in T that have outcome O_i of the chosen test. The decision tree for T consists of a decision node identifying the test and one branch for each possible outcome (examples of this type of nodes are nodes A, B, and C in the decision tree in Figure 7.3a).

The same tree-building procedure is applied recursively to each subset of training samples, so that the i-th branch leads to the decision tree constructed from the subset T_i of training samples. The successive division of the set of training samples proceeds until all the subsets consist of samples belonging to a single class.

The tree-building process is not uniquely defined. For different tests, even for a different order of their application, different trees will be generated. Ideally, we would like to choose a test at each stage of sample-set splitting so that the final tree is small. Since we are looking for a compact decision tree that is consistent with the training set, why not explore all possible trees and select the simplest?

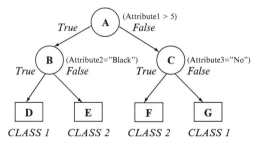

a) Decision tree   b) An example for classification

FIGURE 7.3   Classification of a new sample based on the decision-tree model

Unfortunately, the problem of finding the smallest decision tree consistent with a training data set is NP-complete. Enumeration and analysis of all possible trees will cause a combinatorial explosion for any real-world problem. For example, for a small database with five attributes and only twenty training examples, the possible number of decision trees is greater than 10^6, depending on the number of different values for every attribute. Therefore, most decision tree construction methods are non-backtracking, greedy algorithms. Once a test has been selected using some heuristics to maximize the measure of progress and the current set of training cases has been partitioned, the consequences of alternative choices are not explored. The measure of progress is a local measure, and the gain criterion for a test selection is based on the information available for a given step of data splitting.

Suppose we have the task of selecting a possible test with n outcomes (n values for a given feature) that partitions the set T of training samples into subsets $T_1, T_2, \ldots, T_n$. The only information available for guidance is the distribution of classes in T and its subsets T_i. If S is any set of samples, let *freq*(C_i, S) stand for the number of samples in S that belong to class C_i (out of k possible classes), and let $|S|$ denote the number of samples in the set S.

The original ID3 algorithm used a criterion called *gain* to select the attribute to be tested which is based on the information theory concept: *entropy*. The following relation gives the computation of the entropy of the set S (bits are units):

$$\text{Info}(S) = -\sum_{i=1}^{k} ((\text{freq}(C_i, S)/\ |S|) \cdot \log_2 (\text{freq}(C_i, S)/|S|))$$

Now consider a similar measurement after T has been partitioned in accordance with n outcomes of one attribute test X. The expected information requirement can be found as the weighted sum of entropies over the subsets:

$$\text{Info}_x(T) = -\sum_{i=1}^{n} ((|T_i|/|T|) \cdot \text{Info}(T_i))$$

The quantity

$$\text{Gain}(X) = \text{Info}(T) - \text{Info}_x(T)$$

measures the information that is gained by partitioning T in accordance with the test X. The gain criterion selects a test X to maximize Gain(X), i.e., this criterion will select an attribute with the highest info-gain.

Let us analyze the application of these measures and the creation of a decision tree for one simple example. Suppose that the database T is given in a flat form in which each out of fourteen examples (cases) is described by three input attributes and belongs to one of two given classes: CLASS1 or CLASS2. The database is given in tabular form in Table 7.1.

Nine samples belong to CLASS1 and five samples to CLASS2, so the entropy before splitting is

$$\text{Info}(T) = -9/14 \log_2 (9/14) - 5/14 \log_2 (5/14) = 0.940 \text{ bits}$$

TABLE 7.1.   A simple flat database of examples for training

Database T:

Attribute1	Attribute2	Attribute3	Class
A	70	True	CLASS1
A	90	True	CLASS2
A	85	False	CLASS2
A	95	False	CLASS2
A	70	False	CLASS1
B	90	True	CLASS1
B	78	False	CLASS1
B	65	True	CLASS1
B	75	False	CLASS1
C	80	True	CLASS2
C	70	True	CLASS2
C	80	False	CLASS1
C	80	False	CLASS1
C	96	False	CLASS1

After using Attribute1 to divide the initial set of samples T into three subsets (test x_1 represents the selection one of three values A, B, or C), the resulting information is given by:

$$Info_{x1}(T) = 5/14(- 2/5 \ \log_2 (2/5) - 3/5 \ \log_2 (3/5))$$
$$+ 4/14(- 4/4 \ \log_2 (4/4) - 0/4 \ \log_2 (0/4))$$
$$+ 5/14(- 3/5 \ \log_2 (3/5) - 2/5 \ \log_2 (2/5))$$
$$= 0.694 \ bits$$

The information gained by this test x_1 is

$$Gain(x_1) = 0.940 - 0.694 = 0.246 \ bits$$

If the test and splitting is based on Attribute3 (test x_2 represents the selection one of two values True or False), a similar computation will give new results:

$$Info_{x2}(T) = 6/14(- 3/6 \log_2 (3/6) - 3/6 \log_2 (3/6))$$
$$+ 8/14(- 6/8 \log_2 (6/8) - 2/8 \log_2 (2/8))$$
$$= 0.892 \ bits$$

and corresponding gain is

$$Gain(x_2) = 0.940 - 0.892 = 0.048 \ bits$$

Based on the gain criterion, the decision-tree algorithm will select test x_1 as an initial test for splitting the database T because this gain is higher. To find the optimal test it will be necessary to analyze a test on Attribute2, which is a numeric feature with continuous values. In general, C4.5 contains mechanisms for proposing three types of tests:

1. The "standard" test on a discrete attribute, with one outcome and one branch for each possible value of that attribute (in our example these are both tests x_1 for Attribute1 and x_2 for Attribute3).

2. If attribute Y has continuous numeric values, a binary test with outcomes $Y \leq Z$ and $Y > Z$ could be defined, by comparing its value against a threshold value Z.

3. A more complex test also based on a discrete attribute, in which the possible values are allocated to a variable number of groups with one outcome and branch for each group.

While we have already explained standard test for categorical attributes, additional explanations are necessary about a procedure for establishing tests on attributes with numeric values. It might seem that tests on continuous attributes would be difficult to formulate, since they contain an arbitrary threshold for splitting all values into two intervals. But there is an algorithm for the computation of optimal threshold value Z. The training samples are first sorted on the values of the attribute Y being considered. There are only a finite number of these values, so let us denote them in sorted order as $\{v_1, v_2, \ldots, v_m\}$. Any threshold value lying between v_i and v_{i+1} will have the same effect as dividing the cases into those whose value of the attribute Y lies in $\{v_1, v_2, \ldots, v_i\}$ and those whose value is in $\{v_{i+1}, v_{i+2}, \ldots, v_m\}$. There are thus only $m-1$ possible splits on Y, all of which should be examined systematically to obtain an optimal split. It is usual to choose the midpoint of each interval, $(v_i + v_{i+1})/2$, as the representative threshold. The algorithm C4.5 differs in choosing as the threshold a smaller value v_i for every interval $\{v_i, v_{i+1}\}$, rather than the midpoint itself. This ensures that the threshold values appearing in either the final decision tree or rules or both actually occur in the database.

To illustrate this threshold-finding process, we could analyze, for our example of database T, the possibilities of Attribute2 splitting. After a sorting process, the set of values for Attribute2 is {65, 70, 75, 78, 80, 85, 90, 95, 96} and the set of potential threshold values Z is {65, 70, 75, 78, 80, 85, 90, 95}. Out of these eight values the optimal Z (with the highest information gain) should be selected. For our example, the optimal Z value is Z = 80 and the corresponding process of information-gain computation for the test x_3 (Attribute2 $\leq$ 80 or Attribute2 > 80) is the following:

$$\text{Info}_{x3}(T) = 9/14(-7/9\ \log_2(7/9) - 2/9\ \log_2(2/9))$$
$$+ 5/14(-2/5\ \log_2(2/5) - 3/5\ \log_2(3/5))$$
$$= 0.837 \text{ bits}$$

$$\text{Gain}(x_3) = 0.940 - 0.837 = 0.103 \text{ bits}$$

Now, if we compare the information gain for the three attributes in our example, we can see that Attribute1 still gives the highest gain of 0.246 bits and therefore

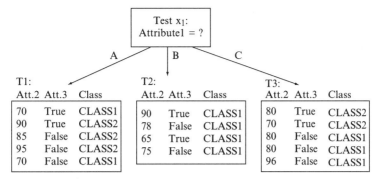

FIGURE 7.4   Initial decision tree and subset cases for a database in Table 7.1

this attribute will be selected for the first splitting in the construction of a decision tree. The root node will have the test for the values of Attribute1, and three branches will be created, one for each of the attribute values. This initial tree with the corresponding subsets of samples in the children nodes is represented in Figure 7.4.

After initial splitting, every child node has several samples from the database, and the entire process of test selection and optimization will be repeated for every child node. Because the child node for test x_1: Attribute1 = B has four cases and all of them are in CLASS1, this node will be the leaf node, and no additional tests are necessary for this branch of the tree.

For the remaining child node where we have five cases in subset T1, tests on the remaining attributes can be performed; an optimal test (with maximum information gain) will be test x_4 with two alternatives: Attribute2 $\leq$ 70 or Attribute2 > 70.

$$\text{Info}(T_1) = -2/15 \ \log_2 (2/5) - 3/15 \ \log_2 (3/5) = 0.940 \text{ bits}$$

Using Attribute2 to divide T_1 into two subsets (test x_4 represents the selection of one of two intervals), the resulting information is given by:

$$\begin{aligned}
\text{Info}_{x4}(T_1) &= 2/5(- 2/2 \ \log_2 (2/2) - 0/2 \ \log_2 (0/2)) \\
&\quad + 3/5(- 0/3 \ \log_2 (0/3) - 3/3 \ \log_2 (3/3)) \\
&= 0 \text{ bits}
\end{aligned}$$

The information gained by this test is maximal:

$$\text{Gain}(x_4) = 0.940 - 0 = 0.940 \text{ bits}$$

and two branches will create the final leaf nodes because the subsets of cases in each of the branches belong to the same class.

A similar computation will be carried out for the third child of the root node. For the subset T_3 of the database T, the selected optimal test x_5 is the test on Attribute3 values. Branches of the tree, Attribute3 = True and Attribute3 = False, will create uniform subsets of cases which belong to the same class. The final decision tree for database T is represented in Figure 7.5.

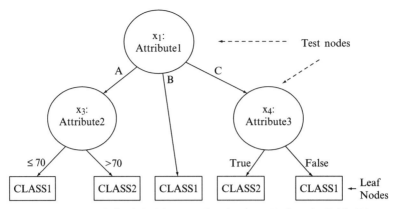

FIGURE 7.5   A final decision tree for database T given in Table 7.1

```
If      Attribute1 = A
        Then
                If      Attribute2 <= 70
                        Then
                                Classification = CLASS1;
                        Else
                                Classification = CLASS2;
Elseif  Attribute1 = B
        Then
                                Classification = CLASS1;
Elseif  Attribute1 = C
        Then
                If      Attribute3 = True
                        Then
                                Classification = CLASS2;
                        Else
                                Classification = CLASS1.
```

FIGURE 7.6   A decision tree in the form of pseudocode for the database T given in Table 7.1

Alternatively, a decision tree can be presented in the form of an executable code (or pseudocode) with *if-then* constructions for branching into a tree structure. The transformation of a decision tree from one representation to the other is very simple and straightforward. The final decision tree for our example is given in pseudocode in Figure 7.6.

While the gain criterion has had some good results in the construction of compact decision trees, it also has one serious deficiency: a strong bias in favor of tests with many outcomes. A solution was found in some kinds of normalization. By analogy with the definition of Info(S), an additional parameter was specified:

$$\text{Split-info}(X) = -\sum_{i=1}^{n}((|T_i|/|T|)\log_2(|T_i|/|T|))$$

This represented the potential information generated by dividing set T into n subsets T_i. Now, a new gain measure could be defined:

$$\text{Gain-ratio(X)} = \text{gain(X)}/ \text{Split-info(X)}$$

This new gain measure expresses the proportion of information generated by the split that is useful, i.e., that appears helpful in classification. The gain–ratio criterion also selects a test that maximizes the ratio given earlier. This criterion is robust and typically gives a consistently better choice of a test than the previous gain criterion. A computation of the gain–ratio test can be illustrated for our example. To find the gain–ratio measure for the test x_1, an additional parameter Split-info(x_1) is calculated:

$$\text{Split-info}(x_1) = -5/14 \, \log_2 (5/14) - 4/14 \, \log_2 (4/14) - 5/14 \, \log_2 (5/14)$$
$$= 1.577 \text{ bits}$$

$$\text{Gain-ratio}(x_1) = 0.246/1.557 = 0.156$$

A similar procedure should be performed for other tests in the decision tree. Instead of gain measure, the maximal gain ratio will be the criterion for attribute selection, along with a test to split samples into subsets. The final decision tree created using this new criterion for splitting a set of samples will be the most compact.

7.3   UNKNOWN ATTRIBUTE VALUES

The previous version of the C4.5 algorithm is based on the assumption that all values for all attributes are determined. But in a data set, often some attribute values for some samples can be missing—such incompleteness is typical in real-world applications. This might occur because the value is not relevant to a particular sample, or it was not recorded when the data was collected, or an error was made by the person the entering data into a database. To solve the problem of missing values, there are two choices:

1. Discard all samples in a database with missing data, or
2. Define a new algorithm or modify an existing algorithm that will work with missing data.

The first solution is simple but unacceptable when large amounts of missing values exist in a set of samples. To address the second alternative, several questions must be answered:

1. How does one compare two samples with different numbers of unknown values?
2. Training samples with unknown values cannot be associated with a particular value of the test, and so they cannot be assigned to any subsets of cases. How should these samples be treated in the partitioning?
3. In a testing phase of classification, how does one treat a missing value if the test is on the attribute with the missing value?

All these and many other questions arise with any attempt to find a solution for missing data. Several classification algorithms that work with missing data are usually based on filling in a missing value with the most probable value, or on looking at the probability distribution of all values for the given attribute. None of these approaches is uniformly superior.

In C4.5, it is an accepted principle that samples with unknown values are distributed probabilistically according to the relative frequency of known values. Let Info(T) and $Info_x(T)$ be calculated as before, except that only samples with known values of attributes are taken into account. Then the gain parameter can reasonably be corrected with a factor F, which represents the probability that a given attribute is known (F = number of samples in the database with a known value for a given attribute / total number of samples in a data set). The new gain criterion will have the form

$$Gain(x) = F(Info(T) - Info_x(T))$$

Similarly, Split–info(x) can be altered by regarding the samples with unknown values as an additional group in splitting. If the test x has n outcomes, its Split-info(x) is computed as if the test divided the data set into n+1 subsets. This modification has a direct influence on the final value of the modified criterion Gain-ratio(x).

Let us explain the modifications of the C4.5 decision-tree methodology applied on one example. The database is similar to previous one (Table 7.1), only there is now one value missing for Attribute1 denoted by "?" as presented in Table 7.2.

The computation of the gain parameter for Attribute1 is similar as before, only the missing value corrects some of the previous steps. Eight out of the thirteen cases with values for Attribute1 belong to CLASS1 and five cases to CLASS2, so the entropy before splitting is

$$Info(T) = -8/13 \log_2 (8/13) - 5/13 \log_2 (5/13) = 0.961 \text{ bits}$$

TABLE 7.2.   A simple flat database of examples
with one missing value
Database T:

Attribute1	Attribute2	Attribute3	Class
A	70	True	CLASS1
A	90	True	CLASS2
A	85	False	CLASS2
A	95	False	CLASS2
A	70	False	CLASS1
?	90	True	CLASS1
B	78	False	CLASS1
B	65	True	CLASS1
B	75	False	CLASS1
C	80	True	CLASS2
C	70	True	CLASS2
C	80	False	CLASS1
C	80	False	CLASS1
C	96	False	CLASS1

After using Attribute1 to divide T into three subsets (test x_1 represents the selection one of three values A, B, or C), the resulting information is given by

$$\begin{aligned} \text{Info}_{x1}(T) \ =\ & 5/13(-2/5\ \log_2(2/5) - 3/5\ \log_2(3/5)) \\ & + 3/13(-3/3\ \log_2(3/3) - 0/3\ \log_2(0/3)) \\ & + 5/14(-3/5\ \log_2(3/5) - 2/5\ \log_2(2/5)) \\ =\ & 0.747\ \text{bits} \end{aligned}$$

The information gained by this test is now corrected with the factor F (F = 13/14 for our example):

$$\text{Gain}(x_1) = 13/14\,(0.961 - 0.747) = 0.199\ \text{bits}$$

The gain for this test is slightly lower than the previous value of 0.216 bits. The split information, however, is still determined from the entire training set and is larger, since there is an extra category for unknown values.

$$\begin{aligned} \text{Split-info}(x1) = & -(5/13\log(5/13) + 3/13\log(3/13) + 5/13\log(5/13) \\ & + 1/13\log(1/13)) \\ = & 1.876 \end{aligned}$$

Additionally, the concept of partitioning must be generalized. With every sample a new parameter, probability, is associated. When a case with known value is assigned from T to subset T_i, the probability of it belonging to T_i is 1, and in all other subsets is 0. When a value is not known, only a weaker probabilistic statement can be made. C4.5 therefore associates with each sample (having a missing value) in each subset T_i a weight w, representing the probability that the case belongs to each subset. To make the solution more general, it is necessary to take into account that the probabilities of samples before splitting are not always equal to one (in subsequent iterations of the decision-tree construction). Therefore, new parameter w_{new} for missing values after splitting is equal to the old parameter w_{old} before splitting multiplied by the probability that the sample belongs to each subset $P(T_i)$, or more formally:

$$w_{new} = w_{old} \cdot P(T_i)$$

After splitting the set T into subsets using test x_1 on Attribute1, the record with the missing value will be represented in all three subsets. The results are given in Figure 7.7. New weights w_i will be equal to probabilities 5/13, 3/13, and 5/13, because the initial (old) value for w is equal to one. The new subsets are given in Figure 7.7. $|T_i|$ can be now reinterpreted in C4.5 not as a number of elements in a set T_i, but as a sum of all weights w for the given set T_i. From Figure 7.7, the new values computed are $|T_1| = 5 + 5/13$, $|T_2| = 3 + 3/13$, and $|T_3| = 5 + 5/13$.

If these subsets are partitioned further by the tests on Attribute2 and Attribute3, the final decision tree for a data set with missing values has the form shown in Figure 7.8.

T_1: (Attribute1 = A)				T_2: (Attribute1 = B)				T_3: (Attribute1 = C)			
Att.2	Att.3	Class	w	Att.2	Att.3	Class	w	Att.2	Att.3	Class	w
70	True	CLASS1	1	*90*	*True*	*CLASS1*	*3/13*	80	True	CLASS2	1
90	True	CLASS2	1	78	False	CLASS1	1	70	True	CLASS2	1
85	False	CLASS2	1	65	True	CLASS1	1	80	False	CLASS1	1
95	False	CLASS2	1	75	False	CLASS1	1	80	False	CLASS1	1
70	False	CLASS1	1					96	False	CLASS1	1
90	*True*	*CLASS1*	*5/13*					*90*	*True*	*CLASS1*	*5/13*

FIGURE 7.7   Results of test x_1 are subsets T_i (initial set T is with missing value).

```
If    Attribute1 = A
          Then
              If      Attribute2 <= 70
                  Then
                          Classification = CLASS1   (2.0 / 0);
                  Else
                          Classification = CLASS2   (3.4 / 0.4);
      Elseif  Attribute1 = B
          Then
                          Classification = CLASS1   (3.2 / 0);
      Elseif  Attribute1 = C
          Then
              If      Attribute3 = True
                  Then
                          Classification = CLASS2   (2.4 / 0);
                  Else
                          Classification = CLASS1   (3.0 / 0).
```

FIGURE 7.8   Decision tree for the database T with missing values

The decision tree in Figure 7.8 has much the same structure as before (Figure 7.6), but because of the ambiguity in final classification, every decision is attached with two parameters in a form ($|T_i|$/E). $|T_i|$ is the sum of the fractional samples that reach the leaf and E is the number of samples that belong to classes other than the nominated class.

For example, (3.4 / 0.4) means that 3.4 (or 3 + 5/13) fractional training samples reached the leaf, of which 0.4 (or 5/13) did not belong to the class assigned to the leaf. It is possible to express the $|T_i|$ and E parameters in percentages:

$3/3.4 \cdot 100\% = 88\%$ of cases at a given leaf would be classified as CLASS2.

$0.4/3.4 \cdot 100\% = 12\%$ of cases at a given leaf would be classified as CLASS1.

A similar approach is taken in C4.5 when the decision tree is used to classify a sample previously not present in a database; that is the *testing phase*. If all attribute values are known then the process is straightforward. Starting with a root node in a decision tree, tests on attribute values will determine traversal through the tree, and at the end, the algorithm will finish in one of leaf nodes that uniquely defines the class of a testing example (or with probabilities, if the training set had missing values). If the value for a relevant testing attribute is unknown, the outcome of the test cannot be determined. Then the system explores all possible outcomes from the test and combines the resulting classification arithmetically. Since there can be multiple paths from the root of a tree or subtree to the leaves, a classification is a class distribution rather than a single class. When the total class distribution for the tested case has been established, the class with the highest probability is assigned as the predicted class.

7.4 PRUNING DECISION TREES

Discarding one or more subtrees and replacing them with leaves simplify a decision tree, and that is the main task in decision-tree pruning. In replacing the subtree with a leaf, the algorithm expects to lower the *predicted error rate and* increase the quality of a classification model. But computation of error rate is not simple. An error rate based only on a training data set does not provide a suitable estimate. One possibility to estimate the predicted error rate is to use a new, additional set of test samples if they are available, or to use the cross-validation techniques explained in Chapter 4. This technique divides initially available samples into equal-sized blocks and, for each block, the tree is constructed from all samples except this block and tested with a given block of samples. With the available training and testing samples, the basic idea of decision tree-pruning is to remove parts of the tree (subtrees) that do not contribute to the classification accuracy of unseen testing samples, producing a less complex and thus more comprehensible tree. There are two ways in which the recursive-partitioning method can be modified:

1. Deciding not to divide a set of samples any further under some conditions. The stopping criterion is usually based on some statistical tests, such as the χ^2 test: *If there are no significant differences in classification accuracy before and after division, then represent a current node as a leaf.* The decision is made in advance, before splitting, and therefore this approach is called *prepruning*.

2. Removing retrospectively some of the tree structure using selected accuracy criteria. The decision in this process of *postpruning* is made after the tree has been built.

C4.5 follows the *postpruning* approach, but it uses a specific technique to estimate the predicted error rate. This method is called *pessimistic pruning*. For every node in a tree, the estimation of the upper confidence limit U_{cf} is computed using the statistical tables for binomial distribution (given in most textbooks on statistics). Parameter U_{cf} is a function of $|T_i|$ and E for a given node. C4.5 uses the default confidence level of 25%, and compares $U_{25\%} (|T_i|/E)$ for a given node T_i with a weighted confidence of its leaves. Weights are the total number of cases for every leaf. If the predicted error for a root node in a subtree is less than weighted sum of $U_{25\%}$ for the leaves (predicted error for the subtree), then a subtree will be replaced with its root node, which becomes a new leaf in a pruned tree.

Let us illustrate this procedure with one simple example. A subtree of a decision tree is given in Figure 7.9, where the root node is the test x_1 on three possible values {1, 2, 3} of the attribute A. The children of the root node are leaves denoted with corresponding classes and $(|T_i|/E)$ parameters. The question is to estimate the

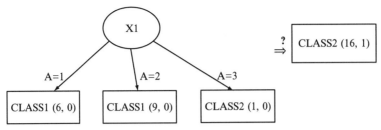

FIGURE 7.9   Pruning a subtree by replacing it with one leaf node

possibility of pruning the subtree and replacing it with its root node as a new, generalized leaf node.

To analyze the possibility of replacing the subtree with a leaf node it is necessary to compute a predicted error PE for the initial tree and for a replaced node. Using default confidence of 25%, the upper confidence limits for all nodes are collected from statistical tables: $U_{25\%}(6,0) = 0.206$, $U_{25\%}(9,0) = 0.143$, $U_{25\%}(1,0) = 0.750$, and $U_{25\%}(16,1) = 0.157$. Using these values, the predicted errors for the initial tree and the replaced node are

$$PE_{tree} = 6 \cdot 0.206 + 9 \cdot 0.143 + 1 \cdot 0.750 = 3.257$$

$$PE_{node} = 16 \cdot 0.157 = 2.512$$

Since the existing subtree has a higher value of predicted error than the replaced node, it is recommended that the decision tree be pruned and the subtree replaced with the new leaf node.

7.5   *C4.5 ALGORITHM*: GENERATING DECISION RULES

Even though the pruned trees are more compact than the originals, they can still be very complex. Large decision trees are difficult to understand because each node has a specific context established by the outcomes of tests at antecedent nodes. To make a decision-tree model more readable, a path to each leaf can be transformed into an IF-THEN production rule. The IF part consists of all tests on a path, and the THEN part is a final classification. Rules in this form are called *decision rules*, and a collection of decision rules for all leaf nodes would classify samples exactly as the tree does. As a consequence of their tree origin, the IF parts of the rules would be mutually exclusive and exhaustive, so the order of the rules would not matter. An example of the transformation of a decision tree into a set of decision rules is given in Figure 7.10, where the two given attributes, A and B, may have two possible values, 1 and 2, and the final classification is into one of two classes.

For our trained decision tree in Figure 7.8, the corresponding decision rules will be

If   Attribute1 = A and Attribute2 ≤ 70
    Then   Classification = CLASS1   (2.0 / 0);

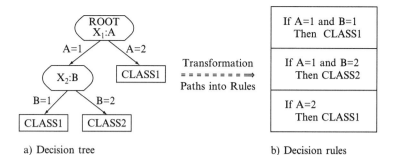

a) Decision tree   b) Decision rules

FIGURE 7.10   Transformation of a decision tree into decision rules

If   Attribute1 = A and Attribute2 > 70
        Then   Classification = CLASS2   (3.4 / 0.4);
If   Attribute1 = B
        Then   Classification = CLASS1   (3.2 / 0);
If   Attribute1 = C and Attribute3 = True
        Then   Classification = CLASS2   (2.4 / 0);
If   Attribute1 = C and Attribute3 = False
        Then   Classification = CLASS1   (3.0 / 0).

Rewriting the tree to a collection of rules, one for each leaf in the tree, would not result in a simplified model. The number of decision rules in the classification model can be extremely large and pruning of rules can improve readability of the model. In some cases, the antecedents of individual rules may contain irrelevant conditions. The rules can be generalized by deleting these superfluous conditions without affecting rule-set accuracy. What are criteria for deletion of rule conditions? Let rule R be

If A Then Class-C

and a more general rule R′ could be

If A′ then Class-C

where A′ is obtained by deleting one condition X from A $(A = A' \cup X)$. The evidence for the importance of condition X must be found in the training samples. Each sample in the database that satisfies the condition A′ either satisfies or does not satisfy the extended conditions A. Also, each of these cases does or does not belong to the designated Class-C. The results can be organized into a contingency 2×2 table:

	Class-C	Other classes
Satisfies condition X	Y_1	E_1
Does not satisfy condition X	Y_2	E_2

There are $Y_1 + E_1$ cases that are covered by the original rule R, where R misclassifies E_1 of them since they belong to classes other than C. Similarly, $Y_1 + Y_2 + E_1 + E_2$ is the total number of cases covered by rule R′, and $E_1 + E_2$ are errors. The criteria for the elimination of condition X from the rule is based on a pessimistic estimate of the accuracy of rules R and R′. The estimate of the error rate of rule R can be set to $U_{cf}(Y_1 + E_1, E_1)$, and for that of rule R′ to $U_{cf}(Y_1 + Y_2 + E_1 + E_2, E_1 + E_2)$. If the pessimistic error rate of rule R′ is no greater than that of the original rule R, then it makes sense to delete condition X. Of course, more than one condition may have to be deleted when a rule is generalized. Rather than looking at all possible subsets of conditions that could be deleted, the C4.5 system performs greedy elimination: at each step, a condition with the lowest pessimistic error is eliminated. As with all greedy searches, there is no guarantee that minimization in every step will lead to a global minimum.

If, for example, the contingency table for a given rule R is given in Table 7.3, then the corresponding error rates are

1. For initially given rule R:

$$U_{cf}(Y_1 + E_1, E_1) = U_{cf}(9, 1) = 0.183$$

2. For a general rule R′ without condition X:

$$U_{cf}(Y_1 + Y_2 + E_1 + E_2, E_1 + E_2) = U_{cf}(16, 1) = 0.157$$

Because the estimated error rate of the rule R′ is lower than the estimated error rate for the initial rule R, a rule set pruning could be done by simplifying the decision rule R and replacing it with R′.

One complication caused by a rule's generalization is that the rules are no more mutually exclusive and exhaustive. There will be the cases that satisfy the conditions of more than one rule, or of no rules. The conflict resolution schema adopted in C4.5 (detailed explanations have not been given in this book) selects one rule when there is "multiple-rule satisfaction". When no other rule covers a sample, the solution is a *default rule* or a *default class*. One reasonable choice for the default class would be the class that appears most frequently in the training set. C.4.5 uses a modified strategy and simply chooses as the default class the one that contains the most training samples not covered by any rule.

The other possibility of reducing the complexity of decision rules and decision trees is a process of grouping attribute values for categorical data. A large number of values causes a large space of data. There is concern that useful patterns may not be detectable because of the insufficiency of training data, or that patterns will be detected but the model will be extremely complex. To reduce the number of attribute values it is necessary to define appropriate groups. The number of possible

TABLE 7.3   Contingency table for the rule R

	Class-C	Other classes
Satisfies condition X	8	1
Does not satisfy condition X	7	0

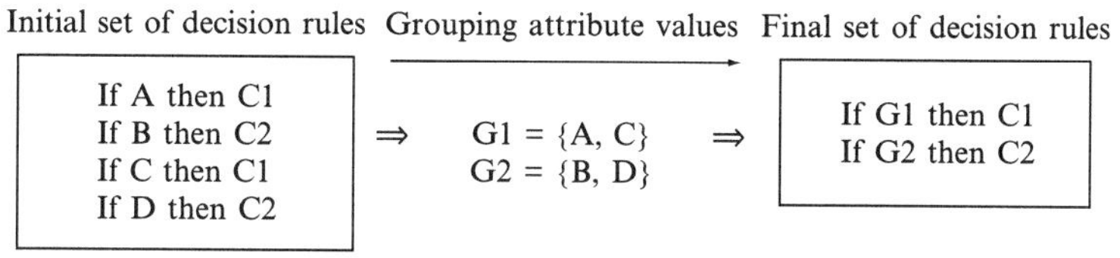

Initial set of decision rules   Grouping attribute values   Final set of decision rules

If A then C1 If B then C2 If C then C1 If D then C2	$\Rightarrow$ G1 = {A, C} G2 = {B, D} $\Rightarrow$	If G1 then C1 If G2 then C2

FIGURE 7.11   Grouping attribute values can reduce decision-rules set

splitting is large: for n values, there exist $2^{n-1} - 1$ nontrivial binary partitions. Even if the values are ordered, there are $n - 1$ "cut values" for binary splitting. A simple example, which shows the advantages of grouping categorical values in decision-rules reduction, is given in Figure 7.11.

C4.5 increases the number of grouping combinations because it does not include only binary categorical data, but also n-ary partitions. The process is iterative, starting with an initial distribution where every value represents a separate group, and then, for each new iteration, analyzing the possibility of merging the two previous groups into one. Merging is accepted if the information gain ratio (explained earlier) is nondecreasing. A final result may be two or more groups that will simplify the classification model based on decision trees and decision rules.

7.6 LIMITATIONS OF DECISION TREES AND DECISION RULES

Decision rule- and decision tree-based models are relatively simple, readable, and their generation is very fast. Unlike many statistical approaches, a logical approach does not depend on assumptions about distribution of attribute values or independence of attributes. Also, this method tends to be more robust across tasks than most other statistical methods. But there are also some disadvantages and limitations of a logical approach, and a data-mining analyst has to be aware of it because the selection of an appropriate methodology is a key step to the success of a data-mining process.

If data samples are represented graphically in an N-dimensional space, where N is the number of attributes, then a logical classifier (decision trees or decision rules) divides the space into regions. Each region is labeled with a corresponding class. An unseen testing sample is then classified by determining the region into which the given point falls. Decision trees are constructed by successive refinement, splitting existing regions into smaller ones that contain highly concentrated points of one class. The number of training cases needed to construct a good classifier is proportional to the number of regions. More complex classifications require more regions that are described with more rules and a tree with higher complexity. All that will require an additional number of training samples to obtain a successful classification.

A graphical representation of decision rules is given by orthogonal hyperplanes in an N-dimensional space. The regions for classification are hyperrectangles in the same space. If the problem at hand is such that the classification hyperplanes are not orthogonal, but are defined through a linear (or nonlinear) combination of attributes, such as the example in Figure 7.12, then that increases the complexity of

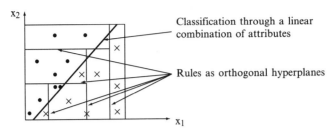

FIGURE 7.12 Approximation of nonorthogonal classification with hyperrectangles

a rule-based model. A logical approach based on decision rules tries to approximate nonorthogonal, and sometimes, nonlinear classification with hyperrectangles; classification becomes extremely complex with large number of rules and a still larger error.

A possible solution to this problem is an additional iteration of the data-mining process: returning to the beginning of preprocessing phases, it is necessary to transform input features into new dimensions that are linear (or nonlinear) combinations of initial inputs. This transformation is based on some domain heuristics and requires emphasis on and effort in the data-preparation process; the reward is a simpler classification model with a lower error rate.

The other type of classification problems, where decision rules are not the appropriate tool for modeling, have classification criteria in the form: *A given class is supported if n out of m conditions are present.* To represent this classifier with rules, it would be necessary to define $\binom{m}{n}$ regions only for one class. Medical diagnostic decisions are a typical example of this kind of classification. If four out of eleven symptoms support diagnosis of a given disease, then the corresponding classifier will generate 330 regions in an 11-dimensional space for positive diagnosis only. That corresponds to 330 decision rules. Therefore, a data-mining analyst has to be very careful in applying the orthogonal-classification methodology of decision rules for this type of nonlinear problems.

Finally, introducing new attributes rather than removing old ones can avoid the sometimes-intensive fragmentation of the n-dimensional space by additional rules. Let us analyze a simple example. A classification problem is described by nine binary inputs $\{A_1, A_2, \ldots, A_9\}$, and the output class C is specified by the logical relation

$$(A_1 \lor A_2 \lor A_3) \land (A_4 \lor A_5 \lor A_6) \land (A_7 \lor A_8 \lor A_9) \to C$$

The above expression can be rewritten in a conjunctive form:

$$((A_1 \land A_4 \land A_7) \lor (A_1 \land A_5 \land A_7) \lor \ldots) \to C$$

and it will have 27 factors with only $\land$ operations. Every one of these factors is a region in a 9-dimensional space and corresponds to one rule. Taking into account regions for negative examples, there exist about fifty leaves in the decision tree (and the same number of rules) describing class C. If new attributes are introduced:

$$B_1 = A_1 \vee A_2 \vee A_3,$$
$$B_2 = A_4 \vee A_5 \vee A_6, \text{ and}$$
$$B_3 = A_7 \vee A_8 \vee A_9$$

the description of class C will be simplified into the logical rule

$$B_1 \wedge B_2 \wedge B_3 \rightarrow C$$

It is possible to specify the correct classification using a decision tree with only four leaves. In a new 3-dimensional space (B_1, B_2, B_3) there will be only four decision regions. This kind of simplification via constructive induction (development of new attributes in the preprocessing phase) can be applied also in a case n-of-m attributes' decision. If none of previous transformations are found appropriate, the only way to deal with the increased fragmentation of an n-dimensional space is to bring more data to bear on the problem.

7.7 ASSOCIATIVE-CLASSIFICATION METHOD

CMAR (Classification based on Multiple Association Rules) is a classification method adopted from the frequent pattern or FP-growth method for generation of frequent itemsets. Although the basic principles of CMAR are explained in this section, for a better understanding of all details we suggest that a reader start with Section 8.6 as an introduction. The main reason we included CMAR methodology in this chapter is its logic-based approach to classification problems, and the possibility of comparing its accuracy and efficiency with the C4.5 methodology.

Suppose data samples are given with n attributes $(A_1, A_2, \ldots, A_n)$. Attributes can be categorical or continuous. For a continuous attribute, we assume that its values are discretized into intervals in the preprocessing phase. A training data set T is a set of samples such that for each sample there exists a class label associated with it. Let $C = \{c_1, c_2, \ldots, c_m\}$ be a finite set of *class labels*.

In general, a pattern $P = \{a_1, a_2, \ldots, a_k\}$ is a set of attribute values for different attributes $(1 \leq k \leq n)$. A sample is said to match the pattern P if it has all the attribute values given in the pattern. For rule R: $P \rightarrow c$, the number of data samples matching pattern P and having class label c is called the *support* of rule R, denoted *sup(R)*. The ratio of the number of samples matching pattern P and having class label c versus the total number of samples matching pattern P is called the *confidence* of R, denoted as *conf(R)*. The association-classification method (CMAR) consists of two phases:

1. Rule generation or training and
2. Classification or testing.

In the first rule generation phase, CMAR computes the complete set of rules in the form R: $P \rightarrow c$, such that sup(R) and conf(R) pass the given thresholds. For a given support threshold and confidence threshold, the associative-classification method finds the complete set of class-association rules (CAR) passing the thresholds. In a

TABLE 7.4   Training database T for the CMAR algorithm

ID	A	B	C	D	Class
01	a_1	b_1	c_1	d_1	A
02	a_1	b_2	c_1	d_2	B
03	a_2	b_3	c_2	d_3	A
04	a_1	b_2	c_3	d_3	C
05	a_1	b_2	c_1	d_3	C

testing phase, when a new (unclassified) sample comes, the classifier, represented by a set of association rules, selects the rule which matches the sample and has the highest confidence, and uses it to predict the classification of the new sample.

We will illustrate the basic steps of the algorithm through one simple example. Suppose that for a given training data set T, as shown in Table 7.4, the support threshold is 2 and the confidence threshold is 70%.

First, CMAR scans the training data set and finds the set of attribute values occurring beyond the threshold support (at least twice in our database). One simple approach is to sort each attribute and to find all frequent values. For our database T, this is a set $F = \{a_1, b_2, c_1, d_3\}$ and it is called a frequent item set. All other attribute values fail the support threshold. Then, CMAR sorts attribute values in F, in support-descending order, i.e., F-list = $\{a_1, b_2, c_1, d_3\}$.

Now, CMAR scans the training data set again to construct an FP-tree. The FP-tree is a prefix tree with respect to the F-list. For each sample in a training data set, attributes values appearing in the F-list are extracted from the sample and sorted according to F-list. For example, for the first sample in database T, (a_1, c_1) are extracted and inserted in the tree as the left-most branch in the tree. The class label of the sample and the corresponding counter are attached to the last node in the path.

Samples in the training data set share prefixes. For example, the second sample carries attribute values (a_1, b_2, c_1) in the F-list and shares a common prefix a_1 with the first sample. An additional branch from the node a_1 will be inserted in the tree with new nodes b_2 and c_1. A new class label B with the count equal to 1 is also inserted at the end of the new path. The final FP-tree for the database T is given in Figure 7.13a.

After analyzing all the samples and constructing an FP-tree, the set of class-association rules can be generated dividing all rules into subsets without overlap. In our example it will be four subsets: a) the rules having d_3 value; b) the rules having c_1 but no d_3; c) the rules having b_2 but neither d_3 nor c_1; and d) the rules having only a_1. CMAR find these subsets one by one.

To find the subset of rules having d_3, CMAR traverses nodes having the attribute value d_3 and looks "upward" the FP-tree to collect d_3-projected samples. In our example, there are three samples represented in the FP-tree, and they are (a_1, b_2, c_1, d_3):C, (a_1, b_2, d_3):C, and (d_3):A. The problem of finding all frequent patterns in the training set can be reduced to mining frequent patterns in the d_3-projected database. In our example, in the d_3-projected database, since the pattern (a_1, b_2, d_3) occurs twice its support is equal to the required threshold value 2. Also, the rule based on this frequent pattern, $(a_1, b_2, d_3) \rightarrow$ C has a confidence 100%

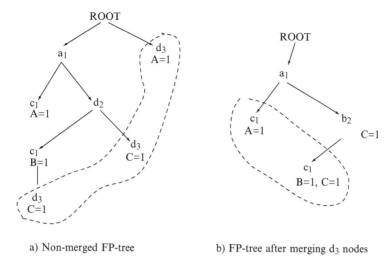

a) Non-merged FP-tree   b) FP-tree after merging d_3 nodes

FIGURE 7.13   FP-tree for the database in Table 7.4

(above the threshold value), and that is the only rule generated in the given projection of the database.

After a search for rules having d_3 value, all the nodes of d_3 and their corresponding class labels are merged into their parent nodes of the FP-tree. The FP-tree is shrunk as shown in Figure 7.13b. The remaining set of rules can be mined similarly repeating the previous procedures for a c_1-projected database, then for the b_2-projected database, and finally for the a_1-projected database. In this analysis, (a_1, c_1) is a frequent pattern with support 3, but all rules are with confidence less than threshold value. The same conclusions can be drawn for pattern (a_1, b_2) and for (a_1). Therefore, the only association rule generated through the training process with the database T is $(a_1, b_2, d_3) \rightarrow C$ with support equal to 2 and 100% confidence.

When a set of rules is selected for classification, CMAR is ready to classify new samples. For the new sample, CMAR collects the subset of rules matching the sample from the total set of rules. Trivially, if all the rules have the same class, CMAR simply assigns that label to the new sample. If the rules are not consistent in the class label, CMAR divides the rules into groups according to the class label and yields the label of the "strongest" group. To compare the strength of groups, it is necessary to measure the "combined effect" of each group. Intuitively, if the rules in a group are highly positively correlated and have good support, the group should have a strong effect. CMAR uses the strongest rule in the group as its representative, i.e., the rule with highest χ^2 test value (adopted for this algorithm for a simplified computation). Preliminary experiments have shown that CMAR outperforms the C4.5 algorithm in terms of average accuracy, efficiency, and scalability.

7.8 REVIEW QUESTIONS AND PROBLEMS

1. Explain the differences between the statistical and logical approaches in the construction of a classification model.

2. What are the new features of the C4.5 algorithm compared to the original Quinlan's ID3 algorithm for decision-tree generation?

3. Given a data set X with 3-dimesional categorical samples:

X:	Attribute1	Attribute2	Class
T	1	C_2
T	2	C_1
F	1	C_2
F	2	C_2

Construct a decision tree using the computation steps given in the C4.5 algorithm.

4. Given a training data set Y:

Y	A	B	C	Class
	15	1	A	C_1
	20	3	B	C_2
	25	2	A	C_1
	30	4	A	C_1
	35	2	B	C_2
	25	4	A	C_1
	15	2	B	C_2
	20	3	B	C_2

a) Find the best threshold (for the maximal gain) for attribute A.
b) Find the best threshold (for the maximal gain) for attribute B.
c) Find a decision tree for data set Y.
d) If the testing set is

A	B	C	Class
10	2	A	C_2
20	1	B	C_1
30	3	A	C_2
40	2	B	C_2
15	1	B	C_1

what is the percentage of correct classifications using the decision tree developed in c).
e) Derive decision rules from the decision tree.

5. Use the C4.5 algorithm to build a decision tree for classifying the following objects:

Class	Size	Color	Shape
A	small	yellow	round
A	big	yellow	round
A	big	red	round
A	small	red	round
B	small	black	round
B	big	black	cube
B	big	yellow	cube
B	big	black	round
B	small	yellow	cube

6. Given a training data set Y* with missing values:

Y*:	A	B	C	Class
	15	1	A	C_1
	20	3	B	C_2
	25	2	A	C_1
	–	4	A	C_1
	35	2	–	C_2
	25	4	A	C_1
	15	2	B	C_2
	20	3	B	C_2

a) Apply a modified C4.5 algorithm to construct a decision tree with the (T_i/E) parameters explained in Section 7.3.

b) Analyze the possibility of pruning the decision tree obtained in a).

c) Generate decision rules for the solution in a). Is it necessary to generate a default rule for this rule-based model?

7. Why is postpruning in C4.5 defined as pessimistic pruning?

8. Suppose that two decision rules are generated with C4.5:

$$\text{Rule1: } (X > 3) \wedge (Y \geq 2) \rightarrow \text{Class1}(9.6/0.4)$$

$$\text{Rule2: } (X > 3) \wedge (Y < 2) \rightarrow \text{Class2}(2.4/2.0).$$

Analyze if it is possible to generalize these rules into one using confidence limit $U_{25\%}$ for the binomial distribution.

9. Discuss the complexity of the algorithm for optimal splitting of numeric attributes into more than two intervals.

10. In real-world data-mining applications, a final model consists of extremely large number of decision rules. Discuss the potential actions and analyses you should perform to reduce the complexity of the model.

11. Search the Web to find the basic characteristics of publicly available or commercial software tools for generating decision rules and decision trees. Document the results of your search.

7.9 REFERENCES FOR FURTHER STUDY

1. Dzeroski S. and N. Lavrac, eds., *Relational Data Mining*, Springer-Verlag, Berlin: Germany, 2001.

   Relational data mining has its roots in inductive logic programming, an area in the intersection of machine learning and programming languages. The book provides a thorough overview of different techniques and strategies used in knowledge discovery from multirelational data. The chapters describe a broad selection of practical, inductive-logic programming approaches to relational data mining, and give a good overview of several interesting applications.

2. Mitchell, T., *Machine Learning*, McGraw Hill, New York: NY, 1997.

   This is one of the most comprehensive books on machine learning. Systematic explanations of all methods and a large number of examples for all topics are the main strengths of the book. Inductive machine-learning techniques are only a part of the book, but for a deeper understanding of current data-mining technology and newly developed techniques, it is very useful to get a global overview of all approaches in machine learning.

3. Quinlan, J. R., *C4.5: Programs for Machine Learning*, Morgan Kaufmann, San Mateo: CA, 1992.

   The book outlines the C4.5 algorithm step by step, with detailed explanations and many illustrative examples. The second part of the book is taken up by the source listing of the C program that makes up the C4.5 system. The explanations in the book are intended to give a broad-brush view of C4.5 inductive learning with many small heuristics, leaving the detailed discussion to the code itself.

4. Russell, S. and P. Norvig, *Artificial Intelligence: A Modern Approach*, Prentice Hall, Upper Saddle River: NJ, 1995.

   The book gives a unified presentation of the artificial intelligence field using an agent-based approach. Equal emphasis is given to theory and practice. An understanding of the basic concepts in AI, including an approach to inductive machine learning, is obtained through layered explanations and agent-based implementations of algorithms.

8 Association Rules

CHAPTER OBJECTIVES

- Explain the local modeling character of association-rule techniques.
- Analyze the basic characteristics of large transactional databases.
- Describe the Apriori algorithm and explain all its phases through illustrative examples.
- Compare the frequent pattern–growth method with the Apriori algorithm.
- Outline the solution for association-rule generation from frequent itemsets.
- Illustrate the possibilities of Web mining using HITS, LOGSOM, and Path Traversal algorithms.
- Formalize a text-mining framework specifying the refining and distillation phases.

Association rules are one of the major techniques of data mining and it is perhaps the most common form of local-pattern discovery in unsupervised learning systems. It is a form of data mining that most closely resembles the process that most people think about when they try to understand the data-mining process; namely, "mining" for gold through a vast database. The gold in this case would be a rule that is interesting, that tells you something about your database that you didn't already know and probably weren't able to explicitly articulate. These methodologies retrieve all possible interesting patterns in the database. This is a strength in the sense that it leaves no stone unturned, but it can be viewed also as a weakness because the user can easily become overwhelmed with a large amount of new information, and an analysis of their usability is difficult and time-consuming.

Besides the standard methodologies such as the *Apriori* technique for association-rule mining, we will explain some data-mining methods related to web mining and text mining in this chapter. The reason we have included these techniques in this chapter is their local-modeling nature and, therefore, their fundamental similarity with the association-rules approach, although the techniques are different.

8.1 MARKET-BASKET ANALYSIS

A market basket is a collection of items purchased by a customer in a single transaction, which is a well-defined business activity. For example, a customer's visits to a grocery store or an online purchase from a virtual store on the Web are typical customer transactions. Retailers accumulate huge collections of transactions by recording business activities over time. One common analysis run against a transactions database is to find sets of items, or *itemsets*, that appear together in many transactions. A business can use knowledge of these patterns to improve the placement of these items in the store or the layout of mail-order catalog pages and Web pages. An itemset containing i items is called an *i-itemset*. The percentage of transactions that contain an itemset is called the itemset's *support*. For an itemset to be interesting, its support must be higher than a user-specified minimum. Such itemsets are said to be frequent.

Why is finding frequent itemsets a nontrivial problem? First, the number of customer transactions can be very large and usually will not fit in the memory of a computer. Second, the potential number of frequent itemsets is exponential to the number of different items, although the actual number of frequent itemsets can be much smaller. Therefore, we want algorithms that are scalable (their complexity should increase linearly, not exponentially, with the number of transactions) and that examine as few infrequent itemsets as possible. Before we explain some of the more efficient algorithms, let us try to describe the problem more formally and develop its mathematical model.

From a database of sales transactions, we want to discover the important associations among items such that the presence of some items in a transaction will imply the presence of other items in the same transactions. Let $I = \{i_1, i_2, \ldots, i_m\}$ be a set of literals, called items. Let DB be a set of transactions, where each transaction T is a set of items such that $T \subseteq I$. Note that the quantities of the items bought in a transaction are not considered, meaning that each item is a binary variable indicating whether an item was bought or not. Each transaction is associated with an identifier called a transaction identifier or TID. An example of the model for such a transaction database is given in Table 8.1.

Let X be a set of items. A transaction T is said to contain X if and only if $X \subseteq T$. An association rule implies the form $X \Rightarrow Y$, where $X \subseteq I$, $Y \subseteq I$, and $X \cap Y = \phi$. The rule $X \Rightarrow Y$ holds in the transaction set DB with *confidence c* if $c \%$ of the transactions in D that contain X also contain Y. The rule $X \Rightarrow Y$ has *support s* in the transaction set D if $s \%$ of the transactions in DB contain $X \cup Y$. Confidence denotes the strength of implication and support indicates the frequency of the patterns occurring in the rule. It is often desirable to pay attention to only those rules that may have a reasonably large support. Such rules with high confidence and strong support are referred to as *strong rules*. The task of mining association rules is essentially to discover strong association rules in large databases. The problem of mining association rules may be decomposed into two phases:

1. Discover the large itemsets, i.e., the sets of items that have transaction support s above a predetermined minimum threshold.

TABLE 8.1   A model of a simple transaction database

Database DB:

TID	Items
001	A C D
002	B C E
003	A B C E
004	B E

2. Use the large itemsets to generate the association rules for the database that have confidence c above a predetermined minimum threshold.

The overall performance of mining association rules is determined primarily by the first step. After the large itemsets are identified, the corresponding association rules can be derived in a straightforward manner. Efficient counting of large itemsets is thus the focus of most mining algorithms, and many efficient solutions have been designed to address previous criteria. The *Apriori* algorithm provided one early solution to the problem, and it will be explained in greater detail in this chapter. Other subsequent algorithms built upon the *Apriori* algorithm represent refinements of a basic solution and they are explained in a wide spectrum of articles including texts recommended in Section 8.12.

8.2 ALGORITHM *APRIORI*

The algorithm *Apriori* computes the frequent itemsets in the database through several iterations. Iteration i computes all frequent i-itemsets (itemsets with i elements). Each iteration has two steps: *candidate generation* and *candidate counting and selection*.

In the first phase of the first iteration, the generated set of candidate itemsets contains all 1-itemsets (i.e., all items in the database). In the counting phase, the algorithm counts their support searching again through the whole database. Finally, only 1-itemsets (items) with s above required threshold will be selected as frequent. Thus, after the first iteration, all frequent 1-itemsets will be known.

What are the itemsets generated in the second iteration? In other words, how does one generate 2-itemset candidates? Basically, all pairs of items are candidates. Based on knowledge about infrequent itemsets obtained from previous iterations, the *Apriori* algorithm reduces the set of candidate itemsets by pruning—a priori—those candidate itemsets that cannot be frequent. The pruning is based on the observation that if an itemset is frequent all its subsets could be frequent as well. Therefore, before entering the candidate-counting step, the algorithm discards every candidate itemset that has an infrequent subset.

Consider the database in Table 8.1. Assume that the minimum support s = 50%; so an itemset is frequent if it is contained in at least 50% of the transactions—in our example, in two out of every four transactions in the database. In each iteration, the *Apriori* algorithm constructs a candidate set of large itemsets, counts the number of occurrences of each candidate, and then determines large itemsets based on the predetermined minimum support s = 50%.

In the first step of the first iteration, all single items are candidates. *Apriori* simply scans all the transactions in a database DB and generates a list of candidates. In the next step, the algorithm counts the occurrences of each candidate and based on threshold s selects frequent itemsets. All these steps are given in Figure 8.1. Five 1-itemsets are generated in C_1 and, of these, only four are selected as large in L_1 because their support is greater than or equal to two, or s $\geq$ 50%.

To discover the set of large 2-itemsets, because any subset of a large itemset could also have minimum support, the *Apriori* algorithm uses $L_1 * L_1$ to generate the candidates. The operation * is defined in general as

$$L_k * L_k = \{X \cup Y \text{ where } X, Y \in L_k, |X \cap Y| = k - 1\}$$

For $k = 1$ the operation represents a simple concatenation. Therefore, C_2 consists of 2-itemsets generated by the operation $|L_1| \cdot (|L_1| - 1)/2$ as candidates in the second iteration. In our example, this number is $4 \cdot 3/2 = 6$. Scanning the database DB with this list, the algorithm counts the support for every candidate and in the end selects a large 2-itemsets L_2 for which $s \geq 50\%$. All these steps and the corresponding results of the second iteration are given in Figure 8.2.

The set of candidate itemsets C_3 is generated from L_2 using the previously defined operation $L_2 * L_2$. Practically, from L_2, two large 2-itemsets with the same first item, such as $\{B, C\}$ and $\{B, E\}$, are identified first. Then, *Apriori* tests whether the 2-itemset $\{C, E\}$, which consists of the second items in the sets $\{B, C\}$ and $\{B, E\}$, constitutes a large 2-itemset or not. Because $\{C, E\}$ is a large itemset by itself, we know that all the subsets of $\{B, C, E\}$ are large, and then $\{B, C, E\}$ becomes a candidate 3-itemset. There is no other candidate 3-itemset from L_2 in our database DB. *Apriori* then scans all the transactions and discovers the large 3-itemsets L_3, as shown in Figure 8.3.

In our example, because there is no candidate 4-itemset to be constituted from L_3, *Apriori* ends the iterative process.

Apriori counts not only the support of all frequent itemsets, but also the support of those infrequent candidate itemsets that could not be eliminated during the pruning phase. The set of all candidate itemsets that are infrequent but whose support is counted by *Apriori* is called the *negative border*. Thus, an itemset is in

1-itemsets C_1
{A}
{C}
{D}
{B}
{E}

1-itemsets	Count	s[%]
{A}	2	50
{C}	3	75
{D}	1	25
{B}	3	75
{E}	3	75

Large 1-itemsets L_1	Count	s[%]
{A}	2	50
{C}	3	75
{B}	3	75
{E}	3	75

a) Generate phase   b1) Count phase   b2) Select phase

FIGURE 8.1   First iteration of the *Apriori* algorithm for a database DB

2-itemsets C_2
{A, B}
{A, C}
{A, E}
{B, C}
{B, E}
{C, E}

2-itemsets	Count	s[%]
{A, B}	1	25
{A, C}	2	50
{A, E}	1	25
{B, C}	2	50
{B, E}	3	75
{C, E}	2	50

Large 2-itemsets L_2	Count	s[%]
{A, C}	2	50
{B, C}	2	50
{B, E}	3	75
{C, E}	2	50

a) Generate phase   b1) Count phase   b2) Select phase

FIGURE 8.2   Second iteration of the *Apriori* algorithm for a database DB

3-itemsets C_3
{B, C, E}

3-itemsets	Count	s[%]
{B, C, E}	2	50

Large 3-itemsets L_3	Count	s[%]
{B, C, E}	2	50

a) Generate phase   b1) Count phase   b2) Select phase

FIGURE 8.3   Third iteration of the *Apriori* algorithm for a database DB

the negative border if it is infrequent, but all its subsets are frequent. In our example, analyzing Figures 8.1 and 8.2, we can see that the negative border consists of itemsets {D}, {A, B}, and {A, E}. The negative border is especially important for some improvements in the *Apriori* algorithm, such as increased efficiency in generation of large itemsets or derivation of negative association rules.

8.3   FROM FREQUENT ITEMSETS TO ASSOCIATION RULES

The second phase in discovering association rules based on all frequent i-itemsets, which have been found in the first phase using the *Apriori* or some other similar algorithm, is relatively simple and straightforward. For a rule that implies $\{x_1, x_2, x_3\} \rightarrow x_4$, it is necessary that both itemset $\{x_1, x_2, x_3, x_4\}$ and $\{x_1, x_2, x_3\}$ are frequent. Then, the confidence c of the rule is computed as the quotient of supports for the itemsets $c = s(x_1, x_2, x_3, x_4)/s(x_1, x_2, x_3)$. Strong association rules are rules with a confidence value c above a given threshold.

For our example of database DB in Table 8.1, if we want to check whether the association rule {B, C} → E is a strong rule, first we select the corresponding supports from tables L_2 and L_3:

$$s(B, C) = 2, s(B, C, E) = 2$$

and using these supports we compute the confidence of the rule:

$$c(\{B, C\} \rightarrow E) = s(B, C, E)/s(B, C) = 2/2 = 1 \text{ (or 100\%)}$$

Whatever the selected threshold for strong association rules (for example, $c_T = 0.8$ or 80%), this rule will pass because its confidence is maximal, i.e., if a transaction contains items B and C, it will also contain item E. Other rules are also possible for our database DB, such as A → C because $c(A \rightarrow C) = s(A, C)/s(A) = 1$, and both itemsets {A} and {A, C} are frequent based on the *Apriori* algorithm. Therefore, in this phase, it is necessary only to systematically analyze all possible association rules that could be generated from the frequent itemsets, and select as strong association rules those that have a confidence value above a given threshold.

Notice that not all the discovered strong association rules (i.e., passing the required support s and required confidence c) are interesting enough to be presented and used. For example, consider the following case of mining the survey-results in a school of 5,000 students. A retailer of breakfast cereal surveys the activities that the students engage in every morning. The data show that 60% of the students (i.e., 3,000 students) play basketball, 75% of the students (i.e., 3,750 students) eat cereal, and 40% of them (i.e., 2,000 students) play basketball and also eat cereal. Suppose that a data-mining program for discovering association rules is run on the following settings: the minimal support is 2,000 (s=0.4) and the minimal confidence is 60% (c=0.6). The following association rule will be produced: "(play basketball) → (eat cereal)", since this rule contains the minimal student support and the corresponding confidence c = 2000/3000 = 0.66 is larger than the threshold value. However, the above association rule is misleading since the overall percentage of students eating cereal is 75%, larger then 66%. That is, playing basketball and eating cereal are in fact negatively associated. Being involved in one itemset decreases the likelihood of being involved in the other. Without fully understanding this aspect, one could make wrong business or scientific decisions from the association rules derived.

To filter out such misleading associations, one may define that an association rule A → B is *interesting* if its confidence exceeds a certain measure. The simple argument we used in the example above suggests that the right heuristic to measure association should be

$$s(A, B)/s(A) - s(B) > d$$

or alternatively:

$$s(A, B) - s(A) \cdot s(B) > k$$

where d or k are suitable constants. The expressions above essentially represent tests of statistical independence. Clearly, the factor of statistical dependence among analyzed itemsets has to be taken into consideration to determine the usefulness of association rules. In our simple example with students this test fails for the discovered association rule

$$s(A, B) - s(A) \cdot s(B) = 0.4 - 0.6 \cdot 0.75 = -0.05 < 0$$

and, therefore, despite high values for parameters s and c, the rule is not interesting. In this case, it is even misleading.

8.4   IMPROVING THE EFFICIENCY OF THE *APRIORI* ALGORITHM

Since the amount of the processed data in mining frequent itemsets tends to be huge, it is important to devise efficient algorithms to mine such data. Our basic *Apriori* algorithm scans the database several times, depending on the size of the largest frequent itemset. Several refinements have been proposed that focus on reducing the number of database scans, the number of candidate itemsets counted in each scan, or both.

Partition-based Apriori is an algorithm that requires only two scans of the transaction database. The database is divided into disjoint partitions, each small enough to fit into available memory. In a first scan, the algorithm reads each partition and computes locally frequent itemsets on each partition. In the second scan, the algorithm counts the support of all locally frequent itemsets toward the complete database. If an itemset is frequent with respect to the complete database, it must be frequent in at least one partition. That is the heuristics used in the algorithm. Therefore, the second scan through the database counts a superset of all potentially frequent itemsets.

In some applications, the transaction database has to be mined frequently to capture customer behavior. In such applications, the efficiency of data mining could be a more important factor than the complete accuracy of the results. In addition, in some applications the problem domain may be vaguely defined. Missing some marginal cases that have confidence and support levels at the borderline may have little effect on the quality of the solution to the original problem. Allowing imprecise results can in fact significantly improve the efficiency of the applied mining algorithm.

As the database size increases, *sampling* appears to be an attractive approach to data mining. A sampling-based algorithm typically requires two scans of the database. The algorithm first takes a sample from the database and generates a set of candidate itemsets that are highly likely to be frequent in the complete database. In a subsequent scan over the database, the algorithm counts these itemsets' exact support and the support of their negative border. If no itemset in the negative border is frequent, then the algorithm has discovered all frequent itemsets. Otherwise, some superset of an itemset in the negative border could be frequent, but its support has not yet been counted. The sampling algorithm generates and counts all such potentially frequent itemsets in subsequent database scans.

Because it is costly to find frequent itemsets in large databases, *incremental updating* techniques should be developed to maintain the discovered frequent itemsets (and corresponding association rules) so as to avoid mining the whole updated database again. Updates on the database may not only invalidate some existing frequent itemsets but also turn some new itemsets into frequent ones. Therefore, the problem of maintaining previously discovered frequent itemsets in large and dynamic databases is nontrivial. The idea is to reuse the information of the old frequent itemsets and to integrate the support information of the new frequent itemsets in order to substantially reduce the pool of candidates to be re-examined.

In many applications, interesting associations among data items often occur at a relatively high *concept level*. For example, one possible hierarchy of food components is presented in Figure 8.4, where M (milk) and B (bread), as concepts in the hierarchy, may have several elementary subconcepts. The lowest level elements in the hierarchy $(M_1, M_2, \ldots, B_1, B_2, \ldots)$ are types of milk and bread defined

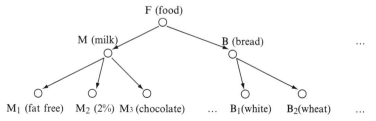

FIGURE 8.4   An example of concept hierarchy for mining multiple-level frequent itemsets

with its bar-code in the store. The purchase patterns in a transaction database may not show any substantial regularities at the elementary data level, such as at the bar-code level (M_1, M_2, M_3, B_1, B_2, ...), but may show some interesting regularities at some high concept level(s), such as milk M and bread B.

Consider the class hierarchy in Figure 8.4. It could be difficult to find high support for purchase patterns at the primitive-concept level, such as chocolate milk and wheat bread. However, it would be easy to find in many databases that more than 80% of customers who purchase milk may also purchase bread. Therefore, it is important to mine frequent itemsets at a generalized abstraction level or at multiple-concept levels; these requirements are supported by the *Apriori* generalized-data structure.

One extension of the *Apriori* algorithm considers an *is-a* hierarchy on database items, where information about multiple abstraction levels already exist in the database organization. An is-a hierarchy defines which items are a specialization or generalization of other items. The extended problem is to compute frequent itemsets that include items from different hierarchy levels. The presence of a hierarchy modifies the notation of when an item is contained in a transaction. In addition to the items listed explicitly, the transaction contains their ancestors in the taxonomy. This allows the detection of relationships involving higher hierarchy levels, since an itemset's support can increase if an item is replaced by one of its ancestors.

8.5   FREQUENT PATTERN–GROWTH METHOD (FP-GROWTH METHOD)

Let us define one of the most important problems with scalability of the *Apriori* algorithm. To generate one frequent pattern of length 100, such as $\{a_1, a_2, \ldots, a_{100}\}$, the number of candidates that has to be generated will be at least

$$\sum_{i=1}^{100} \binom{100}{i} = 2^{100} - 1 \approx 10^{30}$$

and it will require hundreds of database scans. The complexity of the computation increases exponentially! That is only one of the many factors that influence the development of several new algorithms for association-rule mining.

Frequent pattern growth (FP-growth) method is an efficient way of mining frequent itemsets in large databases. The algorithm mines frequent itemsets without the time-consuming candidate-generation process that is essential for *Apriori*. When the database is large, FP-growth first performs a database projection of the frequent items; it then switches to mining the main memory by constructing a compact data structure called the FP-tree. For an explanation of the algorithm, we will use the transactional database in Table 8.2 and the minimum support threshold of 3.

First, a scan of the database T derives a list L of frequent items occurring three or more than three times in the database. These are the items (with their supports):

$$L = \{(f, 4), (c, 4), (a, 3), (b, 3), (m, 3), (p, 3)\}.$$

The items are listed in descending order of frequency. This ordering is important since each path of the FP-tree will follow this order.

Second, the root of the tree, labeled ROOT, is created. The database T is scanned a second time. The scan of the first transaction leads to the construction of the first branch of the FP-tree: $\{(f,1), (c,1), (a,1), (m,1), (p,1)\}$. Only those items that are in the list of frequent items L are selected. The indexes for nodes in the branch (all are 1) represent the cumulative number of samples at this node in the tree, and of course, after the first sample, all are 1. The order of the nodes is not as in the sample but as in the list of frequent items L. For the second transaction, because it shares items f, c, and a it shares the prefix $\{f, c, a\}$ with the previous branch and extends to the new branch $\{(f, 2), (c, 2), (a, 2), (m, 1), (p, 1)\}$, increasing the indexes for the common prefix by one. The new intermediate version of the FP-tree, after two samples from the database, is given in Figure 8.5a. The remaining transactions can be inserted similarly, and the final FP-tree is given in Figure 8.5b.

To facilitate tree traversal, an *item header table* is built, in which each item in list L connects nodes in the FP-tree with its values through node-links. All f nodes are connected in one list, all c nodes in the other, etc. For simplicity of representation only the list for b nodes is given in Figure 8.5b. Using the compact-tree structure, The FP-growth algorithm mines the complete set of frequent itemsets.

According to the list L of frequent items, the complete set of frequent itemsets can be divided into subsets (6 for our example) without overlap: 1) frequent itemsets having item p (the end of list L); 2) the itemsets having item m but not p; 3) the

TABLE 8.2   The transactional database T

TID	Itemset
01	f, a, c, d, g, i, m, p
02	a, b, c, f, l, m, o
03	b, f, h, j, o
04	b, c, k, s, p
05	a, f, c, e, l, p, m, n

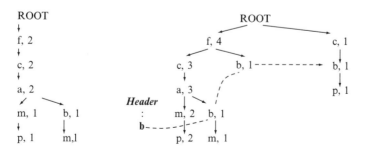

a) FP-tree after two samples   b) Final FP-tree

FIGURE 8.5   FP-tree for the database T in Table 8.2

frequent itemsets with b and without both m and p; ...; 6) the large itemsets only with f. This classification is valid for our example, but the same principles can be applied for other databases and other L lists.

Based on node-link connection, we collect all the transactions that p participates in by starting from the header table of p and following p's node-links. In our example, two paths will be selected in the FP-tree: {(f, 4), (c, 3), (a, 3), (m, 2), ((p, 2)} and {(c, 1), (b, 1), (p, 1)}, where samples with a frequent item p are {(f, 2), (c, 2), (a, 2), (m, 2), ((p, 2) and {(c, 1), (b, 1), (p, 1)}. The given threshold value (3) satisfies only the frequent itemsets *{(c, 3), (p, 3)}*, or the simplified *{c, p}*. All other itemsets with p are below the threshold value.

The next subset of frequent itemsets are those with m and without p. The FP-tree recognizes the paths {(f, 4), (c, 3), (a, 3), (m, 2)} and {(f, 4), (c, 3), (a, 3), (b, 1), (m, 1)}, or the corresponding accumulated samples {(f,2), (c,2), (a,2), (m,2)} and {(f, 1), (c, 1), (a, 1), (b, 1), (m, 1)}. Analyzing the samples we discover the frequent itemset *{(f, 3), (c, 3), (a, 3), (m, 3)}* or, simplified, *{f, c, a, m}*.

Repeating the same process for subsets 3 to 6 in our example, additional frequent itemsets could be mined. These are itemsets *{f, c, a}* and *{f, c}*, but they are already subsets of the frequent itemset *{f, c, a, m}*. Therefore, the final solution in the FP-growth method is the set of frequent itemsets, which is, in our example, *{{c, p}, {f, c, a, m}}*.

Experiments have shown that the FP-growth algorithm is faster than the *Apriori* algorithm by about one order of magnitude. Several optimization techniques are added to the FP-growth algorithm, and there exists other versions for mining sequences and patterns under constraints.

8.6   MULTIDIMENSIONAL ASSOCIATION–RULES MINING

A multidimensional transactional database DB has the schema

$$(ID, A_1, A_2, \ldots, A_n, items)$$

where ID is a unique identification of each transaction, A_i are structured attributes in the database, and items are sets of items connected with the given transaction. The information in each tuple t = (id, a_1, a_2, ..., a_n, items-t) can be partitioned into two: dimensional part (a_1, a_2, ..., a_n) and itemset part (items-t). It is common sense to divide the mining process into two steps: first mine patterns about dimensional information and then find frequent itemsets from the projected subdatabase, or vice versa. Without any preferences in the methodology we will illustrate the first approach using the multidimensional database DB in Table 8.3.

One can first find the frequent multidimensional-value combinations and then find the corresponding frequent itemsets of a database. Suppose that the threshold value for our database DB in Table 8.3 is set to 2. Then, the combination of attribute values that occurs two or more than two times is frequent, and it is called a multidimensional pattern or MD-pattern. For mining MD-patterns, a modified BUC algorithm developed originally by Beyer and Ramakrishnan (it is an efficient "iceberg cube" computing algorithm) can be used. The basic steps of the BUC algorithm are

TABLE 8.3   Multidimensional-transactional database DB

ID	A_1	A_2	A_3	*items*
01	a	1	m	x, y, z
02	b	2	n	z, w
03	a	2	m	x, z, w
04	c	3	p	x, w

First, sort all tuples in the database in alphabetical order of values in the first dimension (A_1). Because the values for the attribute A1 are categorical (characters), sorting is not numeric but alphabetic.

1. The only MD-pattern found for this dimension is (a, *, *) because only the value *a* occurs two times; the other values b and c occur only once and they are not part of the MD-patterns. Value * for the other two dimensions shows that they are not relevant in this first step, and they could have any combination of allowed values.

   Select tuples in a database with found MD-pattern (or patterns). In our database, these are the samples with ID values 01 and 03. Sort the reduced database again with respect to the second dimension (A_2), where the values are 1 and 2. Since no pattern occurs twice, there are no MD-patterns for exact A_1 and A_2 values. Therefore, one can ignore the second dimension A_2 (this dimension does not reduce the database further). All selected tuples are used in the next phase.

   Selected tuples in the database are sorted in alphabetic order of values for the third dimension (in our example A_3). A subgroup (a, *, m) is contained in two tuples and it is an MD-pattern. Since there are no more dimensions in our example, the search continues with the second step.

2. Repeat the processes in step 1; only start not with the first but with the second dimension (first dimension is not analyzed at all in this iteration). In the following iterations, reduce the search process further for one additional dimension at the beginning.

   In our example in the second iteration, starting with attribute A_2, MD-pattern (*, 2, *) will be found. Including dimension A_3, there are no additional MD-patterns. The third and last iteration in our example, starts with the A_3 dimension and the corresponding pattern is (*, *, m).

In summary, the modified BUC algorithm defines a set of MD-patterns with the corresponding projections of a database. The processing tree for our example of database DB is shown in Figure 8.6. Similar trees will be generated for a larger number of dimensions.

When all MD-patterns are found, the next step in the analysis of multidimensional-transactional database is the mining of frequent itemsets in the MD-projected database for each MD-pattern. An alternative approach is based on finding frequent itemsets first and then the corresponding MD-patterns.

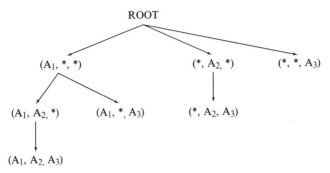

FIGURE 8.6   A processing tree using the BUC algorithm for the database in Table 8.3

8.7   WEB MINING

In a distributed information environment, documents or objects are usually linked together to facilitate interactive access. Examples for such information-providing environments include the World Wide Web (WWW) and on-line services such as America Online, where users, when seeking information of interest, travel from one object to another via facilities such as hyperlinks and URL addresses. The Web is a hypertext body of more than 800 million pages that continues to grow. It exceeds six terabytes of data on about three million servers. Almost a million pages are added daily; typically, pages change every few months and, therefore, several hundred gigabytes are changed every month. As the information offered in the Web grows daily, obtaining that information becomes more and more tedious. Even the largest search engines such as Alta Vista and HotBot index less than 18% of the accessible Web pages as on February 1999, down from 35% in late 1997. The main difficulty lies in the semistructured or unstructured Web content that is not easy to regulate and where enforcing a structure or standards is difficult. A set of Web pages lacks a unifying structure and shows far more authoring style and content variation than that seen in traditional print document collections. This level of complexity makes an "off-the-shelf" database-management and information-retrieval solution very complex and almost impossible to use. New methods and tools are necessary. Web mining may be defined as the use of data-mining techniques to automatically discover and extract information from Web documents and services. It refers to the overall process of discovery, not just to the application of standard data-mining tools. Some authors suggest decomposing Web-mining task into four subtasks:

1. *Resource finding* – This is the process of retrieving data, which is either online or offline, from the multimedia sources on the Web, such as electronic newsletters, electronic newswire, newsgroups, and the text content of HTML documents obtained by removing the HTML tags.

2. *Information selection and preprocessing* – This is the process by which different kinds of original data retrieved in the previous subtask is transformed. These transformations could be either a kind of preprocessing such as removing stop words, stemming, etc. or a preprocessing aimed at obtaining the desired representation,

such as finding phrases in the training corpus, representing the text in the first-order logic form etc.

3. *Generalization* – Generalization is the process of automatically discovering general patterns within individual Web sites as well as across multiple sites. Different general-purpose machine-learning techniques, data-mining techniques, and specific Web-oriented methods are used.

4. *Analysis* – This is a phase in which validation and/or interpretation of the mined patterns is performed.

There are three factors affecting the way a user perceives and evaluates Web sites through the data-mining process: a) Web-page content, b) Web-page design, and c) overall site design including its structure. The first factor concerns the goods, services, or data offered by the site. The other factors concern the way in which the site makes content accessible and understandable to its users. We distinguish between the design of individual pages and the overall site design, because a site is not a simply a collection of pages; it is a network of related pages. The users will not engage in exploring it unless they find its structure simple and intuitive. Clearly, understanding user-access patterns in such an environment will not only help improve the system design (e.g., providing efficient access between highly correlated objects, better authoring design for WWW pages, etc.) but also be able to lead to better marketing decisions. Commercial results will be improved by putting advertisements in proper places, better customer/user classification, and understanding user requirements better through behavioral analysis.

No longer are companies interested in Web sites that simply direct traffic and process orders. Now they want to maximize their profits. They want to understand customer preferences and customize sales pitches to individual users. By evaluating a user's purchasing and browsing patterns, e-vendors want to serve up (in real time) customized menus of attractive offers e-buyers can't resist. Gathering and aggregating customer information into e-business intelligence is an important task for any company with Web-based activities. E businesses expect big profits from improved decision-making, and therefore e-vendors line up for data-mining solutions.

Borrowing from marketing theory, we measure the efficiency of a Web page by its contribution to the success of the site. For an on-line shop, it is the ratio of visitors that purchased a product after visiting this page to the total number of visitors that accessed the page. For a promotional site, the efficiency of the page can be measured as the ratio of visitors that clicked on an advertisement after visiting the page. The pages with low efficiency should be redesigned to better serve the purposes of the site. Navigation-pattern discovery should help in restructuring a site by inserting links and redesigning pages, and ultimately accommodating user-needs and expectations. One possible categorization of Web mining is based on which part of the Web to mine, and it consists of three areas:

1. *Web-content mining* – describes the discovery of useful information from Web documents. Basically, Web content consists of several types of data such as text, image, audio, video, metadata as well as hyperlinks. Research in mining multiple types of data is now termed multimedia-data mining. We could consider

multimedia-data mining as an instance of Web-content mining. The Web content data consist of unstructured data such as free text, semi-structured data such as HTML documents, and a more structured data such as tables and database-generated HTML pages. The goal of Web-content mining is mainly to assist or to improve information-finding or filtering the information. Building a new model of data on the Web, more sophisticated queries other than the keywords-based search could be asked.

2. *Web-structure mining* – tries to discover the model underlying the link structure on the Web. The model is based on the topology of the hyperlinks with or without a description of the links. The model can be used to categorize Web pages and is useful for generating information such as the similarity relationship between Web sites.

3. *Web-usage mining* – tries to make sense of the data generated by the Web surfer's sessions or behaviors. While Web-content mining and Web-structure mining utilize real or primary data on the Web, Web-usage mining mines the secondary data derived from the behaviour of users while interacting with the Web. This includes data from Web server–access logs, proxy-server logs, browser logs, user profiles, registration data, user sessions or transactions, cookies, book-mark data, and any other data that is derived from a person's interaction with the Web.

To deal with problems of Web-page quality, Web-site structure, and their use, two families of Web tools emerge. The first includes tools that accompany the users in their navigation, learn from their behavior, make suggestions as they browse, and, occasionally, customize the user-profile. These tools are usually connected to or built-in into parts of different search engines. The second family of tools ana-lyzes the activities of users off-line. Their goal is to provide an insight in the semantics of a Web site's structure by discovering how this structure is actually utilized. In other words, knowledge of the navigational behavior of users is used to predict future trends. New data-mining techniques are behind these tools, where web log files are analyzed and information uncovered. In the next two sections, we will illustrate Web mining with three techniques that are representative of a large spectrum of Web-mining methodologies developed recently.

8.8   HITS AND LOGSOM ALGORITHMS

To date, index-based search engines for the Web have been the primary tools with which users searched for information. Experienced Web surfers can make effective use of such engines for tasks that can be solved by searching with tightly con-strained keywords and phrases. These search engines are, however, unsuited for a wide range of less precise tasks. How does one select a subset of documents with the most value from the millions that a search engine has prepared for us? To distill a large Web-search topic to a size that makes sense to a human user, we need a means of identifying the topic's most authoritative Web pages. The notion of authority adds a crucial dimension to the concept of relevance: We wish to locate not only a set of relevant pages, but also those that are of the highest quality.

It is important that the Web consists not only of pages, but also hyperlinks that connect one page to another. This hyperlink structure contains an enormous amount of information that can help to automatically infer notions of authority. Specifically, the creation of a hyperlink by the author of a Web page represents an implicit endorsement of the page being pointed to. By mining the collective judgment contained in the set of such endorsements, we can gain a richer understanding of the relevance and quality of the Web's contents. It is necessary for this process to uncover two important types of pages: *authorities*, which provide the best source of information about a given topic and *hubs*, which provide a collection of links to authorities.

Hub pages appear in a variety of forms, ranging from professionally assembled resource lists on commercial sites to lists of recommended links on individual home pages. These pages need not themselves be prominent, and working with hyperlink information in hubs can cause much difficulty. Although many links represent the some kind of endorsement, some of the links are created for reasons that have nothing to do with conferring authority. Typical examples are navigation and paid advertisement hyperlinks. A hub's distinguishing feature is that they are potent conferrers of authority on a focused topic. We can define a *good hub* if it is a page that points to many good authorities. At the same time, a good authority page is a page pointed to by many good hubs. This mutually reinforcing relationship between hubs and authorities serves as the central idea applied in the *HITS algorithm* (*Hyperlink-Induced Topic Search*) that searches for good hubs and authorities. The two main steps of the HITS algorithm are

1. *sampling component*, which constructs a focused collection of Web pages likely to be rich in relevant information, and
2. *weight-propagation component*, which determines the estimates of hubs and authorities by an iterative procedure and obtains the subset of the most relevant and authoritative Web pages.

In the sampling phase, we view the Web as a directed graph of pages. The HITS algorithm starts by constructing the subgraph in which we will search for hubs and authorities. Our goal is a subgraph rich in relevant, authoritative pages. To construct such a subgraph, we first use query terms to collect a root set of pages from an index-based search engine. Since many of these pages are relevant to the search topic, we expect that at least some of them are authorities or that they have links to most of the prominent authorities. We therefore expand the root set into a base set by including all the pages that the root-set pages link to, up to a designated cutoff size. This set typically contains from 1000 to 5000 pages with corresponding links, and it is a final result of the first phase of HITS.

In the weight-propagation phase, we extract good hubs and authorities from the base set V by giving a concrete numeric interpretation to all of them. We associate a non-negative authority weight a_p and a non-negative hub weight h_p with each page p $\in$ V. We are interested only in the relative values of these weights; therefore normalization is applied so that their total sum remains bounded. Since we do not impose any prior estimates, we set all a and h values to a uniform constant initially. The final weights are unaffected by this initialization.

We now update the authority and hub weights as follows. If a page is pointed to by many good hubs, we would like to increase its authority weight. Thus, we update the value of a_p for the page p to be the sum of h_q over all pages q that link to p:

$$a_p = \sum h_q, \quad \forall_q \text{ such that } q \rightarrow p$$

where the notation $q \rightarrow p$ indicates that page q links to page p. In a strictly dual fashion, if a page points to many good authorities, we increase its hub weight

$$h_p = \sum a_q, \quad \forall_q \text{ such that } p \rightarrow q.$$

There is a more compact way to write these updates. Let us number the pages $\{1, 2, \ldots, n\}$ and define their adjacency matrix A to be n × n matrix whose $(i, j)^{th}$ element is equal to 1 if page i links to page j, and 0 otherwise. All pages at the beginning of the computation are both hubs and authorities, and, therefore, we can represent them as vectors

$$a = \{a_1, a_2, \ldots, a_n\} \text{ and}$$
$$h = \{h_1, h_2, \ldots, h_n\}$$

Our update rules for authorities and hubs can be written as

$$a = A^T h$$
$$h = Aa$$

or, substituting one into another relation,

$$a = A^T h = A^T Aa = (A^T A)a$$
$$h = Aa = A A^T h = (A A^T)h$$

These are relations for iterative computation of vectors a and h. Linear algebra tells us that this sequence of iterations, when normalized, converges to the principal eigenvector of $A^T A$. This says that the hub and authority weights we compute are truly an intrinsic feature of the linked pages collected, not an artifact of our choice of initial weights. Intuitively, the pages with large weights represent a very dense pattern of linkage, from pages of large hub weights to pages of large authority weights. Finally, HITS outputs a short list consisting of the pages with the largest hub weights and the pages with the largest authority weights for the given search topic. Several extensions and improvements of the HITS algorithm are available in the literature. Here we will illustrate the basic steps of the algorithm using a simple example.

Suppose that a search engine has selected six relevant documents based on our query, and we want to select the most important authority and hub in the available set. The selected documents are linked into a directed subgraph and the structure is given in Figure 8.7a, while corresponding adjacency matrix A and initial weight vectors a and h are given in Figure 8.7b.

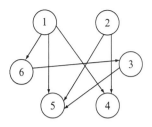

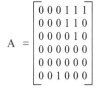

$$A = \begin{bmatrix} 0\,0\,0\,1\,1\,1 \\ 0\,0\,0\,1\,1\,0 \\ 0\,0\,0\,0\,1\,0 \\ 0\,0\,0\,0\,0\,0 \\ 0\,0\,0\,0\,0\,0 \\ 0\,0\,1\,0\,0\,0 \end{bmatrix}$$

$a = \{0.1, 0.1, 0.1, 0.1, 0.1, 0.1\}$
$h = \{0.1, 0.1, 0.1, 0.1, 0.1, 0.1\}$

a) Subgraph of the linked pages

b) Adjacency matrix A and weight vectors for the given graph

FIGURE 8.7   Initialization of the HITS algorithm

The first iteration of the HITS algorithm will give the changes in the a and h vectors:

$$a = \begin{bmatrix} 000000 \\ 000000 \\ 000001 \\ 110000 \\ 111000 \\ 100000 \end{bmatrix} \cdot \begin{bmatrix} 000111 \\ 000110 \\ 000010 \\ 000000 \\ 000000 \\ 001000 \end{bmatrix} \cdot \begin{bmatrix} 0.1 \\ 0.1 \\ 0.1 \\ 0.1 \\ 0.1 \\ 0.1 \end{bmatrix}$$

$$= [0\ 0\ 0.1\ 0.5\ 0.6\ 0.3]$$

$$h = \begin{bmatrix} 000111 \\ 000110 \\ 000010 \\ 000000 \\ 000000 \\ 001000 \end{bmatrix} \cdot \begin{bmatrix} 000000 \\ 000000 \\ 000001 \\ 110000 \\ 111000 \\ 100000 \end{bmatrix} \cdot \begin{bmatrix} 0.1 \\ 0.1 \\ 0.1 \\ 0.1 \\ 0.1 \\ 0.1 \end{bmatrix}$$

$$= [0.6\ 0.5\ 0.3\ 0\ 0\ 0.1]$$

Even this single iteration of the HITS algorithm shows that, in the given set of documents, document-5 has the most authority and document-1 is the best hub. Additional iterations will correct the weight factors for both vectors, but the obtained ranking of authorities and hubs will stay unchanged for this example.

The continuous growth in the size and use of the Internet creates difficulties in the search for information. Resource discovery is frustrating and inefficient when simple keyword searches can convey hundreds of thousands of documents as results. Many of them are irrelevant pages, some of them may have been moved, and some abandoned. While the first Web-mining algorithm HITS is primarily based on static information describing the Web-site structure, the second one LOGSOM uses dynamic information about a user's behavior. LOGSOM is a sophisticated method, which organizes the layout of the information in a user-interpretable graphic form. The LOGSOM system uses self-organizing maps

(SOM) to organize web pages into a two-dimensional table, according to users' navigation patterns.

The system organizes Web pages according to the interest of Web-users by keeping track of their navigation-paths.

The SOM technique is used as the most appropriate technique for the problem of Web-page organization because of its strength not only in grouping data points into clusters, but also in graphically representing the relationship among clusters. The system starts with a Web-log file indicating the date, time, and address of the requested Web pages as well as the IP address of the user's machine. The data are grouped into meaningful transactions, where a transaction is defined by a set of user-requested Web pages. We assume that there is a finite set of unique URLs:

$$U = \{url_1, url_2, \ldots, url_n\}$$

and a finite set of m user transactions:

$$T = \{t_1, t_2, \ldots, t_m\}$$

Transactions are represented as a vector with binary values u_i:

$$t = [u_1, u_2, \ldots, u_n]$$

where

$$u_i = \begin{cases} 1 & \text{if } url_i \in t \\ 0 & \text{otherwise} \end{cases}$$

Preprocessed log files can be represented as a binary matrix. One example is given in Table 8.4.

Since the dimensions of a table (n × m) for real-world applications would be very large, especially as input data to self-organizing maps, a reduction is necessary. By using the K-means clustering algorithm, it is possible to cluster transactions into prespecified number k (k<<m) of transaction groups. An example of a transformed table with new reduced data set is represented in Table 8.5, where the elements in the rows represent the total number of times a group accessed a particular URL (the form of the table and values are only one illustration, and they are not directly connected with the values in Table 8.4).

TABLE 8.4   Transactions described by a set of URLs

	url_1	url_2	$\ldots$	url_n
t_1	0	1		1
t_2	1	1		0
$\ldots$				
t_m	0	0		0

The new, reduced table is the input for SOM processing. Details about application of SOM as a clustering technique and the settings of their parameters are not given in this section. The interested reader may find these details in most textbooks on artificial neural networks. We will explain only the final results and their interpretation in terms of Web-page analysis. Each URL will be mapped onto a SOM based on its similarity with other URLs in terms of user usage or, more precisely, according to users' navigation patterns (transaction group "weights" in Table 8.5). Suppose that the SOM is two-dimensional map with $p \times p$ nodes, where $p \times p \geq n$, then a typical result of SOM processing is given in Table 8.6. The dimensions and values in the table are not the results of any computation with values in previous Tables 8.4 and 8.5, but a typical illustration of the SOM's final presentation.

The SOM organizes Web pages into similar classes based on users' navigation patterns. The blank nodes in the table show that there are no corresponding URLs, while the numbered nodes indicate the number of URLs contained within each node (or within each class). The distance on the map indicates the similarity of the Web pages measured by the user-navigation patterns. For example, the number 54 in the last row shows that 54 Web pages are grouped in the same class because they have been accessed by similar types of people as indicated by their transaction patterns. Similarity here is measured not by similarity of content but by similarity of usage. Therefore, the organization of the web documents in this graphical representation is based solely on the users' navigation behavior. The principles of the SOM methodology have been described briefly in the chapter on artificial neural networks, and interested readers will find several reference texts that will give them a deeper understanding of the technique.

What are the possible applications of the LOGSOM methodology? The ability to identify which Web pages ae being accessed by a company's potential customers gives the company information to make improved decisions. If one Web page

TABLE 8.5   Representing URLs as vectors of transaction group activity

	Transaction Groups			
	1	2	...	k
url_1	15	0		2
url_2	2	1		10
...				
url_n	0	1		2

TABLE 8.6   A typical SOM generated by a description of URLs

	1	2	3	...	p
1	2		1		15
2	3	1	10	...	
...					
p		54		...	11

within a node successfully refers clients to the desired information or desired page, the other pages in the same node are likely to be successful as well. Instead of subjectively deciding where to place an Internet advertisement, the company can now decide objectively, supported directly by the user-navigation patterns.

8.9 MINING PATH–TRAVERSAL PATTERNS

Before improving a company's Web site, we need a way of evaluating its current usage. Ideally, we would like to evaluate a site based on the data automatically recorded on it. Each site is electronically administered by a Web server, which logs all activities that take place in it in a file called a Web server log. All traces left by the Web users are stored in this log. Therefore, from these log files we can extract information that indirectly reflects the site's quality by applying data-mining techniques. We can mine data to optimize the performance of a Web server, to discover which products are being purchased together, or to identify whether the site is being used as expected. The concrete specification of the problem guides us through different data-mining techniques applied to the same Web server log.

While the LOGSOM methodology is concentrated on similarity of Web pages, other techniques emphasize the similarity of a user's paths through the Web. Capturing user-access patterns in a Web environment is referred to as *mining path–traversal patterns*. It represents an additional class of data-mining techniques, which is still in its infancy but showing great promise with spreading Internet applications. Note that because users travel along information paths to search for the desired information, some objects or documents are visited because of their location rather than their content. This feature of the traversal pattern unavoidably increases the difficulty of extracting meaningful information from a sequence of traversal data, and explains the reason why current web-usage analyses are mainly able to provide statistical information for traveling points, but not for traveling paths. However, as these information-providing services become increasingly popular, there is a growing demand for capturing user-traveling behavior to improve the quality of such services.

We first focus on the theory behind the navigational patterns of users in the Web. It is necessary to formalize known facts about navigation: that not all pages across a path are of equal importance and that the users tend to revisit pages previously accessed. To achieve this task, we define a navigation pattern in the Web as a generalized notion of a sequence, the materialization of which is the directed-acyclic graph. A sequence is an ordered list of items, in our case Web pages, ordered by time of access. The log file L is a multiset of recorded sequences. It is not a simple set, because a sequence may appear more than once.

When we want to observe sequence s as a concatenation of the consecutive subsequences x and y, we use the notation

$$s = x\ y.$$

The function *length*(s) returns the number of elements in the sequence s. The function *prefix*(s, i) returns the subsequence comprised of the first i elements of s. If $s' = prefix(s, i)$, we say that s' is a prefix of s and is denoted as $s' \leq s$. Analysis of log files shows that Web users tend to move backwards and revisit pages with a high frequency. Therefore, a log file may contain duplicates. Such revisits may be part of a guided tour or may indicate disorientation. In the first case, their existence is precious as information and should be retained. To model cycles in a sequence, we label each element of the sequence with its occurrence number within the sequence, thus distinguishing between the first, second, third, etc. occurrence of the same page.

Moreover, some sequences may have common prefixes. If we merge all common prefixes together, we transform parts of the log file into a tree structure, each node of which is annotated with the number of sequences having the same prefix up to and including this node. The tree contains the same information as the initial log file. Hence, when we look for frequent sequences, we can scan the tree instead of the original log multiset. On the tree, a prefix shared among k sequences appears and gets tested only once.

Sequence mining can be explained as follows: Given a collection of sequences ordered in time, where each sequence contains a set of Web pages, the goal is to discover sequences of maximal length that appear more frequently than a given percentage threshold over the whole collection. A frequent sequence has maximum value if all sequences containing it have a lower frequency. This definition of the sequence-mining problem implies that the items constituting a frequent sequence need not necessarily occur adjacent to each other. They just appear in the same order. This property is desirable when we study the behavior of Web users because we want to record their intents, not their errors and disorientations.

Many of these sequences even those with the highest frequencies could be of a trivial nature. In general, only the designer of the site can say what is trivial and what is not. The designer has to read all patterns discovered by the mining process and discard unimportant ones. It would be much more efficient to automatically test data-mining results against the expectations of the designer. However, we can hardly expect a site designer to write down all combinations of Web pages that are considered typical; expectations are formed in the human mind in much more abstract terms. Extraction of informative and useful maximal sequences continues to be a challenge for researchers.

Although there are several techniques proposed in the literature, we will explain one of the proposed solutions for mining traversal patterns that consists of two steps:

a) In a first step, an algorithm is developed to convert the original sequence of log data into a set of *traversal subsequences*. Each traversal subsequence represents a maximum forward reference from the starting point of a user access. It should be noted that this step of conversion would filter out the effect of backward references, which are mainly made for ease of traveling. The new reduced set of user-defined forward paths enables us to concentrate on mining meaningful user-access sequences.

b) The second step consists of a separate algorithm for determining the frequent-traversal patterns, termed *large reference sequences*. A large reference sequence is a sequence that appears a sufficient number of times in the log database. In the final phase, the algorithm forms the *maximal references* obtained from large reference sequences. A maximal large sequence is a large reference sequence that is not contained in any other maximal reference sequence.

For example, suppose the traversal log of a given user contains the following path (to keep it simple, Web pages are represented by letters):

$$\text{Path} = \{A\ B\ C\ D\ C\ B\ E\ G\ H\ G\ W\ A\ O\ U\ O\ V\}$$

The path is transformed into the tree structure shown in Figure 8.8. The set of maximum forward references MRF found in the step (a) after elimination of backward references is

$$\text{MFR} = \{ABCD,\ ABEGH,\ ABEGW,\ AOU,\ AOV\}.$$

When maximum forward references have been obtained for all users, the problem of finding frequent-traversal patterns is mapped into one of finding frequently occurring consecutive subsequences among all maximum forward references. In our example, if the threshold value is 0.4 (or 40%), large-reference sequences LRS with lengths 2, 3, and 4 are

$$\text{LRS} = \{AB,\ BE,\ EG,\ AO,\ BEG,\ ABEG\}$$

Finally, with large reference sequences determined, *maximal reference sequences* can be obtained through the process of selection. The resulting set for our example is

$$\text{MRS} = \{ABEG,\ AO\}.$$

In general, these sequences, obtained from large log files, correspond to a frequently accessed pattern in an information-providing service.

The problem of finding large reference sequences is very similar to that of finding frequent itemsets (occurring in a sufficient number of transactions) in association-rule mining. However, they are different from each other in that a reference sequence in the mining-traversal patterns has to be references in a given order whereas a large itemset in mining association rules is just a combination of items in a transaction. The corresponding algorithms are different because they perform

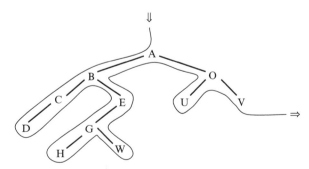

FIGURE 8.8   An example of traversal patterns

operations on different data structures: lists in the first case, sets in the second. As the popularity of Internet applications explodes, it is expected that one of the most important data-mining issues for years to come will be the problem how to effectively discover knowledge on the Web.

8.10   TEXT MINING

Enormous amount of knowledge resides today in text documents that are stored either within the organization or outside of it. Text databases are rapidly growing because of the increasing amounts of information available in electronic form, such as electronic publications, digital libraries, e-mail, and the World Wide Web. Data stored in most text databases are semistructured, and special data-mining techniques, called text mining, have been developed for discovering new information from large collection of textual data.

In general, there are two key technologies that make online text mining possible. One is *Internet searching* capabilities and the other is the *text analysis* methodology. *Internet searching* has been around for a few years. With the explosion of Web sites in the past few years, numerous search engines designed to help users find content appeared practically overnight. Yahoo, Alta Vista, and Excite are three of the earliest. Search engines operate by indexing the content in a particular Web site and allowing users to search these indexes. With the new generation of Internet-searching tools, users can gain relevant information by processing smaller amount of links, pages, and indexes.

Text analysis, as a field, has been around longer than Internet searching. It has been a part of the efforts to make computers understand natural languages and it is commonly thought of as a problem for artificial intelligence. Text analysis can be used anywhere where there is a large amount of text that need to be analyzed. Although automatic processing of documents using different techniques does not allow the depth of analysis that a human can bring to the task, it can be used to extract key points, categorize documents, and generate summaries in a situation when a large number of documents makes manual analysis impossible. Market research, business-intelligence gathering, e-mail management, claim analysis, E-procurement, and automated help desk are only a few of the possible applications where text mining can be deployed successfully.

To understand the details of text documents you can either search for keywords or you can try to categorize the semantic content of the document itself. When identifying keywords in text documents, you are looking at defining specific details or elements within documents that can be used to show connections or relationships with other documents. In the information retrieval (IR) domain, documents have been traditionally represented in the vector space model. Documents are tokenized using simple syntactic rules (such as white-space delimiters in English) and tokens are transformed to canonical form (e.g., "reading" to "read, "is", "was", and "are" to "be"). Each canonical token represents an axis in a Euclidean space. Documents are vectors in this n-dimensional space. If a token t called term occurs n times in document d, then the t-th coordinate of d is simply n. One may choose to normalize the length of the document to 1, using the L_1, L_2, or L_∞ norms:

$$\|d_1\| = \sum_t n(d, t), \ \|d_2\| = \sqrt{\sum_t n(d, t)^2}, \qquad \|d_\infty\| = \max_t n(d, t)$$

where $n(d,t)$ is the number of occurrences of a term t in a document d. These representations do not capture the fact that some terms also called keywords (like "algorithm") are more important than others (like "the" and "is") in determining document content. If t occurs in n_t out of N documents, n_t/N gives sense of rarity, and hence, the importance of the term. The inverse document frequency $IDF = 1 + \log(n_t/N)$ is used to stretch the axes of the vector space differentially. Thus the t-th coordinate of document d may be represented with the value $(n(d, t)/\|d_1\|) \times IDF(t)$ in the weighted vector space model. In spite of being extremely crude and not capturing any aspect of language or semantics, this model often performs well for its intended purpose. Also, in spite of minor variations, all these models of text regard documents as multisets of terms, without paying attention to ordering between terms. Therefore, they are collectively called bag-of-words models. Very often, the outputs from these keyword approaches in document interpretation can be expressed as relational data sets that may be then analyzed using one of the standard data-mining techniques.

Hypertext documents, usually represented as basic components on the Web, are a special type of text-based documents that have hyperlinks in addition to text. They are modeled with varying levels of details, depending on the application. In the simplest model, hypertext can be regarded as directed graph (D, L) where D is the set of nodes representing documents or Web pages, and L is the set of links. Crude models may not need to include the text models at the node level, when the emphasis is on documents' links. More refined models will characterize some sort of joint distribution between the term distribution of a node with those in a certain neighborhood of the document in the graph.

Content-based analysis and partition of documents is a more complicated problem. Some progress has been made along these lines, and new text-mining techniques have been defined, but no standards or common theoretical background has been established in the domain. Generally, you can think of text categorization as comparing a document to other documents or to some predefined set of terms or definitions. The results of these comparisons can be presented visually within a semantic landscape in which similar documents are placed together in the semantic space and dissimilar documents are placed further apart. For example, indirect evidence often lets us build semantic connections between documents that may not even share the same terms. For example, "car" and "auto" terms co-occurring in a set of documents may lead us to believe that these terms are related. This may help us to relate documents with these terms as similar. Depending on the particular algorithm used to generate the landscape, the resulting topographic map can depict the strengths of similarities among documents in terms of Euclidean distance. This idea is analogous to the type of approach used to construct Kohonen feature maps. Given the semantic landscape, you may then extrapolate concepts represented by documents.

The automatic analysis of text information can be used for several different general purposes:

1. To provide an overview of the contents of a large document collection and organize them in the most efficient way;

2. To identify hidden structures between documents or groups of documents;
3. To increase the efficiency and effectiveness of a search process to find similar or related information; and
4. To detect duplicate information or documents in an archive.

Text mining is an emerging set of functionalities that are primarily built on text-analysis technology. Text is the most common vehicle for the formal exchange of information. The motivation for trying to automatically extract, organize, and use information from it is compelling, even if success is only partial. While traditional, commercial text-retrieval systems are based on inverted text indices composed of statistics such as word occurrence per document, text mining must provide values beyond the retrieval of text indices such as keywords. Text mining is about looking for semantic patterns in text, and it may be defined as the process of analyzing text to extract interesting, nontrivial information that is useful for particular purposes.

As the most natural form of storing information is text, text mining is believed to have a commercial potential even higher than that of traditional data mining with structured data. In fact, recent studies indicate that 80% of a company's information is contained in text documents. Text mining, however, is also a much more complex task than traditional data mining as it involves dealing with unstructured text data that are inherently ambiguous. Text mining is a multidisciplinary field involving information retrieval, text analysis, information extraction, clustering, categorization, visualization, machine learning, and other techniques already included in the data-mining "menu"; even some additional specific techniques developed lately and applied on semistructured data can be included in this field.

The text-mining process, graphically represented in Figure 8.9, globally consists of two phases:

- *Text refining* that transforms free-form text documents into a chosen intermediate form, and
- *Knowledge distillation* that deduces patterns or knowledge from an intermediate form.

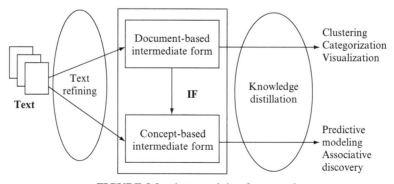

FIGURE 8.9   A text-mining framework

An intermediate form (IF) can be semistructured such as the conceptual-graph representation, or structured such as the relational-data representation. Intermediate forms with varying degrees of complexity are suitable for different mining purposes. They can be classified as *document-based*, wherein each entity represents a document, or *concept–based*, wherein each entity represents an object or concept of interests in a specific domain. Mining a document-based IF deduces patterns and relationships across documents. Document clustering, visualization, and categorization are examples of mining from document-based IFs.

For a fine-grained, domain-specific, knowledge-discovery task, it is necessary to perform a semantic analysis and derive a sufficiently rich representation to capture the relationship between objects or concepts described in the document. Mining a concept-based IF derives patterns and relationships across objects and concepts. These semantic-analysis methods are computationally expensive, and it is a challenge to make them more efficient and scalable for very large text corpora. Text-mining operations such as predictive modeling and association discovery fall in this category. A document-based IF can be transformed into a concept-based IF by realigning or extracting the relevant information according to the objects of interests in a specific domain. It follows that a document-based IF is usually domain-independent and a concept-based is a domain-dependent representation.

Text refining and knowledge-distillation functions as well as the intermediate form adopted are the basis for classifying different text mining-tools and their corresponding techniques. One group of techniques (and recently available commercial products) focuses on document organization, visualization, and navigation. Another group focuses on text-analysis functions, information retrieval, categorization, and summarization.

An important and large subclass of these text-mining tools and techniques is based on document visualization. The general approach here is to organize documents based on their similarities and present the groups or clusters of the documents as 2D or 3D graphics. IBM's Intelligent Miner is probably today one of the most comprehensive text-mining products. It offers a set of text-analysis tools that include tools for feature-extraction, clustering, summarization, and categorization; it also incorporates a text search engine. More examples of text-mining tools are given in Appendix B.

We will conclude this brief introduction to text mining with one very popular text-refining technique. *Latent Semantic Analysis (LSA)* is a method that was originally developed to improve the accuracy and effectiveness of information-retrieval techniques by focusing on semantic meaning of words across a series of usage contexts, as opposed to using simple string-matching operations. LSA is a way of partitioning free text using a statistical model of word usage that is similar to eigenvector decomposition and factor analysis. Rather than focusing on superficial features such as word frequency, this approach provides a quantitative measure of semantic similarities among documents based on a word's context.

Using the LSA method, you first represent the text as a matrix of word occurrences. In this matrix every row represents a unique word in the text and each column corresponds to a meaningful text passage or sample such as a document, paragraph, or sentence that defines a context for the word's usage. The value of each resulting cell in the matrix is the frequency with which a word appears in the given context. LSA then applies a singular value–decomposition (SVD) technique to the matrix. The SVD is a form of factor analysis that decomposes the matrix into a set of orthogonal factors that can be used to approximate the original matrix by linear combination. The resulting matrix will contain far fewer orthogonal factors than original words, and it serves to provide a framework for comparing abstract semantic categories that subsume the individual words contained in the document. You can have a situation in which two different words that are used in the same context across documents will have similar vectors in the LSA representation even if they never appear together in the same document.

Domain knowledge, not used and analyzed by any currently available text-mining tool, could play an important role in the text-mining process. Specifically, domain knowledge can be used as early as in the text-refining stage to improve parsing efficiency and derive a more compact intermediate form. Domain knowledge could also play a part in knowledge distillation to improve learning efficiency. All these ideas are still in their infancy, and we expect that the next generation of text-mining techniques and tools will improve the quality of information and knowledge discovery from text.

8.11   REVIEW QUESTIONS AND PROBLEMS

1. What is the essential difference between association rules and decision rules (described in Chapter 7)?

2. What are the typical industries in which market-basket analysis plays an important role in the strategic decision-making processes?

3. What are the common values for support and confidence parameters in the *Apriori* algorithm? Explain using the retail industry as an example.

4. Why is the process of discovering association rules relatively simple compared to generating large itemsets in transactional databases?

5. Given a simple transactional database X:

X:	TID	Items
	T01	A, B, C, D
	T02	A, C, D, F
	T03	C, D, E, G, A
	T04	A, D, F, B
	T05	B, C, G
	T06	D, F, G
	T07	A, B, G
	T08	C, D, F, G

Using the threshold values support = 25% and confidence = 60%, find:
a) All large itemsets in database X.
b) Strong association rules for database X.
c) Analyze misleading associations for the rule set obtained in b).

5. Given a transactional database Y:

Y:	TID	Items
	T01	A1, B1, C2
	T02	A2, C1, D1
	T03	B2, C2, E2
	T04	B1, C1, E1
	T05	A3, C3, E2
	T06	C1, D2, E2

6. Using the threshold values for support s = 30% and confidence c = 60%, find:

 a) All large itemsets in database Y.

 b) If itemsets are organized in a hierarchy so that A = {A1, A2, A3}, B = {B1, B2}, C = {C1, C2, C3}, D = {D1, D2}, and E = {E1, E2}, find large itemsets that are defined on conceptual level including a hierarchy of items.

 c) Find strong association rules for large itemsets in b).

7. Given a table of linked Web pages:

Page	Linked to the page
A	B, D, E, F
B	C, D, E
C	B, E, F
D	A, F, E
E	B, C, F
F	A, B

 a) Find authorities using two iterations of the HITS algorithm.

 b) Find hubs using two iterations of the HITS algorithm.

8. For the traversal log: {X, Y, Z, W, Y, A, B, C, D, Y, C, D, E, F, D, E, X, Y, A, B, M, N},

 a) Find maximal forward references.

 b) Find large reference sequences if the threshold value is 0.3 (or 30%).

 c) Find maximal reference sequences.

9. Why is the text-refining task very important in a text-mining process? What are results of text refining?

10. Why are the processes of text mining and web mining included in this chapter about association rules?

11. Implement the *Apriori* algorithm and discover large itemsets in transactional database.

12. Implement the HITS algorithm and discover authorities and hubs if the input is the table of linked pages.

13. Develop a software tool for discovering maximal reference sequences in a Web log file.

14. Search the Web to find the basic characteristics of publicly available or commercial software tools for association-rules discovery. Document the results of your search.

8.12   REFERENCES FOR FURTHER STUDY

1. Adamo, J., *Data Mining for Association Rules and Sequential Patterns*, Springer, Berlin, 2001.

    This book presents a collection of algorithms for data mining on the lattice structure of the feature space. Given the computational complexity and time requirements of mining association rules and sequential patterns, the design of efficient algorithms is critical. Most algorithms provided in the book are designed for both sequential and parallel execution, and they support sophisticated data mining of large-scale transactional databases.

2. Chang, G., M. J. Haeley, J. A. M. McHugh, J. T. L. Wang, *Mining the World Wide Web: An Information Search Approach*, Kluwer Academic Publishers, Boston: MA, 2001.

    This book is an effort to bridge the gap between information search and data mining on the Web. The first part of the book focuses on information retrieval on the Web. The ability to find relevant documents on the Web is essential to the process of Web mining. The cleaner the set of Web documents and data, the better the knowledge that can be extracted from it. In the second part of the book, basic concepts and techniques on text mining, Web mining and Web crawling are introduced. A case study, in the last part of the book, focuses on a search engine prototype called EnviroDaemon.

3. Han, J. and M. Kamber, *Data Mining Concepts and Techniques*, Morgan Kaufmann, San Francisco, 2000.

    This book gives a sound understanding of data-mining principles. The primary orientation of the book is for database practitioners and professionals with emphasis on OLAP and data warehousing. In depth analysis of association rules and clustering algorithms is the additional strength of the book. All algorithms are presented in easily understood pseudocode and they are suitable for use in real-world, large-scale data-mining projects including advanced applications such as Web mining and text mining.

4. Mulvenna, M. D. et al., eds., **Personalization on the Net using Web Mining:** *A* **collection of articles**, *CACM* 43, no. 8, 2000.

    This special edition of the CACM journal represents a collection of articles that explains state-of-the-art Web-mining techniques for developing personalization systems on the Internet. New methods are described for analyses of Web-log data in a user-centric manner, influencing Web-page content, Web-page design, and overall Web-site design.

9 Artificial Neural Networks

CHAPTER OBJECTIVES

- Identify basic components of artificial neural networks and their properties and capabilities.
- Describe common learning tasks such as pattern association, pattern recognition, approximation, control, and filtering that are performed by artificial neural networks.
- Compare different artificial neural-network architecture such as feedforward and recurrent networks, and discuss their applications.
- Explain the learning process at the level of an artificial neuron, and its extension for multiplayer, feedforward-neural networks.
- Compare the learning processes and the learning tasks of competitive networks and feedforward networks.
- Discuss the requirements for good generalizations with artificial neural networks, based on heuristic parameter tuning.

Work on artificial neural networks (ANNs) has been motivated by the recognition that the human brain computes in an entirely different way from the conventional digital computer. It was a great challenge for many researchers in different disciplines to model the brain's computational processes. The brain is a highly complex, nonlinear, and parallel information-processing system. It has the capability to organize its components so as to perform certain computations with a higher quality and many times faster than the fastest computer in existence today. Examples of these processes are pattern recognition, perception, and motor control. Artificial neural networks have been studied for more than four decades since Rosenblatt first applied the *single-layer perceptrons* to pattern-classification learning in the late 1950s.

An artificial neural network is an abstract computational model of the human brain. The human brain has an estimated 10^{11} tiny units called neurons. These neurons are interconnected with an estimated 10^{15} links. Similar to the brain, an ANN is composed of artificial neurons (or processing units) and interconnections. When we view such a network as a graph, neurons can be represented as nodes (or vertices) and interconnections as edges. Although the term artificial neural network is most commonly used, other names include "neural network", parallel distributed-processing system (PDP), connectionist model, and distributed adaptive system. ANNs are also referred to in the literature as neurocomputers.

A neural network, as the name indicates, is a network structure consisting of a number of nodes connected through directional links. Each node represents a processing unit, and the links between nodes specify the causal relationship between connected nodes. All nodes are adaptive, which means that the outputs of these nodes depend on modifiable parameters pertaining to these nodes. Although there are several definitions and several approaches to the ANN concept, we may accept the following definition, which views the ANN as a formalized adaptive machine:

DEF: An artificial neural network is a massive parallel distributed processor made up of simple processing units. It has the ability to learn from experiential knowledge expressed through interunit connection strengths, and can make such knowledge available for use.

It is apparent that an ANN derives its computing power through, first, its massive parallel distributed structure and, second, its ability to learn and therefore to generalize. Generalization refers to the ANN producing reasonable outputs for new inputs not encountered during a learning process. The use of artificial neural networks offers several useful properties and capabilities:

1. *Nonlinearity* – An artificial neuron as a basic unit can be a linear- or nonlinear-processing element, but the entire ANN is highly nonlinear. It is a special kind of nonlinearity in the sense that it is distributed throughout the network. This characteristic is especially important, for ANN models the inherently nonlinear real-world mechanisms responsible for generating data for learning.

2. *Learning from examples* – An ANN modifies its interconnection weights by applying a set of training or learning samples. The final effects of a learning process are tuned parameters of a network (the parameters are distributed through the main components of the established model), and they represent implicitly stored knowledge for the problem at hand.

3. *Adaptivity*: An ANN has a built-in capability to adapt its interconnection weights to changes in the surrounding environment. In particular, an ANN trained to operate in a specific environment can be easily retrained to deal with changes in its environmental conditions. Moreover, when it is operating in a nonstationary environment, an ANN can be designed to adopt its parameters in real time.

4. *Evidential Response*: In the context of data classification, an ANN can be designed to provide information not only about which particular class to select for a given sample, but also about confidence in the decision made. This later information may be used to reject ambiguous data, should they arise, and thereby improve the classification performance or performances of the other tasks modeled by the network.

5. *Fault Tolerance*: An ANN has the potential to be inherently fault-tolerant, or capable of robust computation. Its performances do not degrade significantly under adverse operating conditions such as disconnection of neurons, and noisy or missing data. There is some empirical evidence for robust computation, but usually it is uncontrolled.

6. *Uniformity of Analysis and Design*: Basically, artificial neural networks enjoy universality as information processors. The same principles, notation, and the same steps in methodology are used in all domains involving application of artificial neural networks.

To explain a classification of different types of ANNs and their basic principles it is necessary to introduce an elementary component of every ANN. This simple processing unit is called an artificial neuron.

9.1   MODEL OF AN ARTIFICIAL NEURON

An artificial neuron is an information-processing unit that is fundamental to the operation of an ANN. The block diagram (Figure 9.1), which is a model of an artificial neuron shows that it consists of three basic elements:

1. *A set of connecting links* from different inputs x_i (or synapses), each of which is characterized by a weight or strength w_{ki}. The first index refers to the neuron in question and the second index refers to the input of the synapse to which the weight refers. In general, the weights of an artificial neuron may lie in a range that includes negative as well as positive values.

2. *An adder* for summing the input signals x_i weighted by the respective synaptic strengths w_{ki}. The operation described here constitutes a linear combiner.

3. *An activation function* f for limiting the amplitude of the output y_k of a neuron.

The model of the neuron given in Figure 9.1 also includes an externally applied bias, denoted by b_k. The bias has the effect of increasing or lowering the net input of the activation function, depending on whether it is positive or negative.

In mathematical terms, an artificial neuron is an abstract model of a natural neuron, and its processing capabilities are formalized using the following notation. First, there are several inputs x_i, $i = 1, \ldots, m$. Each input x_i is multiplied by the corresponding weight w_{ki} where k is the index of a given neuron in an ANN. The weights simulate the biological synaptic strengths in a natural neuron. The weighted sum of products $x_i w_{ki}$, for $i = 1, \ldots, m$ is usually denoted as *net* in the ANN literature:

$$net_k = x_1 w_{k1} + x_2 w_{k2} + \ldots + x_m w_{km} + b_k$$

Using adopted notation for $w_{k0} = b_k$ and default input $x_0 = 1$, a new uniform version of net summation will be

$$net_k = x_0 w_{k0} + x_1 w_{k1} + x_2 w_{k2} + \ldots + x_m w_{km} = \sum_{i=1}^{m} x_i w_{ki}$$

The same sum can be expressed in vector notation as a scalar product of two m-dimensional vectors:

$$net_k = X \cdot W$$

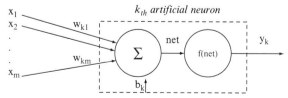

FIGURE 9.1   Model of an artificial neuron

where

$$X = \{x_0, x_1, x_2, \ldots, x_m\}$$
$$W = \{w_{k0}, w_{k1}, w_{k2}, \ldots, w_{km}\}$$

Finally, an artificial neuron computes the output y_k as a certain function of net_k value:

$$y_k = f(net_k)$$

The function f is called the activation function. Various forms of activation functions can be defined. Some commonly used activation functions are given in Table 9.1.

TABLE 9.1   A neuron's common activation functions

Activation Function	Input / Output Relation	Graph
Hard Limit	$y = \begin{cases} 1 & \textit{if net} \geq 0 \\ 0 & \textit{if net} < 0 \end{cases}$	
Symmetrical Hard Limit	$y = \begin{cases} 1 & \textit{if net} \geq 0 \\ -1 & \textit{if net} < 0 \end{cases}$	
Linear	$y = net$	
Saturating Linear	$y = \begin{cases} 1 & \textit{if net} > 1 \\ net & \\ 0 & \textit{if net} < 0 \end{cases}$	if $0 \leq net \leq 1$
Symmetric Saturating Linear	$y = \begin{cases} 1 & \textit{if net} > 1 \\ net & \textit{if} -1 \leq net \leq 1 \\ -1 & \textit{if net} < -1 \end{cases}$	
Log-Sigmoid	$y = 1/(1 + e^{-net})$	
Hyperbolic Tangent Sigmoid	$y = (e^{net} - e^{-net})/(e^{net} + e^{-net})$	

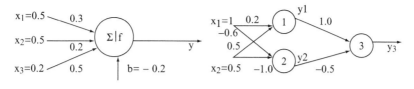

a) A single node   b) Three interconnected nodes

FIGURE 9.2   Examples of artificial neurons and their interconnections

Now, when we introduce the basic components of an artificial neuron and its functionality, we can analyze all the processing phases in a single neuron. For example, for the neuron with three inputs and one output, the corresponding input values, weight factors, and bias are given in Figure 9.2a. It is necessary to find the output y for different activation functions such as Symmetrical Hard Limit, Saturating Linear, and Log-Sigmoid.

1. Symmetrical Hard Limit

$$\text{net} = 0.5 \cdot 0.3 + 0.5 \cdot 0.2 + 0.2 \cdot 0.5 + (-0.2) \cdot 1 = 0.15$$
$$y = f(\text{net}) = f(0.15) = 1$$

2. Saturating Linear

$$\text{net} = 0.15(\text{computation is the same as for case1})$$
$$y = f(\text{net}) = f(0.15) = 0.15$$

3. Log-Sigmoid

$$\text{net} = 0.15(\text{computation is the same as for case1})$$
$$y = f(\text{net}) = f(0.15) = 1/(1 + e^{-0.15}) = 0.54$$

The basic principles of computation for one node may be extended for an artificial neural network with several nodes even if they are in different layers, as given in Figure 9.2b. Suppose that for the given configuration of three nodes all bias values are equal to 0 and activation functions for all nodes aresymmetric saturating linear. What is the final output y_3 from the node 3?

The processing of input data is layered. In the first step, the neural network performs the computation for nodes 1 and 2 that are in the first layer:

$$\text{net}_1 = 1 \cdot 0.2 + 0.5 \cdot 0.5 = 0.45 \Rightarrow y_1 = f(0.45) = 0.45$$
$$\text{net}_2 = 1 \cdot (-0.6) + 0.5 \cdot (-1) = -1.1 \Rightarrow y_2 = f(-1.1) = -1$$

Outputs y_1 and y_2 from the first layer nodes are inputs for node 3 in the second layer:

$$net_3 = y_1 \cdot 1 + y_2 \cdot (-0.5) = 0.45 \cdot 1 + (-1) \cdot (-0.5) = 0.95$$
$$\Rightarrow y_3 = f(0.95) = 0.95$$

As we can see from the previous examples, the processing steps at the node level are very simple. In highly connected networks of artificial neurons, computational tasks are multiplied with an increase in the number of nodes. The complexity of processing depends on the ANN architecture.

9.2   ARCHITECTURES OF ARTIFICIAL NEURAL NETWORKS

The architecture of an artificial neural network is defined by the characteristics of a node and the characteristics of the node's connectivity in the network. The basic characteristics of a single node have been given in a previous section and in this section the parameters of connectivity will be introduced. Typically, network architecture is specified by the number of inputs to the network, the number of outputs, the total number of elementary nodes that are usually equal processing elements for the entire network, and their organization and interconnections. Neural networks are generally classified into two categories on the basis of the type of interconnections: *feedforward* and *recurrent*.

The network is *feedforward* if the processing propagates from the input side to the output side unanimously, without any loops or feedbacks. In a layered representation of the feedforward neural network, there are no links between nodes in the same layer; outputs of nodes in a specific layer are always connected as inputs to nodes in succeeding layers. This representation is preferred because of its modularity, i.e., nodes in the same layer have the same functionality or generate the same level of abstraction about input vectors. If there is a feedback link that forms a circular path in a network (usually with a delay element as a synchronization component), then the network is *recurrent*. Examples of ANNs belonging to both classes are given in Figure 9.3.

Although many neural-network models have been proposed in both classes, the multilayer feedforward network with a backpropagation-learning mechanism is the most widely used model in terms of practical applications. Probably over 90% of commercial and industrial applications are based on this model. Why multilayered

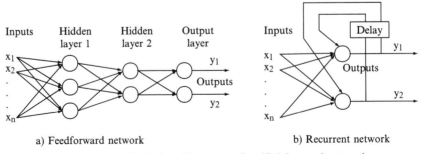

a) Feedforward network   b) Recurrent network

FIGURE 9.3   Typical architectures of artificial neural networks

networks? A simple example will show the basic differences in application require-ments between single layer and multilayer networks.

The simplest and well-known classification problem, very often used as an illus-tration in the neural-network literature, is the exclusive-OR (XOR) problem. The task is to classify a binary input vector X to class 0 if the vector has an even number of 1's or otherwise assign it to class 1. The XOR problem is not linearly separable; this can easily be observed from the plot in Figure 9.4 for a two-dimensional input vector $X = \{x_1, x_2\}$. There is no possibility of obtaining a single linear separation of points that belong to different classes. In other words, we cannot use a single-layer network to construct a straight line (in general, it is a linear hyperplane in an n-dimensional space) to partition the two-dimensional input space into two regions, each containing data points of only the same class. It is possible to solve the problem with a two-layer network, as illustrated in Figure 9.5, in which one possible solution for the connection weights and thresholds is indicated. This network generates a nonlinear separation of points in a 2D space.

The basic conclusion from this example is that single-layered ANNs are a con-venient modeling tool only for relatively simple problems that are based on linear models. For most real-world problems, where models are highly nonlinear, multi-layered networks are better and maybe the only solution.

9.3 LEARNING PROCESS

A major task for an ANN is to learn a model of the world (environment) in which it is embedded and to maintain the model sufficiently consistent with the real world

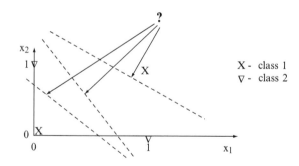

FIGURE 9.4 XOR problem

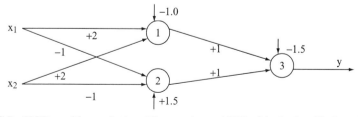

FIGURE 9.5 XOR problem solution: The two-layer ANN with the hardlimit-activation function

so as to achieve the specified goals of the concerned application. The learning process is based on data samples from the real world, and here lies a fundamental difference between the design of an ANN and a classical information-processing system. In the later case, we usually proceed by first formulating a mathematical model of environmental observations, validating the model with real data, and then building (programming) the system on the basis of the model. In contrast, the design of an ANN is based directly on real-life data, with the data set being permitted to "speak for itself". Thus, an ANN not only provides the implicit model formed through the learning process, but also performs the information-processing function of interest.

The property that is of primary significance for an artificial neural network is the ability of the network to learn from its environment based on real-life examples, and to improve its performance through that learning process. An ANN learns about its environment through an interactive process of adjustments applied to its connection weights. Ideally, the network becomes more knowledgeable about its environment after each iteration in the learning process. It is very difficult to agree on a precise definition of the term learning. In the context of artificial neural networks, one possible definition of inductive learning is

DEF: Learning is a process by which the free parameters of a neural network are adapted through a process of stimulation by the environment in which the network is embedded. The type of learning is determined by the manner in which the parameters change.

A prescribed set of well-defined rules for the solution of a learning problem is called a learning algorithm. Basically, learning algorithms differ from each other in the way in which the adjustment of the weights is formulated. Another factor to be considered in the learning process is the manner in which an ANN architecture (nodes and connections) is built.

To illustrate one of the learning rules, consider the simple case of a neuron k, shown in Figure 9.1, constituting the only computational node of the network. Neuron k is driven by input vector X(n), where n denotes discrete time, or, more precisely, the time step of the iterative process involved in adjusting the input weights w_{ki}. Every data sample for ANN training (learning) consists of the input vector X(n) and the corresponding output d(n).

	Inputs	Output
Sample$_k$	$x_{k1}, x_{k2}, \ldots, x_{km}$	d_k

Processing the input vector X(n), a neuron k produces the output that is denoted by $y_k(n)$:

$$y_k = f(\sum_{i=1}^{m} x_i w_{ki})$$

It represents the only output of this simple network, and it is compared to a desired response or target output $d_k(n)$ given in the sample. An error $e_k(n)$ produced at the output is by definition

$$e_k(n) = d_k(n) - y_k(n)$$

The error signal produced actuates a control mechanism of the learning algorithm, the purpose of which is to apply a sequence of corrective adjustments to the input weights of a neuron. The corrective adjustments are designed to make the output signal $y_k(n)$ come closer to the desired response $d_k(n)$ in a step-by-step manner. This objective is achieved by minimizing a cost function $E(n)$, which is the instantaneous value of error energy, defined for this simple example in terms of the error $e_k(n)$:

$$E(n) = (1/2)e_k^2(n)$$

The learning process based on a minimization of the cost function is referred to as *error-correction learning*. In particular, minimization of $E(n)$ leads to a learning rule commonly referred to as the *delta rule* or Widrow-Hoff rule. Let $w_{kj}(n)$ denote the value of the weight factor for neuron k excited by input $x_j(n)$ at time step n. According to the delta rule, the adjustment $\Delta w_{kj}(n)$ is defined by

$$\Delta w_{kj}(n) = \eta \cdot e_k(n) \cdot x_j(n)$$

where η is a positive constant that determines the rate of learning. Therefore, the delta rule may be stated as: *The adjustment made to a weight factor of an input neuron connection is proportional to the product of the error signal and the input value of the connection in question.*

Having computed the adjustment $\Delta w_{kj}(n)$, the updated value of synaptic weight is determined by

$$w_{kj}(n + 1) = w_{kj}(n) + \Delta w_{kj}(n)$$

In effect, $w_{kj}(n)$ and $w_{kj}(n + 1)$ may be viewed as the old and new values of synaptic weight w_{kj}, respectively. From Figure 9.6 we recognize that error-correction learning is an example of a closed-loop feedback system. Control theory explains that the stability of such a system is determined by those parameters that constitute the feedback loop. One of those parameters of particular interest is the learning-rate η. This parameter has to be carefully selected to ensure that the stability of convergence of the iterative-learning process is achieved. Therefore, in practice, this parameter plays a key role in determining the performance of error-correction learning.

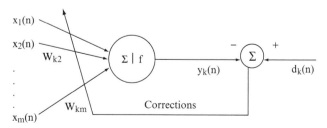

FIGURE 9.6 Error-correction learning performed through weights adjustments

Let us analyze one simple example of the learning process performed on a single artificial neuron in Figure 9.7a, with a set of the three training (or learning) examples given in Figure 9.7b.

The process of adjusting the weight factors for a given neuron will be performed with the learning rate $\eta = 0.1$. The bias value for the neuron is equal 0, and the activation function is linear. The first iteration of a learning process, and only for the first training example, is performed with the following steps:

$$net(1) = 0.5 \cdot 1 + (-0.3) \cdot 1 + 0.8 \cdot 0.5 = 0.6$$

$$\Downarrow$$

$$y(1) = f(net(1)) = f(0.6) = 0.6$$

$$\Downarrow$$

$$e(1) = d(1) - y(1) = 0.7 - 0.6 = 0.1$$

$$\Downarrow$$

$$\Delta w_1(1) = 0.1 \cdot 0.1 \cdot 1 = 0.01 \Rightarrow w_1(2) = w_1(1) + \Delta w_1(1) = 0.5 + 0.01 = 0.51$$
$$\Delta w_2(1) = 0.1 \cdot 0.1 \cdot 1 = 0.01 \Rightarrow w_2(2) = w_2(1) + \Delta w_2(1) = -0.3 + 0.01 = -0.29$$
$$\Delta w_3(1) = 0.1 \cdot 0.1 \cdot 0.5 = 0.005 \Rightarrow w_3(2) = w_3(1) + \Delta w_3(1) = 0.8 + 0.005 = 0.805$$

Similarly, it is possible to continue with the second and third examples ($n = 2$ and $n = 3$). The results of the learning corrections Δw together with new weight factors w are given in Table 9.2.

Error-correction learning can be applied on much more complex ANN architecture, and its implementation is discussed in Section 9.5, where the basic principles of multilayer feedforward ANNs with backpropagation are introduced. This example only shows how weight factors change with every training (learning) sample. We gave the results only for the first iteration. The weight-correction process will continue with either new training samples or use the same data samples in the next iterations. When to finish the iterative process is defined by a special parameter or set of parameters called *stopping criteria*. A learning algorithm may have different stopping criteria, such as the maximum number of iterations, or the threshold level of the weight-factor may change in two consecutive iterations. This parameter of learning is very important for final learning results and it will be discussed in later sections.

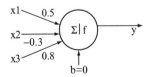

n (sample)	x1	x2	x3	d
1	1	1	0.5	0.7
2	−1	0.7	−0.5	0.2
3	0.3	0.3	−0.3	0.5

a) Artificial neuron with the feedback   b) Training data set for a learning process

FIGURE 9.7   Initialization of the error correction–learning process for a single neuron

TABLE 9.2   Adjustment of weight factors with training examples in Figure 9.7b

Parameter	n = 2	n = 3
x_1	−1	0.3
x_2	0.7	0.3
x_3	−0.5	−0.3
y	−1.1555	−0.18
d	0.2	0.5
e	1.3555	0.68
$\Delta w_1(n)$	−0.14	0.02
$\Delta w_2(n)$	0.098	0.02
$\Delta w_3(n)$	−0.07	−0.02
w1(n + 1)	0.37	0.39
w2(n + 1)	−0.19	−0.17
w3(n + 1)	0.735	0.715

9.4   LEARNING TASKS

The choice of a particular learning algorithm is influenced by the learning task that an ANN is required to perform. We identify six basic learning tasks that apply to the use of different artificial neural networks. These tasks are subtypes of general learning tasks introduced in Chapter 4.

Pattern Association

Association has been known to be a prominent feature of human memory since Aristotle, and all models of cognition use association in one form or the other as the basic operation. Association takes one of two forms: *autoassociation* or *heteroassociation*. In *autoassociation*, an ANN is required to store a set of patterns by repeatedly presenting them to the network. The network is subsequently presented with a partial description or a distorted, noisy version of an original pattern, and the task is to retrieve and recall that particular pattern. *Heteroassociation* differs from *autoassociation* in that an arbitrary set of input patterns is paired with another arbitrary set of output patterns. *Autoassociation* involves the use of unsupervised learning, whereas *heteroassociation* learning is supervised. For both, *autoassociation* and *heteroassociation*, there are two main phases in the application of an ANN for pattern-association problems:

1. The storage phase, which refers to the training of the network in accordance with given patterns, and
2. The recall phase, which involves the retrieval of a memorized pattern in response to the presentation of a noisy or distorted version of a key pattern to the network.

Pattern Recognition

Pattern recognition is also a task that is performed much better by humans than by the most powerful computers. We receive data from the world around us via our senses and are able to recognize the source of the data. We are often able to do so almost immediately and with practically no effort. Humans perform pattern recognition through a learning process; so it is with artificial neural networks.

Pattern recognition is formally defined as the process whereby a received pattern is assigned to one of a prescribed number of classes. An ANN performs pattern recognition by first undergoing a training session, during which the network is repeatedly presented a set of input patterns along with the category to which each particular pattern belongs. Later, in a testing phase, a new pattern is presented to the network that it has not seen before, but which belongs to the same population of patterns used during training. The network is able to identify the class of that particular pattern because of the information it has extracted from the training data. Graphically, patterns are represented by points in a multidimensional space. The entire space, which we call decision space, is divided into regions, each one of which is associated with a class. The decision boundaries are determined by the training process, and they are tested if a new, unclassified pattern is presented to the network. In essence, pattern recognition represents a standard classification task.

Function Approximation

Consider a nonlinear input–output mapping described by the functional relationship

$$Y = f(X)$$

where the vector X is the input and Y is the output. The vector-value function f is assumed to be unknown. We are given the set of labeled examples $\{X_i, Y_i\}$, and we have to design an ANN that approximates the unknown function f with a function F that is very close to original function. Formally:

$$|F(X_i) - f(X_i)| < \varepsilon \quad \text{for all } X_i \text{ from the training set}$$

where ε is a small positive number. Provided that the size of the training set is large enough and the network is equipped with an adequate number of free parameters, the approximation error ε can be made small enough for the task. The approximation problem described here is a perfect candidate for supervised learning.

Control

Control is another learning task that can be done by an ANN. Control is applied to a process or a critical part in a system, which has to be maintained in a controlled condition. Consider the control system with feedback shown in Figure 9.8.

The system involves the use of feedback to control the output y on the level of a reference signal d supplied from the external source. A controller of the system can be realized in an ANN technology. The error signal e, which is the difference between the process output y and the reference value d, is applied to an ANN-based controller for the purpose of adjusting its free parameters. The primary objective of the controller is to supply appropriate inputs x to the process to make its output y track the reference signal d. It can be trained through

1. *Indirect learning* – using actual input–output measurements on the process, an ANN model of a control is first constructed off-line. When the training is finished, the ANN controller may be included into the real-time loop.

2. *Direct learning* – The training phase is on-line, with real-time data, and the ANN controller is enabled to learn the adjustments to its free parameters directly from the process.

Filtering

The term filter often refers to a device or algorithm used to extract information about a particular quantity from a set of noisy data. Working with series of data in time, frequent, or other domain, we may use an ANN as a filter to perform three basic information-processing tasks:

1. *Filtering* – this task refers to the extraction of information about a particular quantity at discrete time n by using data measured up to and including time n.

2. *Smoothing* – this task differs from filtering in that data need not be available only at time n; data measured later than time n can also be used to obtain the required information. This means that in smoothing there is a delay in producing the result at discrete time n.

3. *Prediction* – the task of prediction is to forecast data in the future. The aim is to derive information about what the quantity of interest will be like at some time $n + n_0$ in the future, for $n_0 > 0$, by using data measured up to and including time n. Prediction may be viewed as a form of model building in the sense that the smaller we make the prediction error, the better the network serves as a model of the underlying physical process responsible for generating the data. The block diagram of an ANN for a prediction task is given in Figure 9.8.

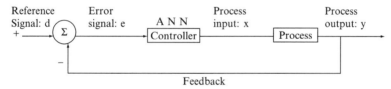

FIGURE 9.8   Block diagram of ANN-based feedback-control system

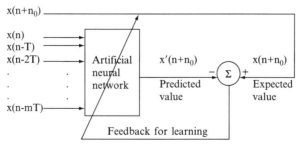

FIGURE 9.9   Block diagram of an ANN-based prediction

9.5 MULTILAYER PERCEPTRONS

Multilayer feedforward networks are one of the most important and most popular classes of ANNs in real-world applications. Typically, the network consists of a set of inputs that constitute the input layer of the network, one or more hidden layers of computational nodes, and finally an output layer of computational nodes. The processing is in a forward direction on a layer-by-layer basis. This type of artificial neural networks are commonly referred to as multilayer perceptrons (MLPs), which represent a generalization of the simple perceptron, a network with a single layer, considered earlier in this chapter.

A multiplayer perceptron has three distinctive characteristics:

1. The model of each neuron in the network includes usually a nonlinear activation function, sigmoidal or hyperbolic.
2. The network contains one or more layers of hidden neurons that are not a part of the input or output of the network. These hidden nodes enable the network to learn complex and highly nonlinear tasks by extracting progressively more meaningful features from the input patterns.
3. The network exhibits a high degree of connectivity from one layer to the next one.

Figure 9.10 shows the architectural graph of a multilayered perceptron with two hidden layers of nodes for processing and an output layer. The network shown here is fully connected. This means that the neuron in any layer of the network is connected to all the nodes (neurons) in the previous layer. Data-flow through the network progresses in a forward direction, from left to right and on a layer-by-layer basis.

Multilayer perceptrons have been applied successfully to solve some difficult and diverse problems by training the network in a supervised manner with a highly popular algorithm known as the *error backpropagation algorithm*. This algorithm is based on the error-correction learning rule and it may be viewed as its generalization. Basically, error backpropagation learning consists of two phases performed through the different layers of the network: a forward pass and a backward pass.

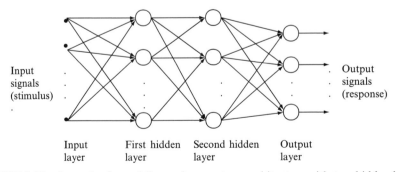

FIGURE 9.10   A graph of a multilayered perceptron architecture with two hidden layers

In the forward pass, a training sample (input data vector) is applied to the input nodes of the network, and its effect propagates through the network layer by layer. Finally, a set of outputs is produced as the actual response of the network. During the forward phase, the synaptic weights of the network are all fixed. During the backward phase, on the other hand, the weights are all adjusted in accordance with an error-correction rule. Specifically, the actual response of the network is subtracted from a desired (target) response, which is a part of the training sample, to produce an error signal. This error signal is than propagated backward through the network, against the direction of synaptic connections. The synaptic weights are adjusted to make the actual response of the network closer to the desired response.

Formalization of the backpropagation algorithm starts with the assumption that an error signal exists at the output of a neuron j at iteration n (i.e., presentation of the *n*th training sample). This error is defined by

$$e_j(n) = d_j(n) - y_j(n)$$

We define the instantaneous value of the error energy for neuron j as $1/2e_j^2(n)$. The total error energy for the entire network is obtained by summing instantaneous values over all neurons in the output layer. These are the only "visible" neurons for which the error signal can be calculated directly. We may thus write

$$E(n) = (1/2)\Sigma e_j^2(n), \quad j \in C$$

where the set C includes all neurons in the output layer of the network. Let N denote the total number of samples contained in the training set. The average squared error energy is obtained by summing E(n) over all n and then normalizing it with respect to size N, as shown by

$$E_{av} = 1/N \sum_{n=1}^{N} E(n)$$

The average error energy E_{av} is a function of all the free parameters of the network. For a given training set, E_{av} represents the cost function as a measure of learning performances. The objective of the learning process is to adjust the free parameters of the network to minimize E_{av}. To do this minimization, the weights are updated on a sample-by-sample basis for one iteration, i.e., one complete presentation of the entire training set of a network has been dealt with.

To obtain the minimization of the function E_{av}, we have to use two additional relations for node-level processing, which have been explained earlier in this chapter:

$$v_j(n) = \sum_{i=1}^{m} w_{ji}(n) \, x_i(n)$$

and

$$y_j(n) = \varphi(v_j(n))$$

where m is the number of inputs for j^{th} neuron. Also, we use the symbol v as a shorthand notation of the previously defined variable *net*. The backpropagation algorithm applies a correction $\Delta w_{ji}(n)$ to the synaptic weight $w_{ji}(n)$, which is proportional to the partial derivative $\delta E(n)/\delta w_{ji}(n)$. Using the chain rule for derivation, this partial derivative can be expressed as

$$\partial E(n)/\partial w_{ji}(n) = \partial E(n)/\partial e_j(n) \cdot \partial e_j(n)/\partial y_j(n) \cdot \partial y_j(n)/\partial v_j(n) \cdot \partial v_j(n)/\partial w_{ji}(n)$$

The partial derivative $\delta E(n)/\delta wji(n)$ represents a sensitive factor, determining the direction of search in weight space. Knowing that the next relations

$$\partial E(n)/\partial e_j(n) = e_j(n) \qquad (\text{from } E(n) = 1/2\Sigma e_j^2(n))$$

$$\partial e_j(n)/\partial y_j(n) = -1 \qquad (\text{from } e_j(n) = d_j(n) - y_j(n))$$

$$\partial y_j(n)/\partial v_j(n) = \varphi'(v_j(n)) \qquad (\text{from } y_j(n) = \varphi(v_j(n)))$$

$$\partial v_j(n)/\partial w_{ji}(n) = x_i(n) \qquad (\text{from } v_j(n) = \Sigma w_{ji}(n) x_i(n))$$

are valid, we can express the partial derivative $\partial E(n)/\partial w_{ji}(n)$ in the form

$$\partial E(n)/\partial w_{ji}(n) = -e_j(n) \cdot \varphi'(v_j(n)) \cdot x_i(n)$$

The correction $\Delta w_{ji}(n)$ applied to $w_{ji}(n)$ is defined by the delta rule

$$\Delta w_{ji}(n) = -\eta \cdot \partial E(n)/\partial w_{ji}(n) = \eta \cdot e_j(n) \cdot \varphi'(v_j(n)) \cdot x_i(n)$$

where η is the learning-rate parameter of the backpropagation algorithm. The use of the minus sign accounts for gradient descent in weight space, i.e., a direction for weight change that reduces the value E(n). Asking for $\varphi'(v_j(n))$ in the learning process is the best explanation for why we prefer continuous functions such as log-sigmoid and hyperbolic as a standard-activation function at the node level. Using the notation $\delta_j(n) = e_j(n) \cdot \varphi_j'(v_j(n))$, where $\delta_j(n)$ is the *local gradient*, the final equation for $w_{ji}(n)$ corrections is

$$\Delta w_{ji}(n) = \eta \cdot \delta_j(n) \cdot x_i(n)$$

The local gradient $\delta_j(n)$ points to the required changes in synaptic weights. According to its definition, the local gradient $\delta_j(n)$ for output neuron j is equal to the product of the corresponding error signal $e_j(n)$ for that neuron and the derivative $\varphi'(v_j(n))$ of the associated activation function.

Derivative $\varphi'(v_j(n))$ can be easily computed for a standard activation function, where differentiation is the only requirement for the function. If the activation function is sigmoid, it means that in the form

$$y_j(n) = \varphi(v_j(n)) = 1/(1 + e^{(-vj(n))})$$

the first derivative is

$$\varphi'(v_j(n)) = e^{(-vj(n))}/(1 + e^{(-vj(n))})^2 = y_j(n)(1 - y_j(n))$$

and a final weight correction is

$$\Delta w_{ji}(n) = \eta \cdot e_j(n) \cdot y_j(n)(1 - y_j(n)) \cdot x_i(n)$$

The final correction $\Delta w_{ji}(n)$ is proportional to the learning rate η, the error value at this node is $e_j(n)$, and the corresponding input and output values are $x_i(n)$ and $y_j(n)$. Therefore, the process of computation for a given sample n is relatively simple and straightforward.

If the activation function is a hyperbolic tangent, a similar computation will give the final value for the first derivative $\varphi'(v_j(n))$:

$$\varphi'(v_j(n)) = (1 - y_j(n)) \, (1 + y_j(n))$$

and

$$\Delta w_{ji}(n) = \eta \cdot e_j(n) \cdot (1 - y_j(n)) \cdot (1 + y_j(n)) \cdot x_i(n)$$

Again, the practical computation of $\Delta w_{ji}(n)$ is very simple because the local-gradient derivatives depend only on the output value of the node $y_j(n)$.

In general, we may identify two different cases of computation for $\Delta w_{ji}(n)$, depending on where in the network neuron j is located. In the first case, neuron j is an output node. This case is simple to handle because each output node of the network is supplied with a desired response, making it a straightforward matter to calculate the associated error signal. All previously developed relations are valid for output nodes without any modifications.

In the second case, neuron j is a hidden node. Even though hidden neurons are not directly accessible, they share responsibility for any error made at the output of the network. We may redefine the local gradient $\delta_j(n)$ for a hidden neuron j as the product of the associated derivative $\varphi'(v_j(n))$ and the weighted sum of the local gradients computed for the neurons in the next layer (hidden or output) that are connected to neuron j

$$\delta_j(n) = \varphi'(v_j(n))\Sigma\delta_k(n) \cdot w_{kj}(n), \quad k \in D$$

where D denotes the set of all nodes on the next layer that are connected to the node j. Going backward, all $\delta_k(n)$ for the nodes in the next layer are known before computation of the local gradient $\delta_j(n)$ for a given node on a layer closer to the inputs.

Let us analyze once more the application of the backpropagation-learning algorithm with two distinct passes of computation that are distinguished for each training example. In the first pass, which is referred to as the forward pass, the function signals of the network are computed on a neuron-by-neuron basis, starting with the nodes on first hidden layer (the input layer is without computational nodes), then the second, etc., until the computation is finished with final output layer of nodes. In this pass, based on given input values of each learning sample, a network computes the corresponding output. Synaptic weights remain unaltered during this pass.

The second, backward pass, on the other hand, starts at the output layer, passing the error signal (the difference between the computed and the desired output value) leftward through the network, layer by layer, and recursively computing the local gradients δ for each neuron. This recursive process permits the synaptic weights of the network to undergo changes in accordance with the delta rule. For the neuron located at the output layer, δ is equal to the error signal of that neuron multiplied by the first derivative of its nonlinearity represented in the activation function. Based on local gradients δ, it is straightforward to compute Δw for each connection to the output nodes. Given the δ values for all neurons in the output layer, we use them in the previous layer before (usually the hidden layer) to compute modified local gradients for the nodes that are not the final, and again to correct Δw for input connections for this layer. The backward procedure is repeated until all layers are covered and all weight factors in the network are modified. Then, the backpropagation algorithm continues with a new training sample. When there are no more training samples, the first iteration of the learning process finishes. With the same samples, it is possible to go through a second, third, and sometimes hundreds of iterations until error energy E_{av} for the given iteration is small enough to stop the algorithm.

The backpropagation algorithm provides an "approximation" to the trajectory in weight space computed by the method of steepest descent. The smaller we make the learning rate parameter η, the smaller the changes to the synaptic weights in the network will be from one iteration to the next and the smoother will be the trajectory in weight space. This improvement, however, is attained at the cost of a slower rate of learning. If, on the other hand, we make η too large in order to speed up the learning process, the resulting large changes in the synaptic weights can cause that the network to become unstable, and the solution will become oscillatory about a minimal point never reaching it.

A simple method of increasing the rate of learning yet avoiding the danger of instability is to modify the delta rule by including a *momentum term*:

$$\Delta w_{ji}(n) = \eta \cdot \delta_j(n) \cdot x_i(n) + \alpha \cdot \Delta w_{ji}(n-1)$$

where α is usually a positive number called momentum constant and $\Delta w_{ji}(n-1)$ is the correction of the weight factor for a previous $(n-1)^{th}$ sample. α, in practice, is usually set to the value between 0.1 and 1. The addition of the momentum term smoothes the weight-updating and tends to resist erratic weight changes because of gradient noise or high-spatial frequencies in the error surface. However, the use of momentum terms does not always seem to speed up training; it is more or less application-dependent. The momentum factor represents a method of averaging; rather than averaging derivatives, momentum averages the weight changes themselves. The idea behind momentum is apparent from its name: including some kind of inertia in weight corrections. The inclusion of the momentum term in the backpropagation algorithm has a stabilizing effect in cases where corrections in weight factors have a high oscillation and show changes in signs, i.e, they are sometimes positive and sometimes negative. The momentum term may also have the benefit of preventing the learning process from terminating in a shallow local minimum on the error surface.

Reflecting practical approaches to the problem of determining the optimal architecture of the network for a given task, the question about values for three parameters: the number of hidden nodes (including the number of hidden layers), learning rate η, and momentum rate α, becomes very important. Usually the optimal architecture is determined experimentally, but some practical guidelines exist. If several networks with different numbers of hidden nodes give close results with respect to error criteria after the training, then the best network architecture is the one with smallest number of hidden nodes. Practically, that means starting the training process with networks that have a small number of hidden nodes, increasing this number, and then analyzing the resulting error in each case. If the error does not improve with the increasing number of hidden nodes, the last analyzed network configuration can be selected as optimal. Optimal learning and momentum constants are also determined experimentally, but experience shows that the solution should be found with η about 0.1 and α about 0.5.

When the artificial neural network is first set up, the initial weight factors must be given. The goal in choosing these values is to begin the learning process as fast as possible. The appropriate method is to take the initial weights as very small evenly distributed random numbers. That will cause the output values to be in a midrange regardless of the values of its inputs, and the learning process will converge much faster with every new iteration.

In backpropagation learning, we typically use the algorithm to compute the synaptic weights by using as many training samples as possible. The hope is that the neural network so designed will generalize the best. A network is said to generalize well when the input–output mapping computed by the network is correct for test data never used earlier in creating or training the network. But the largest number of training samples and the largest number of learning iterations using these samples do not necessarily lead to the best generalization. Additional problems occur during the learning process, and they are briefly described through the following analysis.

The learning process using an ANN may be viewed as a curve-fitting problem. Such a viewpoint then permits us to look on generalization not as a theoretical property of neural networks but as the effect of a good, nonlinear interpolation of the input data. An ANN that is designed to generalize well will produce a correct input–output mapping, even when the input is slightly different from the samples used to train the network, as illustrated in Figure 9.11a. When, however, an ANN learns from too many input–output samples, the network may end up memorizing the training data. Such a phenomenon is referred to as *overfitting* or *overtraining*. This problem has already been described in Chapter 4. When the network is overtrained, it loses the ability to generalize between similar patterns. A smoothness of input–output mapping, on the other hand, is closely related to the generalization abilities of an ANN. The essence is to select, based on training data, the simplest function for generalization; that means the smoothest function that approximates the mapping for a given error criterion. Smoothness is natural in many applications, depending on the scale of the phenomenon being studied. It is therefore important to seek a smooth nonlinear mapping, so that the network is able to classify novel patterns correctly with respect to the training patterns. In Figures 9.11a and 9.11b, a fitting curve with a good generalization and an overfitted curve are represented for the same set of training data.

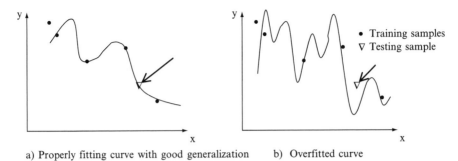

a) Properly fitting curve with good generalization   b) Overfitted curve

FIGURE 9.11 Generalization as a curve fitting problem

To overcome the problem of overfitting, some additional practical recommenda-
tions may be introduced for the design and application of ANN in general and
multiplayer perceptrons in particular. In artificial neural networks, as in all modeling problems, we want to use the simplest network that can adequately represent
the training data set. Don't use a bigger network when a smaller network will
work! An alternative to using the simplest network is to stop the training before
the network overfits. Also, one very important constraint is that the number of
network parameters should be limited. For a network to be able to generalize it
should have fewer parameters (significantly) than there are data points in the
training set. ANN generalization is extremely poor if there is a large input space
with very few training examples.

9.6 COMPETITIVE NETWORKS AND COMPETITIVE LEARNING

Competitive neural networks belong to a class of recurrent networks, and they are
based on algorithms of unsupervised learning, such as the competitive algorithm
explained in this section. In competitive learning, the output neurons of a neural
network compete among themselves to become active (to be "fired"). While in
multiplayer perceptrons several output no~
competitive learning only a si~
are three basic elements necessary to build a network with a competitive learning
rule, a standard technique for this type of artificial neural networks:

1. A *set of neurons* that have the same structure and that are connected with
initially randomly selected weights. Therefore, the neurons respond differently to a
given set of input samples.

2. A *limit value* that is determined on the strength of each neuron.

3. A *mechanism that permits the neurons to compete* for the right to respond to a
given subset of inputs, such that only one output neuron is active at a time. The
neuron that wins the competition is called winner-takes-all neuron.

In the simplest form of competitive learning, an ANN has a single layer of
output neurons, each of which is fully connected to the input nodes. The network

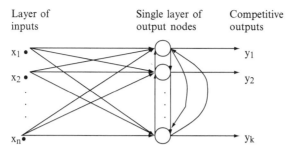

FIGURE 9.12   A graph of a simple competitive network architecture

may include feedback connections among the neurons, as indicated in Figure 9.12. In the network architecture described herein, the feedback connections perform *lateral inhibition*, with each neuron tending to inhibit the neuron to which it is laterally connected. In contrast, the feedforward synaptic connections in the network of Figure 9.12 are all *excitatory*.

For a neuron k to be the winning neuron, its net value net_k for a specified input sample $X = \{x_1, x_2, \ldots, x_n\}$ must be the largest among all the neurons in the network. The output signal y_k of the winning neuron k is set equal to one; the outputs of all other neurons that lose the competition are set equal to zero. We thus write

$$y_k = \begin{cases} 1 \text{ if } net_k > net_j \quad \text{for all } j, j \neq k \\ 0 \text{ otherwise} \end{cases}$$

where the induced local value net_k represents the combined action of all the forward and feedback inputs to neuron k.

Let w_{kj} denote the synaptic weights connecting input node j to neuron k. A neuron then learns by shifting synaptic weights from its inactive input nodes to its active input nodes. If a particular neuron wins the competition, each input node of that neuron relinquishes some proportion of its synaptic weight, and the weight relinquished is then distributed among the active input nodes. According to the standard, competitive-learning rule, the change Δw_{kj} applied to synaptic weight w_{kj} is defined by

$$\Delta w_{kj} = \begin{cases} \eta(x_j - w_{kj}) & \text{if neuron k wins the competition} \\ 0 & \text{if neuron k loses the competition} \end{cases}$$

where η is the learning-rate parameter. The rule has the overall effect of moving the synaptic weights of the winning neuron toward the input pattern X. We may use the geometric analogy represented in Figure 9.13 to illustrate the essence of competitive learning.

Each output neuron discovers a cluster of input samples by moving its synaptic weights to the center of gravity of the discovered cluster. Figure 9.13 illustrates the ability of a neural network to perform clustering through competitive learning. During the competitive-learning process, similar samples are grouped by the network and represented by a single artificial neuron at the output. This grouping,

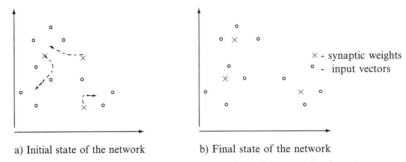

a) Initial state of the network   b) Final state of the network

FIGURE 9.13 Geometric interpretation of competitive learning

based on data correlation, is done automatically. For this function to be performed in a stable way, however, the input samples must fall into sufficiently distinct groups. Otherwise, the network may be unstable.

Competitive (or winner-take-all)-neural networks are often used to cluster input data where the number of output clusters is given in advance. Well-known examples of ANNs used for clustering based on unsupervised inductive learning include Kohonen's learning vector quantization (LVQ), self-organizing map (SOM), and networks based on adaptive-resonance theory models. Since the competitive network discussed in this chapter is very closely related to the Hamming networks, it is worth reviewing the key concepts associated with this general and very important class of artificial neural networks. The Hamming network consists of two layers. The first layer is a standard, feedforward layer and it performs a correlation between the input vector and the preprocessed output vector. The second layer performs a competition to determine which of the preprocessed output vectors is closest to the input vector. The index of the second-layer neuron with a stable, positive output (the winner of the competition) is the index of the prototype vector that best matches the input.

Competitive learning makes efficient adaptive classification, but it suffers from a few methodological problems. The first problem is that the choice of learning rate η forces a trade-off between speed of learning and the stability of the final weight factors. A learning rate near zero results in slow learning. Once a weight vector reaches the center of a cluster, however, it will tend to stay close to the center. In contrast, a learning rate near 1 results in fast but unstable learning. A more serious stability problem occurs when clusters are close together, which causes weight vectors also to become close, and the learning process switches its values and corresponding classes with each new example. Problems with the stability of competitive learning may occur also when a neuron's initial weight vector is located so far from any input vector that it never wins the competition, and therefore it never learns. Finally, a competitive-learning process always has as many clusters as it has output neurons. This may not be acceptable for some applications, especially when the number of clusters is not known or if it is difficult to estimate it in advance.

The following example will trace the steps in the computation and learning process of competitive networks. Suppose that there is a competitive network with three inputs and three outputs. The task is to group a set of 3-dimensional input samples into three clusters. The network is fully connected; there are connections between all inputs and outputs and there are also lateral connections between output nodes. Only local feedback weights are equal to zero, and these connections are not represented in the final architecture of the network. Output nodes are based on a linear-activation function with the bias value for all nodes equal to zero. The weight factors for all connections are given in Figure 9.14, and we assume that the network is already trained with some previous samples.

Suppose that the new sample vector X has components

$$X = \{x_1, x_2, x_3\} = \{1, 0, 1\}$$

In the first, forward phase, the temporary outputs for competition are computed through their excitatory connections and their values are

$$net_1{}^* = 0.5 \cdot x_1 + (-0.5) \cdot x_3 = 0.5 \cdot 1 - 0.5 \cdot 1 = 0$$
$$net_2{}^* = 0.3 \cdot x_1 + 0.7 \cdot x_2 = 0.3 \cdot 1 + 0.7 \cdot 0 = 0.3$$
$$net_3{}^* = 0.2 \cdot x_2 + (-0.2) \cdot x_3 = 0.2 \cdot 0 - 0.2 \cdot 1 = -0.2$$

and after including lateral inhibitory connections:

$$net_1 = net_1{}^* + 0.5 \cdot 0.3 + 0.6 \cdot (-0.2) = 0.03$$
$$net_2 = net_2{}^* + 0.2 \cdot 0 + 0.1 \cdot (-0.2) = 0.28 \text{ (maximum!!)}$$
$$net_3 = net_3{}^* + 0.4 \cdot 0 + 0.2 \cdot 0.3 = -0.14$$

Competition between outputs shows that the highest output value is net_2, and it is the winner. So the final outputs from the network for a given sample will be

$$Y = \{y_1, y_2, y_3\} = \{0, 1, 0\}$$

Based on the same sample, in the second phase of competitive learning, the procedure for a weight factor's correction (only for the winning node y_2) starts. The results of the adaptation of the network, based on learning rate $\eta = 0.2$, are new weight factors:

$$\Delta w_{12} = 0.3 + 0.2(1 - 0.3) = 0.44$$
$$\Delta w_{22} = 0.7 + 0.2(0 - 0.7) = 0.56$$
$$\Delta w_{32} = 0.0 + 0.2(1 - 0.0) = 0.20$$

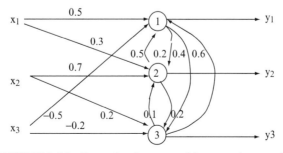

FIGURE 9.14 Example of a competitive neural network

The other weight factors in the network remain unchanged because their output nodes were not the winners in the competition for this sample. New weights are the results of a competitive-learning process only for one sample. The process repeats iteratively for large training data sets.

9.7 REVIEW QUESTIONS AND PROBLEMS

1. Explain the fundamental differences between the design of an artificial neural network and "classical" information-processing systems.

2. Why is the fault-tolerance property one of the most important characteristics and capabilities of artificial neural networks?

3. What are the basic components of the neuron's model?

4. Why are continuous functions such as log-sigmoid or hyperbolic tangent common activation functions in real-world applications of artificial neural networks?

5. Discuss the differences between feedforward and recurrent neural networks.

6. Given a two-input neuron with the following parameters: bias $b = 1.2$, weight factors $W = [w1, w2] = [3, 2]$, and input vector $X = [-5, 6]^T$, calculate the neuron's output for the following activation functions:

   a) A symmetrical hard limit
   b) A log-sigmoid
   c) A hyperbolic tangent

7. Consider a two-input neuron with the following weight factors W and input vector X:

$$W = [3, 2] \quad X = [-5, 7]^T$$

We would like to have an output of 0.5.

   a) Is there a transfer function from Table 9.1 that will do the job if the bias is zero?
   b) Is there a bias that will do the job if the linear-transfer function is used?
   c) What is the bias that will do the job with a log-sigmoid–activation function?

8. Consider a classification problem defined with the set of three-dimensional samples X, where two dimensions are inputs and the third one is the output.

X:	I_1	I_2	O
	−1	1	1
	0	0	1
	1	−1	1
	1	0	0
	0	1	0

a) Draw a graph of the data points X labeled according to their classes. Is the problem of classification solvable with a single-neuron perceptron? Explain the answer.

b) Draw a diagram of the perceptron you would use to solve the problem. Define the initial values for all network parameters.

c) Apply one iteration of the delta-learning algorithm. What is the final vector of weight factors?

9. The one-neuron network is trained to classify input–output samples:

I_1	I_2	O
1	0	1
1	1	−1
0	1	1

Show that this problem cannot be solved unless the network uses a bias.

10. Consider the classification problem based on the set of samples X:

X:	I_1	I_2	O
	−1	1	1
	−1	−1	1
	0	0	0
	1	0	0

a) Draw a graph of the data points labeled according to their classification. Is the problem solvable with one artificial neuron? If yes, graph the decision boundaries.

b) Design a single-neuron perceptron to solve this problem. Determine the final weight factors as a weight vector orthogonal to the decision boundary.

c) Test your solution with all four samples.

d) Using your network classify the following samples: (−2, 0), (1, 1), (0, 1), and (−1, −2).

e) Which of the samples in d) will always be classified the same way, and for which samples will classification vary depending on the solution?

11. Implement the program that performs the computation (and learning) of a single-layer perceptron.

12. For the given competitive network in the figure on the next page:

a) Find the output vector [Y1, Y2, Y3] if the input sample is [X1, X2, X3] = [1, −1, −1].

b) What are the new weight factors in the network?

13. Search the Web to find the basic characteristics of publicly available or commercial software tools that are based on artificial neural networks. Document

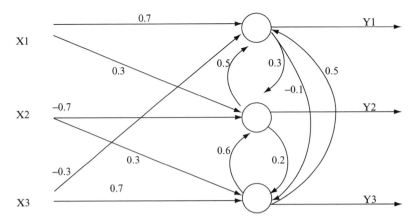

the results of your search. Which of them are for learning with a teacher, and which are support learning without a teacher?

9.8   REFERENCES FOR FURTHER STUDY

1. Engel, A. and Van den Broeck C., *Statistical Mechanics of Learning*, Cambridge University Press, Cambridge: UK, 2001.

   The subject of this book is the contribution made over the last decade to machine learning by researchers applying the techniques of statistical mechanics. The authors provide a coherent account of various important concepts and techniques that are currently only found scattered in papers. They include many examples and exercises to make a book that can be used with courses, or for self-teaching, or as a handy reference.

2. Hagan, M. T., H. B. Demuth, M. Beale, *Neural Network Design*, PWS Publishing Co., Boston, 1996.

   This book provides a clear and detailed survey of basic, artificial neural network architectures and learning rules. The authors emphasize the mathematical analysis of networks, methods for network training, and applications of networks to practical engineering problems. The illustrations and examples support one's intuition and add greatly to the text.

3. Haykin, S., *Neural Networks: A Comprehensive Foundation*, Prentice Hall, Upper Saddle River: NJ, 1999.

   The book provides a comprehensive foundation of artificial neural networks, recognizing the multidisciplinary nature of the subject. The introductory part explains the basic principles of statistical learning theory and the concept of VC-dimension. The main part of the book classifies and explains artificial neural networks as learning machines with and without a teacher. The material presented in the book is supported with a large number of examples, problems, and computer-oriented experiments.

4. Zurada, J. M., *Introduction to Artificial Neural Systems*, West Publishing Co., St. Paul: MN 1992.

   The book is one of the traditional textbooks on artificial neural networks. The text grew out of a teaching effort in artificial neural systems offered for both electrical engineering and computer science majors. The author emphasizes that the practical significance of neural computation becomes apparent for large or very large-scale problems.

10 Genetic Algorithms

CHAPTER OBJECTIVES

- Identify effective algorithms for approximate solutions of optimization problems described with large data sets.

- Compare basic principles and concepts of natural evolution and simulated evolution expressed through genetic algorithms.

- Describe the main steps of a genetic algorithm with illustrative examples.

- Explain standard and nonstandard genetic operators such as a mechanism for improving solutions.

- Discuss a schema concept with don't care values and its application to approximate optimization.

- Apply a genetic algorithm to the traveling salesman problem and optimization of classification rules as examples of hard optimizations.

There is a large class of interesting problems for which no reasonably fast algorithms have been developed. Many of these problems are optimization problems that arise frequently in applications. The fundamental approach to optimization is to formulate a single standard of measurement—a cost function—that summarizes the performance or value of a decision and iteratively improves this performance by selecting from among the available alternatives. Most classical methods of optimization generate a deterministic sequence of trial solutions based on the gradient or higher-order statistics of the cost function. In general, any abstract task to be accomplished can be thought of as solving a problem, which can be perceived as a search through a space of potential solutions. Since we are looking for "the best" solution, we can view this task as an optimization process. For small data spaces, classical, exhaustive search methods usually suffice; for large spaces special techniques must be employed. Under regular conditions, the techniques can be shown to generate sequences that asymptotically converge to optimal solutions, and in certain cases they converge exponentially fast. But the methods often fail to perform adequately when random perturbations are imposed on the function that is optimized. Further, locally optimal solutions often prove insufficient in real-world situations. Despite such problems, which we call *hard-optimization problems*, it is often possible to find an effective algorithm whose solution is approximately optimal. One of the approaches is based on genetic algorithms, which are developed on the principles of natural evolution.

Natural evolution is a population-based optimization process. Simulating this process on a computer results in stochastic-optimization techniques that can often outperform classical methods of optimization when applied to difficult, real-world problems. The problems that the biological species have solved are typified by chaos, chance, temporality, and nonlinear interactivity. These are the characteristics of the problems that have proved to be especially intractable to classical methods of optimization. Therefore, the main avenue of research in simulated evolution is a *genetic algorithm* (GA), which is a new, iterative, optimization method that emphasizes some facets of natural evolution. GAs approximate an optimal solution to the problem at hand; they are by nature stochastic algorithms whose search methods model some natural phenomena such as genetic inheritance and the Darwinian strife for survival.

10.1 FUNDAMENTALS OF GENETIC ALGORITHMS

Genetic algorithms (GA) are derivative-free, stochastic-optimization methods based loosely on the concepts of natural selection and evolutionary processes. They were first proposed and investigated by John Holland at the University of Michigan in 1975. The basic idea of genetic algorithms was revealed by a number of biologists when they used computers to perform simulations of natural genetic systems. In these systems, one or more chromosomes combine to form the total genetic prescription for the construction and operation of some organism. The chromosomes are composed of genes, which may take a number of values called allela values. The position of a gene (its locus) is identified separately from the gene's function. Thus, we can talk of a particular gene, e.g., an animal's eye-color gene with its locus at position 10 and its allela value as blue eyes.

Before going into details of the applications of genetic algorithms in the following sections, let us understand its basic principles and components. GAs encode each point in a parameter or solution space into a binary-bit string called a chromosome. These points in an n-dimensional space do not represent samples in the terms that we defined them at the beginning of this book. While samples in other data-mining methodologies are data sets given in advance for training and testing, sets of n-dimensional points in GAs are a part of a GA and they are produced iteratively in the optimization process. Each point or binary string represents a potential solution to the problem that is to be solved. In GAs, the decision variables of an optimization problem are coded by a structure of one or more strings, which are analogous to chromosomes in natural genetic systems. The coding strings are composed of features that are analogous to genes. Features are located in different positions in the string, where each feature has its own position (locus) and a definite allele value, which complies with the proposed coding method. The string structures in the chromosomes go through different operations similar to the natural-evolution process to produce better alternative solutions. The quality of new chromosomes is estimated based on the "fitness" value, which can be considered as the objective function for the optimization problem. The basic relations between concepts in natural evolution and genetic algorithms are given in Table 10.1. Instead of single a point, GAs usually keep a set of points as a population, which is then evolved repeatedly toward a better overall fitness value. In each generation, the GA constructs a new population using genetic operators such as crossover and mutation. Members with higher fitness values are more likely to survive and participate in mating or *crossover operations*.

TABLE 10.1   Basic concepts in genetic algorithms

Concept in Natural Evolution	Concept in Genetic Algorithms
Chromosome	String
Gene	Features in the string
Locus	Position in the string
Allele	Position value (usually 0 or 1)
Genotype	String structure
Phenotype	Set of characteristics (features)

As a general-purpose optimization tool, GAs are moving out of academia and finding significant applications in many other venues. Typical situations where genetic algorithms are particularly useful are in difficult optimization cases for which analytical methods do not work well. GAs have been quite successfully applied to optimization problems like wire routing, scheduling, adaptive control, game playing, transportation problems, traveling-salesman problems, database query optimization, machine learning,etc. During the last decades, the significance of optimization has grown even further because many important large-scale, combinatorial-optimization problems and highly constrained engineering problems can only be solved approximately. Genetic algorithms aim at such complex problems. They belong to the class of probabilistic algorithms, yet they are very different from random algorithms as they combine elements of directed and stochastic search. Another important property of genetics-based search methods is that they maintain a population of potential solutions while all other methods process a single point of the search space. Because of these characteristics, GAs are more robust than existing directed-search methods.

GAs are popular because they do not depend on functional derivatives and they have the following characteristics:

1. GAs are parallel-search procedures that can be implemented on parallel-processing machines for massively speeding up their operations.
2. GAs are applicable to both continuous- and discrete-optimization problems.
3. GAs are stochastic and less likely to get trapped in local minima, which inevitably are present in any practical, optimization application.
4. GAs' flexibility facilitates both structure and parameter identification in complex models.

The GA theory provides some explanation why, for a given problem formulation, we may obtain convergence to the sought optimal point. Unfortunately, practical applications do not always follow the theory, the main reason being:

1. The coding of the problem often moves the GA to operate in a different space than that of the problem itself.
2. There are practical limits on the hypothetically unlimited number of iterations (generations in the GA).
3. There is a limit on the hypothetically unlimited population size.

One of the implications of these observations is the inability of GAs, under certain conditions, to find the optimal solution or even an approximation to the optimal solution; such failures are usually caused by premature convergence to a local optimum. Don't forget that this problem is common not only for the other optimization algorithms but also for the other data-mining techniques.

10.2 OPTIMIZATION USING GENETIC ALGORITHMS

Let us note first that, without any loss of generality, we can assume that all optimization problems can be analyzed as maximization problems only. If the optimization problem is to minimize a function $f(x)$, this is equivalent to maximizing a function $g(x) = -f(x)$. Moreover, we may assume that the objective function $f(x)$ takes positive values in its domain. Otherwise, we can translate the function for some positive constant C so that it will be always positive; i.e.,

$$\max f^*(x) = \max \{f(x) + C\}$$

If each variable x_i, with real values, is coded as a binary string of length m, then the relation between the initial value and the coded information is

$$x_i = a + decimal(binary - string_i)\{[b - a]/[2^m - 1]\}$$

where the variable x_i can take the values from a domain $D_i = [a, b]$, and m is the smallest integer such that the binary code has the required precision. For example, the value for variable x given on the domain [10, 20] is a binary-coded string with the length equal to 3 and the code 100. While the range of codes is between 000 and 111, the question is what is the real value of the coded variable x? For this example m = 3 and the corresponding precision is

$$[b - a]/[2^m - 1] = (20 - 10)/(2^3 - 1) = 10/7 = 1.42$$

and that is the difference between two successive x values that could be tested as candidates for an extreme. Finally, the attribute with the code 100 has a decimal value

$$x = 10 + decimal (100) \cdot 1.42 = 10 + 4 \cdot 1.42 = 15.68$$

Each chromosome as a potential solution is represented by a concatenation of binary codes for all features in the problem to be optimized. Its total length m is a sum of the features' code lengths m_i:

$$m = \sum_{i=1}^{k} m_i$$

where k is the number of features or input variables for the problem at hand. When we introduce these basic principles of a code construction, it is possible to explain the main steps of a genetic algorithm.

Encoding schemes and initialization

A genetic algorithm starts with designing a representation of a solution for the given problem. A solution here means any value that is a candidate for a correct solution that can be evaluated. For example, suppose we want to maximize function $y = 5 - (x - 1)^2$. Then $x = 2$ is a solution, $x = 2.5$ is another solution, and $x = 3$ is the correct solution of the problem that maximizes y. The representation of each solution for a genetic algorithm is up to the designer. It depends on what each solution looks like and which solution form will be convenient for applying a genetic algorithm. The most common representation of a solution is as a string of characters, i.e., a string of codes for feature representation, where the characters belong to a fixed alphabet. The larger the alphabet, the more the information that can be represented by each character in the string. Therefore, fewer elements in a string are necessary to encode specific amounts of information. However, in most real-world applications, GAs usually use a binary-coding schema.

The encoding process transforms points in a feature space into bit string representation. For instance, a point (11, 6, 9) in a three-dimensional feature space, with ranges [0, 15] for each dimension, can be represented as a concatenated binary string:

$$(11, 6, 9) \Rightarrow (101101101001)$$

in which each feature's decimal value is encoded as a gene composed of four bits using a binary coding.

Other encoding schemes, such as Gray coding, can also be used and, when necessary, arrangements can be made for encoding negative, floating-point, or discrete-value numbers. Encoding schemes provide a way of translating problem-specific knowledge directly into the GA framework. This process plays a key role in determining GAs' performances. Moreover, genetic operators can and should be designed along with the encoding scheme used for a specific application.

A set of all features values encoded into a bit string represents one chromosome. In GAs we are manipulating not a single chromosome but a set of chromosomes called a population. To initialize a population, we can simply set some *pop-size* number of chromosomes randomly. The size of the population is also one of the most important choices faced by any user of genetic algorithms and may be critical in many applications: will we reach the approximate solution at all and if yes, how fast? If the population size is too small, the genetic algorithm may converge too quickly and maybe to a solution that is only the local optimum; if it is too large, the genetic algorithm may waste computational resources and the waiting time for an improvement might be too long.

Fitness evaluation

The next step, after creating a population, is to calculate the fitness value of each member in the population because each chromosome is a candidate for an optimal solution. For a maximization problem, the fitness value f_i of the *i*th member is usually the objective function evaluated at this member (or the point in parameter space). The fitness of a solution is a measure that can be used to compare solutions to determine which is better. The fitness values may be determined from complex analytical formulas, simulation models, or by referring to observations from experiments or real-life problem settings. GAs will work correctly if fitness values are determined appropriately keeping in mind that a selection of the objective function is highly subjective and problem-dependent.

We usually need fitness values that are positive, so some kind of scaling and/or translation of data may become necessary if the objective function is not strictly positive. Another approach is to use the rankings of members in a population as their fitness values. The advantage of this approach is that the objective function does not need to be accurate, as long as it can provide the correct ranking information.

Selection

In this phase, we have to create a new population from the current generation. The selection operation determines which parent chromosomes participate in producing offspring for the next generation. Usually, members are selected for mating with a selection probability proportional to their fitness values. The most common way to implement this method is to set the selection probability p equal to

$$p_i = f_i / \sum_{k=1}^{n} f_k$$

where n is the population size and f_i is a fitness value for the ith chromosome. The effect of this selection method is to allow members with above-average values to reproduce and replace members with below-average fitness values.

For the selection process (selection of a new population with respect to the probability distribution based on fitness values), a roulette wheel with slots sized according to fitness for each chromosome is used. We construct such a roulette wheel as follows:

1. Calculate the fitness value $f(v_i)$ for each chromosome v_i.
2. Find the total fitness of the population:

$$F = \sum_{i=1}^{pop\text{-}size} f(v_i)$$

3. Calculate the probability of a selection p_i for each chromosome v_i:

$$p_i = f(v_i)/F$$

4. Calculate a cumulative probability q_i after each chromosome v_i is included:

$$q_i = \sum_{j=1}^{i} p_j$$

where q increases from 0 to maximum 1. Value 1 shows that all chromosomes from the population are included into a cumulative probability.

The selection process is based on spinning the roulette wheel pop-size times. Each time we select a single chromosome for a new population. An implementation could repeat steps 1 and 2 *pop-size* times:

1. Generate a random number r from the range [0, 1].
2. If $r < q_1$ then select the first chromosome v_1; otherwise select the i-th chromosome v_i such that $q_{i-1} < r \leq q_i$.

Obviously, some chromosomes would be selected more than once. That is in accordance with the theory. GA performs a multidirectional search by maintaining a population of potential solutions and encourages good solutions. The population undergoes a simulated evolution—in each generation the relatively "good" solutions reproduce while the relatively "bad" solutions die. To distinguish between different solutions, we use an objective or evaluation function, which plays the role of an environment.

Crossover

The strength of genetic algorithms arises from the structured information exchange of crossover combinations of highly fit individuals. So what we need is a crossover-like operator that would exploit important similarities between chromosomes. The probability of crossover PC is the parameter that will define the expected number of chromosomes—PC· *pop-size*—which undergo the crossover operation. We define the chromosomes for crossover in a current population using the following iterative procedure. Steps 1 and 2 have to be repeated for all chromosomes:

1. Generate a random number r from the range [0, 1].
2. If $r < PC$, select the given chromosome for crossover.

If PC is set to 1, all chromosomes in the population will be included into the crossover operation; if $PC = 0.5$ only half of the population will perform crossover and the other half will be included into a new population directly without changes.

To exploit the potential of the current gene pool, we use crossover operators to generate new chromosomes that will retain the good features from the previous generation. Crossover is usually applied to selected pairs of parents.

One-point crossover is the most basic crossover operator, where a crossover point on the genetic code is selected at random, and two parent chromosomes are interchanged at this point. In *two-point crossover*, two points are selected and a part of chromosome string between these two points is then swapped to generate two children of the new generation. Examples of one- and two-point crossover are shown in Figure 10.1.

We can define an n-point crossover similarly, where the parts of strings between points 1 and 2, 3 and 4, and finally n-1 and n are swapped. The effect of crossover is similar to that of mating in the natural evolutionary process in which parents pass segments of their own chromosomes on to their children. Therefore, some children are able to outperform their parents if they get "good" genes or genetic traits from their parents.

Selected point for one-point crossover (after fifth position in the string)

a) One-point crossover

Selected points for two-point crossover (after second and fifth positions in the strings)

b) Two-point crossover

FIGURE 10.1 Crossover operators

Mutation

Crossover exploits existing gene potentials, but if the population does not contain all the encoded information needed to solve a particular problem, no amount of gene mixing can produce a satisfactory solution. For this reason, a mutation operator capable of spontaneously generating new chromosomes is included. The most common way of implementing mutation is to flip a bit with a probability equal to a very low, given mutation rate (MR). A mutation operator can prevent any single bit from converging to a value through the entire population and, more important, it can prevent the population from converging and stagnating at any local optima. The mutation rate is usually kept low so good chromosomes obtained from crossover are not lost. If the mutation rate is high (for example above 0.1), GA performance will approach that of a primitive random search. Figure 10.2 provides an example of mutation.

In the natural evolutionary process, selection, crossover, and mutation all occur simultaneously to generate offspring. Here we split them into consecutive phases to facilitate implementation of and experimentation with genetic algorithms. Note that this section only gives a general description of the basics of GAs. Detailed implementations of GAs vary considerably, but the main phases and the iterative process remain.

At the end of this section we can summarize that the major components of GAs include encoding schemas, fitness evaluation, parent selection, and application of crossover operators and mutation operators. These phases are performed iteratively, as represented in Figure 10.3.

It is relatively easy to keep track of the best individual chromosomes in the evolution process. It is customary in genetic algorithm implementations to store"the best ever" individual at a separate location. In that way, the algorithm

Randomly selected mutated bit   Chromosome after mutation
(in the sixth position)

$\Downarrow$ $\Downarrow$

| 1 0 0 1 1 1 1 0 | $\Rightarrow$ | 1 0 0 1 1 0 1 0 |

FIGURE 10.2 Mutation operator

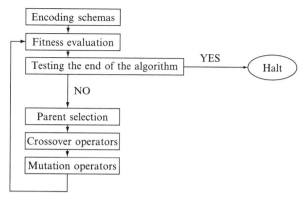

FIGURE 10.3   Major phases of a genetic algorithm

would report the best value found during the whole process, just in the final population.

Optimization under constraints is also the class of problems for which genetic algorithms are an appropriate solution. The constraint-handling techniques for genetic algorithms can be grouped into different categories. One typical way of dealing with GA candidates that violate the constraints is to generate potential solutions without considering the constraints, and then to penalize them by decreasing the "goodness" of the evaluation function. In other words, a constrained problem is transformed to an unconstrained one by associating a penalty with all constraint violations. These penalties are included in the function evaluation, and there are different kinds of implementations. Some penalty functions assign a constant as a penalty measure. Other penalty functions depend on the degree of violation: the larger the violation, the greater the penalty. The growth of the penalty function can be logarithmic, linear, quadratic, exponential, etc., depending upon the size of the violation. Several implementations of GAs' optimization under constraints are given in the texts recommended for further study (Section 10.8).

10.3   A SIMPLE ILLUSTRATION OF A GENETIC ALGORITHM

To apply a genetic algorithm for a particular problem, we have to define or to select the following five components:

1. A genetic representation or encoding schema for potential solutions to the problem.
2. A way to create an initial population of potential solutions.
3. An evaluation function that plays the role of the environment, rating solutions in terms of their "fitness".
4. Genetic operators that alter the composition of offspring.
5. Values for the various parameters that the genetic algorithm uses (population size, rate of applied operators, etc.).

We discuss the main features of genetic algorithms by presenting a simple example. Suppose that the problem is the optimization of a simple function of one variable. The function is defined as

$$f(x) = x^2$$

The task is to find x from the range [0,31] which maximizes the function f(x). We selected this problem because it is relatively easy to analyze optimization of the function f(x) analytically, to compare the results of the analytic optimization with a genetic algorithm, and find the approximate, optimal solution.

Representation
The first step in the GA is to represent the solution alternative (a value for the input feature) in a coded-string format. Typically, the string is a series of features with their values; each feature's value can be coded with one from a set of discrete values called allele set. The allele set is defined according to the needs of the problem, and finding the appropriate coding method is a part of the art of using GAs. The coding method must be minimal but completely expressive. We will use a binary vector as a chromosome to represent real values of the single variable x. The length of the vector depends on the required precision, which, in this example, is selected as 1. Therefore, we need a minimum five-bit code (string) to accommodate the range with required precision:

$$(b - a)/(2^m - 1) \leq \text{ Required precision}$$
$$(31 - 0)/(2^m - 1) \leq 1$$
$$2^m \geq 32$$
$$m \geq 5$$

For this example, the mapping from a real number to a binary code is defined by the relation (because a = 0):

$$\text{Code} = \text{binary} (x_{\text{decimal}})$$

Opposite mapping, from the binary code to the real value of the argument is also unique:

$$x = \text{decimal} (\text{Code}_{\text{binary}})$$

and it will be used only for checking the intermediate results of optimization. For example, if we want to transform the value x = 11 into a binary string, the corresponding code will be 01011. On the other hand, code 11001 represents decimal value x = 25.

Initial population
The initialization process is very simple: we randomly create a population of chromosomes (binary codes) with the given length. Suppose that we decide that the

parameter for the number of strings in the population is equal to four. Then one possible randomly selected population of chromosomes is

$$CR_1 = 01101$$
$$CR_2 = 11000$$
$$CR_3 = 01000$$
$$CR_4 = 10011$$

Evaluation

The evaluation function for binary vectors representing chromosomes is equivalent to the initial function f(x) where the given chromosome represents the binary code for the real value x. As noted earlier, the evaluation function plays the role of the environment, rating potential solutions in terms of their fitness. For our example, four chromosomes CR_1 to CR_4 correspond to values for input variable x:

$$x_1(CR_1) = 13$$
$$x_2(CR_2) = 24$$
$$x_3(CR_3) = 8$$
$$x_4(CR_4) = 19$$

Consequently, the evaluation function would rate them as follows:

$$f(x_1) = 169$$
$$f(x_2) = 576$$
$$f(x_3) = 64$$
$$f(x_4) = 361$$

The results of evaluating the chromosomes initially generated, may be given in a tabular form, and they are represented in Table 10.2. The expected reproduction column shows "the evaluated quality" of chromosomes in the initial population. Chromosomes CR_2 and CR_4 are more likely to be reproduced in the next generation than CR_1 and CR_3.

TABLE 10.2   Evaluation of the initial population

CR_i	Code	x	f(x)	$f(x)/\sum f(x)$	Expected reproduction: f(x)/fav
1	01101	13	169	0.14	0.58
2	11000	24	576	0.49	1.97
3	01000	8	64	0.06	0.22
4	10011	19	361	0.31	1.23
$\sum$			1170	1.00	4.00
Average			293	0.25	1.00
Max			576	0.49	1.97

Alternation

In the alternation phase, the new population is selected based on the population evaluated in the previous iteration. Clearly, the chromosome CR_4 in our example is the best of the four chromosomes, since its evaluation returns the highest value. In the alternation phase, an individual may be selected depending on its objective-function value or fitness value. For maximization problems, the higher the individual's fitness, the more probable that it can be selected for the next generation. There are different schemes that can be used in the selection process. In the simple genetic algorithm we proposed earlier, the roulette wheel–selection technique, an individual is selected randomly depending on a computed probability of selection for each individual. The probability of selection is computed by dividing the individual's fitness value by the sum of fitness values of the corresponding population, and these values are represented in column 5 in Table 10.2.

In the next step we design the roulette wheel, which is, for our problem, graphically represented in Figure 10.4.

Using the roulette wheel, we can select chromosomes for the next population. Suppose that the randomly selected chromosomes for the next generation are CR_1, CR_2, CR_2, CR_4 (the selection is in accordance with the expected reproduction—column 6 in Table 10.2). In the next step, these four chromosomes undergo the genetic operations: crossover and mutation.

Genetic operators

Crossover is not necessarily applied to all pairs of selected individuals. A choice is made depending on a specified probability called crossover probability (PC), which is typically between 0.5 and 1. If crossover is not applied (PC = 0), the offspring are simply a duplication of the parents. For the process of crossover it is necessary to determine the percentage of the population that will perform the crossover. For our particular problem we use the following parameters of the genetic algorithm:

1. Population size, *pop-size* = 4 (the parameter was already used).
2. Probability of crossover, PC = 1.
3. Probability of mutation, PM = 0.001 (the parameter will be used in a mutation operation).

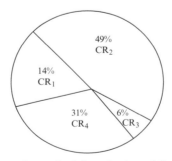

FIGURE 10.4   Roulette wheel for selection of the next population

A value of 1 for the probability of crossover translates into a 100% crossover—all chromosomes will be included in the crossover operation.

The second set of parameters in this phase of a GA is the random selection of parents for crossover and positions in the strings where the crossover will be performed. Suppose that these are randomly selected pairs: $CR_1 - CR_2$ and $CR_2 - CR_4$, and crossover is after the third position in the strings for both pairs. Then the selected strings

$$
\begin{array}{lll}
\text{First pair} & CR_1 = 01101 \\
& CR_2 = 11000 \\
& \qquad\quad \Uparrow
\end{array}
$$

$$
\begin{array}{lll}
\text{Second pair} & CR_2 = 11000 \\
& CR_4 = 10011 \\
& \qquad\quad \Uparrow
\end{array}
$$

will become, after crossover, a new population:

$$
\begin{aligned}
CR_1' &= 01100 \\
CR_2' &= 11001 \\
CR_3' &= 11011 \\
CR_4' &= 10000
\end{aligned}
$$

The second operator that can be applied in every iteration of a GA is mutation. For our example, the mutation operator has a probability of 0.1%, which means that on the 1000 transformed bits, a mutation will be performed only once. Because we transformed only 20 bits (one population of 4×5 bits is transformed into another), the probability that a mutation will occur is very small. Therefore, we can assume that the strings CR_1' to CR_4' will stay unchanged with respect to a mutation operation in this first iteration. It is expected that only one bit will be changed for every 50 iterations.

That was the final processing step in the first iteration of the genetic algorithm. The results, in the form of the new population CR_1' to CR_4', are used in the next iteration, which starts again with an evaluation process.

Evaluation (second iteration)
The process of evaluation is repeated in the new population. These results are given in Table 10.3.

The process of optimization with additional iterations of the GA can be continued in accordance with Figure 10.3. We will stop here with a presentation of computational steps for our example, and give some additional analyses of results useful for a deeper understanding of a genetic algorithm.

Although the search techniques used in the GA are based on many random parameters, they are capable of achieving a better solution by exploiting the best

TABLE 10.3   Evaluation of the second generation of chromosomes

CR_i	Code	x	f(x)	$f(x)/\sum f(x)$	Expected reproduction: $f(x)/f_{av}$
1	01100	12	144	0.08	0.32
2	11001	25	625	0.36	1.44
3	11011	27	729	0.42	1.68
4	10000	16	256	0.14	0.56
$\sum$			1754	1.00	4.00
Average			439	0.25	1.00
Max			729	0.42	1.68

alternatives in each population. A comparison of sums and average and max values from Tables 10.2 and 10.3

$$\sum\nolimits_1 = 1170 \;\Rightarrow\; \sum\nolimits_2 = 1754$$
$$\text{Average}_1 = 293 \;\Rightarrow\; \text{Average}_2 = 439$$
$$\text{Max}_1 = 576 \;\Rightarrow\; \text{Max}_2 = 729$$

shows that the new, second population is approaching closer to the maximum of the function f(x). The best result obtained from the evaluation of chromosomes in the first two iterations is the chromosome $CR3' = 11011$ and it corresponds to the feature's value $x = 27$ (theoretically it is known that the maximum of f(x) is for $x = 31$, where f(x) reaches the value 961). This increase will not be obtained in each GA iteration, but on average, the final population is much closer to a solution after a large number of iterations. The number of iterations is one possible stopping criteria for the GA algorithm. The other possibilities for stopping the GA are when the difference between the sums in two successive iterations is less than the given threshold, when a suitable fitness value is achieved, or when the computation time is limited.

10.4   SCHEMATA

The theoretical foundations of genetic algorithms rely on a binary string representation of solutions, and on the notation of a *schema*—a template allowing exploration of similarities among chromosomes. To introduce the concept of a schema, we have to first formalize some related terms. The search space Ω is the complete set of possible chromosomes or strings. In a fixed-length string l, where each bit (gene) can take on a value in the alphabet A of size k, the resulting size of the search space is k^l. For example, in binary-coded strings where the length of the string is 8 the size of the search space is $2^8 = 256$. A string in the population S is denoted by a vector $x \in \Omega$. So, in the previously described example, x would be an element of $\{0, 1\}^8$. A schema is a similarity template that defines a subset of strings with fixed values in certain positions.

A schema is built by introducing a *don't care* symbol (*) into the alphabet of genes. Each position in the scheme can take on the values of the alphabet (fixed positions) or a "don't care" symbol. In the binary case, for example, the schemata of the length 1 are defined as $H \in \{0, 1, *\}^1$. A schema represents all the strings that match it on all positions other than '*'. In other words, a schema defines a subset of the search space, or a hyperplane partition of this search space. For example, let us consider the strings and schemata of the length ten. The schema

$$(*111100100)$$

matches two strings

$$\{(0111100100), (1111100100)\},$$

and the schema

$$(*1*1100100)$$

matches four strings

$$\{(0101100100), (0111100100), (1101100100), (1111100100)\}.$$

Of course, the schema

$$(1001110001)$$

represents one string only, and the schema

$$(**********)$$

represents all strings of length 10. In general, the total number of possible schemata is $(k + 1)^l$, where k is the number of symbols in the alphabet and l is the length of the string. In the binary example of coding strings, with a length of 10, it is $(2 + 1)^{10} = 3^{10} = 59049$ different strings. It is clear that every binary schema matches exactly 2^r strings, where r is the number of *don't care* symbols in a schema template. On the other hand, each string of length m is matched by 2^m different schemata.

We can graphically illustrate the representation of different schemata for five-bit codes used to optimize the function $f(x) = x^2$ on interval [0, 31]. Every schema represents a subspace in the 2D space of the problem. For example, the schema 1**** reduces the search space of the solutions on the subspace given in Figure 10.5a, and the schema 1*0** has a corresponding search space in Figure 10.5b.

Different schemata have different characteristics. There are three important schema properties: *order* (O), *length* (L), and *fitness* (F). The *order* of the schema S denoted by O(S) is the number of 0 and 1 positions, i.e., fixed positions presented in the schema. A computation of the parameter is very simple: it is the length of the template minus the number of *don't care* symbols. For example, the following three schemata, each of length 10

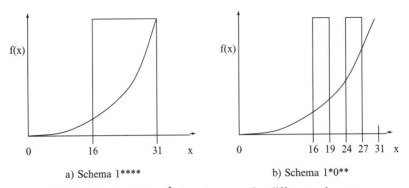

a) Schema 1****   b) Schema 1*0**

FIGURE 10.5 $f(x) = x^2$: Search spaces for different schemata

$$S_1 = (***001*110)$$
$$S_2 = (*****0**0*)$$
$$S_3 = (11101**001)$$

have the following orders:

$$O(S_1) = 10 - 4 = 6, \quad O(S_2) = 10 - 8 = 2, \quad O(S_3) = 10 - 2 = 8$$

The schema S_3 is the most specific one and the schema S_2 is the most general one. The notation of the order of a schema is useful in calculating survival probabilities of the schema for mutations.

The *length* of the schema S, denoted by L(S), is the distance between the first and the last fixed-string positions. It defines the compactness of information contained in a schema. For example, the values of this parameter for the given schemata S_1 to S_3 are

$$L(S_1) = 10 - 4 = 6, \quad L(S_2) = 9 - 6 = 3, \quad L(S_3) = 10 - 1 = 9.$$

Note that the schema with a single fixed position has a length of zero. The length L of a schema is a useful parameter in calculating the survival probabilities of the schema for crossover.

Another property of a schema S is its *fitness* F(S, t) at time t (i.e., for the given population). It is defined as the average fitness of all strings in the population matched by the schema S. Assume there are p strings $\{v_1, v_2, \ldots, v_p\}$ in a population matched by a schema S at the time t. Then

$$F(S, t) = \left[\sum_{i=1}^{p} f(v_i) \right] / p$$

The fundamental theorem of schema construction given in this book without proof explains that the *short* (high O), *low-order* (low L), and *above-average* schemata (high F) receive exponentially increasing number of strings in the next generations of a genetic algorithm. An immediate result of this theorem is that GAs explore the search space by short, low-order schemata which, subsequently, are used for information exchange during crossover and mutation operations. Therefore, a genetic algorithm seeks near-optimal performance through the analysis of these schemata, called the *building blocks*. Note, however, that the building-blocks approach is just a question of empirical results without any proof, and these rules for some real-world problems are easily violated.

10.5   TRAVELING SALESMAN PROBLEM

In this section, we explain how a genetic algorithm can be used to approach the traveling-salesman problem (TSP). Simply stated, the traveling salesman must visit every city in his territory exactly once and then return to the starting point. Given the cost of travel between all the cities, how should he plan his itinerary at minimum total cost for the entire tour? The TSP is a problem in combinatorial optimization and arises in numerous applications. There are several branch-and-bound algorithms, approximate algorithms, and heuristic search algorithms that approach this problem. During the last few years, there have been several attempts to approximate the TSP solution using genetic algorithms.

The TSP description is based on a graph representation of data. The problem could be formalized as: Given an undirected weighted graph, find the shortest route, i.e., a shortest path in which every vertex is visited exactly once, except that the initial and terminal vertices are the same. Figure 10.6 shows an example of such a graph and its optimal solution. A, B, C, etc., are the cities that were visited and the numbers associated with the edges are the cost of travel between the cities.

It is natural to represent each solution of the problem, even if it is not optimal, as a permutation of the cities. The terminal city can be omitted in the representation since it should always be the same as the initial city. For the computation of the total distance of each tour, the terminal city must be counted.

By representing each solution as a permutation of the cities, each city will be visited exactly once. Not every permutation, however, represents a valid solution, since some cities are not directly connected (e.g., A and E in Figure 10.6). One practical approach is to assign an artificially large distance between cities that are

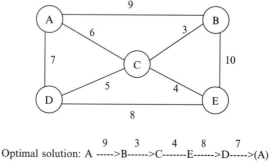

Optimal solution: A -----9----->B------3----->C-------4-------E------8----->D-----7----->(A)

FIGURE 10.6   Graphical representation of the traveling salesman problem with a corresponding optimal solution

not directly connected. In this way, invalid solutions that contain consecutive, non-adjacent cities will disappear, and all solutions will be allowed.

Our objective here is to minimize the total distance of each tour. We can select different fitness functions that will reflect this objective. For example, if the total distance is s then f(s) could be a simple f(s) = s if we minimize the fitness function; alternatives for the maximization of a fitness function are f(s) = 1/s, f(s) = 1/s², f(s) = K − s, where K is a positive constant that makes f(s) ≥ 0. There is no general formula to design the best fitness function. But, when we do not adequately reflect the goodness of the solution in the fitness function, finding an optimal or near-optimal solution will not be effective.

When dealing with permutations as solutions, simple crossover operations will result in invalid solutions. For example, for the problem in Figure 10.6, a crossover of two solutions after the third positions in the strings

A D E B C

A E C D B

will produce new strings

A D E D B

A E C B C

which are invalid solutions because they do not represent permutations of initial elements in the strings. To avoid this problem, a modified-crossover operation is introduced that directly operates on permutations and still gives permutations. This is a *partially matched crossover* (PMX) operation. It can be used not only for the traveling salesman problems, but also for any other problems that involve permutations in a solution's representation. We illustrate the effects of the PMX operation by an example. Assume that two solutions are given as permutations of the same symbols, and suppose that the PMX is a two-point operation. Selecting two strings and two random crossing points is the first step in the process of applying the PMX operation.

A D E B C

A E C D B

The substrings between crossing points are called matching sections. In our example, we have two elements in the matching sections: E B for the first string and C D for the second one. The crossover operation requires an exchange of the symbols E with C, denoted as an ordered pair (E, C), and B with D, represented as (B, D). The next step in the PMX operation is to permute each of these two-element permutations in each string. In other words, it is necessary to exchange the places for pairs (E, C) and (B, D) in both strings. The result of (E, C) changes in the first string is A D C B E, and after second pair (B, D) has been changed, the final version of the first string is A B C D E. The second string after application of the same permutations will become A C E D B first, and then A C E B D finally. If we analyze the two strings obtained by PMX operation

$$\Downarrow \; \Downarrow$$

A B C D E

A C E B D

$$\Uparrow \; \Uparrow$$

we can see that middle parts of the strings were really exchanged as in a standard crossover operation. On the other hand, the two new strings remain as valid permutations, since the symbols are actually permuted within each string.

The other steps of a genetic algorithm applied on the traveling salesman problem are unchanged. A genetic algorithm based on the above operator outperforms a random search for TSP, but still leaves much room for improvement. Typical results from the algorithm, when applied to 100 randomly generated cities, gave, after 20,000 generations, a value of the whole tour 9.4% above minimum.

10.6   MACHINE LEARNING USING GENETIC ALGORITHMS

Optimization problems are one of the most common application categories of genetic algorithms. In general, an optimization problem attempts to determine a solution that, e.g., maximizes the profit in an organization or minimizes the cost of production by determining values for selected features of the production process. Another typical area where genetic algorithms are applied is the discovery of input-to-output mapping for a given, usually complex, system, which is the type of problem that all machine-learning algorithms are trying to solve.

The basic idea of input-to-output mapping is to come up with an appropriate form of a function or a model, which is typically simpler than the mapping given originally — usually represented through a set of input–output samples. We believe that a function best describes this mapping. Measures of the term "best" depend on the specific application. Common measures are accuracy of the function, its robustness, and its computational efficiency. Generally, determining a function that satisfies all these criteria is not necessarily an easy task; therefore, a GA determines a "good" function, which can then be used successfully in applications such as pattern classification, control, and prediction. The process of mapping may be automated, and this automation, using GA technology, represents another approach to the formation of a model for inductive machine learning.

In the previous chapters of the book we described different algorithms for machine learning. Developing a new model (input-to-output abstract relation) based on some given set of samples is an idea that can also be implemented in the domain of genetic algorithms. There are several approaches to GA-based learning. We will explain the principles of the technique that is based on schemata and the possibilities of its application to classification problems.

Let us consider a simple database, which will be used as an example throughout this section. Suppose that the training or learning data set is described with a set of attributes where each attribute has its categorical range: a set of possible values. These attributes are given in Table 10.4.

The description of a classification model with two classes of samples, C1 and C2, can be represented in an *if-then* form where on the left side is a Boolean expression of the input features' values and on the right side its corresponding class:

$$((A_1 = x) \wedge (A_5 = s)) \vee ((A_1 = y) \wedge (A_4 = n)) \Rightarrow C_1$$
$$((A_3 = y) \wedge (A_4 = n)) \vee (A_1 = x) \Rightarrow C_2$$

These classification rules or classifiers can be represented in a more general way: as some strings over a given alphabet. For our data set with six inputs and one output, each classifier has the form

$$(p_1, p_2, p_3, p_4, p_5, p_6): d$$

where p_i denotes the value of the i-th attribute ($1 \leq i \leq 6$) for the domains described in Table 10.4, and d is one of two classes. To describe the classification rules in a given form, it is necessary to include the "don't care" symbol "*" into the set of values for each attribute. For example, the new set of values for attribute A_1 is {x, y, z, *}. Similar extensions are given for other attributes. The rules that were given earlier for classes C_1 and C_2 can be decomposed to the segments under conjunction (AND logical operation) and expressed as

$$(x****s*): C_1$$
$$(y**n**): C_1$$
$$(**yn**): C_2$$
$$(x*****): C_2$$

To simplify the example, we assume that the system has to classify into only two classes: C_1 and *not* C_1. Any system can be easily generalized to handle multiple classes (multiple classification). For a simple classification with a single rule C_1 we

TABLE 10.4 Attributes A_i with possible values for a given data set s

Attributes	Values
A_1	x, y, z
A_2	x, y, z
A_3	y, n
A_4	m, n, p
A_5	r, s, t, u
A_6	y, n

can accept only two values for d: $d = 1$ (member of the class C_1) and $d = 0$ (not a member of the class C_1).

Let us assume that at some stage of the learning process, there is a small and randomly generated population of classifiers Q in the system, where each classifier is given with its strength s:

$$Q_1 \quad (***ms*)\text{: }1, \quad s_1 = 12.3$$
$$Q_2 \quad (**y**n)\text{: }0, \quad s_2 = 10.1$$
$$Q_3 \quad (xy****)\text{: }1, \quad s_3 = 8.7$$
$$Q_4 \quad (*z****)\text{: }0, \quad s_4 = 2.3$$

Strengths s_i are parameters that are computed based on the available training data set. They show the fitness of a rule to the training data set, and they are proportional to the percentage of the data set supported by the rule.

The basic iterative steps of a GA, including corresponding operators, are applied here to optimize the set of rules with respect to the fitness function of the rules to training data set. The operators used in this learning technique are, again, mutation and crossover. However, some modifications are necessary for mutation. Let us consider the first attribute A_1 with its domain {x, y, z, *}. Thus, when mutation is called, we would change the mutated character (code) to one of the other three values that have equal probability. The strength of the offspring is usually the same as that of its parents. For example, if mutation is the rule Q_3 on the randomly selected position 2, replacing the value y with a randomly selected value *, the new mutated classifier will be

$$Q_{3M} \quad (x*****)\text{: }1, \quad s_{3M} = 8.7$$

The crossover does not require any modification. We take advantage of the fact that all classifiers are of equal length. Therefore, to crossover two selected parents, say Q_1 and Q_2

$$\Downarrow$$
$$Q_1 \quad (***ms*)\text{: }1$$
$$Q_2 \quad (**y**n)\text{: }0$$

we generate a random crossover-position point. Suppose that we crossover after the third character in the string as marked, then the offspring are

$$Q_{1c} \quad (*****n)\text{: }0, \quad \text{and}$$
$$Q_{2c} \quad (**yms*)\text{: }1$$

The strength of the offspring is an average (possibly weighted) of the parents' strengths. Now the system is ready to continue its learning process: starting another cycle, and accepting further positive and negative samples from the training set and modifying the strengths of classifiers as a measure of fitness. We can note that the training data set is included in the learning process through evaluation of schema's strengths for each iteration. We expect that the population of classifiers converges to some rules with very high strengths.

One of the possible implementations of the previous ideas is the *GIL system*, which moves the genetic algorithm closer to the symbolic level—mainly by defining specialized operators that manipulate binary strings. Previous symbolic classifiers are translated into binary strings, where for each attribute a binary string of fixed length is generated. The length is equal to the number of possible values for the given attribute. In the string, the required value is set to 1 and all others are set to 0. For example, if attribute A_1 has the value z, it is represented with the binary string 001 (0s are for values x, y). If the value of some attribute is *, that means that all values are possible, so it is represented with value 1 in all positions of the binary string.

For our previous example, with six attributes and a total number of seventeen different values for all attributes, the classifier symbolically represented as

$$(x***r*) \vee (y**n**): 1$$

can be transformed into the binary representation

$$(100|111|11|111|1000|11 \vee 010|111|11|010|1111|11)$$

where bars separate bit-sets for each attribute. The operators of the GIL system are modeled on inductive reasoning, which includes various inductive operators such as RuleExchange, RuleCopy, RuleGeneralization, RuleSpecialization, RuleSplit, SelectorDrop, ReferenceChange, ReferenceExtension, etc. We discuss some of them in turn.

RuleExchange
The RuleExchange operator is similar to a crossover of the classical GA, as it exchanges selected complex between two parent chromosomes. For example, two parents (two rules)

$$\Downarrow$$
$$(100|111|11|111|1000|11\vee010|111|11|010|1111|11) \quad \text{and}$$
$$(111|001|01|111|1111|01\vee110|100|10|010|0011|01)$$
$$\Uparrow$$

may produce the following offspring (new rules)

$$(100|111|11|111|1000|11 \vee 110|100|10|010|0011|01) \quad \text{and}$$
$$(111|001|01|111|1111|01 \vee 010|111|11|010|1111|11).$$

RuleGeneralization
This unary operator generalizes a random subset of complexes. For example, for a parent

$$(100|111|11|111|1000|11 \vee 110|100|10|010|0011|01 \vee$$
$$010|111|11|010|1111|11)$$

and the second and third complexes selected for generalization, the bits are *OR*ed and the following offspring is produced:

$$(100|111|11|111|1000|11 \vee 110|111|11|010|1111|11).$$

RuleSpecialization
This unary operator specializes a random subset of complexes. For example, for a parent

$$(100|111|11|111|1000|11 \vee 110|100|10|010|0011|01 \vee$$
$$010|111|11|010|1111|11)$$

and the second and third complexes selected for specialization, the bits are *AND*ed, and the following offspring is produced:

$$(100|111|11|111|1000|11 \vee 010|100|10|010|0011|01).$$

RuleSplit
This operator acts on a single complex, splitting it into a number of complexes. For example, a parent

$$(100|111|11|111|1000|11)$$

$$==$$

$$\Uparrow$$

~~─ selector):~~

The GIL system is a complex, inductive-learning system based on GA principles. It requires a number of parameters such as the probabilities of applying each operator. The process is iterative. At each iteration, all chromosomes are evaluated with respect to their completeness, consistency, and fitness criteria, and a new population is formed with those chromosomes that are better and more likely to appear. The operators are applied to the new population, and the cycle is repeated.

10.7   REVIEW QUESTIONS AND PROBLEMS

1. Given a binary string that represents a concatenation of four attribute values:

$$\{2, 5, 4, 7\} = \{010101100111\}$$

use this example to explain the basic concepts of a genetic algorithm and their equivalents in natural evolution.

2. If we want to optimize a function f(x) using a genetic algorithm, where the precision requirement for x is six decimal places and the range is $[-1, 2]$, what will be the length of a binary vector (chromosome)?

3. If $v1 = (00110011)$ and $v2 = (01010101)$ are two chromosomes, and suppose that the crossover point is randomly selected after the 5th gene, what are the two resulting offspring?

4. Given the schema (* 1 * 0 0), what are the strings that match with it?

5. What is the number of strings that match with the schema (* * * * * * * *)?

6. The function $f(x) = -x^2 + 16x$ is defined on interval $[0, 63]$. Use two iterations of a genetic algorithm to establish the approximate solution for a maximum of f(x).

7. For the function f(x) given in problem #6, compare three schemata

$$S_1 = (*1*1**)$$
$$S_2 = (*10*1*)$$
$$S_3 = (***1***)$$

with respect to order (O), length (L), and fitness (F).

8. Given a parent chromosome (1 1 0 0 0 1 0 0 0 1), what is the potential offspring (give examples) if the mutation probability is

a) $p_m = 1.0$
b) $p_m = 0.5$
c) $p_m = 0.2$
d) $p_m = 0.1$
e) $p_m = 0.0001$

9. Explain the basic principles of the building-block hypothesis and its potential applications.

10. Perform a partially matched crossover (PMC) operation for two strings S1 and S2, in which two randomly selected crossing points are given:

$$S1 = \{A\ C\ B\ D\ F\ G\ E\}$$
$$S2 = \{B\ D\ C\ F\ E\ G\ A\}$$
$$\uparrow \qquad \uparrow$$

11. Search the Web to find the basic characteristics of publicly available or commercial software tools that are based on genetic algorithms. Document the results of your search.

10.8   REFERENCES FOR FURTHER STUDY

1. Fogel, D. B., ed., *Evolutionary Computation*, IEEE Press, New York, 1998.

   The book provides a collection of thirty landmark papers, and it spans the entire history of evolutionary computation—from today's researches back to its very origins more than forty years ago.

2. Goldenberg, D. E., *Genetic Algorithms in Search, Optimization and Machine Learning*, Addison Wesley, Reading: MA, 1989.

   This book represents one of the first comprehensive texts on genetic algorithms. It introduces in a very systematic way most of the techniques that are, with small modifications and improvements, part of today's approximate-optimization solutions.

3. Michalewicz, Z., *Genetic Algorithms + Data Structures = Evolution Programs*, Springer, Berlin: Germany, 1999.

   This textbook explains the field of genetic algorithms in simple terms, and discusses the efficiency of its methods on many interesting test cases. The importance of these techniques is their applicability to many hard-optimization problems specified with large amounts of discrete data, such as the traveling salesman problem, scheduling, partitioning, and control.

11 Fuzzy Sets and Fuzzy Logic

CHAPTER OBJECTIVES

- Explain the concept of fuzzy sets with formal interpretation in continuous and discrete domains.
- Analyze characteristics of fuzzy sets and fuzzy-set operations.
- Describe the extension principle as a basic mechanism for fuzzy inferences.
- Discuss the importance of linguistic imprecision and computing with them in decision-making processes.
- Construct methods for multifactorial evaluation and extraction of a fuzzy rule–based model from large, numeric data sets.
- Understand why fuzzy computing and fuzzy systems are an important part of data-mining technology.

In the previous chapters, a number of different methodologies for the analysis of large data sets have been discussed. Most of the approaches presented, however, assume that the data is precise. That is, they assume that we deal with exact measurements for further analysis. Historically, as reflected in classical mathematics, we commonly seek a precise and crisp description of things or events. This precision is accomplished by expressing phenomena in numeric or categorical values. But in most, if not all, real-world scenarios, we will never have totally precise values. There is always going to be a degree of uncertainty. However, classical mathematics can encounter substantial difficulties because of this fuzziness. In many real-world situations, we may say that fuzziness is reality whereas crispness or precision is simplification and idealization. The polarity between fuzziness and precision is quite a striking contradiction in the development of modern information-processing systems. One effective means of resolving the contradiction is the fuzzy-set theory, a bridge between high precision and the high complexity of fuzziness.

11.1 FUZZY SETS

Fuzzy concepts derive from fuzzy phenomena that commonly occur in the real world. For example, rain is a common natural phenomenon that is difficult to describe precisely since it can rain with varying intensity, anywhere from a light shower to a torrential downpour. Since the word rain does not adequately or precisely describe the wide variations in the amount and intensity of any rain event, "rain" is considered a fuzzy phenomenon.

Often, the concepts formed in the human brain for perceiving, recognizing, and categorizing natural phenomena are also fuzzy. The boundaries of these concepts are vague. Therefore, the judging and reasoning that emerges from them are also fuzzy. For instance, "rain" might be classified as "light rain", "moderate rain", and "heavy rain" in order to describe the degree of raining. Unfortunately, it is difficult to say when the rain is light, moderate, or heavy, because the boundaries are undefined. The concepts of "light", "moderate", and "heavy" are prime examples of fuzzy concepts themselves. To explain the principles of fuzzy sets, we will start with the basics in classical set theory.

The notion of a set occurs frequently as we tend to organize, summarize, and generalize knowledge about objects. We can even speculate that the fundamental nature of any human being is to organize, arrange, and systematically classify information about the diversity of any environment. The encapsulation of objects into a collection whose members all share some general features naturally implies the notion of a set. Sets are used often and almost unconsciously; we talk about a set of even numbers, positive temperatures, personal computers, fruits, and the like. For example, a classical set A of real numbers greater than 6 is a set with a crisp boundary, and it can be expressed as

$$A = \{x \mid x > 6\}$$

where there is a clear, unambiguous boundary 6 such that if x is greater than this number, then x belongs to the set A; otherwise x does not belong to the set. Although classical sets have suitable applications and have proven to be an important tool for mathematics and computer science, they do not reflect the nature of human concepts and thoughts, which tend to be abstract and imprecise. As an illustration, mathematically we can express a set of tall persons as a collection of persons whose height is more than 6 ft; this is the set denoted by previous equation, if we let A = "tall person" and x = "height". Yet, this is an unnatural and inadequate way of representing our usual concept of "tall person." The dichotomous nature of the classical set would classify a person 6.001 ft tall as a tall person, but not a person 5.999 ft tall. This distinction is intuitively unreasonable. The flaw comes from the sharp transition between inclusions and exclusions in a set.

In contrast to a classical set, a fuzzy set, as the name implies, is a set without a crisp boundary. That is, the transition from "belongs to a set" to "does not belong to a set" is gradual, and this smooth transition is characterized by membership functions that give sets flexibility in modeling commonly used linguistic expressions such as "the water is hot" or "the temperature is high". Let us introduce some basic definitions and their formalizations concerning fuzzy sets.

Let X be a space of objects and x be a generic element of X. A classical set A, $A \subseteq X$, is defined as a collection of elements or objects $x \in X$ such that each x can either belong or not belong to the set A. By defining a *characteristic function* for each element x in X, we can represent a classical set A by a set of ordered pairs (x, 0) or (x, 1), which indicates $x \notin A$ or $x \in A$, respectively.

Unlike the aforementioned conventional set, a fuzzy set expresses the degree to which an element belongs to a set. The characteristic function of a fuzzy set is allowed to have values between 0 and 1, which denotes the degree of membership of an element in a given set. If X is a collection of objects denoted generically by x, then a fuzzy set A in X is defined as a set of ordered pairs:

$$A = \{(x, \mu_A(x)) \mid x \in X\}$$

where $\mu_A(x)$ is called the membership function (or MF for short) for the fuzzy set A. The membership function maps each element of X to a membership grade (or membership value) between 0 and 1.

Obviously, the definition of a fuzzy set is a simple extension of the definition of a classical set in which the characteristic function is permitted to have any value between 0 and 1. If the value of the membership function $\mu_A(x)$ is restricted to either 0 or 1, then A is reduced to a classic set and $\mu_A(x)$ is the characteristic function of A. For clarity, we shall also refer to classical sets as ordinary sets, crisp sets, nonfuzzy sets, or, just, sets.

Usually X is referred to as the universe of discourse, or, simply, the universe, and it may consist of discrete (ordered or nonordered) objects or continuous space. This can be clarified by the following examples. Let X = {San Francisco, Boston, Los Angeles} be the set of cities one may choose to live in. The fuzzy set C = "desirable city to live in" may be described as follows:

Let C = {(San Francisco, 0.9), (Boston, 0.8), (Los Angeles, 0.6)}.

The universe of discourse X is discrete and it contains nonordered objects: three big cities in the United States. As one can see, the membership grades listed above are quite subjective; anyone can come up with three different but legitimate values to reflect his or her preference.

In the next example, let X = {0, 1, 2, 3, 4, 5, 6} be a set of the number of children a family may choose to have. Then the fuzzy set A = "sensible number of children in a family" may be described as follows:

$$A = \{(0, 0.1), (1, 0.3), (2, 0.7), (3, 1), (4, 0.7), (5, 0.3), (6, 0.1)\}$$

Or, in the notation that we will use through this chapter,

$$A = 0.1/0 + 0.3/1 + 0.7/2 + 1.0/3 + 0.7/4 + 0.3/5 + 0.1/6$$

Here we have a discrete-order universe X; the membership function for the fuzzy set A is shown in Figure 11.1(a). Again, the membership grades of this fuzzy set are obviously subjective measures.

Finally, let X = R$^+$ be the set of possible ages for human beings. Then the fuzzy set B = "about 50-years old" may be expressed as

$$B = \{(x, \mu_B(x)) \mid x \in X\}$$

where

$$\mu_B(x) = 1/(1 + ((x - 50)/10)^4)$$

This is illustrated in Figure 11.1(b).

As mentioned earlier, a fuzzy set is completely characterized by its membership function. Since many fuzzy sets in use have a universe of discourse X consisting of the real line R, it would be impractical to list all the pairs defining a membership function. A more convenient and concise way to define a membership function is to express it as a mathematical formula. Several classes of parametrized membership functions are introduced, and in real-world applications of fuzzy sets the shape of membership functions is usually restricted to a certain class of functions that can be specified with only a few parameters. The most well known are triangular, trapezoidal, and Gaussian; Figure 11.2 shows these commonly used shapes for membership functions.

A triangular membership function is specified by three parameters {a, b, c} as follows:

$$\mu(x) = \text{triangle}(x, a, b, c) = \begin{cases} 0 & \text{for} & x \leq a \\ (x - a)/(b - a) & \text{for} & a \leq x \leq b \\ (c - x)/(c - b) & \text{for} & b \leq x \leq c \\ 0 & \text{for} & c \leq x \end{cases}$$

The parameters {a, b, c}, with a < b < c, determine the x coordinates of the three corners of the underlying triangular-membership function.

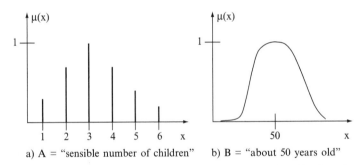

a) A = "sensible number of children"   b) B = "about 50 years old"

FIGURE 11.1   Discrete and continuous representation of membership functions for given fuzzy sets

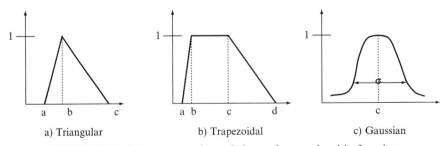

a) Triangular   b) Trapezoidal   c) Gaussian

FIGURE 11.2   Most commonly used shapes for membership functions

A trapezoidal membership function is specified by four parameters $\{a, b, c, d\}$ as follows:

$$\mu(x) = \text{trapezoid } (x, a, b, c, d) = \begin{cases} 0 & \text{for} & x \leq a \\ (x-a)/(b-a) & \text{for} & a \leq x \leq b \\ 1 & \text{for} & b \leq x \leq c \\ (d-x)/d-c) & \text{for} & c \leq x \leq d \\ 0 & \text{for} & d \leq x \end{cases}$$

The parameters $\{a, b, c, d\}$, with $a < b \leq c < d$, determine the x coordinates of the four corners of the underlying trapezoidal membership function. A triangular membership function can be seen as a special case of the trapezoidal form where $b = c$.

Finally, a Gaussian-membership function is specified by two parameters $\{c, \sigma\}$:

$$\mu(x) = \text{gaussian}(x, c, \sigma) = e^{-1/2((x-c)/\sigma)2}$$

A Gaussian membership function is determined completely by c and σ; c represents the membership-function center, and σ determines the membership-function width. Figure 11.3 illustrates the three classes of parametrized membership functions.

From the preceding examples, it is obvious that the construction of a fuzzy set depends on two things: the identification of a suitable universe of discourse and the specification of an appropriate membership function. The specification of membership function is subjective, which means that the membership functions for the same concept (say, "sensible number of children in a family") when specified by different persons may vary considerably. This subjectivity comes from individual differences in perceiving or expressing abstract concepts and has little to do with randomness. Therefore, the *subjectivity* and *nonrandomness* of fuzzy sets is the primary difference between the study of fuzzy sets and the probability theory, which deals with the objective treatment of random phenomena.

There are several parameters and characteristics of membership function that are used very often in some fuzzy-set operations and fuzzy-set inference systems. We will define only some of them that are, in our opinion, the most important:

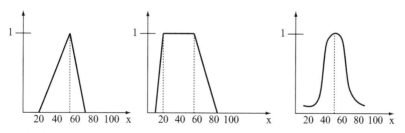

a) triangle (x, 20, 60, 80)   b) trapezoid (x, 10, 20, 60, 90)   c) gaussian (x, 50, 20)

FIGURE 11.3   Examples of parametrized membership functions

1. *Support* – The *support* of a fuzzy set A is the set of all points x in the universe of discourse X such that $\mu_A(x) > 0$:

$$Support(A) = \{x|\mu_A(x) > 0\}$$

2. *Core* – The *core* of a fuzzy set A is the set of all points x in X such that $\mu_A(x) = 1$:

$$Core(A) = \{x|\mu_A(x) = 1\}$$

3. *Normalization* – A fuzzy set A is *normal* if its core in nonempty. In other words, we can always find a point $x \in X$ such that $\mu_A(x) = 1$.

4. *Cardinality* – Given a fuzzy set A in a finite universe X, its cardinality, denoted by Card(A), is defined as

$$Card(A) = \sum \mu_A(x) \text{ where } x \in X$$

Often, *Card*(X) is referred to as the scalar cardinality or the count of A. For example, the fuzzy set $A = 0.1/1 + 0.3/2 + 0.6/3 + 1.0/4 + 0.4/5$ in universe $X = \{1, 2, 3, 4, 5, 6\}$ has a cardinality *Card*(A) = 2.4.

5. *α-cut* – The *α-cut* or *α-level set* of a fuzzy set A is a crisp set defined by

$$A_\alpha = \{x|\mu_A(x) \geq \alpha\}$$

6. *Fuzzy number* – Fuzzy numbers are a special type of fuzzy sets restricting the possible types of membership functions:

    a. The membership function must be normalized (i.e., the core is nonempty) and singular. This results in precisely one point, which lies inside the core, modeling the typical value of the fuzzy number. This point is called the modal value.

    b. The membership function has to monotonically increase left of the core and monotonically decrease on the right. This ensures that only one peak and, therefore, only one typical value exists. The spread of the support (i.e., the nonzero area of the fuzzy set) describes the degree of imprecision expressed by the fuzzy number.

A graphical illustration of some of these basic concepts is given in Figure 11.4.

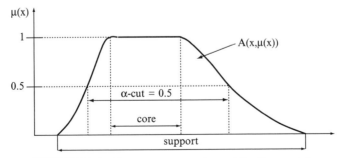

FIGURE 11.4   Core, support, and α-cut for fuzzy set A

11. 2   FUZZY SET OPERATIONS

Union, intersections, and complement are the most basic operations in classic sets. Corresponding to the ordinary set operations, fuzzy sets too have operations, which were initially defined by Zadeh, the founder of the fuzzy-set theory.

The *union* of two fuzzy sets A and B is a fuzzy set C, written as $C = A \cup B$ or $C = A$ *OR* B, whose membership function $\mu_C(x)$ is related to those of A and B by

$$\mu_C(x) = \max(\mu_A(x), \mu_B(x)) = \mu_A(x) \vee \mu_B(x), \forall x \in X$$

As pointed out by Zadeh, a more intuitive but equivalent definition of the union of two fuzzy sets A and B is the "smallest" fuzzy set containing both A and B. Alternatively, if D is any fuzzy set that contains both A and B, then it also contains $A \cup B$.

The *intersection* of fuzzy sets can be defined analogously. The intersection of two fuzzy sets A and B is a fuzzy set C, written as $C = A \cap B$ or $C = A$ *AND* B, whose membership function is related to those of A and B by

$$\mu_C(x) = \min(\mu_A(x), \mu_B(x)) = \mu_A(x) \wedge \mu_B(x), \forall x \in X$$

As in the case of the union of sets, it is obvious that the intersection of A and B is the "largest" fuzzy set that is contained in both A and B. This reduces to the ordinary intersection operation if both A and B are nonfuzzy.

The *complement* of a fuzzy set A, denoted by A', is defined by the membership function as

$$\mu_{A'}(x) = 1 - \mu_A(x), \quad \forall x \in X$$

Figure 11.5 demonstrates these three basic operations: Figure 11.5(a) illustrates two fuzzy sets A and B; Figure 11.5(b) is the complement of A; Figure 11.5(c) is the union of A and B; and Figure 11.5(d) is the intersection of A and B.

Let A and B be fuzzy sets in X and Y domains, respectively. The Cartesian product of A and B, denoted by $A \times B$, is a fuzzy set in the product space $X \times Y$ with a membership function

$$\mu_{A \times B}(x, y) = \min(\mu_A(x), \mu_B(y)) = \mu_A(x) \wedge \mu_B(y), \quad \forall x \in X \text{ and } \forall y \in Y$$

Numeric computations based on these simple fuzzy operations are illustrated through one simple example with a discrete universe of discourse S. Let $S = \{1, 2, 3, 4, 5\}$ and assume that fuzzy sets A and B are given by:

$$A = 0/1 + 0.5/2 + 0.8/3 + 1.0/4 + 0.2/5$$
$$B = 0.9/1 + 0.4/2 + 0.3/3 + 0.1/4 + 0/5$$

Then,

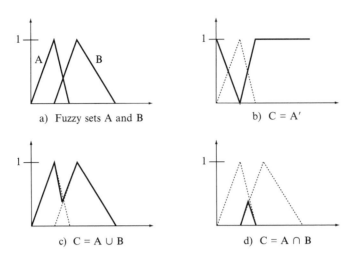

a) Fuzzy sets A and B

b) C = A′

c) C = A ∪ B

d) C = A ∩ B

FIGURE 11.5 Basic operations on fuzzy sets

$$A \cup B = 0.9/1 + 0.5/2 + 0.8/3 + 1.0/4 + 0.2/5$$
$$A \cap B = 0/1 + 0.4/2 + 0.3/3 + 0.1/4 + 0/5$$
$$A' = 1/1 + 0.5/2 + 0.2/3 + 0/4 + 0.8/5$$

and the Cartesian product of fuzzy sets A and B is

$$
\begin{aligned}
A \times B = {}& 0/(1,\ 1) + 0/(1,\ 2) + 0/(1,\ 3) + 0/(1,\ 4) + 0/(1,\ 5) \\
& + 0.5/(2,\ 1) + 0.4/(2,\ 2) + 0.3/(2,\ 3) + 0.1/(2,\ 4) + 0/(2,\ 5) \\
& + 0.8/(3,\ 1) + 0.4/(3,\ 2) + 0.3/(3,\ 3) + 0.1/(3,\ 4) + 0/(3,\ 5) \\
& + 0.9/(4,\ 1) + 0.4/(4,\ 2) + 0.3/(4,\ 3) + 0.1/(4,\ 4) + 0/(4,\ 5) \\
& + 0.2/(5,\ 1) + 0.2/(5,\ 2) + 0.2/(5,\ 3) + 0.1/(5,\ 4) + 0/(5,\ 5)
\end{aligned}
$$

Fuzzy sets, as defined by membership function, can be compared in different ways. Although the primary intention of comparing is to express the extent to which two fuzzy numbers match, it is almost impossible to come up with a single method. Instead, we can enumerate several classes of methods available today for satisfying this objective. One method, distance measures, considers a distance function between membership functions of fuzzy sets A and B and treats it as an indicator of their closeness. Comparing fuzzy sets via distance measures does not place the matching procedure in the set-theory perspective. In general, the distance between A and B, defined in the same universe of discourse X, where X ∈ R, can be defined using the Minkowski distance:

$$D(A,\ B) = \{\Sigma |A(x) - B(x)|^p\}^{1/p},\ x \in X$$

where p ≥ 1. Several specific cases are typically encountered in applications:

1. Hamming distance for p = 1,
2. Euclidean distance for p = 2, and
3. Tchebyshev distance for p = ∞.

For example, the distance between given fuzzy sets A and B, based on Euclidian measure, is

$$D(A, B) = \sqrt{(0 - 0.9)^2 + (0.5 - 0.4)^2 + (0.8 - 0.3)^2 + (1 - 0.1)^2 + (0.2 - 0)^2} = 1.39$$

For continuous universes of discourse, summation is replaced by integration. The more similar the two fuzzy sets, the lower the distance function between them. Sometimes, it is more convenient to normalize the distance function and denote it $d_n(A, B)$, and use this version to express similarity as a straight complement, $1 - d_n(A, B)$.

The other approach to comparing fuzzy sets is the use of possibility and necessity measures. The possibility measure of fuzzy set A with respect to fuzzy set B, denoted by *Pos*(A, B), is defined as

$$Pos(A, B) = \max [\min (A(x), B(x))], x \in X$$

The necessity measure of A with respect to B, *Nec*(A, B), is defined as

$$Nec(A, B) = \min [\max (A(x), 1 - B(x))], x \in X$$

For the given fuzzy sets A and B, these alternative measures for fuzzy-set comparison are

$$Pos(A, B) = \max [\min \{(0, 0.5, 0.8, 1.0, 0.2), (0.9, 0.4, 0.3, 0.1, 0)\}]$$
$$= \max [0, 0.4, 0.3, 0.1, 0] = 0.4$$

$$Nec(A, B) = \min [\max \{(0, 0.5, 0.8, 1.0, 0.2), (0.9, 0.4, 0.3, 0.1, 0)\}]$$
$$= \min [0.1, 0.6, 0.8, 1.0, 1.0] = 0.1$$

An interesting interpretation arises from these measures. The possibility measure quantifies the extent to which A and B overlap. By virtue of the definition introduced, the measure is symmetric. On the other hand, the necessity measure describes the degree to which B is included in A. As seen from the definition, the measure is asymmetrical. A visualization of these two measures is given in Figure 11.6.

A number of simple yet useful operations may be performed on fuzzy sets. These are one-argument mappings, because they apply to a single membership function.

1. *Normalization* – This operation converts a subnormal, nonempty fuzzy set into a normalized version by dividing the original membership function by the height of A

$$Norm A(x) = \{(x, \mu_A(x)/hgt(x) = \mu_A(x)/ \max \mu_A(x)) \text{ where } x \in X\}$$

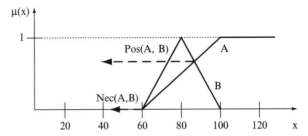

FIGURE 11.6   Comparison of fuzzy sets representing linguistic terms, A = high speed and B = speed around 80 km/h

2. *Concentration* – When fuzzy sets are concentrated, their membership functions take on relatively smaller values. That is, the membership function becomes more concentrated around points with higher membership grades as, for instance, being raised to power two:

$$ConA(x) = \{(x, \mu_A^2(x))\text{ where } x \in X\}$$

3. *Dilation* – Dilation has the opposite effect from concentration and is produced by modifying the membership function through exponential transformation, where the exponent is less than 1

$$DilA(x) = \{(x, \mu_A^{1/2}(x))\text{ where } x \in X\}$$

The basic effects of the previous three operations are illustrated in Figure 11.7.

In practice, when the universe of discourse X is a continuous space (the real axis R or its subset), we usually partition X into several fuzzy sets whose membership functions cover X in a more-or-less uniform manner. These fuzzy sets, which usually carry names that conform to adjectives appearing in our daily linguistic usage, such as "large", "medium", or "small", are called *linguistic values* or linguistic labels. Thus, the universe of discourse X is often called the linguistic variable. Let us give some simple examples.

Suppose that X = "age." Then we can define fuzzy sets "young," "middle aged," and "old" that are characterized by MFs $\mu_{young}(x)$, $\mu_{middle\ aged}(x)$, and $\mu_{old}(x)$, respectively. Just as a variable can assume various values, a linguistic variable

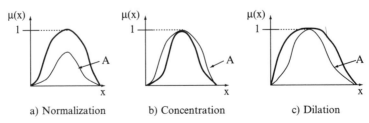

a) Normalization   b) Concentration   c) Dilation

FIGURE 11.7   Simple unary fuzzy operations

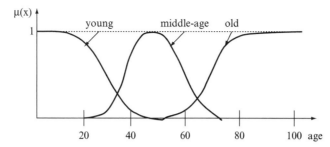

FIGURE 11.8   Typical membership functions for linguistic values "young", "middle aged", and "old"

"age" can assume different linguistic values, such as "young," "middle aged," and "old" in this case. If "age" assumes the value of "young," then we have the expression "age is young," and so also for the other values. Typical membership functions for these linguistic values are displayed in Figure 11.8, where the universe of discourse X is totally covered by the membership functions and their smooth and gradual transition from one to another. Unary fuzzy operations, concentration and dilation, may be interpreted as linguistic modifiers "very" and "more or less", respectively.

A linguistic variable is characterized by a quintuple (x, T(x), X, G, M) in which x is the name of the variable; T(x) is the term set of x—the set of its linguistic values; X is the universe of discourse; G is a syntactic rule which generates the terms in T(x); and M is a semantic rule which associates with each linguistic value A its meaning M(A), where M(A) denotes a membership function for a fuzzy set in X. For example, if age is interpreted as a linguistic variable, then the term set T(age) could be

$$T(age) = \{very\ young,\ young,\ not\ very\ young,\ not\ young,\ \dots\ middle\ aged,\ not$$
$$middle\ aged,\ not\ old,\ more\text{-}or\text{-}less\ old,\ old,\ very\ old\}$$

where each term in T(age) is characterized by a fuzzy set of a universe of discourse X = [0,100]. The syntactic rule refers to the way the linguistic values in the term set T(age) are generated, and the semantic rule defines the membership function of each linguistic value of the term set T(age), such as the linguistic values in Figure 11.8.

11.3   EXTENSION PRINCIPLE AND FUZZY RELATIONS

As in the set theory, we can define several generic relations between two fuzzy sets, such as *equality* and *inclusion*. We say that two fuzzy sets, A and B, defined in the same space X are equal if and only if (iff) their membership functions are identical:

$$A = B \quad iff \quad \mu_A(x) = \mu_B(x),\ \forall x \in X$$

Analogously, we shall define the notion of *containment*, which plays a central role in both ordinary and fuzzy sets. This definition of containment is, of course, a natural extension of the case for ordinary sets. Fuzzy set A is *contained* in fuzzy set B (or, equivalently, A is a subset of B) if and only if $\mu_A(x) \leq \mu_B(x)$ for all x. In symbols,

$$A \subseteq B \Leftrightarrow \mu_A(x) \leq \mu_B(x), \forall x \in X$$

Figure 11.9 illustrates the concept of $A \subseteq B$.

When the fuzzy sets A and B are defined in a finite universe X, and the requirement that for each x in X, $\mu_A(x) \leq \mu_B(x)$ is relaxed, we may define the degree of subsethood DS as

$$DS(A, B) = (1/Card(A))\{Card(A) - \Sigma \max[0, A(x) - B(x)]\}, x \in X$$

DS(A,B) provides a normalized measure of the degree to which the inequality $\mu_A(x) \leq \mu_B(x)$ is violated.

Now we have enough background to explain one of the most important concepts in formalization of a fuzzy-reasoning process. The *extension principle* is a basic transformation of the fuzzy-set theory that provides a general procedure for extending the crisp domains of mathematical expressions to fuzzy domains. This procedure generalizes a common point-to-point mapping of a function f between fuzzy sets. The *extension principle* plays a fundamental role in translating set-based concepts into their fuzzy counterparts. Essentially, the extension principle is used to transform fuzzy sets via functions. Let X and Y be two sets and f a mapping from X to Y:

$$F: X \rightarrow Y$$

Let A be a fuzzy set in X. The extension principle states that the image of A under this mapping is a fuzzy set $B = f(A)$ in Y such that for each $y \in Y$:

$$\mu_B(y) = \max \mu_A(x), \text{ subject to } x \in X \text{ and } y = f(x).$$

The basic idea is illustrated in Figure 11.10. The extension principle easily generalizes to functions of many variables as follows. Let X_i, $i = 1, \ldots, n$, and Y be universes of discourse, and $X = X1 \times X2 \times \ldots \times Xn$ constitute the Cartesian product of the X_is. Consider fuzzy sets A_i in X_i, $i = 1, \ldots, n$ and a mapping $y = f(x)$, where the input is an n-dimensional vector $x = (x_1, x_2, \ldots, x_n)$ and $x \in X$. Fuzzy

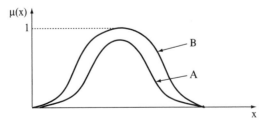

FIGURE 11.9   The concept of $A \subseteq B$ where A and B are fuzzy sets

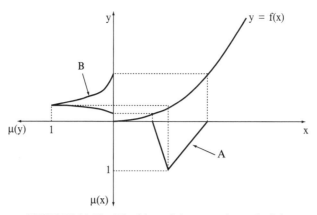

FIGURE 11.10   The idea of the extension principle

sets A1, A2,..., An are then transformed via f, producing the fuzzy set B = f(A1, A2, ..., An) in Y such that for each y ∈ Y:

$$\mu_B(y) = \max_x \{ \min [\mu_{A1}(x_1), \mu_{A2}(x_2), \ldots, \mu_{An}(x_n)] \}$$

subject to x ∈ X and y = f(x). Actually, in the expression above, the min operator is just a choice within a family of operators called triangular norms.

More specifically, suppose that f is a function from X to Y where X and Y are discrete universes of discourse, and A is a fuzzy set on X defined as

$$A = \mu_A(x_1)/x_1 + \mu_A(x_2)/x_2 + \mu_A(x_3)/x_3 + \ldots + \mu_A(x_n)/x_n$$

then the extension principle states that the image of fuzzy set A under the mapping f can be expressed as a fuzzy set B:

$$B = f(A) = \mu_A(x_1)/y_1 + \mu_A(x_2)/y_2 + \mu_A(x_3)/y_3 + \ldots + \mu_A(x_n)/y_n$$

where $y_i = f(x_i)$, i = 1, ..., n. In other words, the fuzzy set B can be defined through the mapped values x_i using the function f.

Let us analyze the extension principle using one example. Suppose that X = {1, 2, 3, 4} and Y = {1, 2, 3, 4, 5, 6} are two universes of discourse, and the function for transformation is y = x + 2. For a given fuzzy set A = 0.1/1 + 0.2/2 + 0.7/3 + 1.0/4 in X, it is necessary to find a corresponding fuzzy set B(y) in Y using the extension principle through function B = f(A). In this case, the process of computation is straightforward and a final, transformed fuzzy set is B = 0.1/3 + 0.2/4 + 0.7/5 + 1.0/6.

Another problem will show that the computational process is not always a one-step process. Suppose that A is given as

$$A = 0.1/-2 + 0.4/-1 + 0.8/0 + 0.9/1 + 0.3/2$$

and the function f is

$$f(x) = x^2 - 3$$

Upon applying the extension principle, we have

$$
\begin{aligned}
B &= 0.1/1 + 0.4/- 2 + 0.8/- 3 + 0.9/- 2 + 0.3/1 \\
&= 0.8/- 3 + (0.4 \vee 0.9)/- 2 + (0.1 \vee 0.3)/1 \\
&= 0.8/- 3 + 0.9/- 2 + 0.3/1
\end{aligned}
$$

where $\vee$ represents the max function. For a fuzzy set with a continuous universe of discourse X, an analogous procedure applies.

Besides being useful in the application of the extension principle, some of the unary and binary fuzzy relations are also very important in a fuzzy-reasoning process. Binary fuzzy relations are fuzzy sets in $X \times Y$ that map each element in $X \times Y$ to a membership grade between 0 and 1. Let X and Y be two universes of discourse. Then

$$R = \{((x, y), \mu_R(x, y)) | (x, y) \in X \times Y\}$$

is a binary fuzzy relation in $X \times Y$. Note that $\mu_R(x, y)$ is in fact a two-dimensional membership function. For example, let $X = Y = R^+$ (the positive real axis); the fuzzy relation is given as R = "y is much greater than x". The membership function of the fuzzy relation can be subjectively defined as

$$
\mu_R(x, y) = \begin{cases} (y - x)/(x + y + 2), & \text{if } y > x \\ 0 & \text{if } y \leq x \end{cases}
$$

If X and Y are a finite set of discrete values such as X {3, 4, 5} and Y = {3, 4, 5, 6, 7}, then it is convenient to express the fuzzy relation R as a relation matrix:

$$
R = \begin{bmatrix} 0 & 0.111 & 0.200 & 0.273 & 0.333 \\ 0 & 0 & 0.091 & 0.167 & 0.231 \\ 0 & 0 & 0 & 0.077 & 0.143 \end{bmatrix}
$$

where the element at row i and column j is equal to the membership grade between the i*th* element of X and the j*th* element of Y.

Common examples of binary fuzzy relations are as follows:

1. x is close to y (x and y are numbers).
2. x depends on y (x and y are categorical data).
3. x and y look alike.
4. If x is large, then y is small.

Fuzzy relations in different product spaces can be combined through a composition operation. Different composition operations have been suggested for fuzzy relations; the best known is the max–min composition proposed by Zadeh. Let R_1

and R_2 be two fuzzy relations defined on $X \times Y$ and $Y \times Z$, respectively. The max–min composition of R_1 and R_2 is a fuzzy set defined by

$$R_1 \circ R_2 = \{[(x, z), \max_y \min(\mu_{R1}(x, y), \mu_{R2}(y, z))] \mid x \in X, y \in Y, z \in Z\}$$

or equivalently,

$$R_1 \circ R_2 = \vee_y[\mu_{R1}(x, y) \wedge \mu_{R2}(y, z)]$$

with the understanding that $\vee$ and $\wedge$ represent max and min, respectively.

When R1 and R2 are expressed as relation matrices, the calculation of $R_1 \circ R_2$ is similar to the matrix-multiplication process, except that $\times$ and $+$ operations are replaced by $\vee$ and $\wedge$, respectively.

The following example demonstrates how to apply the max–min composition on two relations and how to interpret the resulting fuzzy relation $R_1 \circ R_2$. Let $R_1 =$ "x is relevant to y" and $R_2 =$ "y is relevant to z" be two fuzzy relations defined on $X \times Y$ and $Y \times Z$, where $X = \{1, 2, 3\}$, $Y = \{\alpha, \beta, \gamma, \delta\}$, and $Z = \{a, b\}$. Assume that R_1 and R_2 can be expressed as the following relation matrices of μ values:

$$R_1 = \begin{bmatrix} 0.1 & 0.3 & 0.5 & 0.7 \\ 0.4 & 0.2 & 0.8 & 0.9 \\ 0.6 & 0.8 & 0.3 & 0.2 \end{bmatrix}$$

$$R_2 = \begin{bmatrix} 0.9 & 0.1 \\ 0.2 & 0.3 \\ 0.5 & 0.6 \\ 0.7 & 0.2 \end{bmatrix}$$

Fuzzy relation $R_1 \circ R_2$ can be interpreted as a derived relation "x is relevant to z" based on relations R_1 and R_2. We will make a detailed max–min composition only for one element in a resulting fuzzy relation: $(x, z) = (2, a)$.

$$\begin{aligned} \mu_{R1 \circ R2}(2, a) &= \max(0.4 \wedge 0.9, 0.2 \wedge 0.2, 0.8 \wedge 0.5, 0.9 \wedge 0.7) \\ &= \max(0.4, 0.2, 0.5, 0.7) \\ &= 0.7 \end{aligned}$$

Analogously, we can compute the other elements, and the final fuzzy matrix $R_1 \circ R_2$ will be

$$R_1 \circ R_2 = \begin{bmatrix} 0.7 & 0.5 \\ 0.7 & 0.6 \\ 0.6 & 0.3 \end{bmatrix}$$

11.4 FUZZY LOGIC AND FUZZY INFERENCE SYSTEMS

Fuzzy logic enables us to handle uncertainty in a very intuitive and natural manner. In addition to making it possible to formalize imprecise data, it also enables us to do arithmetic and Boolean operations using fuzzy sets. Finally, it describes the inference systems based on fuzzy rules. Fuzzy rules and fuzzy-reasoning processes, which are the most important modeling tools based on the fuzzy set theory, are the backbone of any fuzzy inference system. Typically, a fuzzy rule has the general format of a conditional proposition. A *fuzzy If-then rule*, also known as *fuzzy implication*, assumes the form

If x is A   then y is B

where A and B are linguistic values defined by fuzzy sets on the universes of discourse X and Y, respectively. Often, "x is A" is called the antecedent or premise, while "y is B" is called the consequence or conclusion. Examples of fuzzy If-then rules are widespread in our daily linguistic expressions, such as the following:

1. If pressure is high, then volume is small.
2. If the road is slippery, then driving is dangerous.
3. If a tomato is red, then it is ripe.
4. If the speed is high, then apply the brake a little.

Before we can employ fuzzy If-then rules to model and analyze a fuzzy reasoning-process, we have to formalize the meaning of the expression "If x is A then y is B", sometimes abbreviated in a formal presentation as $A \rightarrow B$. In essence, the expression describes a relation between two variables x and y; this suggests that a fuzzy If-then rule be defined as a binary fuzzy relation R on the product space $X \times Y$. R can be viewed as a fuzzy set with a two-dimensional membership function:

$$\mu_R(x, y) = f(\mu_A(x), \mu_B(y))$$

If we interpret $A \rightarrow B$ as A *entails* B, still it can be formalized in several different ways. One formula that could be applied based on a standard logical interpretation, is

$$R = A \rightarrow B = A' \cup B.$$

Note that this is only one of several possible interpretations for fuzzy implication. The accepted meaning of $A \rightarrow B$ represents the basis for an explanation of the fuzzy-reasoning process using If-then fuzzy rules.

Fuzzy reasoning, also known as approximate reasoning, is an inference procedure that derives its conclusions from a set of fuzzy rules and known facts (they also can be fuzzy sets). The basic rule of inference in a traditional two-valued logic is *modus-ponens*, according to which we can infer the truth of a proposition B from the truth of A and the implication $A \rightarrow B$. However, in much of human reasoning, *modus ponens* is employed in an approximate manner. For example, if we have the rule " if the tomato is red, then it is ripe" and we know that "the tomato is more or less red", then we may infer that "the tomato is more or less ripe". This type of approximate reasoning can be formalized as

Fact: x is A′
Rule: If x is A then y is B

Conclusion: y is B′

where A′ is close to A and B′ is close to B. When A, A′, B, and B′ are fuzzy sets of an approximate universe, the foregoing inference procedure is called approximate reasoning or fuzzy reasoning; it is also called *generalized modus ponens*, since it has *modus ponens* as a special case.

Using the composition rule of inference, we can formulate the inference procedure of fuzzy reasoning. Let A, A′, and B be fuzzy sets on X, X, and Y domains, respectively. Assume that the fuzzy implication A → B is expressed as a fuzzy relation R on X × Y. Then the fuzzy set B′ induced by A′ and A → B is defined by

$$\mu_{B'}(y) = \max_x \min [\mu_{A'}(x), \mu_R(x, y)]$$
$$= \vee_x[\mu_{A'}(x) \wedge \mu_R(x, y)]$$

Some typical characteristics of the fuzzy reasoning process and some conclusions useful for this type of reasoning are

1. $\forall A, \forall A' \rightarrow B' \supseteq B$ (or $\mu_{B'}(y) \geq \mu_B(y)$)
2. If $A' \subseteq A$ (or $\mu_A(x) \geq \mu_{A'}(x)$) $\rightarrow B' = B$

Let us analyze the computational steps of a fuzzy-reasoning process for one simple example. Given the fact A′ = "x is above average height" and the fuzzy rule "if x is high, then his/her weight is also high", we can formalize this as a fuzzy implication A → B. We can use a discrete representation of the initially given fuzzy sets A, A′, and B (based on subjective heuristics):

A′:	x	$\mu(x)$		A:	x	$\mu(x)$		B:	y	$\mu(y)$
	5′6″	0.3			5′6″	0			120	0
	5′9″	1.0			5′9″	0.2			150	0.2
	6′	0.4			6′	0.8			180	0.5
	6′3″	0			6′3″	1.0			210	1.0

$\mu_R(x, y)$ can be computed in several different ways, such as

$$\mu_R(x, y) = \begin{cases} 1 & \text{for } \mu_A(x) \leq \mu_B(y) \\ \mu_B(y) & \text{otherwise} \end{cases}$$

or as the Lukasiewicz-norm:

$$\mu_R(x, y) = \{1 \wedge (1 - \mu_A(x) + \mu_B(y))\}$$

Both definitions lead to a very different interpretation of fuzzy implication. Applying the first relation for $\mu_R(x, y)$ on the numeric representation for our sets A and B, the two-dimensional membership function will be

$$\mu_R(x, y) = \begin{bmatrix} 1 & 1 & 1 & 1 \\ 0 & 1 & 1 & 1 \\ 0 & 0.2 & 0.5 & 1 \\ 0 & 0.2 & 0.5 & 1 \end{bmatrix}$$

Now, using the basic relation for inference procedure, we obtain

$$\mu_{B'}(y) = \max_x \min [\mu_{A'}(x)\mu_R(x, y)]$$

$$= \max_x \min [0.3 \quad 1 \quad 0.4 \quad 0] \cdot \begin{bmatrix} 1 & 1 & 1 & 1 \\ 0 & 1 & 1 & 1 \\ 0 & 0.2 & 0.5 & 1 \\ 0 & 0.2 & 0.5 & 1 \end{bmatrix}$$

$$= \max_x \begin{bmatrix} 0.3 & 0.3 & 0.3 & 0.3 \\ 0 & 1 & 1 & 1 \\ 0 & 0.2 & 0.4 & 0.4 \\ 0 & 0 & 0 & 0 \end{bmatrix}$$

$$= [0.3 \quad 1 \quad 1 \quad 1]$$

The resulting fuzzy set B' can be represented in the form of a table:

B:	y	$\mu(y)$
	120	0.3
	150	1.0
	180	1.0
	210	1.0

or interpreted approximately in linguistic terms: " x's weight is more-or-less high". A graphical comparison of membership functions for fuzzy sets A and A' and B and B' is given in Figure 11.11.

To use fuzzy sets in approximate reasoning (a set of linguistic values with numeric representations of membership functions), the main tasks for the designer of a system are

1. representation of any fuzzy datum, given as a linguistic value, in terms of the codebook A,

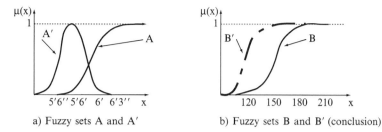

a) Fuzzy sets A and A'   b) Fuzzy sets B and B' (conclusion)

FIGURE 11.11 Comparison of approximate reasoning result B' with initially given fuzzy sets A', A, and B and the fuzzy rule A- > B

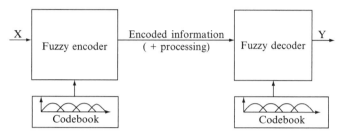

FIGURE 11.12 Fuzzy-communication channel with fuzzy encoding and decoding

2. use these coded values for different communication and processing steps, and

3. at the end of approximate reasoning, transform the computed results back into its original (linguistic) format using the same codebook A.

These three fundamental tasks are commonly referred to as encoding, transmission and processing, and decoding (the terms have been borrowed from communication theory). The encoding activities occur at the transmitter while the decoding take place at the receiver. Figure 11.12 illustrates encoding and decoding with the use of the codebook A. The channel functions as follows. Any input information, whatever its nature, is encoded (represented) in terms of the elements of the codebook. In this internal format, encoded information is sent with or without processing across the channel. Using the same codebook, the output message is decoded at the receiver.

Fuzzy set literature has traditionally used the terms fuzzification and defuzzification to denote encoding and decoding, respectively. These are, unfortunately, quite misleading and meaningless terms because they mask the very nature of the processing that takes place in fuzzy reasoning. They neither address any design criteria nor introduce any measures aimed at characterizing the quality of encoding and decoding information completed by the fuzzy channel.

The next two sections are examples of the application of fuzzy logic and fuzzy reasoning to decision-making processes, where the available data sets are ambiguous. These applications include multifactorial evaluation and extraction of fuzzy rules–based models from large numeric data sets.

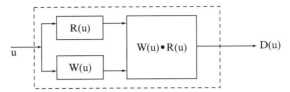

FIGURE 11.13   Multifactorial evaluation model

11.5   MULTIFACTORIAL EVALUATION

Multifactorial evaluation is a good example of the application of the fuzzy-set theory to decision-making processes. Its purpose is to provide a synthetic evaluation matrix of an object relative to an objective in a fuzzy-decision environment that has many factors. Let $U = \{u_1, u_2, \ldots, u_n\}$ be a set of objects for evaluation, let $F = \{f_1, f_2, \ldots, f_m\}$ be the set of basic factors in the evaluation process, and let $E = \{e_1, e_2, \ldots, e_p\}$ be a set of descriptive grades or qualitative classes used in the evaluation. For every object $u \in U$, there is a single-factor evaluation matrix $R(u)$ with dimensions $m \times p$, which is usually the result of a survey. This matrix may be interpreted and used as a two-dimensional membership function for fuzzy relation $F \times E$.

With the preceding three elements, F, E, and R, the evaluation result $D(u)$ for a given object $u \in U$ can be derived using the basic fuzzy-processing procedure: the product of fuzzy relations through max–min composition. This has been shown in Figure 11.13. An additional input to the process is the weight vector $W(u)$ for evaluation factors, which can be viewed as a fuzzy set for a given input u. A detailed explanation of the computational steps in the multifactorial-evaluation process will be given through two examples.

1. A cloth-selection problem

Assume that the basic factors of interest in the selection of cloth consist of f_1 = style, f_2 = quality, and f_3 = price, i.e., $F = \{f_1, f_2, f_3\}$. The verbal grades used for the selection are e_1 = best, e_2 = good, e_3 = fair, and e_4 = poor, i.e., $E = \{e_1, e_2, e_3, e_4\}$. For a particular piece of cloth u, the single-factor evaluation may be carried out by professionals or customers by a survey. For example, if the survey results of the "style" factor f_1 are 60% for the best, 20% for the good, 10% for the fair, and 10% for the poor, then the single-factor evaluation vector $R_1(u)$ is

$$R_1(u) = \{0.6, 0.2, 0.1, 0.1\}$$

Similarly, we can obtain the following single-factor evaluation vectors for f_2 and f_3:

$$R_2(u) = \{0.1, 0.5, 0.3, 0.1\}$$
$$R_3(u) = \{0.1, 0.3, 0.4, 0.2\}$$

Based on single-factor evaluations, we can build the following evaluation matrix:

$$R(u) = \begin{bmatrix} R_1(u) \\ R_2(u) \\ R_3(u) \end{bmatrix} = \begin{bmatrix} 0.6 & 0.2 & 0.1 & 0.1 \\ 0.1 & 0.5 & 0.3 & 0.1 \\ 0.1 & 0.3 & 0.4 & 0.2 \end{bmatrix}$$

If a customer's weight vector with respect to the three factors is

$$W(u) = \{0.4, 0.4, 0.2\}$$

then it is possible to apply the multifactorial-evaluation model to compute the evaluation for a piece of cloth u. "Multiplication" of matrices $W(u)$ and $R(u)$ is based on the max–min composition of fuzzy relations, where the resulting evaluation is in the form of a fuzzy set $D(u) = [d_1, d_2, d_3, d_4]$:

$$D(u) = W(u) \cdot R(u) = [0.4 \quad 0.4 \quad 0.2] \cdot \begin{bmatrix} 0.6 & 0.2 & 0.1 & 0.1 \\ 0.1 & 0.5 & 0.3 & 0.1 \\ 0.1 & 0.3 & 0.4 & 0.2 \end{bmatrix}$$

$$= [0.4 \quad 0.4 \quad 0.3 \quad 0.2]$$

where, e.g., d_1 is calculated through the following steps:

$$d_1 = (w1 \wedge r11) \vee (w2 \wedge r21) \vee (w3 \wedge r31)$$
$$= (0.4 \wedge 0.6) \vee (0.4 \wedge 0.1) \vee (0.2 \wedge 0.1)$$
$$= 0.4 \vee 0.1 \vee 0.1$$
$$= 0.4$$

The values for d_2, d_3, and d_4 are found similarly, where $\wedge$ and $\vee$ represent the operations min and max, respectively. Because the largest components of $D(u)$ are $d_1 = 0.4$ and $d_2 = 0.4$ at the same time, the analyzed piece of cloth receives a rating somewhere between "best" and "good".

2. A problem of evaluating teaching

Assume that the basic factors that influence students' evaluation of teaching are $f_1 =$ clarity and understandability, $f_2 =$ proficiency in teaching, $f_3 =$ liveliness and stimulation, and $f_4 =$ writing neatness or clarity, i.e., $F = \{f_1, f_2, f_3, f_4\}$. Let $E = \{e_1, e_2, e_3, e_4\} = \{\text{excellent, very good, good, poor}\}$ be the verbal grade set. We evaluate a teacher u. By selecting an appropriate group of students and faculty, we can have them respond with their ratings on each factor and then obtain the single-factor evaluation. As in the previous example, we can combine the single-factor evaluation into an evaluation matrix. Suppose that the final matrix $R(u)$ is

$$R(u) = \begin{bmatrix} 0.7 & 0.2 & 0.1 & 0.0 \\ 0.6 & 0.3 & 0.1 & 0.0 \\ 0.2 & 0.6 & 0.1 & 0.1 \\ 0.1 & 0.1 & 0.6 & 0.2 \end{bmatrix}$$

For a specific weight vector $W(u) = \{0.2, 0.3, 0.4, 0.1\}$, describing the importance of the teaching-evaluation factor f_i and using the multifactorial-evaluation model, it is easy to find

$$D(u) = W(u) \cdot R(u) = \begin{bmatrix} 0.2 & 0.3 & 0.4 & 0.1 \end{bmatrix} \cdot \begin{bmatrix} 0.7 & 0.2 & 0.1 & 0.0 \\ 0.6 & 0.3 & 0.1 & 0.0 \\ 0.2 & 0.6 & 0.1 & 0.1 \\ 0.1 & 0.1 & 0.6 & 0.2 \end{bmatrix}$$

$$= \begin{bmatrix} 0.2 & 0.4 & 0.1 & 0.1 \end{bmatrix}$$

Analyzing the evaluation results $D(u)$, because $d_2 = 0.4$ is a maximum, we may conclude that teacher u should be rated as "very good".

11.6 EXTRACTING FUZZY MODELS FROM DATA

In the context of different data-mining analyses, it is of great interest to see how fuzzy models can automatically be derived from a data set. Besides prediction, classification, and all other data-mining tasks, understandability is of prime concern, because the resulting fuzzy model should offer an insight into the underlying system. To achieve this goal, different approaches exist. Let us explain a common technique that constructs grid-based rule sets using a global granulation of the input and output spaces.

Grid-based rule sets model each input variable usually through a small set of linguistic values. The resulting rule base uses all or a subset of all possible combinations of these linguistic values for each variable, resulting in a global granulation of the feature space into rectangular regions. Figure 11.14 illustrates this approach in two dimensions: with three linguistic values (low, medium, high) for the first dimension x_1 and two linguistic values for the second dimension x_2 (young, old).

Extracting grid-based fuzzy models from data is straightforward when the input granulation is fixed, i.e., the antecedents of all rules are predefined. Then, only a

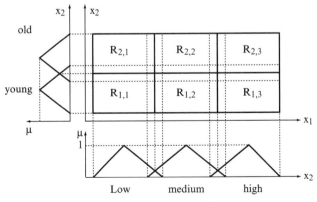

FIGURE 11.14 A global granulation for a two-dimensional space using three membership functions for x_1 and two for x_2

matching consequent for each rule needs to be found. This approach, with fixed grids, is usually called the *Mamdani model*. After predefinition of the granulation of all input variables and also the output variable, one sweeps through the entire data set and determines the closest example to the geometrical center of each rule, assigning the closest fuzzy value output to the corresponding rule. Using graphical interpretation in a 2D space, the global steps of the procedure are illustrated through an example in which only one input x and one output dimension y exist. The formal analytical specification, even with more than one input/output dimension, is very easy to establish.

1. *Granulate the input and output space.* Divide each variable x_i into n_i equidistant, triangular, membership functions. In our example, both input x and output y are granulated using the same four linguistic values: low, below-average, above-average, and high. A representation of the input–output granulated space is given in Figure 11.15.

2. *Analyze the entire data set in the granulated space.* First, enter a data set in the granulated space and then find the points that lie closest to the centers of the granulated regions. Mark these points and the centers of the region. In our example, after entering all discrete data, the selected center points (closest to the data) are additionally marked with **x**, as in Figure 11.16.

3. *Generate fuzzy rules from given data.* The data representative directly selects the regions in a granulated space. These regions may be described with the corresponding fuzzy rules. In our example, four regions are selected, one for each fuzzy input linguistic value, and they are represented in Figure 11.17 with a corresponding crisp approximation (a thick line through the middle of the regions). These regions are the graphical representation of fuzzy rules. The same rules may be expressed linguistically as a set of IF-THEN constructions:

R_1: IF x is *small*   THEN y is *above average*.
R_2: IF x is *below average* THEN y is *above average*.
R_3: IF x is *above average* THEN y is *high*.
R_4: IF x is *high*   THEN y is *above average*.

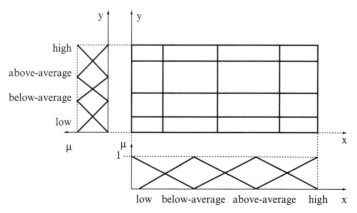

FIGURE 11.15 Granulation of a two-dimensional I/O space

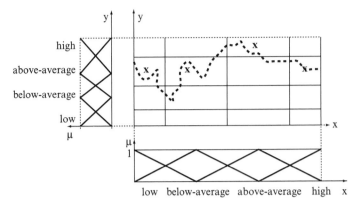

FIGURE 11.16 Selection of characteristic points in a granulated space

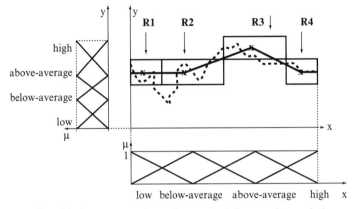

FIGURE 11.17 Graphical representation of generated fuzzy rules and the resulting crisp approximation

Note how the generated model misses the extremes that lie far from the existing rule centers. This behavior occurs because only one pattern per rule is used to determine the outcome of this rule. Even a combined approach would very much depend on the predefined granulation. If the function to be modeled has a high variance inside one rule, the resulting fuzzy rule model will fail to model this behavior.

For practical applications it is obvious, however, that using such a predefined, fixed grid results in a fuzzy model that will either not fit the underlying functions very well or consist of a large number of rules because of small granulation. Therefore, new approaches have been introduced that automatically determine the granulations of both input and output variables based on a given data set. We will explain the basic steps for one of these algorithms using the same data set from the previous example and the graphical representation of applied procedures.

1. Initially, only one membership function is used to model each of the input variables as well as the output variable, resulting in one large rule covering the

entire feature space. Subsequently, new membership functions are introduced at points of maximum error (the maximum distance between data points and the obtained crisp approximation). Figure 11.18 illustrates this first step in which the crisp approximation is represented with a thick line and the selected point of maximal error with an arrow.

2. For the selected point of maximum error, new triangular fuzzy values for both input and output variables are introduced. Processes of granulation, determining fuzzy rules in the form of space regions, and crisp approximation are repeated for a space, with additional input and output fuzzy values for the second step— that means two fuzzy values for both input and output variables. The final results of the second step, for our example, are presented in Figure 11.19.

3. Step 2 is repeated until a maximum number of divisions (fuzzy values) is reached, or the approximation error remains below a certain threshold value. Figures 11.20 and 11.21 demonstrate two additional iterations of the algorithm for a data set. Here granulation was stopped after a maximum of four membership functions was generated for each variable. Obviously this algorithm is able

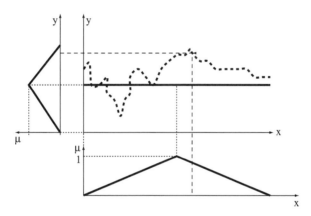

FIGURE 11.18   The first step in automatically determining fuzzy granulation

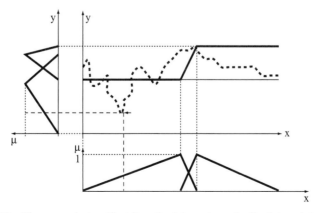

FIGURE 11.19   The second step (first iteration) in automatically determining granulation

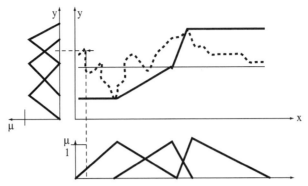

FIGURE 11.20 The second step (second iteration) in automatically determining granulation

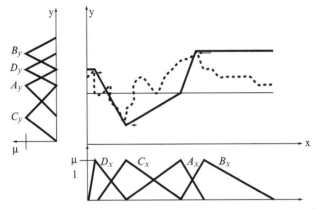

FIGURE 11.21 The second step (third iteration) in automatically determining granulation

to model extremes much better than the previous one with a fixed granulation. At the same time, it has a strong tendency to favor extremes and to concentrate on outliers. The final set of fuzzy rules, using dynamically created fuzzy values A_x to D_x and A_y to D_y for input and output variables, is

R_1: IF x is A_x THEN y is A_y.
R_2: IF x is B_x THEN y is B_y.
R_3: IF x is C_x THEN y is C_y.
R_4: IF x is D_x THEN y is D_y.

11.7 REVIEW QUESTIONS AND PROBLEMS

1. Find some examples of fuzzy variables in daily life.

2. Show graphically and explain why the law of contradiction is violated in the fuzzy set theory.

3. The membership function of a fuzzy set is defined as

$$\mu_A(x) = \begin{cases} 1 & \text{for } 0 < x < 20 \\ (50 - x)/30 & \text{for } 20 \le x < 50 \\ 0 & \text{for } x \ge 50 \end{cases}$$

a) What will be linguistic description of the fuzzy set A if x is the variable "age" in years?

b) Give an analytical description for $\mu_B(x)$ if B is a fuzzy set "age is close to 60 years".

4. Assume you were told that the room temperature is around 70 degrees Fahrenheit. How you would represent this information

a) by a set notation,

b) by a fuzzy set notation.

5. Consider the fuzzy sets A, B, and C defined on the interval x = [0, 10] with corresponding μ functions:

$$\mu_A(x) = x/(x + 2) \qquad \mu_B(x) = 2^{-x} \qquad \mu_C(x) = x^2/24$$

Determine analytically and graphically:

a) A' and B'

b) A $\cup$ C and A $\cup$ B

c) A $\cap$ C and A $\cap$ B

d) A $\cup$ B $\cup$ C

e) A $\cap$ C'

f) Calculate the α-cuts for A, B, and C if $\alpha = 0.2$, $\alpha = 0.5$, and $\alpha = 1$.

6. Consider two fuzzy sets with triangular membership functions A(x, 1, 2, 3) and B(x, 2, 2, 4). Find their intersection and union graphically, and express them analytically using the min and max operators.

7. If X = {3, 4, 5} and Y = {3, 4, 5, 6, 7}, and the binary fuzzy relation R = "Y is much greater than X" is defined by the analytical membership function

$$\mu_R(X, Y) = \begin{cases} (Y - X)/(X + Y + 2) & \text{if } Y > X \\ 0 & \text{if } Y \le X \end{cases}$$

what will be corresponding relation matrix of R (for all discrete X and Y values)?

8. Apply the extension principle to the fuzzy set

$$A = 0.1/\!-2 + 0.4/\!-1 + 0.8/0 + 0.9/1 + 0.3/2$$

where the mapping function $f(x) = x^2 - 3$.

a) What is the resulting image B where B = f(A)?

b) Sketch this transformation graphically.

9. Assume that the proposition "if x is A then y is B" is given where A and B are fuzzy sets:

$$A = 0.5/x_1 + 1/x_2 + 0.6/x_3$$

$$B = 1/y_1 + 0.4/y_2$$

Given a fact expressed by the proposition "x is A*", where

$$A^* = 0.6/x_1 + 0.9/x_2 + 0.7/x_3$$

derive the conclusion in the form "y is B*" using the generalized *modus ponens* inference rule.

10. Solve problem #9 by using

$$A = 0.6/x_1 + 1/x_2 + 0.9/x_3$$

$$B = 0.6/y_1 + 1/y_2$$

$$A^* = 0.5/x_1 + 0.9/x_2 + 1/x_3$$

11. The test scores for the three students are given in the following table:

	Math	Physics	Chemistry	Language
Henry	66	91	95	83
Lucy	91	88	80	73
John	80	88	80	78

Find the best student using multifactorial evaluation, if the weight factors for the subjects are given as the vector W = [0.3, 0.2, 0.1, 0.4].

12. Search the Web to find basic characteristics of publicly available or commercial software tools that are based on fuzzy sets and fuzzy logic. Make a report of your search.

11.8   REFERENCES FOR FURTHER STUDY

1. Klir, G. J. and B. Yuan, *Fuzzy Sets and Fuzzy Logic: Theory and Applications*, Prentice Hall, Upper Saddle River: NJ, 1995.

   The book provides the reader with a comprehensive coverage of the theoretical foundation of fuzzy-set theory and fuzzy logic as well as a broad overview of the increasingly important applications of this relatively novel area. Throughout the book, many examples are used to illustrate concepts, methods, and generic applications. The extensive and carefully selected bibliography is an invaluable resource for further study.

2. Li, H. X. and V. C. Yen, *Fuzzy Sets and Fuzzy Decision-Making*, CRC Press, Boca Raton, 1995.

   The book emphasizes the applications of fuzzy-set theory in the field of management science and decision science, introducing and formalizing the concept of fuzzy decision making. Many interesting methods of fuzzy decisionmaking are developed and illustrated with examples.

3. Pal, S. K. and S. Mitra, *Neuro-Fuzzy Pattern Recognition: Methods in Soft Computing*, John Wiley, New York, 1999.

   The authors consolidate a wealth of information previously scattered in disparate articles, journals, and edited volumes, explaining both the theory of neuro-fuzzy computing and the latest methodologies for performing different pattern-recognition tasks using neuro-fuzzy networks—classification, feature evaluation, rule generation, and knowledge extraction. Special emphasis is given to the integration of neuro-fuzzy methods with rough sets and genetic algorithms to ensure a more efficient recognition system.

4. Pedrycz, W. and F. Gomide, *An Introduction to Fuzzy Sets: Analysis and Design*, MIT Press, Cambridge, 1998.

   The book provides a highly readable, comprehensive, self-contained, updated, and well-organized presentation of the fuzzy-set technology. Both theoretical and practical aspects of the subject are given a coherent and balanced treatment. The reader is introduced to the main computational models, such as fuzzy modeling and rule-based computation, and to the frontiers of the field at the confluence of fuzzy-set technology with other major methodologies of soft computing.

12 VISUALIZATION METHODS

CHAPTER OBJECTIVES

- Recognize the importance of a visual-perception analysis in humans to discover appropriate data-visualization techniques.
- Distinguish between scientific-visualization and information-visualization techniques.
- Understand the basic characteristics of geometric, icon-based, pixel-oriented, and hierarchical techniques in visualization of large data sets
- Explain the methods of parallel coordinates and radial visualization for n-dimensional data sets.
- Analyze the requirements for advanced visualization systems in data mining.

How are humans capable of recognizing hundreds of faces? What is our "channel capacity" when dealing with the visual or any other of our senses? How many distinct visual icons and orientations can humans accurately perceive? It is important to factor all these cognitive limitations when designing a visualization technique that avoids delivering ambiguous or misleading information. Categorization lays the foundation for a well-known cognitive technique: the "chunking" phenomena. How many chunks can you hang onto? That varies among people, but the typical range forms "the magical number seven, plus or minus two". The process of reorganizing large amounts of data into fewer chunks with more bits of information per chunk is known in cognitive science as "recoding". We expand our comprehension abilities by reformatting problems into multiple dimensions or sequences of chunks, or by redefining the problem in a way that invokes relative judgment, followed by a second focus of attention.

12.1 PERCEPTION AND VISUALIZATION

Perception is our chief means of knowing and understanding the world; images are the mental pictures produced by this understanding. In perception as well as art, a meaningful whole is created by the relationship of the parts to each other. Our ability to see patterns in things and pull together parts into a meaningful whole is the key to perception and thought. As we view our environment, we are actually performing the enormously complex task of deriving meaning out of essentially separate and disparate sensory elements. The eye, unlike the camera, is not a mechanism for capturing images so much as it is a complex processing unit that detects changes, forms, and features, and selectively prepares data for the brain to interpret. The image we perceive is a mental one, the result of gleaning what remains constant while the eye scans. As we survey our three-dimensional ambient environment, properties such as contour, texture, and regularity allow us to discriminate objects and see them as constants.

Human beings do not normally think in terms of data; they are inspired by and think in terms of images—mental pictures of a given situation—and they assimilate information more quickly and effectively as visual images than as textual or tabular forms. Human vision is still the most powerful means of sifting out irrelevant information and detecting significant patterns. The effectiveness of this process is based on a picture's submodalities (shape, color, luminance, motion, vectors, texture). They depict abstract information as a visual grammar that integrates different aspects of represented information. Visually presenting abstract information, using graphical metaphors in an immersive 2D or 3D environment, increases one's ability to assimilate many dimensions of the data in a broad and immediately comprehensible form. It converts aspects of information into experiences our senses and mind can comprehend, analyze, and act upon.

We have heard the phrase "Seeing is believing" many times, though merely seeing is not enough. When you understand what you see, seeing becomes believing. Recently, scientists discovered that seeing and understanding together enable humans to discover new knowledge with deeper insight from large amounts of data. The approach integrates the human mind's exploratory abilities with the enormous processing power of computers to form a powerful visualization environment that capitalizes on the best of both worlds. A computer-based visualization technique has to incorporate the computer less as a tool and more as a communication medium. The power of visualization to exploit human perception offers both a challenge and an opportunity. The challenge is to avoid visualizing incorrect patterns leading to incorrect decisions and actions. The opportunity is to use knowledge about human perception when designing visualizations. Visualization creates a feedback loop between perceptual stimuli and the user's cognition.

Visual data-mining technology builds on visual and analytical processes developed in various disciplines including scientific visualization, computer graphics, data mining, statistics, and machine learning with custom extensions that handle very large multidimensional data sets interactively. The methodologies are based on both functionality that characterizes structures and displays data and human capabilities that perceives patterns, exceptions, trends, and relationships.

12.2   SCIENTIFIC VISUALIZATION AND INFORMATION VISUALIZATION

Visualization is defined in the dictionary as "a mental image". In the field of computer graphics, the term has a much more specific meaning. Technically, visualization concerns itself with the display of behavior and, particularly, with making complex states of behavior comprehensible to the human eye. Computer visualization, in particular, is about using computer graphics and other techniques to think about more cases, more variables, and more relations. The goal is to think clearly, appropriately, with insight, and to act with conviction. Unlike presentations, visualizations are typically interactive and very often animated.

Because of the high rate of technological progress, the amount of data stored in databases increases rapidly. This proves true for traditional relational databases and complex 2D and 3D multimedia databases that store images, CAD (Computer-aided design) drawings, geographic information, and molecular biology structure. Many of the applications mentioned rely on very large databases consisting of millions of data objects with several tens to a few hundred dimensions. When confronted with the complexity of data, users face tough problems: Where do I start? What looks interesting here? Have I missed anything? What are the other ways to derive the answer? Is there other data available? People think iteratively and ask ad hoc questions of complex data while looking for insights.

Computation, based on these large data sets and databases, creates content. Visualization makes computation and its content accessible to humans. Therefore, visual data mining uses visualization to augment the data-mining process. Some data-mining techniques and algorithms are difficult for decision-makers to understand and use. Visualization can make the data and the mining results more accessible, allowing comparison and verification of results. Visualization can also be used to steer the data-mining algorithm.

It is useful to develop a taxonomy for data visualization, not only because it brings order to disjointed techniques, but also because it clarifies and interprets ideas and purposes behind these techniques. Taxonomy may trigger the imagination to combine existing techniques or discover a totally new technique.

Visualization techniques can be classified in a number of ways. They can be classified as to whether their focus is geometric or symbolic, whether the stimulus is 2D, 3D, or n-D, or whether the display is static or dynamic. Many visualization tasks involve detection of differences in data rather than a measurement of absolute values. It is the well-known Weber's Law that states that the likelihood of detection is proportional to the relative change, not the absolute change, of a graphical attribute. In general, visualizations can be used to explore data, to confirm a hypothesis, or to manipulate a view.

In *exploratory visualizations*, the user does not necessarily know what s/he is looking for. This creates a dynamic scenario in which interaction is critical. The user is searching for structures or trends and is attempting to arrive at some hypothesis. In *confirmatory visualizations*, the user has a hypothesis that needs only to be tested. This scenario is more stable and predictable. System parameters are often predetermined and visualization tools are necessary for the user to confirm or refute the hypothesis. In *manipulative (production) visualizations*, the user has a validated hypothesis and so knows exactly what is to be presented. Therefore, he focuses on refining the visualization to optimize the presentation. This type is the most stable and predictable of all visualizations.

The accepted taxonomy in this book is primarily based on different approaches in visualization caused by different types of source data. Visualization techniques are divided roughly into two classes, depending on whether physical data is involved. These two classes are *scientific visualization* and *information visualization*.

Scientific visualization focuses primarily on physical data such as the human body, the earth, molecules, and so on. Scientific visualization also deals with multidimensional data, but most of the data sets used in this field use the spatial attributes of the data for visualization purposes; e.g., Computer-Aided Tomography(CAT) and Computer-Aided Design(CAD). Also, many of the Geographical Information Systems (GIS) use either the Cartesian coordinate system or some modified geographical coordinates to achieve a reasonable visualization of the data.

Information visualization focuses on abstract, nonphysical data such as text, hierarchies, and statistical data. Data-mining techniques are primarily oriented toward information visualization. The challenge for nonphysical data is in designing a visual representation of multidimensional samples (where the number of dimensions is greater than three). Multidimensional-information visualizations present data that is not primarily plenary or spatial. One-, two-, and three-dimensional, but also temporal information–visualization schemes can be viewed as a subset of multidimensional information visualization. One approach is to map the nonphysical data to a virtual object such as a cone tree, which can be manipulated as if it were a physical object. Another approach is to map the nonphysical data to the graphical properties of points, lines, and areas.

Using historical developments as criteria, we can divide information-visualization techniques (IVT) into two broad categories: traditional IVT and novel IVT. Traditional methods of 2D and 3D graphics offer an opportunity for information visualization, even though these techniques are more often used for presentation of physical data in scientific visualization. Traditional visual metaphors are used for a single or a small number of dimensions, and they include:

1. *Bar charts* that show aggregations and frequencies.
2. *Histograms* that show the distribution of variables values.
3. *Line charts* for understanding trends in order.
4. *Pie charts* for visualizing fractions of a total.
5. *Scatter plots* for bivariate analysis.

Color-coding is one of the most common traditional IVT methods for displaying a one-dimensional set of values where each value is represented by a different color. This representation becomes a continuous tonal variation of color when real numbers are the values of a dimension. Normally, a color spectrum from blue to red is chosen, representing a natural variation from "cool" to "hot", in other words from the smallest to the highest values.

With the development of large datawarehouses, data cubes became very popular information-visualization techniques. A *data cube*, the raw-data structure in a multidimensional database, organizes information along a sequence of categories. The categorizing variables are called dimensions. The data, called measures, are stored in cells along given dimensions. The cube dimensions are organized into hierarchies and usually include a dimension representing time. The hierarchical levels for the dimension time may be year, quarter, month, day, and hour. Similar hierarchies could be defined for other dimensions given in a datawarehouse. Multi-dimensional databases in modern datawarehouses automatically aggregate measures across hierarchical dimensions; they support hierarchical navigation, expand and collapse dimensions, enable drill-down, drill-up, or drill-across, and facilitate comparisons through time. In a transaction information in the database, the cube dimensions might be product, store, department, customer number, region, month, year. The dimensions are predefined indices in a cube cell and the measures in a cell are roll-ups or aggregations over the transactions. They are usually sums but may include functions such as average, standard deviation, percentage, etc.

For example, the values for the dimensions in a database may be

1. Region: north, south, east, west
2. Product: shoes, shirts
3. Month: January, February, March, ..., December

Then, the cell corresponding to [north, shirt, February] is the total sales of shirts for the northern region for the month of February.

Novel information-visualization techniques can simultaneously represent large data sets with many dimensions on one screen. Some possible classification of these new techniques are

1. Geometric projection techniques
2. Icon-based techniques
3. Pixel-oriented techniques
4. Hierarchical techniques

Geometric projection techniques aim to find interesting projections of multidimensional data sets. We will present some illustrative examples of these techniques.

The Scatter-Plot Matrix Technique is an approach that is very often available in new data-mining software tools. A grid of 2D scatter plots is the standard means of extending a standard 2D scatter plot to higher dimensions. If you have 10-dimensional data, a 10×10 array of scatter plots is used to provide a visualization of each dimension versus every other dimension. This is useful for looking at all possible two-way interactions or correlations between dimensions. Positive and negative correlations, but only between two dimensions, can be seen easily. The standard display quickly becomes inadequate for extremely large numbers of dimensions, and user-interactions of zooming and panning are needed to interpret the scatter plots effectively.

The Survey Plot is a simple technique of extending an n-dimensional point (sample) in a line graph. Each dimension of the sample is represented on a separate axis in which the dimension's value is a proportional line from the center of the axis. The principles of representation are given in Figure 12.1.

This visualization of n-dimensional data allows you to see correlations between any two variables, especially when the data is sorted according to a particular dimension. When color is used for different classes of samples, you can sometimes

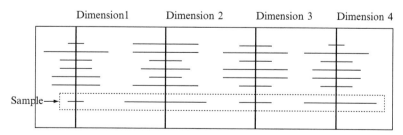

FIGURE 12.1   A 4-dimensional Survey Plot

use a sort to see which dimensions are best at classifying data samples. This technique was evaluated with different machine-learning data sets and it showed the ability to present exact IF-THEN rules in a set of samples.

The *Andrews's curves* technique plots each n-dimensional sample as a curved line. This is an approach similar to a Fourier transformation of a data point. This technique uses the function f(t) in the time domain t to transform the n-dimensional point $X = (x_1, x_2, x_3, \ldots, x_n)$ into a continuous plot. The function is usually plotted in the interval $-\pi \leq t \leq \pi$. An example of the transforming function f(t) is

$$f(t) = x_1/1.41 + x_2 \sin(t) + x_3 \cos(t) + x_4 \sin(2t) + x_5 \cos(2t) + \ldots$$

One advantage of this visualization is that it can represent many dimensions; the disadvantage, however, is the computational time required to display each n-dimensional point for large data sets.

The class of geometric-projection techniques includes also techniques of exploratory statistics such as principal component analysis, factor analysis, and multidimensional scaling. Parallel coordinate–visualization technique and radial-visualization technique belong in this category of visualizations, and they are explained in the next sections.

Another class of techniques for visual data mining is the *icon-based techniques* or iconic-display techniques. The idea is to map each multidimensional data item to an icon. An example is the stick figure technique. It maps two dimensions to the display dimensions and the remaining dimensions are mapped to the angles and/or limb lengths of the stick-figure icon. This technique limits the number of dimensions that can be visualized. A variety of special symbols have been invented to convey simultaneously the variations on several dimensions for the same sample. In 2D displays, these include Chernoff's faces, glyphs, stars, and color mapping. Glyphs represent samples as complex symbols whose features are functions of data. We think of glyphs as location-independent representations of samples. For successful use of glyphs, however, some sort of suggestive layout is often essential, because comparison of glyph shapes is what this type of rendering primarily does. If glyphs are used to enhance a scatter plot, the scatter plot takes over the layout functions. Figure 12.2 shows how the other icon-based technique, called a *star display*, is applied to quality of life measures for various states. Seven dimensions represent seven equidistant radiuses for a circle: one circle for each sample. Every dimension is normalized on interval [0, 1], where the value 0 is in the center of the circle and the value 1 is at the end of the corresponding radius. This representation is convenient for a relatively large number of dimensions but for a very small number of samples. It is usually used for comparative analyses of samples, and it may be included as a part of more complex visualizations.

The other approach is an icon-based, shape-coding technique that visualizes an arbitrary number of dimensions. The icon used in this approach maps each dimension to a small array of pixels and arranges the pixel arrays of each data item into a square or a rectangle. The pixels corresponding to each of the dimensions are mapped to gray scale or color according to the dimension's data value. The small squares or rectangles corresponding to the data items or samples are then arranged successively in a line-by-line fashion.

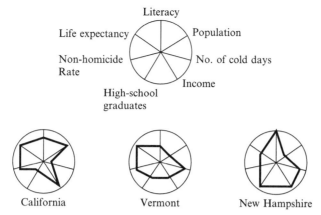

FIGURE 12.2   A star display for data on seven quality-of-life measures for three states

The third class of visualization techniques for multidimensional data aims to map each data value to a colored pixel and present the data values belonging to each attribute in separate windows. Since the *pixel-oriented techniques* use only one pixel per data value, the techniques allow a visualization of the largest amount of data that is possible on current displays (up to about 1,000,000 data values). If one pixel represents one data value, the main question is how to arrange the pixels on the screen. These techniques use different arrangements for different purposes. Finally, the *hierarchical techniques* of visualization subdivide the k-dimensional space and present the subspaces in a hierarchical fashion. For example, the lowest levels are 2D subspaces. A common example of hierarchical techniques is dimensional-stacking representation.

Dimensional stacking is a recursive-visualization technique for displaying high-dimensional data. Each dimension is discretized into a small number of bins, and the display area is broken into a grid of subimages. The number of subimages is based on the number of bins associated with the two "outer" dimensions that are user-specified. The subimages are decomposed further based on the number of bins for two more dimensions. This decomposition process continues recursively until all dimensions have been assigned.

Some of the novel visual metaphors that combine data-visualization techniques are already built into advanced visualization tools, and they include:

1. *Parabox* that combines boxes, parallel coordinates, and bubble plots for visualizing n-dimensional data. It handles both continuous and categorical data. The reason for combining box and parallel-coordinate plots involves their relative strengths. Box plots work well for showing distribution summaries. The strength of parallel coordinates is their ability to display high-dimensional outliers, individual cases with exceptional values. Details about this class of visualization techniques are given in Section 12.3.

2. *Data Constellations*, a component for visualizing large graphs with thousands of nodes and links. Two tables parametrize Data Constellations, one corresponding to nodes and another to links. Different layout algorithms dynamically position the nodes so that patterns emerge (a visual interpretation of outliers, clusters, etc.).

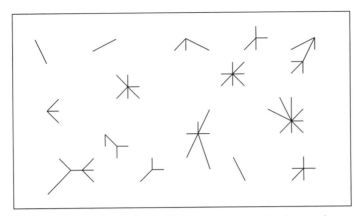

FIGURE 12.3   Data Constellations as a novel visual metaphor

3. *Data Sheet*, a dynamic scrollable-text visualization that bridges the gap between text and graphics. The user can adjust the zoom factor, progressively displaying smaller and smaller fonts, eventually switching to a one-pixel representation. This process is called smashing.

4. *Time Table*, a technique for showing thousands of time-stamped events.

5. *Multiscape* landscape visualization that encodes information using 3D "skyscrapers" on a 2D landscape.

An example of one of these novel visual representations is given in Figure 12.3, where a large graph is visualized using the Data Constellations technique with one possible graph-layout algorithm.

12.3   PARALLEL COORDINATES

Geometric-projection techniques include the parallel coordinate—visualization technique, one of the most frequently used modern visualization tools. The basic idea is to map the k-dimensional space onto the two-display dimensions by using k equidistant axes parallel to one of the display axes. The axes correspond to the dimensions and are linearly scaled from the minimum to the maximum value of the corresponding dimension. Each data item is presented as a polygonal line, intersecting each of the axes at the point that corresponds to the value of the considered dimension.

Suppose that a set of 6-dimensional samples, given in Table 12.1, is a small relational database. To visualize this data, it is necessary to determine the maximum and minimum values for each dimension. If we accept that these values are determined automatically based on a stored database, then graphical representation of data is given on Figure 12.4.

The *anchored-visualization perspective* focuses on displaying data with an arbitrary number of dimensions, say between four and twenty, using and combining multidimensional-visualization techniques such as weighted Parabox, bubble plots, and parallel coordinates. These methods handle both continuous and categorical data. The reason for combining them involves their relative strengths. Box plots works well for showing distribution summaries. Parallel coordinates' strength is their ability to display high-dimensional outliers, individual cases with exceptional values. Bubble plots are used for categorical data and the size of the circles inside the bubbles shows the number of samples and their respective value. The dimensions are organized along a series of parallel axes, as with parallel-coordinate plots. Lines are drawn between the bubble and the box plots connecting the dimensions of each available sample. Combining these techniques results in a visual component that excels the visual representations created using separate methodologies.

An example of multidimensional anchored visualization, based on a simple and small data set, is given in Table 12.2. The total number of dimensions is five, two of them are categorical and three are numeric. Categorical dimensions are represented by bubble plots (one bubble for every value) and numeric dimensions by

TABLE 12.1   Database with 6 numeric attributes

Sample#	Dimensions					
	A	B	C	D	E	F
1	1	5	10	3	3	5
2	3	1	3	1	2	2
3	2	2	1	2	4	2
4	4	2	1	3	1	2

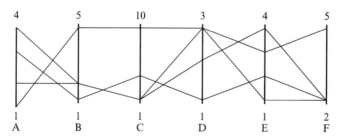

FIGURE 12.4   Graphical representation of 6-dimesional samples from database given in Table 12.1 using a parallel coordinate visualization technique

TABLE 12.2   The database for visualization

Sample#	Dimensions				
	A	B	C	D	E
1	low	low	2	4	3
2	med.	med.	4	2	1
3	high	med.	7	5	9
4	med.	low	1	3	5
5	low	low	3	1	2
6	low	med.	4	3	2

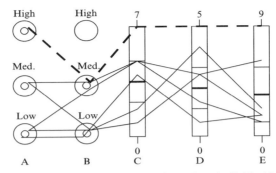

FIGURE 12.5 Parabox visualization of a database given in Table 12.2

boxes. The circle inside the bubbles shows visually the percentage that the given value represents in a database. Lines inside the boxes represent mean value and standard deviation for a given numeric dimension. The resulting representation in Figure 12.5 shows all six 5-dimensional samples as connecting lines. Although the database given in Table 12.2 is small, still, by using anchored representation, we can see that one sample is an outlier for both numeric and categorical dimensions.

The circular-coordinates method is a simple variation of parallel coordinates, in which the axes radiate from the center of a circle and extend to the perimeter. The line segments are longer on the outer part of the circle where higher data values are typically mapped, whereas inner-dimensional values toward the center of the circle are more cluttered. This visualization is actually a star and glyphs visualization of the data superimposed on one another. Because of the asymmetry of lower (inner) data values from higher ones, certain patterns may be easier to detect with this visualization.

12.4 RADIAL VISUALIZATION

Radial visualization is a technique for representation of multidimensional data where the number of dimensions are significantly greater then three. Data dimensions are laid out as points equally spaced around the perimeter of a circle. For example, in the case of an eight-dimensional space, the distribution of dimensions will be given as in Figure 12.6.

A model of springs is used for point-representation. One end of n springs (one spring for each of n dimensions) is attached to n perimeter points. The other end of the springs are attached to a data point. Spring constants can be used to represent values of dimensions for a given point. The spring constant K_i equals the value of the i-th coordinate of the given n-dimensional point where $i = 1, \ldots, n$. Values for all dimensions are normalized to the interval between 0 and 1. Each data point is then displayed in 2D under condition that the sum of the spring forces is equal to 0. The radial visualization of a 4-dimensional point $P(K_1, K_2, K_3, K_4)$ with the corresponding spring force is given in Figure 12.7.

Using basic laws from physics, we can establish a relation between coordinates in an n-dimensional space and in 2D presentation. For our example of 4D representation given in Figure 12.7, point P is under the influence of four forces

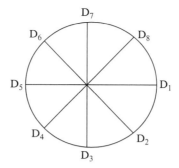

FIGURE 12.6   Radial visualization for an 8-dimensional space

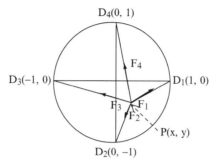

FIGURE 12.7   Sum of the spring forces for the given point P is equal to 0

F_1, F_2, F_3, and F_4. Knowing that every one of these forces can be expressed as a product of a spring constant and a distance, or in a vector form

$$F = K \cdot d$$

it is possible to calculate this force for a given point. For example, force F_1 in Figure 12.7 is a product of a spring constant K_1 and a distance vector between points $P(x, y)$ and $D_1(1,0)$:

$$F_1 = K_1 \cdot [(x - 1)i + yj]$$

The same analysis will give expressions for F_2, F_3, and F_4. Using the basic relation between forces

$$F_1 + F_2 + F_3 + F_4 = 0$$

we will obtain

$$K_1[(x - 1)i + yj] + K_2[xi + (y + 1)j] + K_3[(x + 1)i + yj] + K_4[xi + (y - 1)j] = 0$$

Both the i and j components of the previous vector have to be equal to 0, and therefore:

$$K_1(x - 1) + K_2x + K_3(x + 1) + K_4x = 0$$

$$K_1y + K_2(y + 1) + K_3y + K_4(y - 1) = 0$$

or

$$x = (K_1 - K_3)/(K_1 + K_2 + K_3 + K_4)$$

$$y = (K_4 - K_2)/(K_1 + K_2 + K_3 + K_4)$$

These are the basic relations for representing a 4-dimensional point $P^*(K_1, K_2, K_3, K_4)$ in a 2D space P(x, y) using the radial-visualization technique. Similar procedures may be performed to get transformations for other n-dimensional spaces.

We can analyze the behavior of n-dimensional points after transformation and representation with two dimensions. For example, if all n coordinates have the same value, the data point will lie exactly in the center of the circle. In our 4-dimensional space, if the initial point is $P_1^*(0.6, 0.6, 0.6, 0.6)$, then using relations for x and y its presentation will be $P_1(0, 0)$. If the n-dimensional point is a unit vector for one dimension, then the projected point will lie exactly at the fixed point on the edge of the circle (where the spring for that dimension is fixed). Point $P_2^*(0, 0, 1, 0)$ will be represented as $P_2(-1, 0)$. Radial visualization represents a nonlinear transformation of the data, which preserves certain symmetries. This technique emphasizes the relations between dimensional values, not between separate, absolute values. Some additional features of radial visualization include:

1. Points with approximately equal coordinate values will lie close to the center of the representational circle. For example, $P_3^*(0.5, 0.6, 0.4, 0.5)$ will have 2D coordinates $P_3(0.05, -0.05)$.

2. Points that have one or two coordinate values greater than the others lie closer to the origins of those dimensions. For example, $P_4^*(0.1, 0.8, 0.6, -0.1)$ will have a 2D representation $P_4(-0.36, -0.64)$. The point is in a third quadrant closer to D2 and D3, points where the spring is fixed for the second and third dimensions.

3. An n-dimensional line will map to the line or in a special case to the point. For example, points $P_5^*(0.3, 0.3, 0.3, 0.3)$, $P_6^*(0.6, 0.6, 0.6, 0.6)$, and $P_7^*(0.9, 0.9, 0.9, 0.9)$ are on a line in a 4-dimensional space, and all three of them will be transformed into the same 2D point $P_{567}(0, 0)$.

4. A sphere will map to an ellipse.

5. An n-dimensional plane maps to a bounded polygon.

The *Gradviz method* is a simple extension of a radial visualization that places the dimensional anchors on a rectangular grid instead of the perimeter of a circle. The spring forces work the same way. Dimensional labeling for Gradviz is difficult, but the number of dimensions that can be displayed increases significantly in comparison to the Radviz technique. For example, in a typical Radviz display fifty seems to be a reasonable limit to the points around a circle. However, in a grid layout supported by the Gradviz technique you can easily fit 50×50 grid points or dimensions into the same area.

12.5   KOHONEN SELF-ORGANIZED MAPS

Kohonen neural networks, also called self-organized maps (SOM), are used as a clustering technique based on n-dimensional visualization. The n dimensions of samples are used as n input nodes to the network. The output nodes of the net are arranged in a rectangular grid (for example a 5×6 grid would contain thirty output nodes). The weights of the network are adjusted through the training process so that only one output node is turned on for a given input vector (n-dimensional sample). In a training process, the input vectors that are "closer" to an output node will reinforce the weights to the given output, whereas input vectors further away will turn on other output nodes and corresponding weights. The training stops after a fixed time has elapsed, or when the output nodes become stable for all inputs.

The output nodes of the network generate x and y coordinates for each input vector and they can be used for a 2D display. The design of the Kohonen net is such that similar data samples are mapped to similar x and y coordinates (the same or close outputs). The data elements can be plotted (usually with jittering) on a scatter plot using the x and y coordinates generated from the trained Kohonen network. Also, for some implementations, because several input samples turned out the same output and they are represented with the same (x, y) points in the SOM, this accumulation may be represented by color, or simply by counting (Figure 12.8). The disadvantage of the technique, as with most neural-network techniques, is that the clusters created on the plot are not usually easily described in terms of the original dimensions of samples. The Kohonen network can be considered as a type of nonlinear data projection onto two dimensions. The technique is somewhat similar to a k-means clustering algorithm. The difference (and the advantage) is that the output of a Kohonen SOM is topological: clusters near each other on a 2D representation are similar.

In higher-dimensional spaces, clustering and patterns can exist based on distances between the data points. When these points (samples) are projected linearly, as in a scatter-plot matrix, the true distance between points is often lost in the projection. Kohonen SOM is a nonlinear technique that projects data down to two dimensions while trying to preserve the distances between all initially given n-dimensional

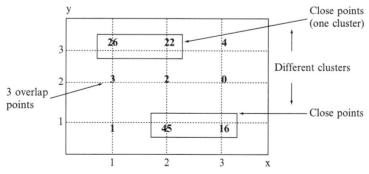

FIGURE 12.8   Trained Kohonen SOM (119 samples) with nine outputs, represented as 3×3 grid (values in nodes are the number of input samples triggered the given output)

samples. These types of visualization techniques could be also classified as "dimensionality reduction–visualization techniques". We have chosen to present Kohonen networks in this chapter about n-dimensional visualization techniques, although there are many arguments that it could be presented either together with other neural networks, or with other clustering algorithms, maybe even as a dimensionality-reduction technique.

12.6 VISUALIZATION SYSTEMS FOR DATA MINING

Many organizations, particularly within the business community, have made significant investments in collecting, storing, and converting business information into results that can be used. Unfortunately, typical implementations of business "intelligence software' have proven to be too complex for most users except for their core reporting and charting capabilities. Users' demands for multidimensional analysis, finer data granularity, and multiple data sources, simultaneously, all at Internet speed, require too much specialist intervention for broad utilization. The result is a report explosion in which literally hundreds of predefined reports are generated and pushed throughout the organization. Every report produces another. Presentations get more complex. Data is exploding. The best opportunities and the most important decisions are often the hardest to see. This is in direct conflict with the needs of front-line decision-makers and knowledge-workers who are demanding to be included in the analytical process.

Presenting information visually, in an environment that encourages the exploration of linked events, leads to deeper insights and more results that can be acted upon. Over the past decade, research on information visualization has focused on developing specific visualization techniques. An essential task for the next period is to integrate these techniques into a larger system that supports work with information in an interactive way, through the three basic components: *foraging the data, thinking about data,* and *acting on data.*

The vision of a visual data-mining system stems from the following principles: simplicity, visibility, user-autonomy, reliability, reusability, availability, and security. A visual data-mining system must be syntactically simple to be useful. Simple doesn't mean trivial or nonpowerful. Simple to learn means use of intuitive and friendly input mechanisms as well as instinctive and easy-to-interpret output knowledge. Simple to apply means an effective discourse between humans and information. Simple to retrieve or recall means a customized data structure that facilitates fast and reliable searches. Simple to execute means a minimum number of steps needed to achieve the results. In short, simple means the smallest, functionally sufficient system possible.

A genuinely visual data-mining system must not impose knowledge on its users, but instead guide them through the mining process to draw conclusions. Users should study the visual abstractions and gain insight instead of accepting an automated decision. A key capability in visual analysis, called visibility, is the ability to focus on particular regions of interest. There are two aspects of visibility: excluding and restoring data. The exclude process eliminates the unwanted data items from the display so that only the selected set is visible. The restore process brings all data back, making them visible again.

A reliable data-mining system must provide estimated error or accuracy of the projected information in each step of the mining process. This error information can compensate for the deficiency that an imprecise analysis of data visualization can cause. A reusable, visual, data-mining system must be adaptable to a variety of environments to reduce the customization effort, provide assured performance, and improve system portability. A practical, visual, data-mining system must be generally and widely available. The quest for new knowledge or deeper insights into existing knowledge cannot be planned. It requires that the knowledge received from one domain adapt to another domain through physical means or electronic connections. A complete, visual, data-mining system must include security measures to protect the data, the newly discovered knowledge, and the user's identity because of various social issues.

Through data visualization we want to understand or get an overview of the whole or a part of the n-dimensional data, analyzing also some specific cases. Visualization of multidimensional data helps decision-makers to

1. slice information into multiple dimensions and present information at various levels of granularity,
2. view trends and develop historical tracers to show operations over time,
3. produce pointers to synergies across multiple dimensions,
4. provide exception-analysis and identify isolated (needle in the haystack) opportunities,
5. monitor adversarial capabilities and developments,
6. create indicators of duplicative efforts,
7. conduct What-If Analysis and Cross-Analysis of variables in a data set.

Visualization tools transform raw experimental or simulated data into a form suitable for human understanding. Representations can take on many different forms, depending on the nature of the original data and the information that is to be extracted. However, the visualization process that should be supported by modern, visualization-software tools can generally be subdivided into three main stages: data preprocessing, visualization mapping, and rendering. Through these three steps the tool has to answer the questions: What should be shown in a plot? How should one work with individual plots? How should multiple plots be organized?

Data preprocessing involves such diverse operations as interpolating irregular data, filtering and smoothing raw data, and deriving functions for measured or simulated quantities. Visualization mapping is the most crucial stage of the process, involving design and adequate representation of the filtered data, which efficiently conveys the relevant and meaningful information. Finally, the representation is often rendered to communicate information to the human user.

Data visualization is essential for understanding the concept of multidimensional spaces. It allows the user to explore the data in different ways and at different levels of abstraction to find the right level of details. Therefore, techniques are most useful if they are highly interactive, permit direct manipulation, and include a rapid response time. The analyst must be able to navigate the data, change its grain (resolution), and alter its representation (symbols, colors, etc.).

Broadly speaking, the problems addressed by current information-visualization tools and requirements for a new generation fall into the following classes:

1. *Presentation graphics* – These generally consist of bars, pies, and line charts that are easily populated with static data and drop into printed reports or presentations. The next generation of presentation graphics enriches the static displays with a 3D or projected n-dimensional information landscape. The user can then navigate through the landscape and animate it to display time-oriented information.

2. *Visual interfaces for information access* – They are focused on enabling users to navigate through complex information spaces to locate and retrieve information. Supported user-tasks involve searching, backtracking, and history-logging. User-interface techniques attempt to preserve user-context and support smooth transitions between locations.

3. *Full visual discovery and analysis* – These systems combine the insights communicated by presentation graphics with an ability to probe, drill-down, filter, and manipulate the display to answer the "why" question as well as the "what" question. The difference between answering a "what" and a "why" question involves an interactive operation. Therefore, in addition to the visualization technique, effective data exploration requires using some *interaction* and *distortion* techniques. The *interaction techniques* let the user directly interact with the visualization. Examples of interaction techniques include interactive mapping, projection, filtering, zooming, and interactive linking and brushing. These techniques allow dynamic changes in the visualizations according to the exploration objectives, but they also make it possible to relate and combine multiple, independent visualizations. Note that connecting multiple visualizations by linking and brushing, e.g., provides more information than considering the component visualizations independently. The *distortion techniques* help in the interactive exploration process by providing a means for focusing while preserving an overview of the data. Distortion techniques show portions of the data with a high level of detail while other parts are shown with a much lower level of detail.

Three tasks are fundamental to data exploration with these new visualization tools:

1. *Finding Gestalt* – Local and global linearities and nonlinearities, discontinuities, clusters, outliers, unusual groups, and so on are examples of gestalt features that can be of interest. Focusing through individual views is the basic requirement to obtain a qualitative exploration of data using visualization. Focusing determines what gestalt of the data is seen. The meaning of focusing depends very much on the type of visualization technique chosen.

2. *Posing queries* – This is a natural task after the initial gestalt features have been found, and the user requires query identification and characterization technique. Queries can concern individual cases as well as subsets of cases. The goal is essentially to find intelligible parts of the data. In graphical data analysis it is natural to pose queries graphically. For example, familiar brushing techniques such as coloring or otherwise highlighting a subset of data means issuing a query about this subset. It is desirable that the view where the query is posed and the view that present the response are linked. Ideally, responses to queries should be instantaneous.

3. *Making comparisons* – Two types of comparisons are frequently made in practice. The first one is a comparison of variables or projections and the second one is a comparison of subsets of data. In the first case, one compares views "from different angles"; in the second, comparison is based on views "of different slices" of the data. In either case, it is likely that a large number of plots are generated, and therefore it is a challenge to organize the plots in such a way that meaningful comparisons are possible.

Visualization has been used routinely in data mining as a presentation tool to generate initial views, navigate data with complicated structures, and convey the results of an analysis. Generally, the analytical methods themselves do not involve visualization. The loosely coupled relationships between visualization and analytical data-mining techniques represent the majority of today's state of the art in visual data mining. The process-sandwich strategy, which interlaces analytical processes with graphical visualization, penalizes both procedures with the other's deficiencies and limitations. For example, because an analytical process can't analyze multimedia data, we have to give up the strength of visualization to study movies and music in a visual data-mining environment. A stronger strategy lies in tightly coupling the visualization and analytical processes into one data-mining tool. Letting human visualization participate in the decision-making in analytical processes remains a major challenge. Certain mathematical steps within an analytical procedure may be substituted by human decisions based on visualization to allow the same procedure to analyze a broader scope of information. Visualization supports humans in dealing with decisions that can no longer be automated.

For example, visualization techniques can be used for efficient process of "visual clustering". The algorithm is based on finding a set of projections $P = [P_1, P_2, \ldots, P_k]$ useful for separating the initial data into clusters. Each projection represents the histogram information of the point-density in the projected space. The most important information about a projection is whether it contains well-separated clusters. Note that well-separated clusters in one projection could result from more than one cluster in the original space. Figure 12.7 shows an illustration of these projections. You can see that the axes' parallel projections don't preserve well the information necessary for clustering. Additional projections A and B, in Figure 12.9, define three clusters in the initial data set.

Visual techniques that preserve some characteristics of the data set can be invaluable for obtaining good separators in a clustering process. In contrast to dimension-reduction approaches such as principal component analyses, this visual approach doesn't require that a single projection preserve all clusters. In the projections, some clusters may overlap and therefore not be distinguishable, such as projection A in Figure 12.9. The algorithm only needs projections that separate the data set into at least two subsets without dividing any clusters. The subsets may then be refined using other projections and possibly partitioned further based on separators in other projections. Based on the visual representation of the projections, it is possible to find clusters with unexpected characteristics (shapes, dependencies) that would be very difficult or impossible to find by tuning the parameter settings of automatic-clustering algorithms.

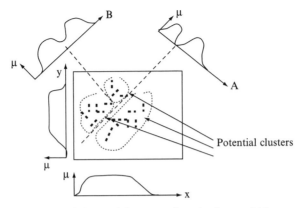

FIGURE 12.9 An example of the need for general projections, which are not parallel to axes, to improve clustering process

12.7   REVIEW QUESTIONS AND PROBLEMS

1. Explain the power of n-dimensional visualization as a data-mining technique. What are the phases of data mining supported by data visualization?

2. What are fundamental experiences in human perception we would build into effective visualization tools?

3. Discuss the differences between scientific visualization and information visualization.

4. The following is the data set X:

X:	Year	A	B
	1996	7	100
	1997	5	150
	1998	7	120
	1999	9	150
	2000	5	130
	2001	7	150

Although the following visualization techniques are not explained with enough details in this book, use your knowledge from earlier studies of statistics and other courses to create 2D presentations:

a) Show a bar chart for the variable A.

b) Show a histogram for the variable B.

c) Show a line chart for the variable B.

d) Show a pie chart for the variable A.

e) Show a scatter plot for A and B variables.

5. Explain the concept of a data cube and where it is used for visualization of large data sets.

6. Use examples to discuss the differences between icon-based and pixel-oriented visualization techniques.

7. Given 7-dimensional samples

X_1	X_2	X_3	X_4	X_5	X_6	X_7
A	1	25	7	T	1	5
B	3	27	3	T	2	9
A	5	29	5	T	1	7
A	2	21	9	F	3	2
B	5	30	7	F	1	7

   a) Make a graphical representation of samples using the parallel-coordinates technique.

   b) Are there any outliers in the given data set?

8. Derive formulas for radial visualization of

   a) 3-dimensional samples

   b) 8-dimensional samples

   c) Using the formulas derived in a) represent samples (2, 8, 3) and (8, 0, 0).

   d) Using the formulas derived in b) represent samples (2, 8, 3, 0, 7, 0, 0, 0) and (8, 8, 0, 0, 0, 0, 0, 0).

9. Implement a software tool supporting a radial-visualization technique.

10. Explain the requirements for full visual discovery in advanced visualization tools.

11. Search the Web to find the basic characteristics of publicly available or commercial software tools for visualization of n-dimensional samples. Document the results of your search.

12.8 REFERENCES FOR FURTHER STUDY

1. Fayyad, V., G. G. Grinstein, A. Wierse, *Information Visualization in Data Mining and Knowledge Discovery*, Morgan Kaufmann, San Diego: CA, 2002.
   Leading researchers from the fields of data mining, data visualization, and statistics present findings organized around topics introduced in two recent international knowledge-discovery and data-mining workshops. The book introduces the concepts and components of visualization, details current efforts to include visualization and user interaction in data-mining, and explores the potential for further synthesis of data-mining algorithms and data-visualization techniques.

2. Gallaghar, R. S., *Computer Visualization: Graphics Techniques for Scientific and Engineering Analysis*, CRC Press, Boca Raton, 1995.

The book is a complete reference book on computer-graphic techniques for scientific and engineering visualization. It explains the basic methods applied in different fields to support an understanding of complex, volumetric, multidimensional, and time-dependent data. The practical computational aspects of visualization such as user-interface, database architecture, and interaction with a model are also analyzed.

3. Spence, R., *Information Visualization*, Addison Wesley, Harlow: England, 2001.

This is the first fully integrated book on the emerging discipline of information visualization. Its emphasis is on real-world examples and applications of computer-generated interactive information visualization. The author also explains how these methods for visualizing information support rapid learning and accurate decision-making.

4. Westphal, C. and T. Blaxton, *Data Mining Solutions: Methods and Tools for Solving Real-World Problems*, John Wiley, New York, 1998.

This introductory book gives a refreshing "out-of-the-box" approach to data mining that will help the reader to maximize time and problem-solving resources and prepare for the next wave of data mining–visualization techniques. An extensive coverage of data mining–software tools is valuable to readers who are planning to set up their own data-mining environment.

13 REFERENCES

CHAPTER 1

1. Adriaans, P. and D. Zantinge, *Data Mining*, Addison-Wesley, New York, 1996.

2. Agosta, L., *The Essential Guide to Data Warehousing*, Prentice Hall, Upper Saddle River: N.J., 2000.

3. An, A. et al., **Applying Knowledge Discovery to Predict Water-Supply Consumption**, *IEEE Expert* (July/Aug1997): 72–78.

4. Barquin, R. and H. Edelstein, *Building, Using, and Managing the Data Warehouse*, Prentice Hall, Upper Saddle River: N.J., 1997.

5. Berson, A., S. Smith, K. Thearling, *Building Data Mining Applications for CRM*, McGraw-Hill, New York, 2000.

6. Bischoff, J. and T. Alexander, *Data Warehouse: Practical Advice from the Experts*, Prentice Hall, Upper Saddle River: N.J., 1997.

7. Brachman, R. J. et al., **Mining Business Databases**, *CACM* 39, no. 11 (1996): 42–48.

8. Djoko, S., D. J. Cook, L. B. Holder, **An Empirical study of Domain Knowledge and its Benefits to Substructure Discovery**, *IEEE Transactions on Knowledge and Data Engineering* 9, no. 4 (1997): 575–585.

9. Fayyad, U. M., G. Piatetsky-Shapiro, P. Smyth, R. Uthurusamy, eds., *Advances in Knowledge Discovery and Data Mining*, AAAI Press / MIT Press, Cambridge, 1996.

10. Fayyad, U. M., G. P. Shapiro, P. Smyth, **From Data Mining to Knowledge Discovery in Databases**, *AI Magazine* (Fall 1996): 37–53.

11. Fayyad, U.M., G. P. Shapiro, P. Smyth, **The KDD Process for Extracting Useful Knowledge from Volumes of Data**, *CACM* 39, no. 11 (1966): 27–34.

12. Friedland, L., **Accessing the Data Warehouse: Designing Tools to Facilitate Business Understanding**, *Interactions* (Jan/Feb 1998): 25–36.

13. Ganti, V., J. Gehrke, R. Ramakrishnan, **Mining Very Large Databases**, *Computer* 32, no. 8 (1999): 38–45.

14. Groth, R., *Data Mining: A Hands-On Approach for Business Professionals*, Prentice Hall, Upper Saddle River: N.J., 1998.

15. Han, J. and M. Kamber, *Data Mining: Concepts and Techniques*, Morgan Kaufmann, San Francisco, 2000.

16. Kaudel, A., M. Last, H. Bunke, eds., *Data Mining and Computational Intelligence*, Physica-Verlag, Heidelberg: Germany, 2001.

17. Maxus Systems International, *What is Data mining*, http://www.maxussystems.com/datamining.html.

18. Ramakrishnan, N. and A. Y. Grama, **Data Mining: From Serendipity to Science**, *Computer* 32, no. 8 (1999): 34–37.

19. Shapiro, G. P., **The Data-Mining Industry Coming of Age**, *IEEE Intelligent Systems* (Nov/Dec 1999): 32–33.

20. Thomsen, E., *OLAP Solution: Building Multidimensional Information System*, John Wiley, New York, 1997.

21. Thuraisingham, B., *Data Mining: Technologies, Techniques, Tools, and Trends*, CRC Press LLC, Boca Raton: FL, 1999.

22. Tsur, S., **Data Mining in the Bioinformatics Domain**, *Proceedings of the 26th YLDB Conference*, Cairo: Egypt, (2000): 711–714.

23. Waltz, D. and S. J. Hong, **Data Mining: A Long Term Dream**, *IEEE Intelligent Systems* (Nov/Dec 1999): 30–34.

CHAPTER 2

1. Adriaans, P. and D. Zantinge, *Data Mining*, Addison-Wesley, New York, 1996.

2. Anand, S. S., D. A. Bell, J. G. Hughes, **The Role of Domain Knowledge in Data Mining**, *Proceedings of the CIKM'95 Conference*, Baltimore: MD, (1995): 37–43.

3. Barquin, R. and H. Edelstein, *Building, Using, and Managing the Data Warehouse*, Prentice Hall, Upper Saddle River: N.J., 1997.

4. Berson, A., S. Smith, K. Thearling, *Building Data Mining Applications for CRM*, McGraw-Hill, New York, 2000.

5. Bischoff, J. and T. Alexander, *Data Warehouse: Practical Advice from the Experts*, Prentice Hall, Upper Saddle River: N.J., 1997.

6. Brachman, R. J. et al., **Mining Business Databases**, *CACM* 39, no. 11 (1996): 42–48.

7. Chen, C. H., L. F. Pau, P. S. P. Wang, *Handbook of Pattern Recognition & Computer Vision*, World Scientific, Singapore, 1993.

8. Dwinnell, W., **Data Cleansing: An Automated Approach**, *PC AI* (Mar/Apr 2001): 21–23.

9. Fayyad, U. M., G. Piatetsky-Shapiro, P. Smyth, R. Uthurusamy, eds., *Advances in Knowledge Discovery and Data Mining*, AAAI Press / MIT Press, Cambridge, 1996.

10. Fayyad, U. M., D. Haussier, P. Stolorz, **Mining Scientific Data**, *CACM* 39, no. 11, (1966): 51–57.

11. Ganti, V., J. Gehrke, R. Ramakrishnan, **Mining Very Large Databases**, *Computer* 32, no. 8 (1999): 38–45.

12. Groth, R., *Data Mining: A Hands-On Approach for Business Professionals*, Prentice Hall, Upper Saddle River: N.J., 1998.

13. Han, J. and M. Kamber, *Data Mining: Concepts and Techniques*, Morgan Kaufmann, San Francisco, 2000.

14. Liu, H. and H. Motoda, *Feature Selection for Knowledge Discovery and Data Mining*, 2nd Print, Kluwer Academic, Boston: MA, 2000.

15. Liu, H. and H. Motoda, eds., *Feature Extraction, Construction and Selection: A Data Mining Perspective*, Kluwer Academic, Boston: MA, 1998.

16. Pass, S., **Discovering Value in a Mountain of Data**, *OR/MS Today* (Oct 1997): 24–28.

17. Pyle, D., *Data Preparation for Data Mining*, Morgan Kaufmann, New York, 1999.

18. Weiss, S. M. and N. Indurkhya, Predictive *Data Mining: a Practical Guide*, Morgan Kaufman, San Francisco, 1998.

19. Westphal, C. and T. Blaxton, *Data Mining Solutions: Methods and Tools for Solving Real-World Problems*, John Wiley, New York, 1998.

CHAPTER 3

1. Adriaans, P. and D. Zantinge, *Data Mining*, Addison-Wesley, New York, 1996.

2. Berson, A., S. Smith, K. Thearling, *Building Data Mining Applications for CRM*, McGraw-Hill, New York, 2000.

3. Brachman, R. J. et al., **Mining Business Databases**, *CACM* 39, no. 11 (1996): 42–48.

4. Chen, C. H., L. F. Pau, P. S. P. Wang, *Handbook of Pattern Recognition & Computer Vision*, World Scientific, Singapore, 1993.

5. Dwinnell, W., **Data Cleansing: An Automated Approach**, *PC AI* (Mar/Apr 2001): 21–23.

6. Fayyad, U. M., G. Piatetsky-Shapiro, P. Smyth, R. Uthurusamy, eds., *Advances in Knowledge Discovery and Data Mining*, AAAI Press / MIT Press, Cambridge, 1996.

7. Groth, R., *Data Mining: A Hands-On Approach for Business Professionals*, Prentice Hall, Upper Saddle River: N.J., 1998.

8. Han, J. and M. Kamber, *Data Mining: Concepts and Techniques*, Morgan Kaufmann, San Francisco, 2000.

9. Jain, A., R. P. W. Duin, J. Mao, **Statistical Pattern Recognition**, *IEEE Transaction on Pattern Analysis and Machine Intelligence* 22, no. 1 (2000): 4–37.

10. Kennedy, R. L. et al., *Solving Data Mining Problems through Pattern Recognition*, Prentice Hall, Upper Saddle River: N.J., 1998.

11. Kil, D. H. and Shin F. B., *Pattern Recognition and Prediction with Applications to Signal Characterization*, AIP Press, Woodburg: NY, 1996.

12. Liu, H. and Motoda H., eds., *Instance Selection and Construction for Data Mining*, Kluwer Academic, Boston: MA, 2001.

13. Liu, H. and H. Motoda, *Feature Selection for Knowledge Discovery and Data Mining*, 2nd Print, Kluwer Academic, Boston: MA, 2000.

14. Liu, H. and H. Motoda, eds., *Feature Extraction, Construction and Selection: A Data Mining Perspective*, Kluwer Academic, Boston: MA, 1998.

15. Maimon, O. and M. Last, *Knowledge Discovery and Data Mining: The Info-Fuzzy Network (IFN) Methodology*, Kluwer Academic, Boston: MA, 2001.

16. Pyle, D., *Data Preparation for Data Mining*, Morgan Kaufmann, New York, 1999.

17. Weiss, S. M. and N. Indurkhya, *Predictive Data Mining: a Practical Guide*, Morgan Kaufmann, San Francisco, 1998.

18. Westphal, C. and T. Blaxton, *Data Mining Solutions: Methods and Tools for Solving Real-World Problems*, John Wiley, New York, 1998.

CHAPTER 4

1. Berbaum, K. S., D. D. Dorfman, E. A. Franken Jr., **Measuring Observer Performance by ROC Analysis: Indications and Complications**, *Investigative Radiology* 2A, (Mar 1989): 228–233.

2. Berthold, M. and D. J. Hand, eds., *Intelligent Data Analysis – An Introduction*, Springer, Berlin, 1999.

3. Bow, S., *Pattern Recognition and Image Preprocessing*, Marcel Dekker, New York, 1992.

4. Cherkassky, V. and F. Mulier, *Learning from Data: Concepts, Theory and Methods*, John Wiley, New York, 1998.

5. Diettrich, T. G., **Machine-Learning Research: Four Current Directions**, *AI Magazine* (Winter 1997): 97–136.

6. Engel, A. and C. Van den Broeck, *Statistical Mechanics of Learning*, Cambridge University Press, Cambridge: England, 2001.

7. Gunopulos, D., R. Khardon, H. Mannila, H. Toivonen, **Data Mining, Hypergraph Traversals, and Machine Learning**, *Proceedings of PODS'97 Conference*, Tucson: AZ (1997): 209–216.

8. Hand, D., H. Mannila, P. Smyth, *Principles of Data Mining*, MIT Press, Cambridge: MA, 2001.

9. Hearst, M., **Support Vector Machines**, *IEEE Intelligent Systems* (July/Aug 1998): 18–28.

10. Hilderman, R. J. and H. J. Hamilton, *Knowledge Discovery and Measures of Interest*, Kluwer Academic, Boston: MA, 2001.

11. Hirji, K. K., **Exploring Data Mining Implementation**, *CACM* 44, no. 7 (2001): 87–93.

12. Kennedy, R. L. et al., *Solving Data Mining Problems through Pattern Recognition*, Prentice Hall, Upper Saddle River: NJ, 1998.

13. Leondes, C. T., *Knowledge-Based Systems: Techniques and Applications*, Academic Press, San Diego, 2000.

14. Luger, G. F. and W. A. Stubblefield, *Artificial Intelligence: Structures and Strategies for Complex Problem Solving*, Addison Wesley Longman, Harlow: England, 1998.

15. Metz, C. E., B. A. Herman, C. A. Roe, **Statistical Comparison of Two ROC-curve Estimates Obtained from Partially-paired Datasets**, *Medical Decision Making* 18, no. 1 (1998) 110–124.

16. Mitchell, T. M., **Does Machine Learning Really Work?** *AI Magazine* (Fall 1997): 11–20.

17. Mitchell, T., *Machine Learning*, McGraw Hill, New York: NY, 1997.

18. Poole, D., A. Mackworth, R. Goebel, *Computational Intelligence: A Logical Approach*, Oxford University Press, New York, 1998.

19. Thrun, S., and C. Faloutsos, **Automated Learning and Discovery**, *AI Magazine* (Fall 1999): 78–82.

20. Zweig, M. and Campbell G., **Receiver-Operating Characteristic (ROC) Plots: A Fundamental Evaluation Tool in Clinical Medicine**, *Clinical Chemistry* 39, no. 4 (1993): 561–576.

CHAPTER 5

1. Bow, S., *Pattern Recognition and Image Preprocessing*, Marcel Dekker, New York, 1992.

2. Brandt, S., *Data Analysis: Statistical and Computational Methods for Scientists and Engineers*, 3rd edn., Springer, New York, 1999.

3. Cherkassky, V. and F. Mulier, *Learning from Data: Concepts, Theory and Methods*, John Wiley, New York, 1998.

4. Christensen, R., *Log-Linear Models*, Springer-Verlag, New York, 1990.

5. Ezawa, K. J. and S. W. Norton, **Constructing Bayesian Network to Predict Uncollectible Telecommunications Accounts**, *IEEE Expert: Intelligent Systems & Their Applications* 11, no. 5 (Oct 1996): 45–51.

6. Golden, B., E. Condon, S. Lee, E. Wasil, **Pre-Processing for Visualization using Principal Component Analysis**, *Proceedings of the ANNEC'2000 Conference*, St. Louis, (2000): 429–436.

7. Gose, E., R. Johnsonbaugh, S. Jost, *Pattern Recognition and Image Analysis*, Prentice Hall, Upper Saddle River: NJ, 1996.

8. Han, J. and M. Kamber, *Data Mining: Concepts and Techniques*, Morgan Kaufmann, San Francisco, 2000.

9. Hand, D., H. Mannila, P. Smyth, *Principles of Data Mining*, MIT Press, Cambridge: MA, 2001.

10. Jain, A., R. P. W. Duin, J. Mao, **Statistical Pattern Recognition**, *IEEE Transaction on Pattern Analysis and Machine Intelligence* 22, no. 1 (2000): 4–37.

11. Kennedy, R. L et al., *Solving Data Mining Problems through Pattern Recognition*, Prentice Hall, Upper Saddle River: N.J., 1998.

12. McCullagh, P. and J. A. Nelder, *Generalized Linear Models*, 2nd edn., Chapman & Hall, London, 1994.

13. Metz, C. E., B. A. Herman, C. A. Roe, **Statistical Comparison of Two ROC-curve Estimates Obtained from Partially-paired Datasets**, *Medical Decision Making* 18, no. 1 (1998) 110–124.

14. Norusis, M. J., *SPSS 7.5: Guide to Data Analysis*, Prentice Hall, Upper Saddle River: N.J., 1997.

15. Smith, M., *Neural Networks for Statistical Modeling*, Van Nostrand Reinhold, New York, 1993.

16. Trueblood, R. P. and J. N. Lovett, *Data Mining and Statistical Analysis using SQL*, Apress, Berkeley: CA, 2001.

17. Walpore, R. E. and R. H. Myers, *Probability and Statistics for Engineers and Scientists*, 4th edn., MacMillan Publishing, New York, 1989.

18. Witten, I. H. and E. Frank, *Data Mining: Practical Machine Learning Tools and Techniques with Java Implementations*, Morgan Kaufmann, New York, 1999.

CHAPTER 6

1. Bow, S., *Pattern Recognition and Image Preprocessing*, Marcel Dekker, New York, 1992.

2. Chen, C. H., L. F. Pau, P. S. P. Wang, *Handbook of Pattern Recognition & Computer Vision*, World Scientific, Singapore, 1993.

3. Dzeroski, S. and Lavrac N., eds., *Relational Data Mining*, Springer, Berlin: Germany, 2001.

4. Gose, E., R. Johnsonbaugh, S. Jost, *Pattern Recognition and Image Analysis*, Prentice Hall, Upper Saddle River: N.J., 1996.

5. Han, J. et al., **Spatial Clustering Methods in Data Mining: A Survey**, in *Geographic Data Mining and Knowledge Discovery*, eds., H. Miller and J. Han,Taylor and Francis, 2001.

6. Han, J. and M. Kamber, *Data Mining: Concepts and Techniques*, Morgan Kaufmann, San Francisco, 2000.

7. Hand, D., H. Mannila, P. Smyth, *Principles of Data Mining*, MIT Press, Cambridge, MA, 2001.

8. Jain, A. K., M. N. Murty, P. J. Flynn, **Data Clustering: A Review**, *ACM Computing Surveys* 31, no. 3 (1999): 264–323.

9. Karypis, G., E. Han, V. Kumar, **Chameleon: Hierarchical Clustering Using Dynamic modeling**, *Computer* 32, no. 8 (1999): 68–75.

10. Moore, S. K., Understanding the Human Genome, *Spectrum* 37, no. 11 (2000): 33–35.

11. Munakata, T., *Fundamentals of the new Artificial Intelligence: Beyond Traditional Paradigm*, Springer, New York, 1998.

12. Norusis, M. J., *SPSS 7.5: Guide to Data Analysis*, Prentice-Hall, Upper Saddle River: New Jersey, 1997.

13. Poole, D., A. Mackworth, R. Goebel, *Computational Intelligence: A Logical Approach*, Oxford University Press, New York, 1998.

14. Westphal, C. and T. Blaxton, *Data Mining Solutions: Methods and Tools for Solving Real-World Problems*, John Wiley, New York, 1998.

15. Witten, I. H. and E. Frank, *Data Mining: Practical Machine Learning Tools and Techniques with Java Implementations*, Morgan Kaufmann, New York, 1999.

CHAPTER 7

1. *Clementine*, http://www.isl.co.uk/clem.html

2. Darlington, J., Y. Guo, J. Sutiwaraphun, H. W. To, **Parallel Induction Algorithms for Data Mining**, *Proceedings of the Third International Conference on Knowledge Discovery and Data Mining KDD'97* (1997): 35–43.

3. Diettrich, T. G., **Machine-Learning Research: Four Current Directions**, *AI Magazine* (Winter 1997): 97–136.

4. Dzeroski, S. and Lavrac N., eds., *Relational Data Mining*, Springer, Berlin: Germany, 2001.

5. Finn, P., S. Muggleton, D. Page, A. Srinivasan, **Pharmacophore Discovery using the Inductive Logic Programming System Prolog**, *Machine Learning*, Special Issue on Applications and Knowledge Discovery 33, no. 1 (1998) 13–47.

6. Hand, D., H. Mannila, P. Smyth, *Principles of Data Mining*, MIT Press, Cambridge: MA, 2001.

7. John, G. H., **Stock Selection Using Rule Induction**, *IEEE Expert: Intelligent Systems & Their Applications* 11, no. 5 (1996): 52–58.

8. King, R. D et al., **Is it better to combine predictions?** *Protein Engineering* 13, no. 1 (2000) 15–19.

9. Leondes, C. T., *Knowledge-Based Systems: Techniques and Applications*, Academic Press, San Diego, 2000.

10. Li, W., J. Han, J. Pei, **CMAR: Accurate and Efficient Classification Based on Multiple Class-Association Rules**, *Proceedings on 2001 International Conference on Data Mining* (ICDM'01), San Jose: CA, 2001.

11. Luger, G. F. and W. A. Stubblefield, *Artificial Intelligence: Structures and Strategies for Complex Problem Solving*, Addison Wesley Longman, Harlow: England, 1998.

12. Maimon, O. and M. Last, *Knowledge Discovery and Data Mining: The Info-Fuzzy Network (IFN) Methodology*, Kluwer Academic, Boston: MA, 2001.

13. McCarthy, J., **Phenomenal Data Mining**, *CACM* 43, no. 8, (2000) 75–79.

14. Mitchell, T. M., **Does Machine Learning Really Work?** *AI Magazine* (Fall 1997) 11–20.

15. Mitchell, T., *Machine Learning*, McGraw Hill, New York: NY, 1997.

16. Poole, D., A. Mackworth, R. Goebel, *Computational Intelligence: A Logical Approach*, Oxford University Press, New York, 1998.

17. Quinlan, J. R., *C4.5: Programs for Machine Learning*, Morgan Kaufmann, San Mateo: CA, 1992.

18. Russell, S. and P. Norvig, *Artificial Intelligence: A Modern Approach*, Prentice Hall, Upper Saddle River: NJ, 1995.

19. Thrun, S. and C. Faloutsos, **Automated Learning and Discovery**, *AI Magazine* (Fall 1999) 78–82.

20. Witten, I. H. and E. Frank, *Data Mining: Practical Machine Learning Tools and Techniques with Java Implementations*, Morgan Kaufmann, New York, 1999.

CHAPTER 8

1. Adamo, J., *Data Mining for Association Rules and Sequential Patterns*, Springer, New York, 2001.

2. Beyer, K. and R. Ramakrishnan, **Bottom-up computation of sparse and iceberg cubes**, *Proceedings of 1999 ACM-SIGMOD International Conference On Management of Data (SIGMOD'99)*, Philadelphia: PA, (1999): 359–370.

3. Bollacker, K. D., S. Lawrence, C. L.Giles, **Discovering Relevant Scientific Literature on the Web**, *IEEE Intelligent Systems* (Mar/Apr 2000): 42–47.

4. Chakrabarti, S., **Data Mining for Hypertext: A Tutorial Survey**, *SIGKDD Explorations* 1, no. 2, (2000): 1–11.

5. Chakrabarti, S et al., **Mining the Web's Link Structure**, *Computer* 32, no. 8, (1999): 60–67.

6. Chang, G., M. J. Haeley, J. A. M. McHugh, J. T. L. Wang, *Mining the World Wide Web: An Information Search Approach*, Kluwer Academic, Boston: MA, 2001.

7. Chen M., J. Park, P. S. Yu, **Efficient Data Mining for Path Traversal Patterns**, *IEEE Transaction on Knowledge and Data Engineering* 10, no. 2, (Mar/Apr 1998): 209–214.

8. *Clementine*, http://www.isl.co.uk/clem.html

9. Cromp, R. F. and W. J. Campbell, **Data Mining of Multidimensional Remotely Sansad Images**, *Proceedings of the CIKM'93 Conference*, Washington D. C., (1993): 471–480.

10. Darlington, J., Y. Guo, J. Sutiwaraphun, H. W. To, **Parallel Induction Algorithms for Data Mining**, *Proceedings of the Third International Conference on Knowledge Discovery and Data Mining* KDD'97, (1997): 35–43.

11. Fayyad, U. M., G. Piatetsky-Shapiro, P. Smyth, R. Uthurusamy, eds., *Advances in Knowledge Discovery and Data Mining*, AAAI Press / MIT Press, Cambridge, 1996.

12. Fukada, T., Y. Morimoto, S. Morishita, T. Tokuyama, **Data Mining Using Two-Dimensional Optimized Association Rules: Scheme, Algorithms, and Visualization**, *Proceedings of SIGMOD'96 Conference*, Montreal: Canada (1996): 13–23.

13. Han, E., G. Karypis, V. Kumar, **Scalable Parallel Data Mining for Association Rules**, *Proceedings of the SIGMOD'97 Conference*, Tucson: AZ 1(997): 277–288.

14. Han, J. and M. Kamber, *Data Mining: Concepts and Techniques*, Morgan Kaufmann, San Francisco, 2000.

15. Han, J. and K. Koperski, N. Stefanovic, **GeoMiner: A System Prototype for Spatial Data Mining**, *Proceedings of the SIGMOD'97 Conference*, Tucson: AZ, (1997):553–556.

16. Han, J., S. Nishio, H. Kawano, W. Wang, **Generalization-Based Data Mining in Object-Oriented Databases Using an Object Cube Model**, *Proceedings of the CASCON'97 Conference*, Canada, (Nov 1997): 221–252.

17. Han, J. and J. Pei, **Mining Frequent Patterns by Pattern-Growth: Methodology and Implications**, *SIGKDD Explorations* 2, no. 2 (2000): 14–20.

18. Han, J., **Towards On-Line Analytical Mining in Large Databases**, *SIGMOD Record* 27, no. 1 (1998): 97–107.

19. Hedberg, S. R., **Data Mining Takes Off at the Speed of the Web**, *IEEE Intelligent Systems*, (Nov/Dec 1999): 35–37.

20. Hilderman, R. J. and H. J. Hamilton, *Knowledge Discovery and Measures of Interest*, Kluwer Academic, Boston: MA, 2001.

21. Kasif, S., Datascope: **Mining Biological Sequences**, *IEEE Intelligent Systems*, (Nov/Dec1999): 38–43.

22. Kosala R. and H. Blockeel, **Web Mining Research: A Survey**, *SIGKDD Explorations* 2, no. 1 (2000): 1–15.

23. Kowalski, G. J. and M. T. Maybury, *Information Storage and Retrieval Systems: Theory and Implementation*, Kluwer Academic, Boston: MA, 2000.

24. Liu, B., W. Hsu, L. Mun, H. Lee, **Finding Interesting Patterns Using User Expectations**, *IEEE Transactions on Knowledge and Data Engineering* 11, no. 6 (1999): 817–825.

25. McCarthy, J., **Phenomenal Data Mining**, *CACM* 43, no. 8, (2000): 75–79.

26. Moore, S. K., **Understanding the Human Genome**, *Spectrum* 37, no. 11 (2000): 33–35.

27. Mulvenna, M. D et al., eds., **Personalization on the Net using Web Mining, a collection of articles**, *CACM* 43, no. 8, (2000): 123–158

28. Ng, R. T., L. V. S. Lakshmanan, J. Han, A. Pang, **Exploratory Mining and Optimization of Constrained Association Queries** (*Technical Report, University of British Columbia and Concordia University*, 1997): 1–38

29. Park, J. S., M. Chen, P. S. Yu, **Efficient Parallel Data Mining for Association Rules**, *Proceedings of the CIKM'95 Conference*, Baltimore: MD, (1995): 31–36.

30. Pinto, H et al., **Multi-dimensional Sequential Pattern Mining**, *Proceedings of the 2001 International Conference On Information and Knowledge Management (CIKM'01)*, Atlanta: GA, (2001).

31. Salzberg, S. L., **Gene Discovery in DNA Sequences**, *IEEE Intelligent Systems*, (Nov/Dec1999): 44–48.

32. Spiliopoulou, M., **The Laborious Way from Data Mining to Web Log Mining**, *Computer Systems in Science & Engineering* 2 (1999): 113–125.

33. Thuraisingham, B., *Managing and Mining Multimedia Databases*, CRC Press LLC, Boca Raton: FL, 2001.

34. Witten, I. H. and E. Frank, *Data Mining: Practical Machine Learning Tools and Techniques with Java Implementations*, Morgan Kaufmann, New York, 1999.

CHAPTER 9

1. Benitez, J. M., J. L. Castro, I. Requena, **Are Artificial neural networks Black Boxes?** *IEEE Transactions on Neural Networks* 8, no. 5 (1997): 1156–1164.

2. Berthold, M. and D. J. Hand, eds., *Intelligent Data Analysis – An Introduction*, Springer, Berlin: Germany 1999.

3. Cherkassky V. and F. Mulier, *Learning from Data: Concepts, Theory and Methods*, John Wiley, New York, 1998.

4. *Clementine*, http://www.isl.co.uk/clem.html

5. Embrechts, M. J., **Neural Network for Data Mining**, in *Intelligent Engineering Systems through Artificial Neural Networks*, P. Chen, Fernandez B. R., Gosh J., eds., ASME Press (1995): 771–778.

6. Engel, A. and C. Van den Broeck, *Statistical Mechanics of Learning*, Cambridge University Press, Cambridge: England, 2001.

7. Fayyad, U. M., G. Piatetsky-Shapiro, P. Smyth, R. Uthurusamy, eds., *Advances in Knowledge Discovery and Data Mining*, AAAI Press / MIT Press, Cambridge: MA 1996.

8. Finn, P., S. Muggleton, D. Page, A. Srinivasan, **Pharmacophore Discovery using the Inductive Logic Programming System Prolog**, *Machine Learning*, Special Issue on Applications and Knowledge Discovery 33, no. 1 (1998): 13–47.

9. Fu, L., **An Expert Network for DNA Sequence Analysis**, *IEEE Intelligent Systems*, (Jan/Feb1999): 65–71.

10. Fu, L., *Neural Networks in Computer Intelligence*, McGraw-Hill, New York, 1994.

11. Hagan, M. T., H. B. Demuth, M. Beale, *Neural Network Design*, PWS Publishing, Boston, 1996.

12. Hand, D., H. Mannila, P. Smyth, *Principles of Data Mining*, MIT Press, Cambridge: MA, 2001.

13. Haykin, S., *Neural Networks: A Comprehensive Foundation*, Prentice Hall, Upper Saddle River: N.J., 1999.

14. Jang, J. R. and C. Sun, **Neuro-Fuzzy Modeling and Control**, *Proceedings of the IEEE* 83, no. 3, (1995): 378–406.

15. Jang, J. S. R., C. T. Sun, E. Mizutani, *Neuro-Fuzzy and Soft Computing: A Computational Approach to Learning and Machine Intelligence*, Prentice Hall, Upper Saddle River: N.J., 1997.

16. Kantardzic, M., A. A. Aly, A. S. Elmaghraby, **Visualization of Neural-Network Gaps Based on Error Analysis**, *IEEE Transaction on Neural Networks* 10, no. 2 (1999) 419–426.

17. Kaudel, A., M. Last, H. Bunke, eds., *Data Mining and Computational Intelligence*, Physica-Verlag, Heidelberg: Germany, 2001.

18. King, R. D et al., **Is it better to combine predictions?** *Protein Engineering* 13, no. 1 (2000), 15–19.

19. Munakata, T., *Fundamentals of the new Artificial Intelligence: Beyond Traditional Paradigm*, Springer, New York, 1998.

20. Pal, S. K., S. Mitra, *Neuro-Fuzzy Pattern Recognition: Methods in Soft Computing*, John Wiley, New York, 1999.

21. Smith, M., *Neural Networks for Statistical Modeling*, Van Nostrand Reinhold, New York, 1993.

22. Van Rooij, A. J. F., L. C. Jain, R. P. Johnson, *Neural Network Training Using Genetic Algorithms*, World Scientific, Singapore, 1996.

23. Zurada, J. M., *Introduction to Artificial Neural Systems*, West Publishing, St. Paul: MN 1992.

CHAPTER 10

1. Fogel, D. B., ed., *Evolutionary Computation*, IEEE Press, New York, 1998.

2. Fogel, D., **An Introduction to Simulated Evolutionary Optimization**, *IEEE Transactions on Neural networks* 5, no. 1, (1994): 3–14.

3. Fogel, D. B., **Evolutionary Computing**, *Spectrum* 37, no. 2, (2000): 26–32.

4. Goldenberg, D. E., *Genetic Algorithms in Search, Optimization and Machine Learning*, Addison Wesley, Reading: MA, 1989.

5. Kaudel, A., M. Last, H. Bunke, eds., *Data Mining and Computational Intelligence*, Physica-Verlag, Heidelberg: Germany, 2001.

6. Michalewicz, Z., *Genetic Algorithms + Data Structures = Evolution Programs*, Springer, Berlin: Germany, 1999.

7. Munakata, T., *Fundamentals of the new Artificial Intelligence: Beyond Traditional Paradigm*, Springer, New York, 1998.

8. Van Rooij, A. J. F., L. C. Jain, R. P. Johnson, *Neural Network Training Using Genetic Algorithms*, World Scientific, Singapore, 1996.

CHAPTER 11

1. Chen, C. H., L. F. Pau, P. S. P. Wang, *Handbook of Pattern Recognition & Computer Vision*, World Scientific, Singapore, 1993.

2. Chen, S., **A Fuzzy Reasoning Approach for Rule-Based Systems Based on Fuzzy Logic**, *IEEE Transaction on System, Man, and Cybernetics* 26, no. 5, (1996), 769–778.

3. Jang, J. R. and C. Sun, **Neuro-Fuzzy Modeling and Control**, *Proceedings of the IEEE* 83, no. 3, (1995): 378–406.

4. Jang, J. S. R., C. T. Sun, E. Mizutani, *Neuro-Fuzzy and Soft Computing: A Computational Approach to Learning and Machine Intelligence*, Prentice Hall, Upper Saddle River: N.J., 1997.

5. Kaudel, A., M. Last, H. Bunke, eds. *Data Mining and Computational Intelligence*, Physica-Verlag, Heidelberg: Germany, 2001.

6. Klir, G. J. and B. Yuan, *Fuzzy Sets and Fuzzy Logic: Theory and Applications*, Prentice Hall, Upper Saddle River: N.J., 1995.

7. Koczy, L. T. and K. Hirota, **Size Reduction by Interpolation in Fuzzy Rule Bases**, *IEEE Transaction on System, Man, and Cybernetics* 27, no. 1, (1997): 14–25.

8. Lee, E. S. and H. Shih, *Fuzzy and Multi-level Decision Making: An Interactive Computational Approach*, Springer, London, 2001.

9. Li, H. X. and V. C. Yen, *Fuzzy Sets and Fuzzy Decision-Making*, CRC Press, Boca Raton: FL, 1995.

10. Lin, T. Y. and N. Cerone, *Rough Sets and Data Mining*, Kluwer Academic, Boston: MA, 1997.

11. Maimon, O. and M. Last, *Knowledge Discovery and Data Mining: The Info-Fuzzy Network (IFN) Methodology*, Kluwer Academic, Boston: MA, 2001.

12. Mendel, J., **Fuzzy Logic Systems for Engineering: A Tutorial**, *Proceedings of the IEEE* 83, no. 3 (1995): 345–377.

13. Miyamoto, S., *Fuzzy Sets in Information Retrieval and Cluster Analysis*, Kluwer Academic, Dordrecht: Netherlands, 1990.

14. Munakata, T., *Fundamentals of the new Artificial Intelligence: Beyond Traditional Paradigm*, Springer, New York, 1998.

15. Pal, S. K. and S. Mitra, *Neuro-Fuzzy Pattern Recognition: Methods in Soft Computing*, John Wiley, New York, 1999.

16. Pedrycz, W. and F. Gomide, *An Introduction to Fuzzy Sets: Analysis and Design*, MIT Press, Cambridge: MA, 1998.

17. Pedrycz, W. and J. Waletzky, **Fuzzy Clustering with Partial Supervision**, *IEEE Transaction on System, Man, and Cybernetics* 27, no. 5 (1997) 787–795.

18. Yager, R. R., **Targeted E-commerce Marketing Using Fuzzy Intelligent Agents**, *IEEE Intelligent Systems* (Nov/Dec 2000): 42–45.

19. Yeung, D. S. and E. C. C. Tsang, **A Comparative Study on Similarity-Based Fuzzy Reasoning Methods**, *IEEE Transaction on System, Man, and Cybernetics* 27, no. 2 (1997) 216–227.

20. Zadeh, L. A., **Fuzzy Logic = Computing with Words**, *IEEE Transactions on Fuzzy Systems* 4, no. 2 (1996): 103–111.

21. Zadeh, L. A., **Knowledge Representation in Fuzzy Logic**, *IEEE Transactions on Knowledge and Data Engineering* 1, no. 1 (1989): 89–99.

CHAPTER 12

1. Barry, A. M. S., *Visual Intelligence*, State University of New York Press, New York, 1997.

2. Buja, A., D. Cook, D. F. Swayne, *Interactive High-Dimensional Data Visualization*, http://www.research.att.com/andreas/xgobi/heidel.

3. Chen, C and R. J. Paul, **Visualizing a Knowledge Domain's Intellectual Structure**, *Computer* 36 no. 3, (2001): 65–72.

4. Eick, S. G., **Visual Discovery and Analysis**, *IEEE Transaction on Visualization and Computer Graphics* 6, no. 1 (2000): 44–57.

5. Eick, S. G., **Visualizing Multi-dimensional Data**, *Computer Graphics* (Feb 2000): 61–67.

6. Estrin, D et al., **Network Visualization with Nam, the VINT Network Animator**, *Computer* 33, no. 11 (2000): 63–68.

7. Faloutsos, C. and K. Lin, **FastMap: A Fast Algorithm for Indexing, Data-Mining and Visualization of Traditional and Multimedia Datasets**, *Proceedings of SIGMOD'95 Conference*, San Jose: CA (1995): 163–174.

8. Fayyad, U.M., G. G. Grinstein, A. Wierse, eds., *Information Visualization in Data Mining and Knowledge Discovery*, Morgan Kaufmann, San Francisco: CA, 2002.

9. Gallaghar, R. S., *Computer Visualization: Graphics Techniques for Scientific and Engineering Analysis*, CRC Press, Boca Raton: FL, 1995.

10. Hinneburg, A., D. A. Keim, M. Wawryniuk, **HD-Eye: Visual Mining of High-Dimensional Data**, *IEEE Computer Graphics and Applications* (Sept/Oct 1999): 22–31.

11. Hofman, P., *Radviz*, http:www.cs.uml.edu/phoffman/viz.

12. IBM, *Parallel Visual Explorer at Work in the Money Market*, http://www.ibm.com/news/950203/pve-03html.

13. Inselberg A. and B. Dimsdale, **Visualizing Multi-Variate Relations with Parallel Coordinates**, *Proceedings of the Third International conference on Human-Computer Interaction*, New York, (1989): 460–467.

14. Mackinlay, J. D., **Opportunities for Information Visualization**, *IEEE Computer Graphics and Applications* (Jan/Feb 2000): 22–23.

15. Pu, P. and G. Melissargos, **Visualizing Resource Allocation Tasks**, *IEEE Computer Graphics and Applications* (July/Aug 1997): 6–9.

16. Roth, S. F et al., **Towards an Information Visualization Workspace: Combining Multiple Means of Expressions**, *Human-Computer Interaction Journal* (July 1997): 61–70.

17. Spence, R., *Information Visualization*, Addison Wesley, Harlow: England, 2001.

18. Thomsen, E., *OLAP Solution: Building Multidimensional Information System*, John Wiley, New York, 1997.

19. Wong, P. C., **Visual Data Mining**, *IEEE Computer Graphics and Applications* (Sept/Oct 1999): 20–21.

APPENDIX A
Data-Mining Tools

A1 COMMERCIALLY AND PUBLICLY AVAILABLE TOOLS

This summary of some publicly available commercial data-mining products is being provided to help readers better understand what software tools can be found on the market and what their features are. It is not intended to endorse or critique any specific product. Potential users will need to decide for themselves the suitability of each product for their specific applications and data-mining environments. This is primarily intended as a starting point from which users can obtain more information. There is a constant stream of new products appearing in the market and hence this list is by no means comprehensive. Because these changes are very frequent, the author suggests two Web sites for information about the latest tools and their performances: http://www.kdnuggets.com *and* http://www.knowledgestorm.com.

AgentBase/Marketeer

AgentBase/Marketeer is, according to its designers, the industry's first second-generation data-mining product. It is based on emerging intelligent-agent technology. The system comes with a group of wizards to guide a user through different stages of data mining. This makes it easy to use. AgentBase/Marketeer is primarily aimed at marketing applications. It uses several data-mining methodologies whose results are combined by intelligent agents. It can access data from all major sources, and it runs on Windows95, Windows NT, and the Solaris operating system.

ANGOSS Knowledge Miner

ANGOSS Knowledge Miner combines ANGOSS Knowledge Studio with proprietary algorithms for clickstream analysis; it interfaces to Web log–reporting tools.

Autoclass III

Autoclass is an unsupervised Bayesian classification system for independent data. It seeks a maximum posterior probability to provide a simple approach to problems such as classification, clustering, and general mixture separation. It works on Unix platforms.

BusinessMiner

BusinessMiner is a single-strategy, easy-to-use tool based on decision trees. It can access data from multiple sources including Oracle, Sybase, SQL Server, and Teradata. BusinessMiner runs on all Windows platforms, and it can be used stand-alone or in conjunction with OLAP tools.

CART

CART is a robust data-mining tool that automatically searches for important patterns and relationships in large data sets and quickly uncovers hidden structures even in highly complex data sets. It works on the Windows, Mac, and Unix platforms.

Clementine

Clementine is a comprehensive toolkit for data mining. It uses neural networks and rule-induction methodologies. The toolkit includes data manipulation and visualization capabilities. It runs on Windows and Unix platforms and accepts the data from Oracle, Ingres, Sybase, and Informix databases. A recent version offers sequence association and clustering for Web-data analyses.

Darwin (now part of Oracle)

Darwin is an integrated, multiple-strategy tool that uses neural networks, classification and regression trees, nearest-neighbor rule, and genetic algorithms. These techniques are implemented in an open client/server architecture with a scalable, parallel-computing implementation. The client-side unit can work on Windows and the server on Unix. Darwin can access data from a variety of networked data sources including all major relational databases. It is optimized for parallel servers.

DataEngine

DataEngine is a multiple-strategy data-mining tool for data modeling, combining conventional data-analysis methods with fuzzy technology, neural networks, and advanced statistical techniques. It works on the Windows platform.

Data Mining Suite

Data Mining Suite is a comprehensive and integrated set of data-mining tools. The main tools are IDIS (Information Discovery System) for finding classification rules, IDIS-PM (Predictive Modeler) for prediction and forecasting, and IDIS-Map for finding geographical patterns. Data Mining Suite supports client/server architecture and runs on all major platforms with different database-management systems. It also discovers patterns of users' activities on Web sites.

Data Surveyor

Data Surveyor is a single-strategy (classification) tool. It consists of two components: a front-end and a back-end. The front-end is responsible for data mining using the tree-generation methodology. The back-end consists of a fast, parallel, database server where the data are loaded from a user's databases. The back-end runs on parallel Unix servers and the front-end works with Unix and Windows platforms.

DataMind

DataMind's architecture consists of two components: DataCruncher for server-side data mining and DataMind Professional for client-side specification and viewing results. It can implement classification, clustering, and association-rule technologies. DataMind can be set up to mine data locally or on a remote server, where data are organized using any of the major relational databases.

Datasage

Datasage is a comprehensive data-mining product whose architecture incorporates a data mart in its data-mining server. The user accesses Datasage through an interface operating as a thin client, using either a Windows client or a Java-enabled browser client.

DBMiner

DBMiner is a publicly available tool for data mining. It is a multiple-strategy tool and it supports methodologies such as clustering, association rules, summarization, and visualization. DBMiner uses Microsoft SQL Server 7.0 Plato and runs on different Windows platforms.

Decision Series

Decision Series is a multiple-strategy tool that uses artificial neural networks, clustering algorithms, and genetic algorithms to perform data mining. It can operate on scalable, parallel platforms to provide speedy solutions. It runs on standard industry platforms such as HP, SUN, and DEC, and it supports most of the commercial, relational database–management systems.

Decisionhouse

Decisionhouse is a suite of tightly integrated tools that primarily support classification and visualization processes. Various aspects of data preparation and reporting are included. It works on the Unix platform.

Delta Miner

Delta Miner is a multiple-strategy tool supporting clustering, summarization, deviation-detection, and visualization processes. A common application is the analysis of financial controlling data. It runs on Windows platforms and it integrates new search techniques and "business intelligence" methodologies into an OLAP front-end.

Emerald

Emerald is a publicly available tool still used as a research system. It consists of five different machine-learning programs supporting clustering, classification, and summarization tasks.

Evolver

Evolver is a single-strategy tool. It uses genetic-algorithm technology to solve complex optimization problems. This tool runs on all Windows platforms and it is based on data stored in Microsoft Excel tables.

GainSmarts

GainSmarts uses predictive-modeling technology that can analyze past purchases and demographic and lifestyle data to predict the likelihood of response and other characteristics of customers.

IBM Datajoiner

Datajoiner allows the user to view multivendor—relational and nonrelational, local and remote—geographically distributed databases as local databases to access and join tables without knowing the source locations.

IBM Intelligent Miner

Intelligent Miner is an integrated and comprehensive set of data-mining tools. It uses decision trees, neural networks, and clustering. The latest version includes a wide range of text-mining tools. Most of its algorithms have been parallelized for scalability. A user can build models using either a GUI or an API. It works only with DB2 databases.

KATE

KATE is a single, rule-based strategy tool consisting of four components: KATE-editor, KATE-CBR, KATE-Datamining, and KATE-Runtime. It runs on Windows and Unix platforms, and it is applicable to several databases.

Kensington 2000

Kensington 2000 is an internet-based knowledge-discovery and -management platform for the analyses of large and distributed data sets.

Kepler

Kepler is an extensible, multiple-strategy data-mining system. The key element of its architecture is extensibility through a "plug-in" interface for external tools without redeveloping the system core. The tool supports data-mining tasks such as classification, clustering, regression, and visualization. It runs on Windows and Unix platforms.

Knowledge Seeker

Knowledge Seeker is a single-strategy desktop or client/server tool relying on a tree-based methodology for data mining. It provides a nice GUI for model building and letting the user explore data. It also allows users to export the discovered data model as text, SQL query, or Prolog program. It runs on Windows and Unix platforms, and accepts data from a variety of sources.

MATLAB NN Toolbox

A MATLAB extension implements an engineering environment (i.e. a computer-based environment for engineers to help them solve their common tasks) for research in neural networks and its design, simulation, and application. It offers various network architectures and different learning strategies. Classification and function approximations are typical data-mining problems that can be solved using this tool. It runs on Windows, Mac, and Unix platforms.

Marksman

Marksman is a single-methodology tool based on artificial neural networks. It provides a number of useful data-manipulation features, which are very important in preprocessing. Its design is optimized for the database-analysis needs of direct-marketing professionals, and it runs on PC/Windows platforms.

MARS

MARS is a logistic-regression tool for binary classification. It automatically handles missing values, detection of interactions between input variables, and transformation of variables.

MineSet

MineSet is comprehensive tool for data mining. Its features include extensive data manipulation and transformation capabilities, various data-mining approaches, and powerful visualization capabilities. MineSet supports client/server architecture and runs on Silicon Graphics platforms.

NETMAP

NETMAP is a general purpose, information-visualization tool. It is most effective for large, qualitative, text-based data sets. It runs on Unix workstations.

Neuro Net

NeuroNet is a publicly available software for experimentation with different artificial neural-network architectures and types.

NeuroSolutions V3.0

NeuroSolutions V3.0 combines a modular, icon-based artificial neural-network design, and it solves data-mining problems such as classification, prediction, and function approximation. Its implementations are based on advanced learning techniques such as recurrent backpropagation and backpropagation through time. The tool runs on all Windows platforms.

OC1

OC1 is publicly available software for data mining. It is specially designed as a decision tree induction system for applications where the samples have continuous feature values.

OMEGA

OMEGA is a system for developing, evaluating, and implementing predictive models using the genetic-programming approach. It is suitable for the classification and visualization of data. It runs on all Windows platforms.

Partek

Partek is a multiple-strategy data-mining product. It is based on several methodologies including statistical techniques, neural networks, fuzzy logic, genetic algorithms, and data visualization. It runs on UNIX platforms.

Pattern Recognition Workbench (PRW)

Pattern Recognition Workbench (PRW) is a comprehensive multiple-strategy tool. It uses neural networks, statistical pattern recognition, and machine-learning methodologies. It runs on all Windows platforms using a spreadsheet-style GUI. PRW automatically generates alternative models and searches for the best solution. It also provides a variety of visualization tools to monitor model building and interpret results.

Readware Information Processor

Readware Information Processor is an integrated text-mining environment for intranets and the Internet. It classifies documents by content, providing a literal and conceptual search. The tool includes a ConceptBase with English, French, and German lexicons.

SAS (Enterprise Miner)

SAS (Enterprise Miner) represents one of the most comprehensive sets of integrated tools for data mining. It also offers a variety of data manipulation and transformation features. In addition to statistical methods, the SAS Data Mining Solution employs neural networks, decision trees, and SAS Webhound that analyzes Web-site traffic. It runs on Windows and Unix platforms and it provides a user-friendly GUI front-end to the SEMMA (Sample, Explore, Modify, Model, Assess).

Scenario

Scenario is a single-strategy tool that uses the tree-based approach to data mining. The GUI relies on wizards to guide a user through different tasks, and it is easy to use. It runs on Windows platforms.

Sipina-W

Sipina-W is publicly available software that includes different traditional data-mining techniques such as CART, Elisee, ID3, C4.5, and some new methods for generating decision trees.

SNNS

SNNS is a publicly available software. It is a simulation environment for research on and application of artificial neural networks. The environment is available on Unix and Windows platforms.

SPIRIT

SPIRIT is a tool for exploration and modeling using Bayesian techniques. The system allows communication with the user in the rich language of conditional events. It works on Windows platforms.

SPSS

SPSS is one of the most comprehensive integrated tools for data mining. It has data-management and data-summarization capabilities and includes tools for both discovery and verification. The complete suite includes statistical methods, neural networks, and visualization techniques. It is available on a variety of commercial platforms.

S-Plus

S-Plus is an interactive, object-oriented programming language for data mining. Its commercial version supports clustering, classification, summarization, visualization, and regression techniques. It works on Windows and Unix platforms.

STATlab

STATlab is a single-strategy tool that relies on interactive visualization to help a user perform exploratory data analysis. It can import data from common relational databases and it runs on Windows, Mac, and Unix platforms.

STATISTICA-Neural Networks

STATISTICA-Neural Networks is a single-strategy tool includes a standard backpropagation-learning algorithm and iterative procedures such as Conjugate Gradient Descent and Levenberg-Marquardt. It runs on all Windows platforms.

Strategist

Strategist is a tool based on Bayesian-network methodology to support different dependency analyses. It provides the methodology for integration of expert judgments and data-mining results, which are based on modeling of uncertainties and decision-making processes. It runs on all Windows platforms.

Syllogic

Syllogic Data Mining Tool is a toolbox that combines many data-mining methodologies and offers a variety of approaches to uncover hidden information. It includes several data-preprocessing and -transformation functions. It is available on Windows NT and Unix platforms and it supports most of the commercial relational databases.

Teradata Warehouse Miner

Teradata Warehouse Miner provides different statistical analyses, decision-tree methods, and regression methodologies for in-place mining on a Teradata database-management system.

TiMBL

TiMBL is a publicly available software. It includes several memory-based learning techniques for discrete data. A representation of the training set is explicitly stored in memory, and new cases are classified by extrapolation from the most similar cases.

TOOLDIAG

TOOLDIAG is a publicly available tool for data mining. It consists of several programs in C for statistical pattern recognition of multivariate numeric data. The tool is primary oriented toward classification problems.

WINROSA

WINROSA is a software tool that complements many other tools available for building fuzzy logic systems. It automatically generates fuzzy rules from the available data set. It works on Windows platforms.

Viscovery©SOMine

This single-strategy data-mining tool is based on self-organizing maps and is uniquely capable of visualizing multidimensional data. Viscovery©SOMine supports clustering, classification, and visualization processes. It works on all Windows platforms.

Weka (2.2)

Weka is a software environment that integrates several machine-learning tools within a common framework and a uniform GUI. Classification and summarization are the main data-mining tasks supported by the Weka system.

WUM

WUM 6.0 is a publicly available integrated environment for Web-log preparation, querying, and visualization of summarized activities on a Web site.

A2   WEB SITE LINKS

General Web sites

Web site	Description
www.cs.bham.ac.uk/~anp/	A major server of KDD and OLAP information that is a repository of papers, bibliographies, and has links to conferences, software, and other Web sites.
www.ics.uci.edu	A comprehensive machine-learning site. Popular for its large repository of standard data sets and machine-learning programs for experimental evaluation.

Web site	Description
www.ortech-engr.com/fuzzy/ reservoir.html	Newsgroup about fuzzy logic and fuzzy set theory
www.aic.nrl.navy.mil/galist/	Newsgroup about genetic algorithms.
www.emsl.pnl.gov:2080/proj/neuron/ neural/newsgroups.html	Newsgroup about artificial neural networks.
www.mathworks.com/matlabcentral/	Newsgroup about MATLAB and SIMULINK.
www.knowledgestorm.com/	An online resource that provides "one-stop shopping" for managers, system builders, researchers, and users who wish to study the empirical behavior of information systems.
ftp.abo.fi/pub/iasmr/who.txt	This is a list of who-is-who in the community of fuzzy logic researchers.
www.cs.ualberta.ca/~holte/mlj/	*Kluwer Machine Learning Journal*: A journal on robotics, computer and information science, artificial intelligence, machine learning, expert systems, and cognitive science.
http://megaputer.com/	A comprehensive list of links to machine-learning resources on the WWW. The links are sorted into various categories such as software, bibliographies, data sets, conferences, people, etc.
www.the-data-mine.com/bin/view/Main/ WebHome	A valuable site for business users of data mining. It contains pointers to all kinds of end-user tool vendors, infrastructure-technology vendors, and function-and industry-specific tool vendors.
www.almaden.ibm.com/cs/quest/	An online resource for research in data mining using IBM Intelligent Miner. It contains Synthetic Data Generation Codes for associations, sequential patterns, and classification.
www.cs.cmu.edu/Groups/AI/html	This address collects files, programs, and publications of interest to the artificial-intelligence research community.
http://www-2.cs.cmu.edu/afs/ cs.cmu.edu/project/ai-repository/ai/ html/air.html	An online resource to A.I. programs, software, data sets, bibliographies, and links.
www.datamining.org	This is a site run by a group of users and international data-mining tool providers. It is geared more for business users, and it provides links to many data-mining sites.

Web site	Description
www.ieee-nns.org/	IEEE Transactions on Neural Networks: A journal that covers the latest topics on artificial neural networks and their applications.
www.iospress.nl/site/html/ 1088467x.html	Journal of Intelligent Data Analysis: An E-journal to examine issues related to the research and applications of A.I.-techniques in data analysis.
www.cs.umd.edu/users/nfa/ dm_ people_ papers.html	An online resource for basic information on current research and results in the data-mining field.
www.ics.uci.edu/~mlearn/MLList.html	A mailing list focusing on the scientific study of machine learning.
www.ieee.org/pub_preview/ fuzz_toc.html	*IEEE Transactions on Fuzzy Systems*: A journal that covers the latest topics on fuzzy logic and fuzzy systems.
www.jair.org	*Journal of AI Research* The journal includes research articles, technical notes, surveys, and expository articles in the field of machine learning.
www.kdnuggets.com	This site contains information about data-mining activities and pointers to past and current research. It maintains a guide to commercial and public-domain tools for data mining. It also provides links to companies supporting software, consulting, and data-mining services.
www.ncc.up.pt/liacc/ML/	Research on evaluation and characterization of learning systems using various machine-learning methods including neural networks and statistical approaches. It contains about twenty different algorithms and data sets.
www.pcwebopedia.com/ data_mining.htm	This site provides news, articles, and other useful sites in data-mining applications.
www.digimine.com/usama/datamine/	*Journal of Data Mining and Knowledge Discovery:* The journal consolidates papers in both the research and practice of knowledge discovery, surveys of implementation techniques and application papers
www.research.microsoft.com/datamine	The site provides a good starting point for those who want to get more information about data mining. It contains different topics from conferences, journals, services, and products to discussions and references.

Web site	Description
www.santafe.edu/~kurt/ dmvendors.shtml	A frequently visited site for basic information about the data-mining field with a large number of pointers to data-mining products and vendors.
www.stat.ufl.edu/vlib/statistics.html	An up-to-date online resource to statistical software, data sets, and links.
www.elsevier.com/inca/publications/ store/5/0/5/7/8/7/	*International Journal of Approximate Reasoning*
www.elsevier.nl/catalogue/SAE/515/ 08410/08417/505545/505545.html	*International Journal on Fuzzy Sets and Systems*
http://ejournals.wspc.com.sg/ijns/ ijns.html	*International Journal of Neural Systems*
http://ejournals.wspc.com.sg/ijufks/ ijufks.html	*International Journal of Uncertainty, Fuzziness and Knowledge-Based Systems*
http://tatooine.fortunecity.com/halley/ 421/nfsc.htm	A detailed list of more than 100 research groups all over the world working on neuro-fuzzy logic and soft computing.
http://ai.iit.nrc.ca/misc.html	A list of links to other A.I.-and statistics-related sites. It also contains recent publications and e-maillists.
www.emsl.pnl.gov	Neural Networks at Pacific Northwest National Laboratory.
www.cs.gmu.edu/research/gag	George Mason University Genetic Algorithms Research.
www.marketingtools.com	Getting Marketing Information.
http://otal.umd.edu/Olive/Multi-D.html	A list of projects and products for multidimensional visualization.

Web Sites for Data-Mining Software Tools and Data Sets

Web site	Data-Mining Tool
www.spss.com/clementine	Clementine
www.datamining.com	Data Mining Suite
www.hnc.com	DataBase Mining Marksman
www.datamind.co.uk/Merchant/ index.html	DataMind
www.vignette.com/CDA/Site/ 0%2C2097%2C1-1-30-72-407- 1107%2CFF.html	Datasage
www.jda.com/	Decision series
www.pilotsw.com	Discovery
www.software.ibm.com	Intelligent Miner
www.acknosoft.com	KATE Tools
www.ncr.com	Knowledge Discovery Workbench
www.angoss.com	Knowledge Seeker
www.sgi.com	MineSet

Web site	Data-Mining Tool
http://netmap.sourceforge.net/	NETMAP
www.capgemini.com	OMEGA
www.partek.com	Partek
http://www.unicacorp.com/index3.html	PRW
www.sas.com	SAS Enterprise Miner
www.cognos.com	Scenario
www.spss.com	SPSS
www.statview.com/	StatView
http://www.syllogic.com/	Tolkien
www.mathsoft.com/	Mathcad
www.prevision.com/	Strategy Science
www.prevision.com/	MarketSmart
http://kmi.open.ac.uk/projects/bkd/	Bayesian Knowledge Discoverer
www.eudaptics.co.at/	Viscovery©SOMine
www.mathworks.com/	MATLAB NN Toolbox
www.neuralware.com/	NeuralWorks Professional II/PLUS
www.nd.com/products.htm	NeuroSolutions v3.0
www.wardsystems.com/	NeuroShell2/NeuroWindows
www.statsoftinc.com/	STATISTICA: Neural Networks
www.palisade.com/	@RISK 4.5
www.angoss.com/ProdServ/ AnalyticalTools/index.html#seeker	KnowledgeSEEKER
www.quadstone.com/	Decisionhouse
www.salford-systems.com/	CART
http://www.dataengine.de/english/sp/ index.htm	DataEngine
www.wizsoft.com	WizWhy
www.bissantz.de/	Delta Miner
www.oracle.com	Darwin (Oracle)
www.dialogis.de/	D-Miner
www.mitgmbh.de/	DataEngine
www.lans.ece.utexas.edu/winsnns.html	SNNS
http://allanon.gmd.de/de/projekte.html	Descartes
http://ic.arc.nasa.gov/ic/projects/bayes- group/autoclass/	AutoClass
http://aic.gmu.edu/mresearch.html	Emerald
www.dbminer.com	DBMiner
http://eewww.eng.ohio-state.edu/~lih/ dm.html	MLC++
www.mathworks.com/fuzzytbx.html	Fuzzy Logic Toolbox
http://fuzzy.cs.uni-magdeburg.de/ nefclass/	NEFCLASS
http://websom.hut.fi/websom/	Websom
http://www.cis.hut.fi/research/ demos.shtml	FastICA
http://www.genesis-sim.org/GENESIS/	GENESIS
http://www-2.cs.cmu.edu/~dv/	Dv
www.ics.uci.edu/~mlearn/ MLSummary.html	Data Sets for Machine Learning

Web site	Data-Mining Tool
http://www.ics.uci.edu/~smyth/courses/ics278/dmlinks.html	Data Mining Resources
http://vasc.ri.cmu.edu/cgi-bin/demos/findface.cgi	Face Detection Data Sets
www.cs.utoronto.ca/neuron/delve/delve.html	DELVE Data Set
www.attar.com	XpertRule
http://scanner-group.mit.edu/htdocs/DATAMINING/Datamining/DMProducts.html	Data Mining Products
www.ics.uci.edu/~mlearn/	Standard Data Sets for Experimental Evaluation of Machine Learning Techniques
www.gmd.de/ml-archive	Data Sets for Machine Learning
http://www.inf.ufes.br/~thomas/home/tooldiag.html	TOOLDIAG
http://www.altaanalytics.com/	NetMap
www.belmont.com	CrossGraphs
www.mapinfo.com	MapInfo
http://megaputer.com/	PolyAnalyst
www.ics.uci.edu	The Machine Learning Database Repository
www.census.gov	U. S. Census Bureau Data Sets
lib.stat.cmu.edu/datasets	Sample Data Sets for Data Mining (StatLib)
www.cs.bham.ac.uk	The Data Mine
info.gte.com	Knowledge Discovery Mine
www.visualizetech.com	DataVista
http://www.trajecta.com/	Trajecta Intelligent Intuition
http://www.sphinxvision.com/	SphinxVision
www.incontext.ca	WebAnalyzer

Data-Mining Vendors

Data-Mining Vendor	Address	Web Site
Angoss Software International LTC.	34 St. Patrick Street, Suite 200 Toronto, Ontario Canada M5T 1V1	www.angoss.com
Attar Software USA	Two Deerfoot Trial on Partridge Hill Harward, MA 01451, USA	www.attar.com
Business Objects, Inc.	20813 Stevens Creek Blvd., Suite 100 Cupertino, CA 95014, USA	www.businessobjects.com

Data-Mining Vendor	Address	Web Site
Cognos Corp.	67 S. Bedford St., Suite 200 W. Burlington, MA 01803, USA	www.cognos.com
DataMind Corp.	2121 S. El Camino Real, Suite 1200 San Mateo, CA 94403, USA	
HNC Software Inc.	5930 Cornerstone Court West San Diego, CA 92121, USA	www.hnc.com
HyperParallel	282 Second Street, 3rd Floor San Francisco, CA 94105, USA	
IBM Corp.	Old Orchard Road Armonk, NY 10504, USA	www.ibm.com
Integral Solutions Ltd.	Berk House, Basing View Basingstoke Hampshire RG21 4RG, UK	www.isl.co.uk
Information Discovery, Inc.	703B Pier Avenue, Suite 169 Hermosa Beach, CA 90254, USA	www.datamining.com
Isoft	Bridgewater House 58-60 Whitworth Street Manchester M1 6LT England	http://www.isoftplc.com/ ie_ind.htm
NeoVista Solutions, Inc.	10710 N. Tantau Ave. Cupertino, CA 95014, USA	http://www.jda.com/
Neural Applications Corp.	2600 Crosspark Rd. Coralville, IA 52241, USA	www.neural.com
NeuralWare Inc.	202 Park West Drive Pittsburgh, PA 15275, USA	www.neuralware.com
Pilot Software, Inc.	One Canal Park Cambridge, MA 02141, USA	www.pilotsw.com
Red Brick Systems, Inc.	485 Alberto Way Los Gatos, CA 95032, USA	www.redbrick.com
Silicon Graphics Computer Systems	2011 N. Shoreline Blvd. Mountain View, CA 94043, USA	www.sgi.com
SPSS, Inc.	444 N. Michigan Ave. Chicago, IL 60611-3962, USA	www.spss.com
SAS Institute Inc.	SAS Campus Dr. Cary, NC 27513-2414, USA	www.sas.com
Thinking Machine Corp.	14 Crosby Dr. Bedford, MA 01730, USA	www.think.com
Trajecta	611 S. Congress, Suite 420 Austin, TX 78704, USA	www.trajecta.com

Data-Mining Vendor	Address	Web Site
Daisy Analysis Ltd.	East Green Farm, Great Bradley Newmarket, Suffolk CB8 9LU, UK	www.daisy.co.uk
Visible Decisions, Inc.	200 Front Street West, Suite 2203, P.O.Box 35 Toronto, Ont M5V 3K2, Canada	www.vdi.com
Maxus Systems International Inc.	610 River Terrace Hoboken, NJ 07030, USA	www.maxussystems.com
United Information Systems, Inc.	10401 Fernwood Road, #200 Bethesda, MD 20817, USA	www.unitedis.com/
ALTA Analytics, Inc.	929 Eastwind Dr., Suite 203 Westerville, OH 43081, USA	
Visualize, Inc.	1819 East Morten, Suite 210 Phoenix, AZ 85020, USA	www.visualizetech.com
Data Description, Inc.	840 Hanshaw Road, Suite 9 Ithaca, NY 14850, USA	www.datadesk.com
i2 Ltd.	Breaks House Mill Court, Great Shelford Cambridge, CB2, SLD, UK	www.i2.co.uk
Harlequin Inc.	One Cambridge Center, 8th Floor Cambridge, MA 02142, USA	
Advanced Visual Systems, Inc.	300 Fifth Avenue Waltham, MA 02154, USA	www.avs.com
ORION Scientific Systems	19800 Mac Arthur Blvd. Suite 480 Irvine, CA 92612, USA	www.orionsci.com
Belmont Research, Inc.	84 Sherman St. Cambridge, MA 02140, USA	www.belmont.com/
Spotfire, Inc.	28 State Street, Suite 1100 Boston, MA 02109, USA	www.ivee.com
Precision Computing, Inc.	P. O. Box 1193 Sierra Vista, AZ 85636, USA	www.crimelink.com
Information Technology Institute	11 Science Park Road Singapore Science Park II Singapore 117685	
NCO Natural Computing	Deurtschherrnufer 31 60594 Frankfurt, Germany	
Imagix Corp.	6025 White Oak Lane San Luis Obispo, CA 93401, USA	www.imagix.com
Helsinki University of Technology	Neural Networks Research Center, P. O. Box 1000, FIN-02015 HUT, Finland	websom.hut.fi
Amtec Engineering, Inc.	P. O. Box 3633 Bellevue, WA 98009-3633, USA	www.amtec.com
IBM-Haifa Research Laboratory	Matam, Haifa 31905 Israel	www.ibm.com/java/ mapuccino

Data-Mining Vendor	Address	Web Site
Infospace, Inc.	181 2nd Avenue, Suite 218 San Mateo, CA 94401, USA	www.infospace-inc.com
Research Systems, Inc.	2995 Wilderness Place Boulder, CO 80301, USA	www.rsinc.com
GR-FX Pty Limited	P. O. Box 2121 Clovelly, NSW, 2031 Australia	www.gr-fx.com
Analytic Technologies	104 Pond Street Natick, MA 01760, USA	analytictech.com
The GIFIC Corp.	405 Atlantic Street Melbourne Beach, FL 32951 USA	www.gific.com
Inxight Software Inc.	3400 Hillview Avenue Palo Alto, CA 94304, USA	www.inxight.com
ThemeMedia Inc.	8383 158th Avenue NE, Suite 320 Redmond, WA 98052, USA	
Neovision Hypersystems, Inc.	50 Broadway, 34th Floor New York, NY 10004, USA	www.neovision.com
Artificial Intelligence Software SpA	Via Carlo Esterle 9-20132 Milano, Italy	www.iunet.it/ais
SRA International, Inc.	2000 15th Street Arlington, VA 22201, USA	www.knowledge discovery.com
Quadstone Ltd.	16 Chester Street, Edinburgh EH3 7RA, Scotland	www.quadstone.co.uk
Data Junction Corp.	2201 Northland Drive Austin, TX 78756, USA	www.datajunction.com
Semio Corp.	1730 South Amphlett Blvd. #101 San Mateo, CA 94402, USA	www.semio.com
Visual Numerics, Inc.	9990 Richmond Ave., Suite 400 Houston, TX 77042-4548, USA	www.vni.com
Perspecta, Inc	600 Townsend Street, Suite 170E San Francisco, CA 94103-4945 USA	www.perspecta.com
Dynamic Diagrams	12 Bassett Street Providence, RI 02903, USA	www.dynamicdiagrams. com
Presearch Inc.	8500 Executive Park Avenue Fairfax, VA 22031, USA	www.presearch.com
InContext Systems	6733 Mississauga Road, 7th floor Mississauga, Ontario L5N 6J5 Canada	www.incontext.ca
Cygron Research & Development, Ltd.	Szeged, Pf.: 727 H-6701 Hungary	www.tiszanet.hu/cygron/

Data-Mining Vendor	Address	Web Site
NetScout Systems, Inc.	4 Technology Park Drive Westford, MA 01886, USA	http://www.netscout.com/
Advanced Visual Systems	300 Fifth Ave. Waltham, MA 02154, USA	www.avs.com
Alta Analytics, Inc	555 Metro Place North Suite 175 Dublin, OH 43017, USA	
MapInfo Corp.	1 Global View Troy, NY 12180, USA	www.mapinfo.com
Information Builders, Inc.	1250 Broadway, 30th Floor New York, NY 10001-3782, USA	http://www. informationbuilders. com/
Prism Solutions, Inc.	1000 Hamlin Court Sunnyvale, CA 94089, USA	
Oracle Corp.	500 Oracle Parkway Redwood Shores, CA 94086 USA	www.oracle.com
Evolutionary Technologies, Inc.	4301 Westbank Drive Austin, TX 78746, USA	www.eti.com/home/ home.htm
Information Advantage, Inc.	12900 Whitewater Drive, Suite 100 Minnetonka, MN 55343, USA	
IntelligenceWare, Inc.	55933 W. Century Blvd., Suite 900 Los Angeles, CA 90045, USA	
Microsoft Corporation	One Microsoft Way Redmond, WA 98052, USA	http:// www.microsoft.com/
Computer Associates International, Inc.	One Computer Associates Plaza Islandia, NY 11788-7000, USA	http://www.cai.com/

APPENDIX B
Data-Mining Applications

Many businesses and scientific communities are currently employing data-mining technology. Their number continues to grow, as more and more data-mining success stories become known. Here we present a small collection of real-life examples of data-mining implementations from the business and scientific world. We also present some pitfalls of data mining to make readers aware that this process needs to be applied with care and knowledge (both, about the application domain and about the methodology) to obtain useful results.

In the previous chapters of this book, we have studied the principles and methods of data mining. Since data mining is a young discipline with wide and diverse applications, there is a still a serious gap between the general principles of data mining and the domain-specific knowledge required to apply it effectively. In this appendix, we examine a few application domains illustrated by the results of data-mining systems that have been implemented.

B1 DATA MINING FOR FINANCIAL DATA ANALYSIS

Most banks and financial institutions offer a wide variety of banking services such as checking, savings, business and individual customer transactions, investment services, credits, and loans. Financial data, collected in the banking and financial industry, are often relatively complete, reliable, and of a high quality, which facilitates systematic data analysis and data mining to improve a company's competitiveness.

In the banking industry, data mining is used heavily in the areas of modeling and predicting credit fraud, in evaluating risk, in performing trend analyses, in analyzing profitability, as well as in helping with direct-marketing campaigns. In the financial markets, neural networks have been used in forecasting stock prices, options trading, rating bonds, portfolio management, commodity-price prediction, and mergers and acquisitions analyses; it has also been used in forecasting financial disasters. Daiwa Securities, NEC Corporation, Carl & Associates, LBS Capital Management, Walkrich Investment Advisors, and O'Sallivan Brothers Investments are only a few of the financial companies who use neural-network technology for data mining. A wide range of successful business applications has been reported, although the retrieval of technical details is not always easy. The number of investment companies and banks that mine data is far more extensive that the list mentioned earlier, but you will not often find them willing to be referenced. Usually, they have policies not to discuss it. Therefore, finding articles about banking companies who use data mining is not an easy task, unless you look at the US

Government Agency SEC reports of some of the data-mining companies who sell their tools and services. There, you will find customers such as Bank of America, First USA Bank, Wells Fargo Bank, and U.S. Bancorp.

The widespread use of data mining in banking has not been unnoticed. The journal *Bank Systems & Technology* commented that data mining was the most important application in financial services in 1996. For example, fraud costs industries billions of dollars, so it is not surprising to see that systems have been developed to combat fraudulent activities in such areas as credit card, stock market, and other financial transactions. Fraud is an extremely serious problem for credit-card companies. For example, Visa and Master-Card lost over $700 million in 1995 from fraud. A neural network–based credit card fraud-detection system implemented in Capital One has been able to cut the company's losses from fraud by more than fifty percent. Several successful data-mining systems are explained here to support the importance of data-mining technology in financial institutions.

US Treasury Department

Worth particular mention is a system developed by the Financial Crimes Enforcement Network (FINCEN) of the US Treasury Department called "FAIS". FAIS detects potential money-laundering activities from a large number of big cash transactions. The Bank Secrecy Act of 1971 required the reporting of all cash transactions greater than $10,000, and these transactions, of about fourteen million a year, are the basis for detecting suspicious financial activities. By combining user expertise with the system's rule-based reasoner, visualization facilities, and association-analysis module, FIAS uncovers previously unknown and potentially high-value leads for possible investigation. The reports generated by the FIAS application have helped FINCEN uncover more than 400 cases of money-laundering activities, involving more than $1 billion in potentially laundered funds. In addition, FAIS is reported to be able to discover criminal activities that law enforcement in the field would otherwise miss, e.g., connections in cases involving nearly 300 individuals, more than eighty front operations, and thousands of cash transactions.

Mellon Bank, USA

Mellon Bank has used the data on existing credit-card customers to characterize their behavior and they try to predict what they will do next. Using IBM Intelligent Miner, Mellon developed a credit card–attrition model to predict which customers will stop using Mellon's credit card in the next few months. Based on the prediction results, the bank can take marketing actions to retain these customers' loyalty.

Capital One Financial Group

Financial companies are one of the biggest users of data-mining technology. One such user is Capital One Financial Corp., one of the nation's largest credit-card issuers. It offers 3000 financial products, including secured, joint, co-branded, and college-student cards. Using data-mining techniques, the company tries to help market and sell the most appropriate financial product to 150 million potential prospects residing in its over 2-terabyte Oracle-based datawarehouse. Even after a customer has signed up, Capital One continues to use data mining for tracking the ongoing profitability and other characteristics of each of its customers. The use of data mining and other strategies has helped Capital One expand from $1 billion to $12.8 billion in managed loans over eight years. An additional successful data-mining application at Capital One is fraud detection.

American Express

Another example of data mining is at American Express, where datawarehousing and data mining are being used to cut spending. American Express has created a single Microsoft SQL Server database by merging its worldwide purchasing system, corporate purchasing card, and corporate card databases. This allows American Express to find exceptions and patterns to target for cost cutting.

MetLife, Inc.

MetLife's Intelligent Text Analyzer has been developed to help automate the underwriting of 260,000 life insurance applications received by the company every year. Automation is difficult because the applications include many free-form text fields. The use of keywords or simple parsing techniques to understand the text fields has proven to be inadequate, while the application of full semantic natural-language processing was perceived to be too complex and unnecessary. As a compromise solution, the "information-extraction" approach was used in which the input text is skimmed for specific information relevant to the particular application. The system currently processes 20,000 life-insurance applications a month and it is reported that 89% of the text fields processed by the system exceed the established confidence-level threshold.

B2   DATA MINING FOR THE TELECOMMUNICATIONS INDUSTRY

The telecommunication industry has quickly evolved from offering local and long-distance telephone services to providing many other comprehensive communication services including voice, fax, pager, cellular phone, images, e-mail, computer and Web-data transmission, and other data traffic. The integration of telecommunications, computer networks, Internet, and numerous others means of communication and computing is underway. The U.S. Telecommunication Act of 1996 allowed Regional Bell Operating Companies to enter the long-distance market as well as offer "cable-like" services. The European Liberalization of Telecommunications Services has been effective from the beginning of 1998. Besides deregulation, there has been a sale by the Federal Communication Commission (FCC) of airwaves to companies pioneering new ways to communicate. The cellular industry is rapidly taking on a life of its own. With all this deregulation of the telecommunication industry, the market is expanding rapidly and becoming highly competitive.

The hypercompetitive nature of the industry has created a need to understand customers, to keep them, and to model effective ways to market new products. This creates a great demand for data mining to help understand the new business involved, identify telecommunication patterns, catch fraudulent activities, make better use of resources, and improve the quality of services. In general, the telecommunications industry is interested in answering some strategic questions through data-mining applications such as:

- How does one retain customers and keep them loyal as competitors offer special offers and reduced rates?
- Which customers are most likely to churn?
- When is a high-risk investment, such as new fiber optic lines, acceptable?
- How does one predict whether customers will buy additional products like cellular services, call waiting, or basic services?
- What characteristics differentiate our products from those of our competitors?

Companies like AT&T, AirTouch Communications, and AMS Mobile Communication Industry Group have announced the use of data mining to improve their marketing activities. There are several companies including Lightbridge and Verizon that use data-mining technology to look at cellular fraud for the telecommunications industry. Another trend has been to use advanced visualization techniques to model and analyze wireless-telecommunication networks. Selected examples of data-mining applications in the telecommunication industry follow.

Cablevision Systems, Inc.

Cablevision Systems Inc., a cable TV provider from New York, was concerned about its competitiveness after deregulation allowed telecom companies into the cable industry. As a consequence, it decided that it needed a central data repository so that its marketing people could have faster and more accurate access to data. Using data mining, the marketing people at Cablevision were able to identify nine primary customer segments among the company's 2.8 million customers. This included customers in the segment that are likely to "switch" to another provider. Cablevision also focused on those segments most likely to buy its offerings for new services. The company has used data-mining to compare the profiles of two sets of targeted customers—those who bought new services and those who did not. This has led the company to make some changes in its messages to customers, which, in turn, has led to a thirty percent increase in targeted customers signing up for new services.

Worldcom

Worldcom is another company that has found great value in data mining. By mining databases of its customer-service and telemarketing data, Worldcom has discovered new ways to sell voice and data services. For example, it has found that people who buy two or more services were likely to be relatively loyal customers. It also found that people were willing to buy packages of products such as long-distance, cellular-phone, Internet, and other services. Consequently, Worldcom started to offer more such packages.

BBC TV

TV-program schedulers would like to know the likely audience for a proposed program and the best time to show it. The data for audience prediction are fairly complex. Factors, which determine the audience share gained by a particular program, include not only the characteristics of the program itself and the time at which is shown, but also the nature of the competing programs in other channels. Using Clementine, Integral Solutions Limited developed a system to predict television audiences for the BBC. The prediction accuracy was reported to be the same as that achieved by the best performance of BBC's planners.

B3   DATA MINING FOR THE RETAIL INDUSTRY

Slim margins have pushed retailers into datawarehousing earlier than other industries. Retailers have seen improved decision-support processes leading directly to improved efficiency in inventory management and financial forecasting. The early adoption of datawarehousing by retailers has allowed them a better opportunity to take advantage of data mining. The retail industry is a major application area for data mining since it collects huge amounts of data on sales, customer-shopping history, goods transportation, consumption patterns, and service records, and so on. The quantity of data collected continues to expand rapidly, especially due to the increasing availability and popularity of business conducted on the Web, or e-commerce. Today, many stores also have Web sites where customers can make purchases online. A variety sources and types of retail data provide a rich source for data mining.

Retail data mining can help identify customer-buying behaviors, discover customer-shopping patterns and trends, improve the quality of customer services, achieve better customer retention and satisfaction, enhance goods consumption, design more effective goods transportation and distribution policies, and, in general, reduce the cost of business and increase profitability. In the forefront of applications that have been adopted by the retail industry are direct-marketing applications. The direct-mailing industry is an area where data mining is widely used. Almost every type of retailer uses direct marketing, including catalogers, consumer retail chains, grocers, publishers, B2B marketers, and packaged goods manufacturers. The claim could be made that every Fortune 500 company has used some level of data mining in their direct-marketing campaigns. Large retail chains and groceries stores use vast amounts of sale data that is "information rich". Direct marketers are mainly concerned about customer segmentation, which is a clustering or classification problem.

Retailers are interested in creating data-mining models to answer questions such as:

- What are the best types of advertisements to reach certain segments of customers?
- What is the optimal timing at which to send mailers?
- What is the latest product trend?
- What types of products can be sold together?
- How does one retain profitable customers?
- What are the significant customer segments that buy products?

Data mining helps to model and identify the traits of profitable customers, and it also helps to reveal the "hidden relationship" in data that standard-query processes have not found. IBM has used data mining for several retailers to analyze shopping patterns within stores based on point-of-sale (POS) information. For example, one retail company with $2 billion in revenue, 300,000 UPC codes, and 129 stores in 15 states found some interesting results: "...we found that people who were coming into the shop gravitated to the left-hand side of the store for promotional items, and they were not necessarily shopping the whole store." Such information is used to change promotional activities and provide a better understanding of how to lay out a store in order to optimize sales. Additional real-world examples of data-mining systems in retail industry follow.

Safeway, UK

Grocery chains have been another big user of data-mining technology. Safeway is one such grocery chain with more than $10 billion in sales. It uses Intelligent Miner from IBM to continually extract business knowledge from its product-transaction data. For example, the data-mining system found that the top-spending 25% customers very often purchased a particular cheese product ranked below 200 in sales. Normally, without the data-mining results, the product would have been discontinued. But the extracted rule showed that discontinuation would disappoint the best customers, and Safeway continues to order this cheese, though it is ranked low in sales. Thanks to data mining, Safeway is also able to generate customized mailing to its customers *by applying the sequence-discovery function of Intelligent Miner, allowing the company to maintain its competitive edge.*

RS Components, UK

RS Components, a UK-based distributor of technical products such as electronic and electrical components and instrumentation, has used the IBM Intelligent Miner to develop a system to do cross selling (suggested related products on the phone when customers ask for one set of products), and in warehouse product allocation. The company had one warehouse in Corby before 1995 and decided to open another in the Midlands to expand its business. The problem was how to split the products into these two ware-houses so that the number of partial orders and split shipments could be minimized. Remarkably, the percentage of split orders is just about 6% after using the patterns found by the system, much better than expected.

B4 DATA MINING IN HEALTHCARE AND BIOMEDICAL RESEARCH

With the amount of information and issues in the healthcare industry, not to mention the pharmaceutical industry and biomedical research, opportunities for data-mining applications are extremely widespread, and benefits from the results are enormous. Storing patients' records in electronic format and the development in medical-information systems cause a large amount of clinical data to be available online. Regularities, trends, and surprising events extracted from these data by data-mining methods are important in assisting clinicians to make informed decisions, thereby improving health services.

Clinicians evaluate a patient's condition over time. The analysis of large quantities of time-stamped data will provide doctors with important information regarding the progress of the disease. Therefore, systems capable of performing temporal abstraction and reasoning become crucial in this context. Although the use of temporal-reasoning methods requires an intensive knowledge-acquisition effort, data mining has been used in many successful medical applications, including data validation in intensive care, the monitoring of children's growth, analysis of diabetic patient's data, the monitoring of heart-transplant patients, and intelligent anesthesia monitoring.

Data mining has been used extensively in the medical industry. Data visualization and artificial neural networks are especially important areas of data mining applicable in the medical field. For example, NeuroMedicalSystems used neural networks to perform a pap smear diagnostic aid. Vysis Company uses neural networks to perform protein analyses for drug development. The University of Rochester Cancer Center and the Oxford Transplant Center use KnowledgeSeeker, a decision-tree-based technology, to help with their research in oncology.

The past decade has seen an explosive growth in biomedical research, ranging from the development of new pharmaceuticals and advances in cancer therapies to the identification and study of the human genome. The logic behind investigating the genetic causes of diseases is that once the molecular bases of diseases are known, precisely targeted medical interventions for diagnostics, prevention, and treatment of the disease themselves can be developed. Much of the work occurs in the context of the development of new pharmaceutical products that can be used to fight a host of diseases ranging from various cancers to degenerative disorders such as Alzheimer's Disease.

A great deal of biomedical research has focused on DNA-data analysis, and the results have led to the discovery of genetic causes for many diseases and disabilities. An important focus in genome research is the study of DNA sequences since such sequences form the foundation of the genetic codes of all living organisms. What is DNA? Deoxyribonucleic acid, or DNA, forms the foundation for all living organisms. DNA contains the instructions that tell cells how to behave and is the primary mechanism that permits us to transfer our genes to our offspring. DNA is built in sequences that form the foundations of our genetic codes, and that are critical for understanding how our genes behave. Each gene comprises a series of building blocks called nucleotides. When these nucleotides are combined, they form long, twisted, and paired DNA sequences or chains. Unraveling these sequences has become a challenge since the 1950s when the structure of the DNA was first understood. If we understand DNA sequences, theoretically, we will be able to identify and predict faults, weaknesses, or other factors in our genes that can affect our lives. Getting a better grasp of DNA sequences could potentially lead to improved procedures to treat cancer, birth defects, and other pathological processes. Data-mining technologies are only one weapon in the arsenal used to understand these types of data, and the use of visualization and classification techniques is playing a crucial role in these activities.

It is estimated that humans have around 100,000 genes, each one having DNA that encodes a unique protein specialized for a function or a set of functions. Genes controlling production of hemoglobin, regulation of insulin, and susceptibility to Huntington's chorea are among those that have been isolated in recent years. There are seemingly endless varieties of ways in which nucleotides can be ordered and sequenced to form distinct genes. Any one gene might comprise a sequence containing hundreds of thousands of individual nucleotides arranged in a particular order. Furthermore, the process of DNA sequencing used to extract genetic information from cells and tissues usually produces only fragments of genes. It has been difficult to tell using traditional methods where these fragments fit into the overall complete sequence from which they are drawn. Genetic scientists face the difficult task of trying to interpret these sequences and form hypotheses about which genes they might belong to, and the disease processes that they may control. The task of identifying good candidate gene sequences for further research and development is like finding a needle in a haystack. There can be hundreds of candidates for any given disease being studied. Therefore, companies must decide which sequences are the most promising ones to pursue for further development. How do they determine which ones would make good therapeutic targets? Historically, this has been a process based largely on trial and error. For every lead that eventually turns into a successful pharmaceutical intervention that is effective in clinical settings, there are dozens of others that do not produce the anticipated results. This is a research area that is crying out for innovations that can help to make these analytical processes more efficient. Since pattern analysis, data visualization, and similarity-search techniques have been developed in data mining, this field has become a powerful infrastructure for further research and discovery in DNA sequences. We will describe one attempt to innovate the process of mapping human genomes that has been undertaken by Incyte Pharmaceuticals, Inc. in cooperation with Silicon Graphics.

Incyte Pharmaceuticals, Inc.

Incyte Pharmaceuticals is a publicly held company founded in 1991, and it is involved in high-throughput DNA sequencing and development of software, databases, and other products to support the analysis of genetic information. The first component of their activities is a large database called LiveSeq that contains more than three million human-gene sequences and expression records. Clients of the company buy a subscription to the database and receive monthly updates that include all of the new sequences identified since the last update. All of these sequences can be considered as candidate genes that might be important for future genome mapping. This information has been derived from DNA sequencing and bioanalysis of gene fragments extracted from cell and tissue samples. The tissue libraries contain different types of tissues including normal and diseased tissues, which are very important for comparison and analyses.

To help impose a conceptual structure of the massive amount of information contained in LifeSeq, the data have been coded and linked to several levels. Therefore, DNA sequences can be grouped into many different categories, depending on the level of generalization. LifeSeq has been organized to permit comparisons of classes of sequence information within a hypothesis-testing mode. For example, a researcher could compare gene sequences isolated from diseased and nondiseased tissue from an organ. One of the most important tools that is provided in LifeSeq is a measure of similarity among sequences that are derived from specific sources. If there is a difference between two tissue groups for any available sequences, this might indicate that these sequences should be explored more fully. Sequences occurring more frequently in the diseased sample might reflect genetic factors in the disease process. On the other hand, sequences occurring more frequently in the nondiseased sample might indicate mechanisms that protect the body from the disease.

Although it has proved invaluable to the company and their clients in its current incarnation, additional features are being planned and implemented to extend the LifeSeq functionality into research areas such as:

- *Identifying co-occurring gene sequences.*
- *Tying genes to disease stage.*
- *Using LifeSeq to predict molecular toxicology.*

Although the LifeSeq database is an invaluable research resource, queries to the database often produce very large data sets that are difficult to analyze in text format. For this reason, Incyte developed the LifeSeq 3D application that provides visualization of data sets, and also allows users to cluster or classify and display information about genes. The 3D version has been developed using the Silicon Graphics MineSet tool. This version has customized functions that let researchers explore data from LifeSeq and discover novel genes within the context of targeted protein functions and tissue types.

B5   DATA MINING IN SCIENCE AND ENGINEERING

Enormous amounts of data have been generated in science and engineering, e.g., in cosmology, molecular biology, and chemical engineering. In cosmology, advanced computational tools are needed to help astronomers understand the origin of large-scale cosmological structures as well as the formation and evolution of their astrophysical components (galaxies, quasars, and clusters). Over three terabytes of image data have been collected by the Digital Palomar Observatory Sky Survey, which contain on the order of two billion sky objects. It has been a challenging task for astronomers to catalog the entire data set, i.e., a record of the sky location of each object and its corresponding classification such as a star or a galaxy. The Sky Image Cataloguing and Analysis Tool (SKICAT) has been developed to automate this task. The SKICAT system integrates methods from machine learning, image processing, and classification and analysis of data in databases, and it is reported to be able to classify objects, replacing visual classification, with high accuracy.

In molecular biology, recent technological advances are applied in such areas as molecular genetics, protein sequencing, and macro-molecular structure determination as was mentioned earlier. Artificial neural networks and some advanced statistical methods have shown particular promise in these applications. In chemical engineering, advanced models have been used to describe the interaction among various chemical processes, and also new tools have been developed to obtain a visualization of these structures and processes. Let us have a brief look at a few important cases of data-mining applications in engineering problems. Pavilion Technologies' Process Insights, an application-development tool that combines neural networks, fuzzy logic, and statistical methods has been successfully used by Eastman Kodak and other companies to develop chemical manufacturing and control applications to reduce waste, improve product quality, and increase plant throughput. Historical process data is used to build a predictive model of plant behavior and this model is then used to change the control set points in the plant for optimization.

DataEngine is another data-mining tool that has been used in a wide range of engineering applications, especially in the process industry. The basic components of the tool are neural networks, fuzzy logic, and advanced graphical user interfaces. The tool has been applied to process analysis in the chemical, steel, and rubber industries, resulting in a saving in input materials and improvements in quality and productivity. Successful data-mining applications in some industrial complexes and engineering environments follow.

Boeing

To improve its manufacturing process, Boeing has successfully applied machine-learning algorithms to the discovery of informative and useful rules from its plant data. In particular, it has been found that it is more beneficial to seek concise predictive rules that cover small subsets of the data, rather than generate general decision trees. A variety of rules were extracted to predict such events as when a manufactured part is likely to fail inspection or when a delay will occur at a particular machine. These rules have been found to facilitate the identification of relatively rare but potentially important anomalies.

Southern California Gas Company

The Southern California Gas Company is using SAS software as a strategic marketing tool. The company maintains a data mart called the Customer Marketing Information Database that contains internal billing and order data along with external demographic data. According to the company, it has saved hundreds of thousands of dollars by identifying and discarding ineffective marketing practices.

WebWatcher

Despite the best effort of Web designers, we all have had the experience of not being able to find a certain Web page we want. A bad design for a commercial Web site obviously means the loss of customers. One challenge for the data-mining community has been the creation of "adaptive Web sites"; Web sites that automatically improve their organization and presentation by learning from user-access patterns. One early attempt is WebWatcher, an operational tour guide for the WWW. It learns to predict what links users will follow on a particular page, highlight the links along the way, and learn from experience to improve its advice-giving skills. The prediction is based on many previous access patterns and the current user's stated interests. It has also been reported that Microsoft is to include in its electronic-commerce system a feature called Intelligent Cross Sell that can be used to analyze the activity of shoppers on a Web site and automatically adapt the site to that user's preferences.

B6 PITFALLS OF DATA MINING

Despite the above and many other success stories often presented by vendors and consultants to show the benefits that data mining provides, this technology has several pitfalls. When used improperly, data mining can generate lots of "garbage". As one professor from MIT pointed out: "Given enough time, enough attempts, and enough imagination, almost any set of data can be teased out of any conclusion." David J. Lainweber, managing director of First Quadrant Corp. in Pasadena, California, gives an example of the pitfalls of data mining. Working with a United Nations data set, he found that historically, butter production in Bangladesh is the single best predictor of the Standard & Poor's 500–stock index. This example is similar to another absurd correlation that is heard yearly around Super Bowl time—a win by the NFC team implies a rise in stock prices. Peter Coy, Business Week's associate economics editor, warns of four pitfalls in data mining:

1. It is tempting to develop a theory to fit an oddity found in the data.
2. One can find evidence to support any preconception if you let the computer churn long enough.
3. A finding makes more sense if there is a plausible theory for it. But a beguiling story can disguise weaknesses in the data.

4. The more factors or features in a data set the computer considers, the more likely the program will find a relationship, valid or not.

It is crucial to realize that data mining can involve a great deal of planning and preparation. Just having a large amount of data alone is no guarantee of the success of a data-mining project. In the words of one senior product manager from Oracle: "Be prepared to generate a lot of garbage until you hit something that is actionable and meaningful for your business."

This appendix is certainly not an inclusive list of all data-mining activities, but it does provide examples of how data-mining technology is employed today. We expect that new generations of data-mining tools and methodologies including Web-mining and text-mining techniques will increase and extend the spectrum of application domains.

Index

About the Author

Mehmed Kantardzic received B.S., M.S., and Ph.D. degrees in computer science from the University of Sarajevo, Bosnia. Until 1994, he was an Associate Professor at the University of Sarajevo, Faculty of Electrical Engineering. In 1995 Dr. Kantardzic joined the University of Louisville, and since 2001 he has been an Associate Professor at the Computer Engineering and Computer Science Department, University of Louisville, and the Director of the Data Mining Lab. His research interests are: data mining and knowledge discovery, soft computing, visualization of neural network generalizations, multimedia technologies on Internet, and distributed intelligent systems. Dr. Kantardzic has recently focused his work on application of data mining technologies in biomedical research. Dr. Kantardzic is the author of five books, and he initiated and led more than 30 research and development projects. He has also published more than 120 articles in refereed journals and conference proceedings. Dr. Kantardzic is a member of IEEE, ISCA, and SPIA, and he was Program Chair for ISCA'99 Conference in Denver, CO, and General Chair for the International Conference on Intelligent Systems 2001 in Arlington, VA.